T0269839

LINCOLN
THE FIRE OF GENIUS

LINCOLN
THE FIRE OF GENIUS

How Abraham Lincoln's Commitment to Science and
Technology Helped Modernize America

DAVID J. KENT

Foreword by
Sidney Blumenthal

Essex, Connecticut

An imprint of Globe Pequot, the trade division of
The Rowman & Littlefield Publishing Group, Inc.
4501 Forbes Blvd., Ste. 200
Lanham, MD 20706
www.rowman.com

Distributed by NATIONAL BOOK NETWORK

Copyright © 2022 by David J. Kent

All rights reserved. No part of this book may be reproduced in any form or by any electronic or
mechanical means, including information storage and retrieval systems, without written permission
from the publisher, except by a reviewer who may quote passages in a review.

British Library Cataloguing in Publication Information available

Library of Congress Cataloging-in-Publication Data

Names: Kent, David J., author. | Blumenthal, Sidney, writer of foreword.
Title: Lincoln : the fire of genius / David J. Kent ; foreword by Sidney Blumenthal.
Description: Essex, Connecticut : Lyons Press, [2022] | "How Abraham Lincoln's commitment to
     science and technology helped modernize America." | Includes bibliographical references and
     index.
Identifiers: LCCN 2022010003 (print) | LCCN 2022010004 (ebook) | ISBN 9781493063833
     (cloth) | ISBN 9781493063888 (epub)
Subjects: LCSH: Lincoln, Abraham, 1809–1865. | Science—United States—History—19th cen-
     tury. | Presidents—United States—Biography. | Patent lawyers—Illinois—Biography.
Classification: LCC E457.2 .K46 2022 (print) | LCC E457.2 (ebook) | DDC 973.7092 [B]—
     dc23/eng/20211119
LC record available at https://lccn.loc.gov/2022010003
LC ebook record available at https://lccn.loc.gov/2022010004

♾️™ The paper used in this publication meets the minimum requirements of American National
Standard for Information Sciences—Permanence of Paper for Printed Library Materials, ANSI/
NISO Z39.48-1992.

For Ru
Without whom this book could not have been written

CONTENTS

Author's Note

As do all good scientists and historians, I have relied on a myriad of primary source materials for this book. Spelling, grammar, and sentence structure were not standardized in the nineteenth century, and many of the people who knew Lincoln in his early years had limited literacy. For ease of reading and to limit distraction, I have corrected minor spelling and writing idiosyncrasies unless the language was critical to the original understanding.

Foreword

Two paintings depicting Abraham Lincoln issuing proclamations of emancipation are displayed in Washington, one prominently and the other virtually unknown. The first was painted by the portrait artist Francis B. Carpenter, who inveigled Lincoln to spend six months in the White House creating a tribute to what he called "an act unparalleled for moral grandeur in the history of mankind" and titled *First Reading of the Emancipation Proclamation of President Lincoln*. Poised with quill pen, Lincoln is surrounded by his cabinet secretaries as he prepares to sign the earthshaking piece of paper he holds in his hand. Unveiled in the White House in 1864 with Lincoln present, the picture was exhibited to awestruck crowds around the country, lithographs popularly sold, and the canvas can now be viewed on the Senate side of the Capitol.

The other painting, less recognized, hangs within the second marble monument to Lincoln on the national mall and within sight of the Lincoln Memorial. That monument is the architecturally notable building of the National Academy of Sciences, an institution created by Lincoln on March 3, 1863, two months after he signed the Emancipation Proclamation. In its boardroom hangs a painting that imagines the moment of the academy's founding, by the artist Albert Herter in 1924. Just as in Carpenter's *First Reading*, the document that Lincoln is about to sign is at the center of the picture. Lincoln is not seated in Herter's design but standing, looking straight ahead. The Lincoln in this portrait is directly drawn from Alexander Gardner's famous photograph of Lincoln taken in 1863. Instead of being surrounded by his cabinet secretaries, assembled around Lincoln are the most distinguished scientists of the age, who were the first members of the academy. They are his cabinet for the emancipation of science.

The Lincoln honored in the Herter portrait was a man of science himself, the greatest patron of science, and applied science to win the Civil War. Science was for Lincoln an instrument of emancipation. Just after his loss to his rival Senator Stephen A. Douglas in the 1858 contest for the Senate from Illinois, he delivered his lecture "On Discoveries and Inventions," in which he explained how the invention of the printing press ended "the dark ages," spread literacy, and gave the "great mass of men" a new sense of "equality." "To emancipate the mind from this false underestimate of itself, is the great task which printing came into the world to perform," Lincoln said. "It is difficult for us, *now* and *here*, to conceive how strong this slavery of the mind was; and how long it did, of necessity, take, to break its shackles, and to get a habit of freedom of thought, established. It is, in this connection, a curious fact that a new country is most favorable—almost necessary—to the emancipation of thought, and the consequent advancement of civilization and the arts."

Lincoln the "hayseed," as he once self-deprecatingly dubbed himself, the rail-splitter from the prairie, the bumptious backwoods humorist, and country courthouse lawyer was also the self-made man with a fierce and insatiable desire for education. He was a believer in evidence and facts, trial and error, cause and effect, law and logic. The scientific method suited his temperament. He saw it as a revolutionary tool.

Throughout his life, from his earliest days as a boatman plying the Sangamon River to captain of the ship of state, Lincoln was a student of modern technology, the industrial revolution, and the latest scientific developments. As a young man, he applied for a patent to lift boats through shoals, the only president ever to hold one. As a lawyer, he represented hundreds of patent cases. While other attorneys on the circuit snored in the rooms they shared, he pored over Euclid by candlelight. He more than grasped how railroads were rapidly changing the country and was the lawyer for the Rock Island Railroad in the key case that allowed bridges to span the Mississippi River and steam westward.

President Lincoln's interest was more than a fascination with how things worked. He understood that winning the war meant making a new nation. He established the land grant colleges to teach scientific agriculture, oversaw the greatest organization of natural resources, men, and materiel in human history; acted as the de facto chief of ordnance and tested the latest weaponry, including rapid-firing rifles; personally ran the naval board constructing ironclad warships, which sparked a new phase of the industrial revolution; created the first air force with balloons; and spent long evenings with Joseph Henry, secretary of the Smithsonian Institution. And then, Lincoln founded the National Academy of Sciences.

Lincoln the patent lawyer constantly encouraged innovation as president. One measure of the difference between Lincoln's America and the Confederacy was that during the war the United States government issued more than 30,000 patents while the Confederacy only issued 266. In his lecture of 1859, Lincoln described how the inventor "added the fuel of *interest* to the *fire* of genius, in the discovery and production of new and useful things." That motto today is engraved on the U.S. Patent Office.

It became more than an accident of time and sheer coincidence that an ocean apart Abraham Lincoln and Charles Darwin were born on the same day, February 12, 1809. The child born to a poor dirt farmer in Kentucky and the one born into a wealthy English family wrought revolutions and emancipations. Lincoln was the vindicator of liberal democracy of, by, and for the people. Darwin was the scientific voyager of *On the Origin of Species* and *The Descent of Man*, of evolution, natural selection, and the diversity of life. But in Lincoln's case the division between statesmanship and science is unnatural. David J. Kent's invaluable history shows us how Lincoln's fire of genius was to fuse those elements in order to create a "new birth of freedom."

Sidney Blumenthal, former senior adviser to President Bill Clinton and Hillary Clinton and former journalist for the New Yorker, *the* Washington Post, *and the* New Republic, *author of political classics* The Permanent Campaign *and* The Rise of the Counter-Establishment, *has published three books of a projected five-volume political life of Abraham Lincoln:* A Self-Made Man, Wrestling with His Angel, *and* All the Powers of Earth.

INTRODUCTION

ABRAHAM LINCOLN IS OFTEN LISTED AS AMERICA'S GREATEST PRESI-
dent. Most of us know the story of Lincoln—born in a log cabin, labored
as a poor farm boy until escaping to become a lawyer and politician and,
eventually, president of the United States. We know he married Mary
Todd, saved the Union during the Civil War, and emancipated the
enslaved. He is the most well-known president in our history. And yet,
perhaps not so well known as we think.

Lincoln's life spanned one of the greatest periods of scientific and
technological growth in our national history. Lincoln not only lived
through it, he recognized and encouraged it. Most know he grew up on
farms, but not how much science he learned there. Most know his formal
education "did not amount to one year," but not how his self-study led
to an understanding and skill in mathematics far above his peers. Most
know he completed two flatboat trips, but not the extent of his life on
the waters. Many have heard he is the only president with a patent, but
not how he pressed for technological improvements that would change
the face of the Midwest and, in the process, grow Chicago from a tiny
lakeside hamlet into a pivotal hub for transportation and economic development. Some may know about his life as a lawyer on the circuit, but not
how he set legal precedents critical to the future of westward American
expansion. We know he emancipated the slaves, but not how science and
technology facilitated the expansion of slavery in the United States, and
Lincoln's struggles to contain it.

The science of the early nineteenth-century United States was far
behind that of Europe. Most American men of science received their
training by studying with the great scientists in Germany, England, or
France. Science was the realm of the elite, wealthy men with the money
and leisure time to spend hours studying what was often esoteric, of little
value to the immediate needs of the majority of Americans. Most pure
science never trickled down to the masses. In fact, Europeans and some

eastern United States scientists saw little need to bring science to the public, who they felt were too ignorant and incapable to make use of it. Renowned scientists like James Hall, James Dana, John Torrey, and Asa Gray all preferred writing for other scientists only, the "ivory tower" in which scientific jargon limited comprehension only to those trained in the particular fields of endeavor. To satisfy the "vulgar appetites of the people," James Dana complained, required science to be "diluted and mixed with a sufficient amount of the *spirit of the age*." Some exceptions like mathematician Elias Loomis felt that the "scientific taste of the community" was important to cultivate. Others such as Louis Agassiz conducted public lectures, believing that education of the masses was an overall benefit to society. But mostly, science was a luxury of the leisure class.[1]

Many politicians also thought America was becoming too democratic, that too much power was devolving to the masses. The aging Charles Carroll, a signer of the Declaration of Independence, warned Alexis de Tocqueville in 1831 that "a mere democracy is but a mob." He disdained the masses and longed for the "old aristocratic institutions" that helped make him wealthy and politically powerful. Lincoln felt differently. While he would himself warn against the dangers of mob rule, he joined former president James Madison in his faith in the people's power of self-government.[2]

Lincoln was not a scientist. He was not even the first president to have an interest in science. Thomas Jefferson was more of an inventor, concocting everything from clocks to a revolving bookstand, a plow, and scientific instruments, although he never obtained any patents. Jefferson, like George Washington before him, did some surveying, a hobby that Lincoln would learn as a trade early in his adult life. Jefferson also kept meticulous records of the weather around Monticello, his Virginia estate. Jefferson's scientific knowledge was unequalled in his time. But Jefferson believed the economy should be primarily based on agriculture. While he claimed to envision "the rolling out of a republic in which small independent farmers would become foot-soldiers of the infant nation and the guardians of its liberty," in reality he owned a large plantation and enslaved more than six hundred men, women, and children in his lifetime. Slave labor enabled Jefferson the privilege of intellectual pursuit.[3]

Jefferson may have been more of a scientist than Lincoln, but Jefferson saw science as a benefit for the few while Lincoln saw its potential to benefit the many.

Lincoln had more in common with our sixth president, John Quincy Adams. Adams was not a scientist himself but wrote a treatise on the reform of weights and measures. His nearly religious promotion of astronomical observatories helped create the study of astronomy in America, pushing in an 1843 oration the practical value of astronomy. He reminded humanity to look "heavenward" as if "the special purpose of their creation" was "observation of the stars." During his tenure as a congressman following his presidency, Adams fought against both anti-British and antifederalist biases to get the Smithson bequest devoted to scientific research.[4] Like Adams, Lincoln saw science and technology as something that could improve the lives of all Americans. He saw a mechanism by which all men could better their condition.

Lincoln often spoke endearingly of Jefferson, but always about Jefferson's role in the founding of our nation, and especially the principle that "all men are created equal" from the Declaration of Independence. Lincoln once noted that he "never had a feeling politically that did not spring from the sentiments embodied in the Declaration of Independence." He believed the declaration applied to all men and that the document "contemplated the progressive improvement in the condition of all men everywhere." To Lincoln, that included black as well as white men.[5] Lincoln parted with Jefferson when it came to economics. Unlike Jefferson, Lincoln saw the future of the United States being driven by industrialization spurred on by discoveries in science and technology. During Lincoln's lifetime, the United States, especially in the North, moved from a purely agricultural economy to one built on manufacturing and industrialization of work and transport. While this was more prevalent in the more refined East, eventually even the frontier of Lincoln's youth in Kentucky and Indiana would see the shift. Lincoln played a role in making that happen. He was more Hamiltonian than Jeffersonian in his economic beliefs.[6]

These beliefs were the result, and the driver, of Lincoln's naturally inquisitive and mechanical mind. Lincoln grew from an inconsequential life of subsistence farming on the frontier outskirts of civilization to the most powerful man in the United States, taking the reins of an out-of-control country in the midst of tearing itself apart.

Like an arranged marriage gone bad, the nation found itself growing into two distinct sections over the first half of the nineteenth century. One section embraced free society and industrialization; the other section hunkered down into an aristocratic hierarchy focused on a plantation-based agricultural economy. Technological advances and social constraints served to expand the divisions between the two sections. Growth of the United States westward with the Louisiana Purchase, followed by the spoils of the Mexican War, created a third section—the federal territories—that exacerbated the economic, social, and political tensions between the two populated regions.[7] Commercial interactions between the North and the South, and mutual thirst for the West, tied the sections together while creating the conditions for their split.

From his vantage point in Springfield, Illinois, at the crossroads between the old agricultural past and the new technological future, Lincoln sought to constrain the growth of slavery, the singular driving issue rending the fabric of America woven from the threads of the Declaration of Independence and fashioned by the loom of the Constitution. Lincoln would grow and learn and put himself into a position to save the world's last best hope.

FROM LOG CABIN TO WHITE HOUSE

It all began on a farm in Kentucky. Born on the Sinking Spring farm, Lincoln's first memories were of the nearby farm at Nolin Creek where the family moved because of a land dispute. Facing losses from faulty land titles and finding Kentucky's acceptance of slavery morally repugnant, the family moved across the border to the newly formed free state of Indiana. Here the teenage Lincoln toiled from dawn to dusk clearing land, building cabins, splitting rails, and working as a hired hand to needy neighbors, with any money earned immediately handed over to his father. Formal education was limited to a few months a year when itinerant schoolmasters might find enough parents willing to subscribe to lessons in reading, writing, and arithmetic. But farming was not all labor; it provided myriad lessons in forest ecology, civil engineering, agronomy, hydrology, and disease. The curious mind of Lincoln absorbed these sciences and applied them to his life as he matured. Later, as president, he would expand the use of science in agriculture to improve productivity and reduce the manual labor of farming life. For education, Lincoln went beyond the formal classroom, borrowing every book he could find and reading to learn all he could. He became fascinated with astronomy, a captivation that he carried for the rest of his life and inspired his oldest son even more passionately. He studied Euclid's geometry in his spare time to improve his logical thinking. He never stopped learning, always looking for things he did not know and then mastering them.

Approaching adulthood offered more exposure to science and technology. He worked as a ferryman across the Ohio River, dug canals to bypass rapids, plied the Sangamon River as a steamboat pilot, and steered flatboats down the mighty Mississippi to New Orleans. While there, he saw a world far more diverse and industrious than he had ever experienced. It changed his life, and he dedicated himself to bringing that industriousness to the greater country.

Returning from his second flatboat trip, he set out to begin a life on his own. He found himself in New Salem, a small merchant and mill town that serviced the surrounding farming community. He worked several trade jobs before successfully being elected a representative in the Illinois State Legislature. Over four terms, Lincoln grew into leadership positions on the two major issues of the day—transfer of the state capital from Vandalia to Springfield, and a program of internal improvements designed to apply technology to transportation and economic development. Lincoln went to Washington and served a single term as the only Whig congressman from Illinois. He argued again for internal improvements and gained notoriety—and a certain amount of ridicule—with his challenge to President Polk's war with Mexico. On his way back to Springfield between congressional sessions, he stopped at Niagara Falls long enough to inspire a partial discourse on the power of the falls. This incomplete treatise showed his tendency to apply mathematics to the world around him, as he calculated the flow of water over the precipice. He also observed a stranded vessel, which with his previous experience hanging up a flatboat on a mill dam, inspired the patent that distinguishes him from every other president.

While in New Salem, Lincoln began the study of the law. Moving to Springfield, he joined a law practice with a senior partner, then after a few years signed on with a different senior partner. Eventually, he opened his own law practice with a junior partner, William Herndon, who worked with Lincoln the rest of his legal career, then became an indefatigable chronicler of Lincoln's life after his demise. Lincoln took on a number of patent, scientific, and technological cases, reflecting both his growing expertise and the increasing technological advancement of society. Among them are many lucrative cases working both for and against the railroads as they grew into the transformational drivers of economic expansion.

While in the state legislature, as a U.S. congressman, and then increasingly during the 1850s, Lincoln jumped into what rapidly became the dominant issue of the time—slavery. The 1854 Kansas-Nebraska Act and repeal of the Missouri Compromise "aroused him as he had never been before," after which the fight to put slavery on the course of its ultimate extinction became his all-consuming focus.[8] As he delved into the debate, Lincoln became intimately aware of the science behind slavery. He began to understand the scientific and religious debates of the origins of man, how technology led to the expansion of slavery, and how pseudoscientific arguments were used to rationalize the enslavement of nearly four million men and women.

Shortly after losing his Senate race to Stephen A. Douglas, Lincoln took his scientific knowledge on the road, presenting a lecture on "discoveries and inventions" tracing the historical growth of science and technology over the course of man's development. Article 1, Section 8, of the U.S. Constitution gives Congress the power "to promote the Progress of Science and useful Arts, by securing for limited Times to Authors and Inventors the exclusive Right to their respective Writings and Discoveries."[9] This is the basis for today's copyright and patent protection. Lincoln highlighted the importance of the patent laws in his science lecture, and as president he signed into existence the National Science Foundation, whose charter reiterated the constitutional authority "to promote the progress of science."

Science and technology became critically important during the Civil War. New weapons, new scientific issues to be solved, and new strategies to be implemented all came into focus. Lincoln led the way, often against the headwinds of military tradition. Seeing the need for long-term scientific infrastructure, Lincoln and the Republican majority in Congress took steps to institutionalize science and technology, putting the United States on a path to modern society. Even today, Lincoln continues to influence medical research and investigation as modern genetic and DNA testing delves into the Lincoln family's apparent health problems. Fascination with our sixteenth president never ends, and science is keeping pace with that fascination.

Today some politicians disdain science. Abraham Lincoln appreciated science and technology. He was curious about mechanical things. He read books on a variety of scientific topics. He promoted internal improvements, dug deep into mathematics, was a strategic thinker who could boil every issue down to its root causes, and then seek a way to resolve them. He understood the base instincts that allowed a small number of wealthy plantation owners to control the federal, state, and individual mindsets on slavery. Firmly planted within the limits of the Constitution, Lincoln sought to promote the fundamental principles of America as defined in the Declaration of Independence's "all men are created equal." It would take logic, perseverance, science, technology, and ultimately, political options only available to him as commander-in-chief during a time of insurrection to end the institution most in conflict with our national principles.

Recent debates over the fate of Confederate monuments and the distrust of many for science even during a global pandemic show that political partisanship and passions still dominate the country, much as they did during the Civil War. Historical context is both necessary and desired. Past presidents like Abraham Lincoln embraced science and technology as a means to improving the condition of all Americans. This is that story.

Part I

The Science of Frontier Life

CHAPTER 1

Farming Science

NINE-YEAR-OLD ABE LINCOLN CONTINUED HIS CHORES WHILE HIS mother Nancy wasted away in agony. In less than a week, she was dead from a disease no one understood.[1] Abe paused long enough to whittle wooden pegs to hold her coffin together and helped his father put her in the ground.[2] A formal funeral had to wait; the struggle for existence would not. Plowing, grubbing, girdling, shucking, splitting, and swinging an axe at a defiant forest were still required as his remaining family carved out a meager existence. This was the life and death of subsistence farming on the frontier. Not the place one anticipates much science, and yet a deep understanding of the unforgiving environment, soil properties, and the special characteristics of trees was a necessity for survival. As much as he grew to despise it, the farm taught Lincoln lessons he carried throughout his lifetime, providing the foundation for his later political and economic views.

Long before the term "scientist" was coined in 1834, scholarly men were mostly eastern U.S. and European elites with access to the leisure time and money required to study nature. Much of this early study was in agronomy, the science of farming. While formal science did not readily trickle down to the wilderness, farmers were inherently accustomed to the natural world. Survival required a firm grasp of the nuances of seasons, climate, and agronomic principles.[3] Lincoln began learning these important environmental realities at a very young age. He also started to see how bringing science to the masses, not just the privileged wealthy, could help all Americans "better their condition." Over time, Lincoln developed an appreciation that served him well throughout his legal and political careers, culminating in the role science and technology played in the American Civil War.

"It is a great piece of folly to attempt to make anything out of me or my early life," Lincoln wrote when asked for a presidential campaign autobiography, adding, "it can be condensed into a single sentence . . . 'The short and simple annals of the poor.'"[4] The self-effacing Lincoln was belittling his early life to maintain his rail-splitter campaign persona; in truth, his father, Thomas, was a successful farmer and carpenter. While primitive by today's standards, farming underwent rapid development in Lincoln's lifetime, a period that saw steady progress in technological advancement.[5] Nineteenth-century America evolved from a subsistence farming and barter economy to a manufacturing and agricultural market economy, a trend Lincoln actively encouraged.[6] Regardless of increased industrialization, the vast majority of the national economy remained agricultural, and much of this early technological improvement directly aided farmers: better plows, amended tilling practices, and enhanced nutrient management.[7]

For the first half of the nineteenth century, subsistence farming was the typical condition of men as the United States expanded westward, first with the Louisiana Purchase and then after the war with Mexico. Pioneers moved into virgin territory, laid claim to a parcel of land—usually on some form of credit—and started a farm from scratch. This involved clearing land of trees and brush, building a log cabin, planting and harvesting crops, and scraping out a living. Each step required knowledge of the local ecosystem (what trees for the cabin and fences, edible vs. nonedible plants), hydrology (soil types, drainage, and water sources), crop management (planting, weeding, and harvesting), and the quirks of climate.

The lessons started early. Abe was born on Sinking Spring farm in Kentucky, moving shortly thereafter to the farm on Knob Creek that stirred his earliest memories. While the soil was better than the "uncompromising homestead of infertile ground" of Sinking Spring, the location was less desirable overall. The new farm contained only three small fields in a valley surrounded by high hills, thus subject to repeated flooding after heavy rain. Abe remembered a summer in which his father was planting corn while Abe dropped pumpkin seeds into nearby furrows. A week later: "there came a big rain in the hills, it did not rain a drop in the valley, but the water coming down through the gorges washed ground, corn, pumpkin seeds and all clear off the field."[8] This incident taught Abe a brutal lesson in farming: one poorly timed deluge could disrupt an entire summer's crop. Of course, drought could have similarly devastating effects, as could insect infestation or poor soil quality. Rarely was there a year without calamity.

Not long after this, Thomas lost three-quarters of his land, "partly on account of slavery," but mostly because of Kentucky's inadequate survey-ing and land title system.[9] Although only seven years old at the time, Lin-coln could sense the importance of skilled surveyors, a lesson he carried into manhood. He likely also noticed another scientific factor influenc-ing the Lincoln family's decision to move to greener pastures—climatic extremes.

That summer of 1816 brought unusually severe cold to the Lincolns' drafty log cabin. Deep freezes, each lasting a week in June, July, and August, stunted crops. The end of summer brought two killer frosts that killed off much of what was left of the year's growth.[10] Crop failures led to hoarding and hunger. Prices for agricultural commodities such as wheat, vegetables, meat, butter, milk, and flour soared. Animals, both wild and domesticated, scraped by on inadequate forage. It was a terrible year for farmers.[11]

The "year without a summer" was so extensive that widespread cold and famine spread across the United States, Asia, and Europe, with history-changing effects. Farmers in New England gave up and moved west, beginning a process of westward migration that altered the course of the growing nation.[12] Loss of crops in the Yunnan province of China led family farms to switch to the more durable and profitable opium crop, giving rise to the "Golden Triangle" of opium production.[13] In Switzer-land, the damp dreariness of Lake Geneva kept nineteen-year-old Mary Wollstonecraft inside a chalet with future husband Percy Shelley and prominent poet Lord Byron. Challenged to while away the bleakness by writing ghost stories, Mary Wollstonecraft Shelley brought to life a cre-ation called *Frankenstein: Or, The Modern Prometheus*.[14]

No one understood it at the time, but modern scientists now know the disruption was caused by a geological phenomenon half a world away.[15] Mount Tambora, a massive volcano on the Indonesian island of Sumbawa, erupted in early April 1815, reducing the volcanic peak's height from over 14,000 feet to less than 10,000 in seconds. The colossal eruption destroyed local villages, killing over 10,000 people, while spewing 100 cubic kilometers of molten rock, ash, and pumice over 800 miles away.[16] Ten times the explosive power of the 1883 eruption of Krakatoa (made more famous by the invention of the telegraph), Tambora sent toxic clouds into the atmosphere that affected global climate patterns for several years. By the spring and summer of 1816, a persistent sulfate aerosol veil often described as a "dry fog" settled in over the eastern United States.[17]

Tambora's climate-altering effect on top of the recent crop losses solidified Thomas's tentative deliberations, and the Lincolns moved to Indiana in December. After the rough year, November and December proved mercifully warmer than normal, again a lingering effect of the Mount Tambora eruption.[18]

LEARNING FOREST ECOLOGY

Moving at this time of year was typical. Crops had been harvested and preserved for the long winters. The drier autumn made roads passable compared to the mud that inevitably mired travel in the rainy spring. The winter also allowed time to rid the new land of trees and prepare the soil in time for spring planting.[19]

Before farming anything, the Lincolns needed to clear the land. By the time they moved to Indiana, the rapidly growing Abe "had an axe put into his hands at once; and from that till within his twenty-third year, he was almost constantly handling that most useful instrument—less, of course, in plowing and harvesting seasons."[20] Farming was Lincoln's introduction to hard work. It was also an education in temperate forestry.

Lincoln later recalled that the family "settled in an unbroken forest" and that "the clearing away of surplus wood was the great task at hand."[21] Thomas took Abe into the forest and schooled him to recognize the types of trees. The exact species varied by local geography and climate, but one visitor described southern Indiana as "covered with heavy timber—comprising oaks, beeches, ash, three kinds of nut trees." He also noted the presence of "gum trees, hackberry, sycamore, persimmons, wild cherries, apples and plums, also wild grape vines of enormous diameter and heights," plus "a large number of maple and sugar trees . . . and a kind of poplar."[22] Other observers mentioned the presence of hickory, black walnut, locust, dogwood, cherry, sassafras, and elm.[23] A variety of oak trees were present, including white, black, and Jack oak. The undergrowth was densely packed with spice wood, various briers, grape vines, sumac bushes, and dry brush, a diversity that is largely lost today.[24]

Abe quickly learned the relevant ecology. Hickory, walnut, and white oak have taproot systems where large roots descend straight down deep into the earth. Red oak, locust, sycamore, and many pines have heart root systems characterized by many primary roots that may be visible on the surface and spread out below, with numerous secondary roots extending downward in search of water. Maples, hackberry, poplar, ash, gum, and dogwood have a flat root, one that spreads out in a shallow fan around the tree. Each of these required a different strategy for removal, with big hardwoods like oak or ash particularly difficult to remove.[25] Abe became so knowledgeable that during his presidency he settled a dispute between visitors at the Soldiers' Home. "I know all about trees in right of being a backwoodsman," he said. "I'll show you the difference between spruce, pine, and cedar, and this shred of green, which is neither one nor the other, but a kind of illegitimate cypress." He had learned his lessons well.[26]

"Abe could sink an axe deeper in wood more than any man I ever saw," recalled the aptly named William Wood, for whom Lincoln periodically worked as a teenager.[27] Abe's relative Dennis Hanks later remarked, "My, how he could chop! . . . If you heard his fellin' trees in a clearin' you would say there was three men at work by the way the trees fell."[28] But swinging an axe was not the only way to remove a tree from the dense forest. To save time for planting, farmers like the Lincolns learned they could use a process called girdling for some of the larger trees, especially walnuts, hickories, and beeches. Girdling, or "ring-barking," involves stripping bark with its underlying xylem and phloem from completely around the circumference of the tree. Since xylem and phloem are the layers that transport water and nutrients to other parts of the tree, interrupting the line of cells kills the tree above the area girdled. Death of the tree takes time, so girdling is best used for preparing larger trees for removal years in the future.[29]

ENGINEERING A LOG CABIN

With stacks of trees dragged to their homestead clearing, building the cabin helped teach Abe more forest ecology, some basic mathematics, and even a little civil engineering. Constructing a log cabin was a combination of art, science, and seat-of-the-pants innovation based on what materials were available. Thomas built his Kentucky and Indiana cabins with strong hardwoods like white oak, although American chestnut could also be used if abundant. The shakes, or shingles, that made up the roof were usually tulip poplar or cedar. Other species of trees could be substituted if these were not available.[30]

Abe rapidly learned the key factors in choosing appropriate trees for the cabin. While the Lincolns may not have had much choice, trees grown in higher elevations were preferable because they grew slower and thus had denser wood with tighter growth rings that resist cracking and warping as they dry. Cutting the logs in winter was also beneficial, as the cold months limited the amount of sap flowing, again resulting in lower-moisture logs that limit cracking as they dry. Depending on the species, cut trees were air-dried for one or two years. This is one reason the Lincolns lived in a primitive half-faced camp their first year, so they could stockpile newly cut trees for use in later construction.[31] Without knowing the scientific details, Abe learned that trees produce their own natural decay resistance to ward off insects and fungi. Older trees have higher concentrations of these natural toxins, so the greater the heartwood the greater the protection. Faster-growing trees like pines generally have more sapwood, which makes them more susceptible to decay.

Even a simple square or rectangular cabin is more complicated than stacking logs. The building lot had to be tamped to flatness, and the land around this rudimentary foundation had to be canted at a slight angle to ensure rainwater did not pool at the base of the cabin or seep inside. The first step was to lay the mudsill, thick and strong timbers serving as the lowest threshold supporting the foundation of the cabin. Then it was time to final cut and lay out the logs in the square or rectangular shape of the house. Thomas had several choices: round logs or hewn, various notch styles, covered windows or not, loft or no loft, and more, beginning with calculating how many logs were needed. The illiterate Thomas probably eyeballed the measurements, but long before they moved to Illinois Abe may have used a more precise calculation method, extrapolating from his limited formal schooling and autodidactic study. Lincoln later joked, however, that because of the unlimited forest available to a western pioneer building a log cabin, "when he commenced he didn't know how much timber he would need, and when he had finished, he didn't care how much he had used up."[32]

Once all the walls, gables, and fireplace were built, the whole house had to be chinked. No matter how tight you secure the logs to each other by hewing, shaping, and notching, there will be gaps that need to be filled to keep out rain, insects, and snakes. Abe added hay or horsehair to the local red clay as reinforcement while it dried, much like modern rebar strengthens the surrounding concrete.[33]

AGRONOMY AND HYDROLOGY

Survival of the family depended on the ability to produce adequate food for the household, and these became Abe's initial lessons in agronomy. The first crops were planted while stumps were still in the fields, often carving paths around the remnants like a Zen Garden around boulders. Any suitable soil was chopped up and plowed so that seeds could be put in the ground as soon as possible. Abe took on this chore at a young age. "A boy that could not plow by the time he was eight, was not much of a boy," offered one frontiersman.[34] The Lincolns planted a hardy variety of corn as their first crop because it provided food for the family, additional fodder for any animals they might obtain, and could be sold for the cash needed to buy any household supplies they could not grow, hunt, or manufacture themselves.[35] Wheat probably did not get planted for a few years as, ironically, the soil was initially too rich in nutrients.[36] The Lincolns constantly battled weeds and resurgent tree shoots as the nascent corn, potatoes, greens, beans, peas, carrots, squash, cabbages, okra, and pumpkins struggled to get a foothold. While waiting for the food to grow, the family foraged. Abe learned which plants could be eaten safely, such as berries, sweet acorns called chinquapins, nuts, tubers, mushrooms, wild asparagus, plums, and herbs.[37] Since berry patches also tended to attract bears, Lincoln learned to forage with his elder cousin John Hanks manning the family musket.[38] Pioneer farmers like the Lincolns could get a lot of food out of a small piece of land if they were attentive. Given the calorie-burning hard labor that was the norm for frontier life, food tended to be simple, salty, and substantial (i.e., fatty).[39]

Hunting was another necessary skill. Close relative Dennis Hanks remembers Thomas getting "no small amusement and pleasure" from hunting everything from turkeys to bears.[40] The hunting gene apparently was not passed on to Abe, however, who after shooting and killing a turkey never again "pulled a trigger on any larger game."[41] Any game killed provided meat for food, fat for candles and grease, and buckskin for clothing.[42] In the early 1800s game was plentiful, and Lincoln later recalled that the Little Pigeon Creek area was "a wild region, with many bears and other wild animals still in the woods."[43] In addition to bear, the family could count on bagging deer, opossum, squirrel, rabbit, boar, beaver, badger, and occasionally elk.[44] An animal most pioneers tried to avoid was the panther—what today we call a mountain lion or cougar. On a trip back to his old Indiana homestead in 1846, Lincoln wrote a long poem, part of which recalled, "The panther's scream, filled the night with fear / And bears preyed on the swine."[45]

Hydrology was also important. The availability of water for drinking, cooking, and washing was critical to a successful household, as was water for the animals and rudimentary irrigation. At Sinking Spring farm, abundant pure water was retrieved from the namesake karst spring. In karst topography, cracks appear in the rock as weak carbonic acid formed from carbon dioxide in the water leaches through the topsoil and slowly dissolves the underlying limestone. Eventually, a natural drainage system forms, leading to the spring spitting from the ground into a natural rock pit near the cabin. Any water not captured by the Lincolns seeped into the earth, eventually leaking into the Nolin River.[46]

At Knob Creek, the stream provided convenient clean freshwater.[47] At Little Pigeon Creek in Indiana, Thomas's attempt to dig wells yielded water unusable unless boiled, and then still had particles to be strained before use.[48] For drinking water, Abe had to hike a mile through the woods to fill buckets from a spring, then haul them back to the cabin twice a day.[49]

One of the most critical shortages was salt, useful for both flavoring and preservation. Abe often went to the salt lick, a natural outcropping of rock providing essential elements such as phosphorus, sodium, calcium, iron, zinc, and essential trace elements like selenium. Because licks attracted wildlife, they were a great place to wait for deer, which to the deer's misfortune, became dinner for the Lincolns.[50] Salt was also used for preservation of meat because it inhibited the growth of microorganisms by drawing water out of the cells. This kept meat and vegetables from spoiling during long periods between successful hunts and harvests.[51]

DEALING WITH DISEASE

Death was a fact of life for pioneers. Abe's sister Sarah died giving birth to her first child, who perished with her. Ague (a form of malaria), consumption (tuberculosis), cholera, and smallpox were common occurrences.[52] Diseases that prematurely ended the lives of pioneers included many we have largely eradicated today but for which understanding of the cause was lacking in the nineteenth century: measles, mumps, chicken pox, smallpox, diphtheria, influenza, typhoid, tetanus, polio, and many others. Doctors did little more than prescribe herb pastes or attach leeches for bloodletting, so it was largely up to women like Abe's mother, Nancy, and stepmother, Sarah, to handle illnesses in the family, for which they relied on a variety of home remedies derived from over two hundred kinds of herbs and roots.[53] Castoreum extracted from the glands of beavers was also seen as a wonder cure for a variety of ailments.[54]

Abe's mother died from what pioneers variously called puking fever, the trembles, the staggers, or the slows because of its assorted symptoms. Most commonly, the disease was referred to as "the milk sick." The disease was so prevalent that the names Milk Sick Ridge, Milk Sick Cove, and Milk Sick Holler are still found in the South.[55] Early in October, Thomas and Elizabeth Sparrow, relatives of Nancy who had joined them in Indiana the previous year, died of the milk sickness. Within two weeks, Nancy began showing symptoms and, after a week of agony, died.[56]

While the Lincolns and others knew vaguely it was associated with milk, no one had yet connected the disease with the ultimate source. Some had noticed the seasonality of the disease and that it seemed to occur more often in years in which natural forage vegetation was in short supply. Less than normal rain in 1818 had resulted in dusty conditions and low crop yields. As a result, the Lincolns' livestock instinctively foraged for food wherever they could find it, often into the underbrush of the neighboring forest. What they found was a weedy plant now known to be white snakeroot (current scientific name *Ageratina altissima*).[57]

While early observations suggesting plants as a source occurred before Nancy's death, it was not until 1834 that a physician and scientist named Anna Pierce Hobbs Bixby learned the connection to white snakeroot and led a campaign to eradicate the weed from her Rock Creek, Illinois, community.[58] Ohio farmer William J. Vermilya independently implicated white snakeroot in 1837. Given the lack of scientific infrastructure, these early discoveries were insufficient to settle the issue, and as late as 1841 the Kentucky legislature was offering $2,000 to anyone "who shall, within five years after the passage of this act" succeed in discovering "the true cause of the disease, now known to be caused by the poisonous effects of the wild, flowering white snakeroot transmitted by the milk, butter, and flesh of cattle consuming the plant."[59]

That "true cause" was a natural toxin called tremetone that remained active even after the plant was dried for hay. Sometimes farmers noticed listlessness, trembling, and peculiar odors in the breath of cattle, sheep, and horses. The tremetone easily passed into the milk, which was how most humans were exposed to the toxin.[60] Milk sickness was not a pleasant disease. One of the symptoms is an acetone-like odor (similar to today's nail polish remover). Persistent vomiting, abdominal pains, muscle stiffness, and eventually tremors, respiratory distress, and agonizing pain were obvious to the Lincoln family. Not seen was the intense inflammation of Nancy's gastrointestinal tract, enlarged liver and kidneys, and swelling of her heart. Milk sickness was a painful death.[61]

The definitive conclusion that milk sickness was caused by tremetone was not made until the early twentieth century.[62] In 1818, all the preadolescent Abe could do was helplessly watch his mother die. Death from the lack of scientific knowledge was one reason Lincoln later supported the greater use of science in agriculture—and the broad dissemination of information to farms of all sizes throughout the nation.

ON THE MOVE AGAIN

In 1830 the Lincoln family abruptly abandoned their partially constructed new cabin and moved to Illinois.[63] After fourteen years in Indiana, Thomas faced the usual reality: tilling the soil year after year oxidizes out organic matter and depletes the bacteria necessary for nutrient replenishment. The result is a dead soil unable to sustain crop growth.[64]

Weather again affected the move. The wet spring made the 225-mile journey difficult. Road conditions could be summarized in a single word—mud. After a two-week trek in handmade oxen-pulled wooden wagons, they settled about ten miles west of Decatur, Illinois, on "the North side of the Sangamon river at the junction of the timber-land and prairie."[65]

Although now a legal adult, Lincoln trekked westward with his family and once again set to preparing the land, breaking the tough prairie soil, building a cabin, splitting fence rails, and putting crops in the ground. He was "the toughest looking man I ever saw," observed one neighbor.[66]

The Illinois landscape presented a distinct contrast from the land they had known on previous farms. They built their cabin on hillier ground in the central forest–grasslands transition where the native forest met the tallgrass prairie extending westward into the Great Plains.[67] These fertile plains were leveled by glaciers during the last ice age, resulting in many square miles of flat land with rolling hills.[68]

Without knowing the scientific terms, Lincoln discovered that the prairie provided a loamy soil called mollisol that is highly fertile and rich in calcium and magnesium. Unlike the overstressed thin soils of the East, prairie soils have a deep, organics-rich topsoil providing substantial nutrients for new crops. The dense forests had been replaced with wide grasslands.

In Lincoln's time, the tallgrass prairies were a complex ecosystem supporting a wide variety of wildlife, although the term *tallgrass* oversimplifies the high species diversity present on the native prairie.[69] In contrast to today's monocultures of corn, wheat, or soybeans, Lincoln's prairie was a polyculture of many grasses dominated by big and little bluestem, Indian grass, prairie cord grass, dropseed, porcupine grass, sideoats grama, needle grass, and more. A native prairie in Lincoln's time held about 150 kinds of grasses, with about ten dominating specialty niches.[70] This diversity provides a more resilient natural resistance to diseases and insect pests while better preserving the topsoil layer in which crops are grown. Polycultures in general are better for natural water storage, nutrient recycling, pest control, and adaptivity.[71]

Lincoln discovered that the bulk of tallgrass plants exists below the surface. Grasses several feet tall can have up to fourteen feet of roots extending into the earth. These roots store carbon, nourish the soil, increase bioproductivity, and prevent erosion while serving as a carbon sink for storing biomass below ground.[72] Unfortunately for Lincoln, the tangled roots and deep mucky soil made plowing extremely difficult, often requiring joint oxen teams borrowed from neighbors to break the prairie for planting.[73]

Cast-iron plows had been available since the late 1700s, although the Lincolns probably used a simple wooden plow for much of their time in Kentucky and Indiana. Cast iron was sturdier than wood, but the metal wore down over time and the brittleness of cast iron caused it to break on large rocks. Many farmers also shunned it because they thought the iron poisoned the soil. By the 1820s, a man named Jethro Wood invented a cast-iron plow with separate parts such that those most exposed to wear and breakage could easily be replaced in the field.[74] Already, technology was making its way into agriculture on a rudimentary level.

To Lincoln's misfortune, the invention of the steel plow by transplanted Illinoisan John Deere did not occur until long after Lincoln had left the farm. Deere's plow more easily shed the soil as the moldboard moved through it, thus saving hours of backbreaking labor. With these improvements, steel plows halved the number of oxen or horses needed over iron plows.[75] Lincoln followed these developments attentively, later promoting plow advancements in his science lectures. He may not have been consciously thinking about it at the time, but Lincoln was absorbing the key scientific and technological knowledge he came to encourage later in life.

Then the bane of farmers—extreme weather—again made their lives difficult. Years earlier, they left Kentucky after the "year without a summer"; now they faced the "winter of deep snow."

In 1830, soon after arriving in Illinois, a desperate summer besieged the family with swarms of disease-laden mosquitoes the locals called gallnippers. Many of the extended Lincoln family were inflicted with ague, a broad name for malaria characterized by chills, fevers, and profuse sweating. By the time they recovered their health, winter had hit with a vengeance. The first flakes fell in early December, dumping three feet of snow that was rapidly covered by a thick crust of ice made thicker with nineteen subsequent storms.[76] Soon, snow drifts deep enough to cover fence rails trapped the family in their cabin. Temperatures fell below zero repeatedly. Unable to be forage or be fed, the Lincolns' livestock starved to death, often simply freezing in place.

Eventually, the situation became so dire that Lincoln was sent out to ask their neighbor, Sheriff William Warnick, for spare food. Crossing the frozen Sangamon River, Lincoln slipped and got his feet wet. By the time he reached the Warnick cabin two miles away, his feet were frostbitten. Mrs. Warnick kept Lincoln at the cabin for over a week and applied a mixture of "goose grease, skunk oil, and rabbit fat" until he was able to walk again.[77]

A welcome spring brought relief from the cold and snow, but then the massive snowmelt engorged rivers and streams, flooding the lowlands and turning the roads into impassable mud. After this trying introduction to Illinois, Thomas Lincoln decided he was better off in Indiana and started back east. He got as far as Coles County in eastern Illinois and remained there the rest of his life, sharing their larger "saddlebag" log cabin with as many as eighteen members of the extended family. Rather than move with them, Lincoln finally set out to make a life of his own, soon settling in New Salem.

Beginnings of the Industrial-Agronomic Split
Lincoln's farming experience could be characterized as pioneer exploitation. Land was cleared and crops were planted, not for the long term but only until the land was no longer optimum. Then the homesteader moved

to the next plot of land, often in the next state being carved out of the Northwest Territories. This was subsistence farming on the frontier.[78]

In slaveholding states, the opposite trend occurred. Small farms were acquired by rich planters and turned into plantations. Tobacco, sugar beets, and cotton grew to take up thousands, then millions, of acres, leading to significant soil nutrient depletion and destructive disease infestations.[79] Slave labor became the mainstay for cultivating such huge expanses, the powerful plantation interests disdaining industrialization as encouraging a more democratic society. The inherent conflict between individual farms and shops of free men paid for their labor versus aristocratic plantations relying on forced slave labor set up contrasts in the moral, economic, and technological systems that seemed unsolvable without violent upheaval.[80]

Industrialization had reached the United States soon after the colonies had successfully split from the British crown. In 1789, Samuel Slater had memorized the plans of an English textile mill and opened a cotton-spinning plant in Rhode Island.[81] Within two decades, hundreds of such mills spread out across New England, and textile production rapidly grew to be the new nation's largest industry. While small farms still dominated the northern states, the concept of factories began taking hold. The cotton production of the South fed the textile mills of the North.

When the Lincolns lived in rural Kentucky and Indiana, the most they saw of industrialization was a blacksmith who could forge iron plows, horseshoes, tools, and household goods. Over time, industrialization gradually expanded west through the new states organized as Ohio, Indiana, Illinois, Michigan, and Wisconsin. Mechanization of farmwork advanced as Deere's new plow, McCormick's reaper, and other industrial enhancements made farming easier and more efficient. Lincoln was a spectator to these events as he grew up, but he slowly realized that internal and personal improvements were necessary if the frontier and its people were to reach their full potential. Lincoln's eyes were opening to a rapidly changing world.

As an adult, Lincoln abandoned his reliance on the soil and reaped the greener pastures of law and politics. He never again tilled the land, but he had grown an appreciation of the need for more systematic approaches to farming. He would become a champion of scientific farming and technological improvements for the rest of his life.[82]

In a moment of exasperation while hired out to the Crawford family in Indiana, a teenage Abraham Lincoln cried out, "I don't always intend to delve, grub, shuck corn, split rails, and the like." Lincoln was making it clear he intended to better his condition.[83] To accomplish that, he needed what neither his father nor his stepmother could provide—an education.

CHAPTER 2

Educating Lincoln: From Readin' to Euclid

"UPON THE SUBJECT OF EDUCATION," ABRAHAM LINCOLN WROTE IN HIS "Communication to the People of Sangamo County" in 1832, "I can only say that I view it as the most important subject which we as a people can be engaged in."[1] Yet later, when asked to provide a short biographical entry for the *Dictionary of the American Congress*, Lincoln wrote simply: "Education defective."[2]

Reflecting on his upbringing, Lincoln thought "that the aggregate of all his schooling did not amount to one year." Recognizing that his lack of formal education was a weight on his ability to move ahead in the world, he later admitted: "He regrets his want of education, and does what he can to supply the want."[3]

This well-worn characterization of Lincoln's education is largely true, but also deceptively incomplete. Lincoln's limited formal schooling was as much the norm for children on the frontier as it was a contrast with the classical education available to eastern elites.

Thomas Jefferson, for example, had begun his formal education at the age of five, receiving extensive instruction in reading, writing, and mathematics but also training in the natural sciences and languages such as Latin, Greek, and French. Jefferson had access to a significant library of books spanning every topic. He went on to study mathematics, metaphysics, and philosophy at the College of William & Mary. As with many of the wealthy class, Jefferson had a distinct advantage—hundreds of enslaved men and women laboring on the family plantation gave him plenty of free time.[4]

Lincoln and his peers had none of these advantages. His formal schooling was limited by the lack of trained teachers and free time away from daily chores, especially during planting, weeding, and harvesting seasons. Frontier children mostly learned "by littles."[5] Yet Lincoln clearly outclassed the majority of his pioneer friends. Not satisfied with rote learning of basic skills, Lincoln squeezed in self-study in grammar, science, mathematics, technology, and the law.[6] His natural talent was supplemented with an autodidactic determination to teach himself. Despite the lack of privilege, he became a lifelong learner who far exceeded the constraints of frontier life.

Lincoln's mother, Nancy, could not write, but she "could read a little" and often read him Bible stories to instill in him moral values and a love of words.[7] His more cultivated stepmother, Sarah, provided books and encouraged his reading and writing. Whether his father, Thomas, supported his pursuit of knowledge is hotly debated. Thomas, who according to Lincoln "grew up literally without education" and "never did more in the way of writing than to bunglingly sign his own name," preferred that young Abe put his effort into breaking sod and trimming brush. Realizing Lincoln's potential, Sarah induced Thomas to permit Abe to read and study at home to supplement school learning. Reluctant at first, Thomas eventually came to encourage his son's studies.[8] Lincoln later gave his father even more credit, suggesting to a colleague that Thomas wanted Lincoln to have better educational opportunities than his own meager upbringing.[9]

Lincoln's education may have been deficient in formal schooling, but he made the best of the little he had and excelled at self-study and learning from day-to-day experiences. A typical day for a frontier farmer was to rise before dawn, work until nightfall, and fall dead asleep in a communal cabin after a fat-filled dinner. Because this routine was constant from early spring plowing until after fall harvesting, scholastic opportunities were largely limited to winter.

Often illiterate themselves, parents relegated their children's academic learning to itinerate teachers offering limited scholastics before moving on to the next village. A retired Thomas Jefferson had unsuccessfully advocated for public schools in the East as early as 1810, and the idea remained unattainable in the often transient and consistently poorer western territories and emerging states.[10] Churches often sponsored schools, with the requisite emphasis on religious training as much as spelling and reading. Most schools were by subscription, teachers only providing instruction when enough parents were willing to pay to make it worthwhile. Often the payment was in grain or produce, and the teacher usually boarded with local families.[11]

Finding a competent teacher was a challenge. In an autobiographical sketch written in 1859, Lincoln recalled in his frontier vernacular that "no qualification was ever required of a teacher beyond readin, writin, and cipherin, to the Rule of Three. If a straggler supposed to understand latin, happened to so-joun in the neighborhood, he was looked upon as a wizzard."[12]

As a very young boy in Kentucky, Lincoln and his sister, Sarah, did briefly attend two A.B.C. schools, so called because the schoolmaster's primary goal was to impress upon students the alphabet and rudimentary reading. Zachariah Riney set up in a tiny dirt-floored schoolhouse without windows about three miles from the Lincoln cabin, a distance Lincoln usually covered on foot.[13] Lincoln later ventured even farther from home as a student of Caleb Hazel. While Lincoln later referred to Riney "in terms of grateful respect," Hazel was less impressive, his abilities described as to "perhaps teach spelling & indifferent writing & perhaps could Cipher to the rule of three—but had no other qualifications of a teacher."[14] A large man in a time of rampant corporal punishment, Hazel was better qualified for punishing wayward students than raising their education levels. According to Lincoln's childhood friend Austin Gollaher, Hazel was so limited that when his "most advanced pupils finished" the spelling book, "he started them once more in words of one syllable."[15] This limited instruction was too often the norm, and the precocious Lincoln quickly realized he could learn faster than any available teacher could teach. Likely he attended school with Hazel simply to keep his sister company on the long walks to and from the schoolhouse. By the time he left Kentucky, Lincoln could probably read and spell a little.

After a four-year delay upon moving to Indiana, Lincoln again picked up sporadic formal education, squeezing sessions around his increasing role as a family laborer and hired hand. Lincoln remembered his teachers over the next decade as Andrew Crawford, James Swaney, and Azel Dorsey.[16] As with Kentucky, Indiana schools were "blab schools," so called because students of all ages worked at their own pace in a single room, reading their lessons out loud. The resulting din made individual instruction impossible. His law partner William Herndon later complained that Lincoln annoyingly read aloud throughout his adult life. Lincoln argued: "When I read aloud two senses catch the idea: first, I see what I read; second, I hear it, and therefore I can remember it better."[17]

While he complained that frontier schooling offered "absolutely nothing to excite ambition for education," Lincoln never stopped teaching himself whatever intrigued him, which he "picked up from time to time under the pressure of necessity."[18]

Most pioneers relied on spelling books to learn reading and writing. Lincoln relied primarily on *Dilworth's Spelling Book*, featuring tables of letters, syllables, and monosyllabic words of two, three, four, and five or more letters. Each section was followed by reading lessons with texts such as "When we go out, and when we come in, we are not out of the eye of God." The focus was as much on developing a moral compass as on spelling. The book then expands into multisyllabic words with accents on different syllables, again with biblical insight in the lessons. Students progressing through the book learn about pronouns, verbs, and other parts of speech before reading practice in the form of verse, prose, and fables.[19] Lincoln further honed his speaking skills with William Scott's *Lessons in Elocution*, likely brought to Indiana by his stepmother. *Lessons* provides eight rules of speaking that teach articulation, pronunciation, cadence, and other elements of speaking style. Packed with an exhaustive compilation of poetry and prose, *Lessons* may be the initial source of Lincoln's interest in poets such as Robert Burns, Thomas Gray, Alexander Pope, and Lord Byron, although he likely also enjoyed the pithy maxims that abound in the book.[20]

Lincoln supplemented these with books borrowed from neighbors and teachers. In Indiana he read standards such as *Aesop's Fables*, John Bunyan's *The Pilgrim's Progress*, Daniel Defoe's *Robinson Crusoe*, Benjamin Franklin's *Autobiography*, and two books called *Life of George Washington*, one by David Ramsay and the other by Mason Locke "Parson" Weems.[21] William Herndon later confirmed with Elizabeth Crawford that one famous story was true: Lincoln had borrowed the Weems *Life of George Washington* from her husband, Josiah. After accidentally allowing the book to get wet, Lincoln admitted his guilt, and Josiah had him "pull fodder" for a day or two to make amends. Crawford then allowed Lincoln to keep the damaged book.[22] Lincoln advanced so far in his studies that he served as an amanuensis for his Indiana neighbors, writing letters for the still largely illiterate populace, many of whom had arrived like the Lincolns from Kentucky.[23]

By the time he was living in New Salem, Illinois, Lincoln realized his command of the English language remained stilted from his backwoods Kentucky and Hoosier upbringing. He sought to correct this deficiency while boarding with an educator fittingly named Mentor Graham.[24] Graham helped Lincoln work through Kirkham's *English Grammar in Familiar Lectures*, in which "the learner should commence, *not by committing and rehearsing*, but by reading attentively the first *two* lectures several times over. He ought then to parse, according to the *systematic order*, the examples given for that purpose." Kirkham once dramatically claimed: "Grammar is the science of language."[25] Lincoln told his friend Bill Green, "If that is what they call a science, I'll subdue another."[26] As Lincoln read and practiced, he would begin to learn a systematic and logical method of study that would suit him for the rest of his life.

This systematic method led Lincoln to more concrete sciences, beginning with arithmetic. "We had an old dog-eared arithmetic in our house, and father determined that somehow, or somehow else, I should cipher clear through that book."[27] That arithmetic book was *The New Complete System of Arithmetick* by Nicholas Pike and is generally accepted to be the primary arithmetic book from which Lincoln studied. Evidence shows he also had access to Nathan Daboll's *Schoolmaster's Assistant: Being a Plain Practical System of Arithmetic*.[28]

Lincoln's stepmother, Sarah, gave Lincoln's childhood "copy book" (now more accurately referred to as a "ciphering book") to William Herndon following Lincoln's assassination. Originally about 100 pages sewn together, the book Herndon received had "ten or twelve leaves," the rest having been lost. Herndon apparently gave individual pages to friends of Lincoln as thanks for providing in-depth interviews or correspondence. The eleven pages, now broken into fragments and strewn across at least ten manuscript collections, are organized in the standard *abbaco* curriculum, with the four arithmetical operations, plus compound operations, reduction, practice, rules of three, loss and gain, and so on.[29] One page contains examples and problems in which the young Lincoln has written "The Single Rule of Three" at the top with great literary flourish. The arithmetical operations of addition, subtraction, multiplication, and division are easy to understand. But what is the rule of three?

The rule of three is a fairly elegant mathematical technique with a long history, perhaps known to Hebrews as early as the 15th century BCE. By the sixth century BCE, it was used by Vedic mathematicians, and China had adopted it by the seventh century CE. Eventually it came to Europe. By Lincoln's time, it was considered "high math" for the frontier. In short, the rule of three is defined as "the product of the means in a proportion equals the product of the extremes—used for finding the fourth term of a proportion where three are given." More simply, "a mathematical rule asserting that the value of one unknown quantity in a proportion is found by multiplying the denominator of each ratio by the numerator of the other."

Okay, perhaps not so simply. The rule of three is a way of solving "proportions," what we today call ratios. It is a form of cross-multiplication in which the problem is set up such that the unknown quantity is the last "extreme" in a series of numbers exhibiting a proportional relationship. The basic form is

$$\frac{a}{b} = \frac{c}{x}$$

The idea is to determine the value of x when you know the values of a, b, and c. The rule of three states that you simply rearrange this simple ratio formula into

$$x = \frac{bc}{a}$$

Another way of looking at it is by laying out the three known terms in a linear sequence (a → b → c) and then multiplying the last term (*c*) by the middle term (*b*) before dividing that product by the first term (*a*). For example, to cipher to the rule of three for 3, 9, and 2 is to complete the phrase "3 is to 9 as 2 is to __." In other words, 3/9 = 2/*x*, and *x* is calculated to be 6.[30]

Today we would do this sort of thing fairly easily using algebra, but given the dearth of formal education back in Lincoln's day, the rule of three provided a relatively simple process for working through several types of problems without a great deal of knowledge of proportions. Lincoln would use it often.

STUDYING THE SCIENCES

This takes us to the limits of Lincoln's education according to his autobiographical statement. A closer look at these pages shows that Lincoln was less than forthcoming, intentionally downplaying his expertise for political expediency. The ciphering book includes an additional page covering his practice with the double rule of three, a slightly more complicated skill than he suggested. There are also several fragmented pages in which he practices both simple and compound interest and calculation of a discount rate.[31] Based on these few entries, only a fraction of the original 100-page volume, Lincoln clearly gained more intense mathematical knowledge than suggested in his biographical sketch. Early twentieth-century researcher M. L. Houser went so far as to suggest Lincoln received a "collegiate education" before he was eighteen years old. Taking Lincoln at his word that he ciphered clear through Pike's *Arithmetick*, with additional study in Daboll's book, he would have covered more advanced skills such as reduction (converting unlike numbers), vulgar (simple) fractions, decimals (called decimal fractions), duodecimals, and the inverse rule of three. He likely studied square and cube roots (and their extraction), permutations, and involutions. The two books also provided instruction in practical mathematics that he would find useful in his later life as a store clerk, including gauging the volume of casks used for liquid goods, ways to calculate payments, and general bookkeeping skills. Pike's book provides information on mechanical powers of levers, an introduction to physics that Lincoln would have found useful in loading and unloading flatboats. From Daboll's book, he could have learned geometrical progression, or how to determine the sum of the terms in any series of numbers increasing or decreasing by one common multiplier.[32]

Lincoln continued to seek out books to borrow, reportedly telling a friend that "My Best Friend is a person who will give me a book I have not read."[33] Relative Dennis Hanks suggested Lincoln was aware of the town of New Harmony in Indiana, an intellectual utopia boasting a center for learning and research with an extensive library. There is no conclusive evidence that Lincoln visited the town, but its community of scientists and educators would clearly have appealed to him.[34]

Lincoln's quest for the exact sciences continued as he served four terms in the Illinois State Legislature, then one term in the U.S. Congress. He slowly gained confidence that he was more advanced than most of his peers in the West but realized he remained woefully deficient in knowledge and logical skills compared to many of his eastern-educated congressional colleagues. Feeling the need to improve his thinking skills, Lincoln "studied and nearly mastered the first Six-books of Euclid Geometry."

At first glance the idea of studying a geometry textbook seems odd for a lawyer and politician. But Euclid is about more than just geometry. It is about the progression from a premise to a demonstrable conclusion. It is about logic.

Euclid was a Greek mathematician active in Alexandria in what is now Egypt during the reign of Ptolemy I, roughly 325–270 BCE.[35] Euclid's *Elements* is an epic mathematical treatise, both a history and basis for development of logic and modern science. The thirteen books are a collection of definitions, postulates, propositions, and mathematical proofs. *Elements* was second only to the Bible in the number of editions published since its first printing in 1482. Euclid was the first to present mathematics in a single, logically coherent reference, including a system of rigorous mathematical proofs that continue to be used twenty-three centuries later.[36]

In studying Euclid, Lincoln was following in the footsteps of Thomas Jefferson, who found Euclid in his later years as a means of developing his logical skills, although Jefferson added a racist spin by arguing that only those with superior reasoning capacity (for example, wealthy white landowners like himself) could understand Euclid.[37] William Herndon noted that once back on the circuit in Illinois, while others were soundly, if not soundlessly, sleeping, Lincoln would stay up much of the night analyzing abstract propositions from Euclid. Eventually, Lincoln could "demonstrate all the propositions in the six books."[38] So what is in these six books? According to John Casey's 1885 edition: geometry, the science of figured space in one, two, or three dimensions. Book 1 focuses on the theory of angles, triangles, parallel lines, and parallelograms. It includes a series of postulates, that is, the presumed truth of something based on logical reasoning. There are also axioms, which are statements or propositions regarded as self-evidently true without the need for a definitive proof. One example is to acknowledge that if one thing and a second thing are both equal to a third thing, then the first and second things are also equal to each other.[39] Also covered are the Pythagorean theorem and the sum of the angles of a triangle. The second book does the same for rectangles and squares, concluding with a construction of the "golden ratio."[40] Book 3 deals with circles, including finding their center, inscribing angles, and drawing tangents. Book 4 is inscription and circumscription of triangles and of regular polygons. Book 5 describes a theory of proportion much more sophisticated than Lincoln's simple rule of three. The sixth book then applies proportions to plane geometry. Throughout the six books, Euclid provides a basis for reasoning, logic, and mathematical proofs supporting basic truths.[41]

This is sophisticated mathematics for a frontier lawyer. Lincoln never learned the remaining seven books of Euclid's *Elements*, but he clearly integrated Euclid's logical progressions into his thinking and applied them in both his legal and political careers. In his debates with Stephen A. Douglas, for example, Lincoln employed Euclidean logic and examples to counter Douglas's attempt to dismiss a given fact by simply declaiming the speaker's character. Recalling a lesson from Book 1 of *Elements*, Lincoln retorted that "Euclid proves that all the angles in a triangle are equal to two right angles. Euclid has shown you how to work it out. Now, if you undertake to disprove that proposition, and to show that it is erroneous, would you prove it to be false by calling Euclid a liar?"[42] Researchers David Hirsch and Dan Van Haften suggest Lincoln so ingrained the logic of Euclidean geometry into his thought processes that the structure is embedded in such memorable Lincoln speeches as the Gettysburg Address, the Cooper Union speech, and both Inaugural Addresses.[43]

Euclid, along with Henry Philip Tappan's *Elements of Logic*, may have helped refine Lincoln's logical thought, but he had a naturally inquisitive inclination from a young age.[44] Stepmother Sarah told Herndon that Lincoln liked to eavesdrop on the conversations of his parents and adult visitors. "He was a silent and attentive observer," she said, "never speaking or asking questions till they were gone, and then he must understand everything, even to the smallest thing, minutely and exactly." He would then repeat it to himself "again and again" until it was fixed in his mind.[45] Lincoln acknowledged that not understanding something would drive him to distraction. "I can say this," he related to Reverend J. P. Gulliver in 1860,

> *that among my earliest recollections I remember how, when a mere child, I used to get irritated when anyone talked to me in a way I could not understand. I don't think I ever got angry at anything else in my life. But that always disturbed my temper, and has ever since. I remember going to my little bedroom, after hearing the neighbors talk of an evening with my father, and spending no small part of the night walking up and down, and trying to make out what was the exact meaning of some of their, to me, dark sayings. I could not sleep, though I often tried to, when I go on such a hunt after an idea, until I had caught it; and when I thought I had got it, I was not satisfied until I had repeated it over and over, until I had put it in language plain enough, as I thought, for any boy I knew to comprehend. This was a kind of passion with me, and it has stuck by me; for I am never easy now, when I am handling a thought, till I have bounded it North, and bounded it South, and bounded it East, and bounded it West.*[46]

When his closest friend, Joshua Speed, remarked that Lincoln's mind "was a wonder" and that he seemed to grasp new concepts quickly, Lincoln retorted that Speed was mistaken. Instead, he said he was slow to learn, but once learned "he was slow to forget." Lincoln explained that "his mind was like a piece of steel, very hard to scratch anything on it, and yet, almost impossible after you get it there to rub it out."[47] This characteristic was observed by friends and rivals alike throughout his political life and presidency. The *New York World*, for example, noted in 1862 that Lincoln generally turned over an important subject many times in his thoughts before reaching a decision, but once made, "the Alps or the Andes are not more firmly planted on their bases than are his deliberate decisions."[48] Mentor Graham told Herndon that "Lincoln was the most studious, straight-forward young man in the pursuit of a knowledge of literature than any among the five thousand I have taught in the schools." He went on to say that "his method of doing anything was very systematic."[49]

This systematic, analytical, almost scientific mind drove his need for self-improvement. The fact that it took some effort to ingrain a new concept into his mentality, but once there it was retained forever, points to his phenomenal memory. Lincoln's habit of reading the same book repeatedly, and turning it over in his mind until he had it down, led to a deeper understanding of the material. Once in, it stayed in, and could be recalled in greater detail. This is why Lincoln could recite long poems of dozens of stanzas in their entirety, yet another way he trained his mind. He understood the motivations of individuals, both friend and foe, on a variety of issues because he could recall their specific circumstances, arguments, and beliefs. Fellow politicians were impressed with his ability to remember them. In one example, soon after arriving in Washington for his inauguration, he attended an informal reception with members of Congress working to ward off the impending civil war. As Lincoln was introduced to the delegates by their last names, he was able to fill in their first names and many of their family histories. Doing so ingratiated him and often led to more respectful, and productive, interactions.[50]

Mathematics was not the only analytical science that Lincoln studied, as evidenced by his astonishing number of references to science in later life. Where he attained that knowledge is still mysterious. Mentor Graham told William Herndon that Lincoln had read books on science to boost his knowledge of men and things more than any other man Graham had known.[51] Another New Salemite, Robert Rutledge, confirmed that Lincoln studied "Natural Philosophy [natural science, especially physics], Astronomy, Chemistry &c" while clerking for Denton Offutt.[52] Neither offered the names of any specific books, but clearly Lincoln had spent time reading about these sciences.

Lincoln had attained some knowledge of basic astronomy in Indiana. By his nineteenth year, he had reached his adult six-foot-four-inch height, his 160 pounds glued to a taut muscular frame. Awkward in movement and dress, the uniqueness of his mind managed to impress at least some of the girls. One acquaintance, Anna "Kate" Roby, found him more scientifically instructive than romantic as they sat on the banks of the Ohio River. After Roby noted in awe that the moon was going down, Lincoln lapsed into a rather clinical discourse on the nature of planetary movement: "That's not so," he said, "it don't really go down; It seems so." He went on to explain: "The Earth turns from west to East and the revolution of the Earth carries us under, as it were: we do the sinking as you call it. The moon as to us is comparatively still. The moons sinking is only an appearance." Notwithstanding the rudimentary nature of this description, Roby concluded that "Abe knew the general laws of astronomy and the movements of the heavenly bodies," which she attributed to him being better read than anyone else in the region—"a learned boy among us unlearned folks." What he read to gain this knowledge is unknown, but Roby admitted that "No man could talk to me that night as he did unless he had known something of geography as well as astronomy."[53] At least one early researcher suggested Lincoln had access in Indiana to John O'Neill's New and Easy System of Geography and Popular Astronomy. The book provides a basic introduction to geographical terms and how to read maps, plus an extensive history of each continent. This is followed by an extensive discussion of popular astronomy, the basics of the earth and moon's movement, the causes of solar and lunar eclipses, and explanations of comets, meteors, and constellations. There are even chapters on the moon's effect on tides, calculations of longitude, and weather prediction.[54]

He expanded his understanding after moving to Illinois. Lincoln's fellow circuit-riding colleague Leonard Swett said he observed Lincoln with "a geometry," or "an astronomy," that he would read between county courthouses.[55] This could have been a copy of O'Neill but may also have been *An Introduction to Astronomy* by Denison Olmsted, released in 1839, which Lincoln definitely owned because a copy with Lincoln's signature was offered for sale in 1926.[56] In a much more comprehensive volume than O'Neill's, Olmsted delves deeply into every aspect of astronomy, which may explain Lincoln's growing understanding of astronomical phenomena over the elementary level expressed to Kate Roby. Lincoln never faltered in his growing interest in astronomy up to and including his time as president.[57]

Lincoln's access to scientific literature continued to expand in Illinois. New Salem supplied him with learned patrons with libraries Lincoln could only have dreamed of in Indiana. He also made his first foray into public speaking. Boarding with James Rutledge, the village's founder, Lincoln was invited by Rutledge to join New Salem's Literary and Debating Society. Already largely known for his humorous stories and awkward physical mannerisms, Lincoln surprised the club with his "splendid style," to the "infinite astonishment of his friends." He demonstrated he could pursue discussion with logical reason and concise argument. Rutledge acknowledged that "there was more in Abe's head than wit and fun, that he was already a fine speaker; that all he lacked was culture to enable him to reach the high destiny which he knew was in store for him."[58] Lincoln so enjoyed the science of debating that he reportedly walked six miles to attend a separate debating society and "practice polemics." Often on contentious topics and a supreme test of wits, some of these polemical debates were more entertainment than the best farces played in eastern theaters.[59]

New Salem's debating society was part of a lyceum movement spreading across the nation during the nineteenth century. Lyceum associations hosted traveling guest lecturers as well as discussions by local members. Topics ranged from philosophical deliberations on slavery and female voting to recent scientific explorations to political discourses. About a fifth of lyceum lectures were focused on science. Strict rules of decorum were observed, with members required to engage in civil debate, declamation, composition, criticism, and lecturing. Papers were solicited and read aloud at meetings to stir debate. Lincoln would present a lyceum address of his own in 1838 on "The Perpetuation of Our Political Institutions." The lyceum movement was Lincoln's inspiration for his own later venture into scientific lecturing.[60]

The move to Springfield further increased Lincoln's access to scientific knowledge. There he read Francis Bacon's *Essays*, a series of philosophical evaluations on every facet of life and death. Bacon is best known for his *Novum Organum*, a treatise outlining a new system of logic that was instrumental in the development of the scientific method. Whether Lincoln read the *Novum* in addition to *Essays* is uncertain, but the analytical and logical progression Bacon discusses was reflected in Lincoln's own thinking processes. As Lincoln biographer Sidney Blumenthal notes, "Lincoln applied the empirical and inductive Baconian scientific method by idiosyncratic means." In "his external affairs he had no method, system, or order," according to fellow circuit lawyer Henry Whitney, "but in his mental processes and operations he had a most complete method, system, and order . . . inside [his mind] was all symmetry and precision."[61]

Lincoln also read George Brewster's *A New Philosophy of Matter*, an intriguing scientific philosophy in which Brewster argues there are three "creative" powers in the universe—"Ponderable Matter," "Imponderable Matter," and "Mind." The first is controlled by the second, which consists of forces such as electricity, magnetism, light, gravitation, and capillary attraction. All are controlled by the final creative power, "Mind." This is a rather esoteric and dense book that Lincoln probably only scanned but found intriguing. Most likely it gave him a sense of the physical sciences of electricity and magnetism that would become important during the Civil War.[62]

Lincoln may have also read *On the Correlation of Physical Forces* by William Grove, although there remains some uncertainty. Grove's book describes the principle of conservation of energy and was written in 1846, a year before the principle's description by German physicist Hermann von Helmholz, who is generally credited with its discovery. At least one historian suggests Lincoln also read a copy of Robert Bell's *Eminent Literary and Scientific Men* while he was in Springfield.[63]

More certain is that he read a series of books called the *Annual of Scientific Discovery: or, Year-Book of Facts in Science and Art*, a compilation of scientific advances for each year running from 1850 to 1871, edited by David A. Wells. Herndon recalls that he brought a volume of the annual to the office one day, and Lincoln interrupted his own newspaper reading to look at it. After reading the introduction and first chapter, he told Herndon they must buy the rest of the set. The book's object was to explain the "failures and successes" of the experiments of philosophers and scientists around the world. Contributors to the annual included some of the greatest scientific minds of the time, including Louis Agassiz and Jeffries Wyman, both of whom would later serve Lincoln in scientific roles during the Civil War. Among the study summaries was a list of new patents and a bibliography of recent scientific publications.[64]

Lincoln probably did not read each annual cover to cover but rather scanned for the entries he found most useful. Among them he could choose sections on mechanics, chemistry, astronomy, meteorology, zoology, botany, mineralogy, geology, and geography. Two or three hundred pages per year cataloged scientific and technological news for both general readers and specialists.[65] "I have wanted such a book for years," Lincoln said, "because I sometimes make experiments & have thoughts about the physical world that I do not know to be true nor false." Lincoln saw the books as a way to "correct my Errors and save time & expense—I can see where the scientists and philosophers have failed and avoid the rock on which they split or can see the means of their success and take advantage of their brains—toil and knowledge."[66] He added that

> *the history of failures shows what cannot be done, as general rule and puts the artist—scientist & philosopher on his guard & sets him a thinking on the right line. We always hear of the successes of life & experiment, but scarcely ever of the failures. Were the failures published to the world as well as the successes much brain work & pain work—as well as money & time would be saved.*[67]

The value of these annuals in developing Lincoln's scientific knowledge and broad thinking cannot be overestimated. Lincoln was so enthralled with the work that as president he appointed Wells chairman of the National Revenue Commission.[68]

Other than a few gilded volumes ornamenting his home parlor table, Lincoln himself had only a limited personal library. Lincoln's science knowledge was facilitated by Herndon's ever-expanding book collection, which was at least partially stored in their shared law office.[69] A voracious reader and a determined science aficionado, Herndon had significant natural science knowledge in botany, geology, and ornithology.[70] Lincoln no doubt borrowed as needed from Herndon's collection. When not perusing the books himself, Lincoln would sprawl across the office sofa and engage in hours of discourse on history, literature, philosophy, and science with Herndon.[71] These sessions boosted Lincoln's knowledge in many areas of science and technology.

In 1873 Herndon put up for auction about a thousand volumes from his library.[72] The auction list gives a sense for what scientific volumes may have been available to Lincoln, although there is no way to know which ones he actually read. We do know that Lincoln was fond of astronomy, and Herndon's auction list contains at least one astronomy text published while the two of them practiced law: Elias Loomis's 1856 book *The Recent Progress of Astronomy*.[73] Herndon specifically queried several of Lincoln's friends to determine how much geology Lincoln may have studied. Joseph Gillespie and David Davis independently suggested Lincoln was not much interested in geology despite his friendships with several prominent Illinois geologists and access to as many as a dozen geology books in Herndon's library. Later events showed that Lincoln developed at least some understanding of geology beyond the normal levels of his peers.

Lincoln was less inclined toward theoretical or speculative sciences and was not particularly interested in the natural science volumes in Herndon's library. He was mainly drawn to practical sciences, those areas of study that he felt could be useful in daily life. These included a broad interest in mechanics and technology. David Davis noted that Lincoln studied the "exact sciences," and "he had a good mechanical mind and knowledge." Joseph Gillespie told Herndon that Lincoln "wanted something solid to rest upon, hence his bias for mathematics and physical sciences." That Lincoln was drawn to mechanics and inventions should not be surprising, and both served him well in patent law and the later war.[74]

Lincoln's interest in science was not simply "science for science's sake." He was developing his interests in such a way to put practical applications in play for the common man, not merely as an intellectual exercise of the leisure class like Thomas Jefferson. His scientific learning continued throughout his life, including in the White House, where as president he routinely withdrew science-related books from the Library of Congress.

In his "Communication to the People of Sangamo County," Lincoln did not presume to dictate any specific plan or system to achieve education, but he did say that "every man should receive at least a moderate education, and thereby be enabled to read the histories of his own and other countries, by which he may duly appreciate the value of our free institutions."[75] In a eulogy to his beau ideal of a statesman, Henry Clay, Lincoln noted that like himself, Clay had little formal schooling but did what he could through self-study to "supply the want."[76] "In this country," Lincoln said, "one can scarcely be so poor, but that, if he will, he can acquire sufficient education to get through the world respectably."[77] Lincoln's goal, therefore, was not simply that people could read and write but that they could use those abilities to be more informed and responsible citizens. He wanted the public, and society, to follow his own determination to improve himself, and he advocated for higher standards for teachers and schools.[78] He saw the world rapidly changing as science and technology expanded the reach of even frontier farmers. Only twenty-three years old at the time, Lincoln had a long road ahead of him to achieve his own heights of education. While he would immerse himself in more books along the way, that road would take him out into the real world and, briefly, to a life on the waters.

Part II

Expanding Interests in Science and Technology

CHAPTER 3

Life on the Waters

THE LINCOLN FAMILY FARMS ARE NAMED AFTER THE WATERWAYS FLOW-
ing through their land, in part because access to drinking water was the
first necessity for any frontier family. Such waterways were often also the
most dependable means of marking land on homestead surveys. Although
the smaller streams, brooks, creeks, branches, fords, forks, rivers, and runs
could change course somewhat over time, they remained convenient
borders between neighboring claims. These waterways also provided the
water for mills, transportation, and the site of ferry landings to identify
villages and individual cabins deeper in the woods.[1]

While he was born on the Sinking Spring farm near the South Fork
of the Nolin River in Hardin County, Kentucky, the first home Lincoln
recalls is the Knob Creek farm about fifteen miles northeast. It was here
the child Abe had his first exposure to river life, which the adult Lincoln
later remembered as "three, or three and a half miles South or South-
West of Atherton's ferry on the Rolling Fork."[2] The ferry aided travelers
crossing the Rolling Fork River for places east, but also served as an inter-
mediate transport for more extensive travels downstream to the Salt River
and on to the Ohio River.

When the family moved to Indiana, they spent their first night of
the trip with William Atherton, who extolled his ferry service with the
young Abe present.[3] The Lincoln family reached the broad Ohio River
several days later. Rain had swelled the river, delaying the crossing long
enough for other families to join them on the Kentucky banks until it was
safe to cross. Loading their wagons and livestock aboard a flatboat run by
Hugh Thompson's Ferry on the Indiana side, the family landed a half mile

downstream of Troy at the mouth of the Anderson River, a small tributary into the Ohio. The exact form of this flatboat ferry is unknown, but certain regulations were required for licensed ferry boat operators, including posting a bond in case of accidents, so the ferry would have been considerable size. The fare was probably around twenty-five cents per person, extra for horses and wagons.[4] This was Lincoln's first experience on a flatboat, and although too young to remember it in detail, his precocious mind would have picked up on the difficulties of maintaining a safe crossing as skittish horses panicked with the unsteady bobbing on the swollen river.

When Lincoln was seventeen, his father hired him out to James Taylor for six to nine months. Lincoln worked Taylor's farm, split rails, and did a variety of odd jobs, including running the ferry for Taylor at the mouth of the Anderson River. He would ferry people and goods between the Indiana and Kentucky shores of the Ohio River, approximately the same route his family had taken on the now-defunct Thompson Ferry.[5] Again the type of boat is not identified but was probably a substantial-sized flatboat to handle the breadth and turbulence of the Ohio. He also used a smaller rowboat to ferry people from one side of the Anderson to the other, approximately 100 feet apart. At the time, the Anderson River was designated as a navigable stream and in fact was the "most considerable stream" flowing into the Ohio between the Blue River and the Wabash. Settlements had cropped up on either side of the Anderson, with Troy being the largest on the eastern side. The Taylor family lived on the western bank in Maxville, a small settlement that belies its grandiose name. Likely Lincoln spent free time in Troy, listening to stories from river navigators about their exploits on "The Big Muddy," one of the many nicknames for the Mississippi River.[6] While working for Taylor, he received six dollars per month. He was paid extra for less pleasant work, including thirty-one cents a day for the brutal business of butchering hogs.[7] For the Anderson crossing, he received six and a quarter cents for each round trip. The distance traveled was so short that one passenger noted how, with Lincoln's long arms, he could move the boat from shore to shore "with one sweep of the oars."[8]

About a year after his first hire out to Taylor, Lincoln returned for a second time on the orders of his father. Near Troy he constructed a small flatboat for selling supplies down the river. Lincoln was tending to the boat one day when he was approached by two men dragging large trunks who hired him to ferry them out to a steamboat stopped midriver. Anxious to earn some extra money, Lincoln loaded the trunks onto his flatboat, helped the two gentlemen take seats, and rowed them out to the steamer. Immediately after the men and their heavy baggage were on board the steamship, it "put on steam again" to head downstream.

"Wait," Lincoln said, "you have forgotten to pay me."

Each of them took from his pocket a silver half-dollar and threw it to the bottom of Lincoln's boat. Lincoln "could scarcely believe [his] eyes." He, a poor boy, "had earned a dollar in less than a day; that by honest work I had earned a dollar."

Equivalent to about twenty-six dollars today, Lincoln's first dollar helped him understand the importance of the river to commerce. He saw the world grow substantially that day, how the river could transport people and goods for vast distances with significant monetary gain. He learned that a cash-based economy could be more lucrative than the labor-based family farming that had been his lot in life to that point. Lincoln admitted that the incident made him "a more hopeful and thoughtful boy" from that time on.[9] As he was still a teenager, and as required by law until he reached the age of twenty-one, his first dollar was turned over to his father, along with all the wages earned working for hire. But the experience guided his future thinking.

Lincoln continued to learn the river with each additional ferry run for Taylor. He also got his first taste of the law when he was sued by John T. Hall and his brother Len, owners of ferry rights from the Kentucky side of the river. The brothers claimed that by ferrying people out to waiting steamships, Lincoln was encroaching on their business. The case was brought before Judge Samuel Pate in Kentucky for violating a Kentucky law barring anyone other than those so appointed from "setting any person over any river or creek" for a fee. Lincoln, who had been sitting in on local trials as entertainment, noted that he had not set any person entirely over any river; he had, in fact, only ferried them halfway across, dropping them at steamers in the channel and returning to the original Indiana riverbank. Amused by the strength of the logic, the judge dismissed the case.[10] Lincoln probably took the incident more seriously than the judge. There were legal ramifications to life on the water. He would remember this lesson.

Lincoln gained his first experience with canal boats during this eighteenth year. Canal traffic was just becoming a major form of transportation and would see a surge in construction during the 1830s, only to fall to competition with the railroads by 1840, leaving 3,326 miles of largely incomplete or unused canal ways.[11] The 363-mile Erie Canal in upstate New York had been completed two years earlier, and smaller canals were being built to accommodate local traffic or bypass obstructions. Such was the case in 1827 when Lincoln and his stepbrother John D. Johnston trekked a hundred miles east to work on the Louisville and Portland Canal at the Ohio River just above Louisville, Kentucky. Both strapping men found work digging a two-mile-long canal designed to bypass a natural obstruction to navigation called the Falls of the Ohio. The Falls were more like broken rapids, dropping only twenty-six feet over a distance of two miles, similar to the Great Falls Lincoln would see on the Potomac years later in Washington, D.C. After decades of political and engineering disagreement, construction of the canal finally began the year before Lincoln and Johnston were hired, and the canal was made operational in 1830, although not fully completed until 1833, six years behind schedule. Lincoln and Johnston seem not to have worked long on the canal, as they returned to Indiana to continue their farmwork and outside hired labor. But Lincoln did earn payment in silver dollars and lingered long enough to understand the importance of canals for commerce and for improved river navigation. Yet another lesson on the waters.[12]

CHASING THE FATHER OF WATERS

Up to this point, Lincoln's involvement on the waters was limited to smaller streams and crossing the Ohio from bank to bank. What he really craved, according to neighbor William Wood, was to take a job as a river hand down the Ohio River. He yearned to experience more of the world than just the farm and the opposite banks.[13] When he was nineteen, he had his first opportunity to go significantly downriver on a flatboat, a trip that would take him nearly 1,300 miles to New Orleans.

As Lincoln was already learning, bodies of water were highways for transport and commerce. He had gone from the small Nolin River to the slightly larger Anderson River to the broad Ohio. He had heard stories of an even broader river, the Father of Waters, the Mississippi River.[14] Lincoln had seen steamboats on the Ohio—the first one up the river in 1811 was the *New Orleans*—but the main mode of transportation for the working class were the flatboats farmers used to carry goods downstream to distant cities, where they could sell excess produce, livestock, and manufactured goods.[15] Lincoln wanted to explore the river life, in part because it would take him to an outside world, light-years beyond the small existence he had so far experienced.

James Gentry was a successful merchant not far from where the Lincolns lived in Indiana. In early 1828, he arranged for his twenty-one-year-old son Allen, who had already completed one trip to New Orleans, to captain a second trip with a load of produce and merchandise destined for Louisiana sugar plantations. He hired Lincoln as a reliable—and strong—bow hand working the foremost oar, for which he would be paid eight dollars per month, plus his return fare home.[16]

Lincoln was not the first in the family with this opportunity. His father, Thomas, had made at least one flatboat trip in March 1806 while living in Elizabethtown, Kentucky, mere weeks before marrying Nancy Hanks. Thomas was hired by Elizabethtown merchants Bleakley & Montgomery to help build a flatboat, then was employed with Isaac Bush to float down the Ohio and Mississippi Rivers to New Orleans with a load of goods, principally pork. The Bush connection would be fruitful; he was the brother of Sarah Bush Johnston, whom Thomas would later marry after their respective first spouses died.[17] The pork probably came from Thomas Lincoln himself. Store records show that in mid-February, Thomas sold Bleakley & Montgomery "2400 pounds of pork at 15 pence and 494 pounds of beef at 15 pence." The store turned around and sold Thomas a saw, a plane, an auger, and an adze, exactly the tools needed to build a boat, while crediting Bush's account for construction of the flatboat at nearby West Point.[18]

Thomas was adamantly antislavery, but slavery provided an impetus for making the grueling trip south on the river. Large plantations meant concentrations of enslaved people, and that higher population density required a substantial investment in food. At the same time, these plantations focused their energies and acreage on nonfood commodities like tobacco, sugarcane, and cotton. To make up their need, they bought or traded for edible produce coming down the river.

Leaving around the first of March, Thomas and Isaac finished their business in New Orleans and then walked the entire distance back to Kentucky, arriving home about two months later. One relative suggested Thomas made at least two, and possible several, flatboat trips to New Orleans when he lived in Kentucky and Indiana, with little profit. On one occasion he sold an "entire load on credit & never realized a cent for the same."[19]

Lincoln and Allen Gentry hoped to be more successful. A typical investment for Allen's father required about seventy-five dollars (over $2,000 today) for the flatboat alone. The cargo could be worth over three thousand dollars ($82,000 today).[20] A successful trip could be immensely profitable, an unsuccessful one financially devastating.

Building the flatboat was the first chore. Unlike keelboats, which were long and narrow with a central ridge keel under the hull to maintain stability and easy steering, flatboats were entirely flat on the bottom like a raft. They had simple square sides, with angled bow and stern. They could range from fifteen to thirty feet wide and from forty to 120 feet long. Lengthy oars called sweeps extended from the sides for stability. In the back was a wide-bladed steering oar, in the front an oar called a gouger to throw the boat in any direction to avoid snags, trees, and stumps.[21]

While that sounds simple, Gentry and Lincoln had to use their full extent of "woods craft" knowledge learned felling forests and building log cabins.[22] One circuit-riding colleague of Lincoln described the basic construction of the flatboat for that era:

Two flat pieces of timber from thirty to fifty feet in length, two to three feet in breadth, and foot in thickness were hewed out of poplar log; one edge was level, the other two were beveled at each end. These pieces were called gunwales—pronounced gunnels. Into these gunwales, at suitable distances, were mortised cross-pieces of oak, fourteen feet long, six inches wide, and three inches thick, in addition to head blocks at each end, six- or eight-inches square. A stout frame being thus made, two-inch oak planks were fastened longitudinally to the oak cross-pieces by means of wooden pins an inch square, systematically cut out from tough species of timber termed "pin oak," and driven by a heavy maul through an auger hole bored through both planks. The bottom, consisting of two-inch oak plank, was then fastened on to these longitudinal planks and rabbeted into the gunwales, the same being made water-tight by oakum and pitch. Thus far, no iron was used in the construction, and no iron tools employed beyond crosscut saw, mill saw, an axe, broad-axe, an augur, and a draw-knife.

This boat was launched by simply turning it over by two windlasses and levers so as to lie bottom side down in the river. Uprights consisting of 4 x 4 scantling were then mortised into the upper edge of the gunwales, and one-and-one-half-inch poplar plank securely fastened longitudinally thereon, and the seams caulked with oakum, and pitched. When produce was to be her cargo, a false bottom was put in, as it was impossible to construct such boats so that they would be entirely water-tight. Finally, a ridge-pole was placed longitudinally, and a roof was added. A cabin was improvised in one corner by the use of rough boards, and four huge oars were rigged, two on the sides, one at the bow, and one at the stern. A "check post" and coil of rope were then provided, and the craft was in commission.[23]

A small woodstove was installed for cooking. Because Lincoln and Gentry were its sole crew, their flatboat was probably about eighteen feet wide and sixty-five feet long, and they likely omitted the side sweeps, controlling the boat solely with the steering and gouger oars.[24]

This deceptively simple boat provided a significant showcase of construction and navigation. Lincoln and Gentry had to consider structural stresses on the frame to avoid any twisting that might open up leaks between the boards. Flipping the hull into the water required an understanding of leverage and the windlass, the latter being a rudimentary block and tackle, perhaps even a rope thrown over a tree branch or wooden frame. When a boat had them, sweeps needed to be almost twice as wide as the width of the hull in order to create enough physical force against the water to maintain positioning in the river. The gouger must be strong and thick enough to jab into shallow mud to jolt the flatboat to the side when necessary. Like the steering oar at the stern, the gouger required almost superhuman strength to ensure boat stability and direction. Lincoln and Gentry would use both their brains and their brawn throughout the voyage.

Most likely, the two men departed Rockport in the spring to take advantage of high waters. The winter of 1828 had been rather mild, with an early spring bringing rapid tree growth. Corn crops were already beginning to grow in Louisiana.[25] With the Ohio River cresting over its banks, the high waters offered smoother and faster sailing to the Mississippi River and on to New Orleans. The two men loaded the flatboat with James Gentry's cargo, which included corn and hay for the mules on sugar plantations and meat and potatoes for the enslaved workers.[26] They also likely carried "barrel pork," a preserved pork similar to bacon that Southern planters preferred as a low-cost, high-energy food for slaves.[27] Since much of the sugar was grown north of New Orleans in places like Natchez, Mississippi, and Baton Rouge, Louisiana, the two men likely made several stops to sell their wares or barter for products they could sell farther downstream, including cotton, tobacco, and sugar.[28] The flatboat was well battered by floating debris by the time they reached New Orleans about 1,300 miles distant. Once there, Lincoln and Gentry lingered long enough to sell their remaining stock before the flatboat was sold off to be taken apart for building houses, repairing docks, or fueling the boilers of steamboats. The two men then took a steamboat back to Rockport, Indiana.

Three years later, after moving to Illinois, Lincoln again made a flatboat trip to New Orleans. A local entrepreneur and schemer named Denton Offutt approached Lincoln's relative John Hanks about manning such a journey. Hanks then recruited Lincoln and brother-in-law John Johnston, all of whom now lived in a wooded area west of Decatur near the banks of the Sangamon River. Because of the previous "winter of deep snow," melting snowpack made the roads impassable by the first of March 1831, forcing the three men to purchase a canoe and paddle down the

Sangamon River as far as Springfield, where they expected to find a fully loaded flatboat. Offutt, however, had somehow forgotten to arrange for it, but offered to pay the three men to construct one.[29]

Frustrated by the delay but eager to continue, Lincoln, Hanks, and Johnston were joined by local carpenters Charles Cabanis and John Roll. While they largely followed the standard design, there were some differences that were in part influenced by Lincoln's experience building log cabins and fence rails. Because this trip was to include livestock—live hogs in addition to wet and dry goods—the men constructed small corrals and troughs in the boat. They also added a wooden mast and sail to help them maneuver when the wind was gentle enough to push the boat but not wreck it.[30] After about six weeks of construction, they shoved the eighteen-foot-wide-by-eighty-foot-long boat into the Sangamon River just below Sangamotown.[31] They floated the Sangamon River as it wound northwest until meeting the Illinois River near Beardstown, which then turned south until its confluence with the mighty Mississippi River north of Alton for their final thousand miles on the waters to New Orleans. Along the way, they would pass St. Louis (where John Hanks turned back because his wife was due to give birth), Memphis, Vicksburg, Natchez, and Baton Rouge, giving Lincoln a glimpse of cities that would become important strategic points in the later Civil War.

Contrary to any naïve expectation of a lazy float down a broad flowing river, dangerous conditions abounded for flatboat men. Smaller rivers like the Sangamon and Illinois were filled with debris-induced dangers, and large, faster, and deeper rivers like the Mississippi offered their own hazards. Now traveling by flatboat to New Orleans a second time, Lincoln developed an intuitive sense of hydrography, the science behind the observation of physical features of the river. Lincoln was said to have a "quick river eye," a necessary skill to keep from getting hung up on obstructions, or worse, sunk.[32] The flatboat had to move fast enough to most efficiently use the valuable time, while slow enough to keep control around loops, turns, and cutbacks. Lincoln later recalled his critical role in the trip, where he "acted both as the engineer and the engine."[33]

Trees and driftwood were common obstructions, collecting in shallows and channels and impeding navigation.[34] Wrecks of boats with less adept crews could quickly end the trip downstream or upend the cargo. Large trees might drift down the river until they rooted themselves into the sediment to create "planters" that could spike up through the hull of an unsuspecting boat.[35]

Sandbars were a danger at every meander in the constantly shifting "shape" of the river, which riverboat pilots had to learn, and relearn, for every stretch of the river and with the changing seasons. The shape was affected by currents, eddies, and even the cast of light from different phases of the moon or stars on dark nights.[36] Each bend in the river offered its own hazards, including point bars sneaking out from the convex side of the bend with its opposing cut bank on the concave side. And then there were the chutes—sometimes called "shoots" or cutoffs—in which a break in the bank or levee creates an unexpected rapid flow of water out of the river into the surrounding floodplain. All rivers naturally carve shortcuts over time, cutting through meandering loops to create a straighter pathway for the water while isolating the original loop as a new oxbow lake. Unexpected chutes, however, can be disastrous to a flatboat that finds itself suddenly in a farmer's field a mile from the river.[37]

As he moved down the river, Lincoln came to understand why the Mississippi was the central artery of commerce in the Midwest, allowing farmers from western New York, Ohio, Indiana, and Illinois to transport their produce to New Orleans. In the city itself, Lincoln discovered the existence of a cosmopolitan multiethnic society. Ships from this crucial port did trade with the Caribbean and South America, as well as up the East Coast of the United States to Europe and Africa. Transferring cargo to wagons for the land crossing over the central American isthmus in what is now Panama allowed reloading of ships on the Pacific Ocean for ports up the West Coast and to Asia.[38] Lincoln's world enlarged immeasurably in New Orleans. No longer simply subsistence farming and small towns as far as you could walk or ride on horseback, life on the river showed Lincoln a glimpse of upper society. There were wealthy sugar plantation owners who purchased or traded for pork and potatoes. There were poverty-stricken families, both black and white, desperate to barter whatever little they had for whatever little they could get. The river was an economic engine as well as transportation, but he recognized the benefits were unequal in distribution. It made Lincoln think about his own situation, his limited formal schooling and opportunities, and how he might better his condition.[39]

Upon arrival in New Orleans, Lincoln and his companions had to compete with hundreds of other flatboats for space at the piers, two to three deep along the docks for over a mile at the landing site. After crawling over other boats, the men bartered and sold whatever remained of their wares, plus anything acquired along the way. Eventually, they would sell the boat itself, sometimes whole to a wealthy buyer but usually piecemeal, taking it apart board by board to sell as lumber or fuel. Overall, they could net a return of about a quarter of the construction cost.[40] On each occasion, the crews lingered in New Orleans for as long as they could afford before setting out for home.

The experience gave Lincoln his first real taste of slavery in its fullest expression. He saw enslaved people struggling to exist and avoid beatings on the sugar plantations. He and Allen Gentry survived an attack on their boat by a group of slaves desperate to escape. In New Orleans Lincoln reportedly witnessed a slave auction in progress, which reinforced his belief that slavery was immoral.[41] Beyond slavery, Lincoln experienced a cultural diversity in New Orleans more foreign than anything he experienced before or after. Here he saw sailors and merchants from ports in Spain, Portugal, France, and elsewhere in Europe, each spouting an unfamiliar language beyond his comprehension. Then there was the cacophony of mixed-heritage residents, including Creole, Cajun, Indigenous, and mixtures of African with all of the above.[42] While Lincoln lacked most of the typical vices of the day, New Orleans was rife with every depravity imaginable, not the least of which were rampant gambling, thievery, prostitution, and murder. All of this gave him insight into human nature, both the good and the bad, that informed his relationships with people the rest of his life. He would remember that different people had different backgrounds and different motivations for making decisions.

Lincoln and his companions returned back north on steamboats, an improvement on his father's need to walk the entire way home from New Orleans. Steamboats had begun plying the Mississippi, Ohio, and other inland waterways in the early nineteenth century. In 1811, the steamboat

New Orleans traveled all the way from its namesake city to Cincinnati. Flatboats remained the standard for going downstream, but steam was necessary to push a vessel upstream against the strong current.

Like many poor farmers returning from their flatboat journey south, Lincoln worked as a boat hand as the steamboat forced itself upstream against the current. Periodically, the boat would stop to take on cordwood for the boilers; much later, steamers shifted to coal as fuel. Sometimes a local boat would pull alongside the moored steamer to offload cordwood for fuel, just as Lincoln had done on the Ohio River back in Indiana.[43] Other times Lincoln would be set ashore with an axe to cut wood. All steamboats burned the wood to produce steam, which then moved pistons that turned paddles. Steamers at the time were either side-wheelers, with massive wooden paddle wheels on either side of the boat to pull the boat through the water, or stern-wheelers, with a single paddle system in the rear pushing the boat.[44]

Lincoln likely spent some travel time chatting with the engine room workers to learn how the steamboat engines worked. He discovered that steamers were notoriously dangerous. In addition to getting caught on snags and other obstructions like flatboats, steamers produced immense amounts of heat under pressure. Boilers too-frequently exploded or accidentally set the boat afire. Lincoln probably also hung around the pilot house, learning the ins and outs of steering the boat through narrow channels and obstructions. River piloting was both a science and an art. It took a steady eye and a natural feel for the waters moving under the boat.[45] And Lincoln was eager to learn.

Lincoln evidently learned his lessons well because back in Illinois he quickly became a reliable river pilot of his own. A local pilot was necessary because the river channels moved over time, sometimes suddenly after massive storms.[46] Someone who could observe the same stretch of river over time was invaluable. Lincoln had moved to New Salem on the Sangamon River, a small winding waterway that many believed was navigable. He quickly learned its specific idiosyncrasies, which came in handy when a steamboat named the *Talisman* attempted to travel up the Illinois River from Beardstown and then the Sangamon River with the goal of reaching Springfield, thus opening up direct commerce to New Orleans.

While relatively small for a steamboat, the *Talisman* spanned almost the width of the narrow Sangamon. Lincoln and others served as axemen to clear the tangle of overhanging trees obstructing the vessel's passage, along with accumulating ice and driftwood. The boat eventually reached Portland Landing, about seven miles north of Springfield, and prepared to move into the city proper once it loaded up with more fuel wood.[47]

But then the water level began dropping and the crew rushed to get the *Talisman* back downstream. Lincoln was hired as an assistant pilot to Rowan Herndon, cousin of future law partner William Herndon. They proceeded slowly, but the boat still received significant damage from overhanging branches and drifting fallen trees as the riverbanks seemed to close in on them. According to Herndon, the steamboat then got hung up on the Cameron and Rutledge Mill dam in New Salem, which had to be broken up by throwing the anchor over it and yanking a breech in the dam. The boat continued to struggle its way back to Beardstown. There Lincoln collected his fee of forty dollars and walked the sixty miles back to New Salem. The incident ended aspirations of making the Sangamon navigable to Springfield. To put an exclamation on the idea, the *Talisman* burned to cinders at the wharf in St. Louis a few months later.[48]

The *Talisman* was the second time Lincoln had lodged a boat on the dam in New Salem. As he worked to free the *Talisman*, he would have recalled hanging over the same mill dam a year before on his second flatboat trip to New Orleans. He had taken charge on that incident as well, transferring their cargo to smaller boats to lighten the load and reportedly borrowing an auger from the local carpenter to bore a drainage hole. Both cases reinforced his growing understanding of the importance of navigable rivers to aid in transportation and commerce. His time on the waters made him begin to see the desperate need to improve navigability of rivers, dig canals, and build roads. Not only would these improvements make life easier, they would help stimulate the economy in Illinois and other western states. The two dam incidents would also stick in his mind years later when, yet again, he would witness a steamboat run aground, forced to use debris to coax it off an obstruction. It gave him ideas. But that would come later. For now, despite his own experiences on the mill dam, New Salem attracted him as a place finally to set out on his own after an early lifetime of indenture to his family. He would settle in New Salem with the promise of a job from Denton Offutt, the same man who hired him to take the flatboat to New Orleans. Like the flatboat, that job would be slow to appear, but it would lead Lincoln to a series of increasingly technical trades that would continue to open Lincoln's eyes to the future.

CHAPTER 4

The Technical Trades

"Come to New Salem," Offutt had offered. "You can clerk at the store I am about to open." Offutt had been impressed with the young man's maturity, and Lincoln had felt an immediate connection to the residents of New Salem in the short time he was hung up on the dam. They had pitched in to help offload the cargo and got him and his fellow flatboaters back on track for the long trip to New Orleans. Starting his new life in New Salem seemed like a good idea.

After saying goodbye to his father and stepmother, Lincoln walked back to New Salem, only to find that the consistently erratic Offutt had not yet procured the goods for the store. Lincoln did odd jobs in exchange for room and board. Much of his early labor involved rail splitting, a skill he had advanced to a level as high as his disdain for it. Splitting a rail was a mix of science and art. Unlike some popular depictions of Lincoln swinging an axe, splitting a log was done with a maul, a kind of mallet or sledgehammer, and a wedge.[1] The thin edge of the wedge would be inserted in an initial hatchet cut, then struck with the maul to split the log along its natural cleavage. Logs would be split into halves, then quarters, and even eighths for large trees. The resulting ten- to twelve-foot-long rails were then stacked in a zigzag pattern to create a relatively effective fence line without nails.[2] But as good as Lincoln was at it, this was exactly the kind of farmwork he was trying to escape. "Without means and out of business," he would have to find a trade if Offutt did not come through soon.[3]

NONSTARTERS

Lincoln briefly considered apprenticing as a blacksmith. Most subsistence farmers also doubled as tradesmen, working as coopers (barrel makers), tanners (leather makers), distillers (whiskey), brickmakers, shoemakers, or blacksmiths.[4] His exposure to the trade went back to Indiana. He and Dennis Hanks had spent many evenings in the Gentryville general store and at Baldwin's blacksmith shop trading stories and "yarns," so Lincoln had seen many an hour of blacksmithing in action.[5]

Blacksmiths were accorded an honored place in the village. They forged the plows, the tools, and the cookware needed to sustain life on the frontier. The village blacksmith was a "gunsmith, farrier, coppersmith, millwright, machinist, and surgeon general to all broken tools and implements," as one scholar put it. He could be called on to forge such a variety of implements as nails, horseshoes, chains, bullet molds, yoke rings, bear traps, bells, saws, and all the metal parts of looms, spinning wheels, and sausage grinders.[6] Lincoln had been familiar with the cast-iron plows he used when he was young. With its relatively high carbon content (over 2 percent), cast iron tends to be brittle, which caused problems for Lincoln back on the farm. On the other hand, iron could be cast into a variety of shapes using molds. As a blacksmith, Lincoln also could have learned how to work with wrought iron, which with its very low carbon content (less than 0.08 percent) was much tougher, easier to hammer into useful shapes, could be drawn out into thin wires, was corrosion resistant, and was more easily welded.[7]

Later, during the Civil War, Lincoln evoked his short-lived blacksmithing experience to describe his relationship with George B. McClellan, the man he assigned as general-in-chief of the Union Army but later described as "having the slows" because of his lack of aggressiveness in battle. Lincoln recalled a blacksmith in his boyhood days who tried to put to a purposeful use a big piece of wrought iron he had in the shop. Firing up the forge, the blacksmith put the iron on the anvil determined to make a sledgehammer out of it. Giving up on that after a while, he decided to draw it out and make a clevis (a U-shaped fastener). After a few whacks and pumping the bellows to heighten the fire, he again stopped. "Okay, maybe a bolt." Working it hard for a while longer, it now was too thin even for a bolt. Frustrated with his lack of success trying to make something useful happen, he proclaimed, "Darn you, I'm going to make a fizzle of you." And with that he dunked it into the water and let it fizz. McClellan, Lincoln told his friend, was someone who should have been productive, but no amount of working him hard could make him useful. McClellan's career soon fizzled out.[8]

Being a blacksmith was respectable, but it was also hard work. The idea of toiling over a hot forge, slinging a heavy hammer for hours on end while sweat poured from his skin, was unappealing. Given his distaste for the hard labor of subsistence farming, Lincoln chose not to pursue blacksmithing. He would find some other trade.

Another option for Lincoln was carpentry. His father, Thomas, had learned carpentry as a youth from Joseph Hanks, his future wife's uncle, in Elizabethtown, Kentucky.[9] Thomas's level of proficiency as a carpenter has been debated by historians, with some suggesting he did yeoman work but was not particularly adept or prosperous. People who knew him said that Thomas was a tolerable "cabinet & house carpenter," capable of framing windows, doors, and floors and constructing rudimentary tables and other basic needs such as coffins.[10]

Other historians have suggested Thomas was a skilled cabinetmaker and owned "the best set of carpenter's tools in Hardin County" when he lived in Kentucky. Some claim even that he considered himself a carpenter by trade rather than a farmer. Thomas had made cupboards and other furniture for neighbors in Indiana, including several seven-foot-tall corner cupboards constructed out of fine cherrywood.[11] There appear to be at least twelve surviving examples of Thomas Lincoln's cabinetmaking skill, many of which are on display in museums like the Abraham Lincoln Presidential Library and Museum in Springfield, Illinois, and the Henry Ford Museum and Greenfield Village in Michigan, including an elegant fall-front desk.[12] Thomas did explain to a young Lincoln which trees were good for cabinetmaking, including various oak, walnut, and cherry trees that were "splendid material for all kinds of cabinet work."[13] Lincoln spent a great deal of time whipsawing planks with his father to construct cabins, floors, doors, and windows. Recent discoveries have unearthed the heavy wooden-handled, iron-bladed froe Lincoln used to split shingles for the family cabin, complete with his initials, "AL," etched into the back of the blade. One walnut corner cupboard made for Indiana neighbors Josiah and Elizabeth Crawford is sometimes identified as having been made by Abraham, but Elizabeth definitively confirmed it was the work of Thomas Lincoln. In truth, while Lincoln had assisted his father's cabinetmaking on occasion, he never developed significant interest in carpentry. At best he was more interested in the mathematical preciseness of angles, which encouraged his further study of geometry but not cabinetmaking.[14]

THE MILLS

Considering his experiences getting stuck on the mill dam not once, but twice, it was perhaps fated that Lincoln also found work at the mill in New Salem. Tens of thousands of water mills were constructed as farmers slowly moved their way inland from the inhospitable coasts during the early nineteenth century. These mills transformed the geography of the land and changed the flow of rivers.[15] Water was diverted to turn great waterwheels for gristmills to grind corn, wheat, and other grains. Designs of the basic gristmills were simple: water flowed past a vertical paddle wheel, which turned a shaft that turned a large millstone. The rough surface of the millstone would grind against a second, stationary, stone. Any grain placed between the two stones would be ground into the soft powder we call flour. Early mills were dependent on the rate of flow of the water source, but eventually they included wooden gears to better control the rotation and grinding capacity.[16] Some mills were modified to saw lumber. Sawmills worked similarly, with a crank and connecting rod transforming the circular movement of the wheel to the back-and-forth movement of a straight saw. Later in Lincoln's life, mills were converted to steam power, but early on he had to do grinding manually with a crank or by having a horse or mule walk in circles to turn the millstone.

Lincoln was no stranger to mills. Thomas had helped build the mill in Elizabethtown, Kentucky, working alongside enslaved men whose meager pay went to their masters and drove Thomas's wages down.[17] Later in Little Pigeon Creek, Thomas built a horse-powered mill for grinding corn for the community. "Many corn dodgers [were] made from that old mill," a neighbor recalled.[18] Lincoln was usually the one tasked with carting the family corn to the mill for grinding.

Running the hand-operated mill was hard work, and Lincoln could only grind fifteen to twenty bushels of corn in a day. On the rare occasions that there was wheat to grind, the mill lacked the capability to sift the flour from the bran, which made for lumpy bread.[19] Still, Lincoln looked forward to the seven-mile trek. At least for a while it got him away from the drudgery of the farm. It gave him the greatest pleasure of his boyhood days, reported Herndon.[20]

That pleasure came with its risks. One day when he was ten, Lincoln straddled his old flea-bitten gray mare, tossed a large bag of corn on its haunches behind him, and rode several miles to Noah Gordon's mill. Finding a long line, he spent the afternoon relating humorous stories while he waited his turn. As sundown approached, Lincoln finally hitched up the old mare to the log arm that turned the grinding stone as the horse walked slowly in circles. Riding this arm, he could coax along the horse's pace with a few well-placed snaps of his whip. "Get up, you old hussy," Lincoln admonished with each gentle lash. On and on this went for the interminable time needed to grind the corn, each whip snap accompanied by the admonition. Lincoln was in the midst of repeating the exclamation, yelling out, "Get up . . ." when suddenly "the old jade, resenting the continued use of the goad, elevated her shoeless hoof and striking the young engineer in the forehead, sent him sprawling to the earth."[21]

Seeing the incident, Noah Gordon rushed in to pick up the "bleeding, senseless boy" he thought was dead, immediately sending for his father. Lincoln was still unconscious when Thomas arrived and remained such throughout the night. Around daybreak, Lincoln suddenly stirred from his apparent demise, "jerked for an instant," and with no preamble or awareness blurted out the words, ". . . you old hussy" to finish the exclamation so unceremoniously interrupted the night before.[22]

Lincoln survived the ordeal with no apparent permanent injury, although some speculate it might be the reason for his asymmetrical facial structure. He later admitted in an autobiographical statement that he was "apparently killed for a time."[23]

The inquisitive Lincoln never forgot this event and considered it one of the most remarkable incidents in his life. On slow days he entertained Herndon with speculation as to the psychological phenomenon he had experienced, that is, the blurting out of the rest of his "Get up, you old hussy" admonition after twelve hours of unconsciousness. Setting his scientific mind to the task, Lincoln thought, "Just before I struck the old mare my will through the mind had set the muscles of my tongue to utter the expression, and when her heels came in contact with my head the whole thing stopped half-cocked, as it were, and was only fired off when the mental energy or force returned."[24] Perhaps not ready for publication in a scientific paper, his thoughts demonstrate a formulation of a hypothesis to be tested.

In any case, not long after Lincoln had settled in New Salem, Offutt rented the Rutledge and Cameron flour and saw mills and set Lincoln to manage them. New Salem at this time consisted of about twenty-five families, most of them tradesmen or storekeepers, and served as the commercial hub for the region. Farmers from miles around came for supplies and to grind their corn or cut their lumber. There were also two doctors, a shoemaker, a carpenter, a teacher, a tavern (that is, an inn), and a wool-carding mill.[25] The flour mill was the only one around for many miles and was operated by water diverted from the Sangamon River. Lincoln did manual labor like unloading sacks of wheat from farmers' wagons, but also got to use his arithmetic learning by measuring out the bushels and calculating the amount due.[26] One day he again demonstrated both his brawn and brains by devising an arrangement of ropes and straps, harnessed about his hips to lift a box of stones weighing around a thousand pounds. He was already building an awareness of basic physics, learning that levers and pulleys could be used to enhance one's physical strength.[27]

PASSING TIME AS A MERCHANT

Lincoln worked occasionally in Abner Ellis's store while waiting for Offutt, so Lincoln already knew the basics of merchant life by the time Offutt finally acquired the merchandise.[28] Farmers grew or hunted most of their own food, while their wives sewed most of the family clothing. Offutt's store was one of three or four in small New Salem, and they stayed open largely by stocking the kinds of goods that were harder to find. Eastern goods were too expensive and unnecessary for the still-frontier Illinois, but farmers commonly traded produce for iron goods such as plow blades, pots, and pans. Women purchased fine textiles made in New England cotton mills, with the bolts of fabric brought home to stitch everything from dresses to pantaloons. Coffee was a big seller since it could not be grown in the temperate climates of the Midwest. Other sales included lard, bacon, firearms, beeswax, and honey.

Unfortunately, there were no laws controlling the purity of food products, so it was common for unscrupulous merchants to stretch their flour with a little white plaster or sell dyed navy beans, dry-roasted peas, or even small pebbles as "coffee."[29] Lincoln quickly earned a reputation as an honest broker in New Salem, a merchant everyone could trust.

Lincoln worked for Offutt for about six months in the fall of 1831 and winter of 1832 at a pay of fifteen dollars per month, during which time he became friends with William Berry.[30] Around the end of this time, it was clear Offutt's store was failing, so Lincoln signed on to fight in the Black Hawk War. By the time he returned three months later, the three stores still existing in New Salem were owned by Samuel Hill, Reuben Radford, and the Herndon brothers. One of the brothers sold his share to William Berry, the other to Lincoln on credit. Berry and Lincoln were in business. Not long after, Radford's store was vandalized, and in a fit of frustration he sold it to William Greene, who resold it the same day to Berry and Lincoln. Consolidating their now combined stock, Berry and Lincoln moved into the larger Radford store and essentially held a merchandizing monopoly in the town.

Much of the business was done on credit and barter. Although he was not yet a lawyer, Lincoln himself drew up and attested to the mortgage as Greene deeded part of his property to Radford in payment for two notes to cover the $400 cost of buying the store. Later that same day, Berry and Lincoln purchased the store from Greene for $750, paying $265 in cash (likely from Berry), and assumed payment for two notes of $188.50 each. Berry then gave Greene a horse, saddle, and bridle for the remainder. They soon after bought additional merchandise, again on credit, thus putting them "deeper and deeper in debt."[31]

Lincoln at least was able to use his rudimentary formal education during this time as a storekeeper. The simple rule of three he learned in Indiana usually sufficed for people who were used to trading hogs for farming supplies but now had to start paying for them in cash—or more often, on credit, with a promise to pay later. The final page of Lincoln's ciphering book shows the calculation of a discount rate with the example: "Bought goods to the value of £109-10[5] to be paid at 9 months what present money will discharge the same if I am allowed 6 per cent per annum discount." The rule of three and higher math skills likely came in handy. For example, if Lincoln knew three bushels of corn cost $1.80 and wanted to know how much twelve bushels would cost, the rule of three would quickly allow him to write out[32]

$$\frac{3}{\$1.80} = \frac{12}{x}$$

Rearranged, this becomes

$$x = \frac{\$1.80 * 12}{3}$$

and calculates to

$$x = \$7.20$$

While Berry was the son of a prominent Presbyterian minister, he was often described negatively due to his intemperance, although this is disputed by his family heirs.[33] Neither man seemed particularly adept at running a store. Whatever Berry's perceived incapacities, Lincoln tended to sell too much on credit while being less adamant about collecting payment. More often than not, Lincoln simply paid too little attention to the business. Henry C. Whitney, who later spent much time on the legal circuit with him, suggested that Lincoln "attended perfunctorily to the wants of the customers" and was "quite apt to be diverted by something he 'was put in mind of' or by some scientific or educational diversion."[34] In time, these burdens and mismanagement led to the store failing. As Lincoln succinctly put it, "The store winked out."[35] Berry died in 1835, and with the store being sued for past due bills, Lincoln carried what he referred to as his "national debt" of $1,100, slowly paying it off over many years.[36]

POSTMASTER

His short-lived mercantile career gave him a political advantage as the store was the center of life and commerce in the area serviced by New Salem. Lincoln made a lot of friends in the community through his visibility. Since Lincoln was more literate than many of his fellow villagers, people eagerly enlisted him to write family letters for them. It seemed a natural development for Lincoln to become postmaster when an opening became available. Postmaster was one of tens of thousands of positions officially appointed by the president of the United States, who at that time was Democrat Andrew Jackson. An avowed follower of Henry Clay of the Whig Party, Lincoln later acknowledged that his appointment as postmaster was "too insignificant to make his politics an objection."[37] He served as part-time postmaster for about three years, conducting business from the store and continuing his duties even after he was elected to the state legislature.

With mail arriving only once or twice a week, Lincoln had plenty of time to read the newspapers before delivering them to their subscribers, which pleased him more than any other aspect of the job.[38] Among them were the *Louisville Journal*, *St. Louis Republican*, *New York Telescope*, and the *Washington National Intelligencer*. He also read the *Congressional Globe*, which he continued to have access to once he became a state legislator.[39] Always honest, in late 1835 he wrote to the publisher of the *Globe* to say, "Your subscriber at this place, John C. Vance, is dead; and no person takes the paper from the office. Respectfully, A. Lincoln P.M."[40] Not only did he read the local *Sangamo Journal*, he often published editorials in it, both anonymously and as himself.[41]

Letters were delivered by a carrier on horseback and, later, by stagecoach. Lincoln's job as postmaster was to count the number of pages, determine how far it had traveled from the post bill that accompanied every letter, calculate the postage, and mark it in the upper right-hand corner. Postage stamps did not exist until 1847, and the addressee rather than the sender was responsible for the cost. In practice, the postmaster was required to pay the postage and collect reimbursement from the recipient upon physical delivery. Postage varied with the distance traversed and the number of pages in a letter. Each single sheet was six cents for the first thirty miles, ten cents for thirty to eighty miles, and continued up incrementally, capping at twenty-five cents for more than four hundred miles. Authors tended to write in small print and often wrote crossways to squeeze as much as possible on a single sheet. Envelopes were not used; the letter was simply folded and sealed. Lincoln was required to report all transactions to Washington on a quarterly basis.[42]

The calculation of payment for postmaster duties was complicated. Lincoln would receive as pay 30 percent of the quarterly receipts up to one hundred dollars. That dropped to only 25 percent for receipts on one hundred to four hundred dollars per quarter, and further down as the receipts rose. No postmaster was to receive more than two thousand dollars per quarter, plus up to another five hundred dollars per quarter as their share of newspaper receipts. In practice the amounts were much lower, and Lincoln likely made less than twenty dollars per year as postmaster.[43]

As with other aspects of his life, Lincoln was scrupulously honest. He always kept the postmaster money in a blue sock in a wooden chest under the counter. No one showed up to collect the receipts after the New Salem post office was closed and moved to Petersburg. One of Lincoln's close friends, Dr. Anson Henry, reported that months later, when the Post Office Department sent an agent to Springfield, where Lincoln now lived, to collect the money, Henry was shocked that Lincoln could immediately go to his trunk in the boarding house, pull out the blue sock, and dump out the exact amount due in the exact silver and copper coins he had been paid in. Lincoln said, "I never make use of money that does not belong to me."[44]

Being postmaster was not particularly profitable, but it did give Lincoln opportunity to converse with people in the district, which he would use to his advantage when he ran for elective office. The postal system improved as occasional riders switched to stagecoaches and eventually to railroads. By 1851 a prepaid three-cent stamp could take a letter almost anywhere in the United States, leading to faster communication, less expensive freight transportation, and greater scientific exchange across the nation. Lincoln would take note of these changes as his political career expanded. Even years later he retained his interest in the post office, often visiting the small post office just off the House chambers in the Capitol when he was a congressman and taking great care in choosing honest and industrious postmasters under his jurisdiction.[45]

SURVEYOR

Another income opportunity relied on his analytical skills. Despite Lincoln's early formal studies in mathematics, his tutor Mentor Graham claimed that he did "not think Lincoln was anything of an arithmetician—especially so of geometry and trigonometry—before he came to my house." Whether Graham gave him instruction is debatable, but Lincoln did learn these necessary mathematical skills a year or two later when he began an assistantship under John Calhoun, the county surveyor.[46]

Lincoln may have also received some early exposure to surveying as far back as Indiana according to his neighbors. Part of the reason his father had moved to Indiana was due to Kentucky's inadequate surveying and land title system. From Parson Weems's book, Lincoln knew George Washington had been a surveyor, as had Thomas Jefferson. Surveying was a critically important element in the growth of the United States. The southern territories had only loose guidelines for delineating property, hence the uncertainty of land titles experienced by Thomas Lincoln in Kentucky. In contrast, Congress had passed the Northwest Ordinance in 1787, stipulating specific surveying and tract requirements for the area now encompassed by Indiana, Ohio, Illinois, Michigan, and Wisconsin. Thomas could be more certain that any property he bought in Indiana would not be taken from him, and indeed he held the Pigeon Creek farm for the entire fourteen years the family lived in the Hoosier state. Still, the towns themselves were often laid out haphazardly, and there was a significant need for surveyors to organize the land even as speculators from the East flowed into Illinois. Accuracy and honesty were essential.[47]

"The Surveyor of Sangamon," Lincoln later wrote in a third-person autobiography, "offered to depute to A[braham] that portion of his work which was within his part of the country. He accepted, procured a compass and chain, studied Flint, and Gibson a little, and went at it. This procured bread, and kept soul and body together."[48]

Calhoun was a devout Democrat, and again the Whiggish Lincoln only took the job after he was assured his politics would not be held against him. Lincoln also realized the mathematical requirements of surveying were beyond the rudimentary "long measure" and "land measure" of his Indiana youth. Biographer Carl Sandburg suggested that Lincoln "had to transfer his blank ignorance of the science and art of surveying into a thorough working knowledge and skill."[49] Lincoln initially turned to "Flint," lent to him by Calhoun. Flint was *A System of Geometry and Trigonometry with a Treatise on Surveying*, published in 1804 by Abel Flint. The first chapter focuses on geometry, which it describes as "a Science which treats of the properties of magnitude" or the study of properties and relations of points, lines, surfaces, solids, and higher dimensional analogs.[50] Flint would have been Lincoln's first exposure to geometry, as his study of Euclid did not come until much later. Flint's second chapter deals with trigonometry, "that part of practical Geometry by which the sides and angles of triangles are measured." Trigonometry made use of proportions such that "three things being given, either all sides, or sides and angles, a fourth may be found; either by measuring with a scale and dividers ... or more accurately by calculation with logarithms, or with natural sines."[51] Lincoln quickly had to learn about such mathematical processes as converging of meridians, the curvature of parallels of latitude, and the calculation of sines and cosines.[52] The next section of Flint includes practical applications of these mathematical concepts to "measuring, laying out, and dividing land." The appendix then explains more about logarithms and includes many tables of useful data for use in surveying.

That was still not enough. Lincoln also studied Gibson "a little," referring to the 1814 publication *The Theory and Practice of Surveying* by Robert Gibson. This book covers many of the same mathematics, including geometry, trigonometry, and logarithms. It then goes into practical applications of surveying. Like Flint, Gibson provides many examples, such as reducing square rods to acres, finding the area of a rectangle or triangle, and how to survey a triangular field. Then there were areas with irregular or curved boundaries, which are usually measured by establishing a base line and taking offsets at regular intervals from the base line to the boundary. Lincoln had to apply more complicated calculation techniques such as trapezoidal methods, a one-third rule, or the coordinate method.[53]

Having taught himself the mathematics behind surveying, he now needed the equipment. Basic surveying equipment of the time consisted of a compass, a Gunter's chain, a set of marking pins, two or more plumb bobs, a few flag or range poles, an axe, and stakes, not to mention a horse for travel and notebooks to record the surveys.[54] Lincoln obtained these items secondhand and on credit, which would come back to haunt him.

As with all compasses, Lincoln's was encased in brass so that it would not interfere with the magnetic needle, an issue he would need to revisit during the Civil War. The compass manufactured by Rittenhouse and Company was attached to a Jacob staff by a ball-and-socket joint to secure the instrument for measurement of magnetic north. Two upright standards allowed Lincoln to sight through the slits toward the range pole set in the distance. Lincoln used a Gunter's chain to measure distance. This item consists of 100 pieces of linked chain totaling four rods or sixty-six feet long, each link being 7.92 inches. Eighty chains make one mile.[55]

Early on, Lincoln may have sought out assistance from Mentor Graham. According to Graham's daughter, after surveying a plot of land, Lincoln would call on her father to check his calculations and confirm the correct number of acres. Sometimes they would "sit up till midnight or later calculating the figures."[56] One technical issue Lincoln encountered was determining true north. All compasses measure magnetic north, which is several degrees off of the true pole, which reflects where the axis of rotation meets the surface. Magnetic north moves over time, and its difference from true north is measured as a declination, that is, the number of degrees (the angle) away from true north.[57]

Over the three years he was deputy surveyor, Lincoln surveyed the towns of New Boston, Bath, Albany, and Huron. He also resurveyed the city of Petersburg. The city had been surveyed years previously, but Lincoln was asked to repeat the survey because the city had grown substantially, in part as New Salem faded away and its residents moved to nearby Petersburg.[58] He also laid out the area that town fathers decided to name after its surveyor—Lincoln, Illinois. Lincoln christened the town with the juice from a watermelon.[59] Beyond towns, he surveyed and laid out numerous roads and private properties, including a bridge over the Salt River at Musick Crossing.[60] In one case, he found in resurveying some land that the seller had by error granted more land than he received payment for. Lincoln convinced his client, the descendant of the original buyer, to pay the cost of the additional land to the seller's heirs.[61] For his surveying services, Lincoln was paid $2.50 for each quarter section of land and as little as twenty-five cents for smaller lots.[62]

Overall, Lincoln found surveying profitable both financially and in building relationships for his later political activities. "Mr. Lincoln was a good surveyor," one investor noted, "he did it all himself, without help from anybody except chainmen."[63] The chainmen were men or boys who carried chains, drove stakes, and blazed trees for Lincoln, always with an ear out to hear Lincoln's stories and jokes.[64] Others were equally impressed with Lincoln's honesty and industriousness. Whenever there was a dispute, both parties relied on Lincoln to settle the matter with his compass and chain.[65]

Lincoln still owed Thomas Watkins for the horse and supplies he purchased on credit. In a pique of irritation one day, Watkins sued Lincoln for payment. Other creditors piled on and also sued Lincoln for past-due bills. Eventually, Lincoln's surveying tools and horse, along with two lots of property in New Salem, were seized by Sangamon County Sheriff Garret Elkin and sold off at auction. By this time Lincoln had made many friends. One of them, James Short, realized that Lincoln would be unable to make a living without his surveying business, and so bought all his possessions for $120 and immediately returned them to Lincoln. With the utmost gratitude, Lincoln continued to work and eventually repaid Short after moving to Springfield and making more substantial money as a lawyer.[66]

This early experience as a surveyor instilled in Lincoln an understanding of the growing frontier. Springfield supplanted Vandalia as the capital of Illinois, and Chicago was starting to blossom into a significant city. More people were migrating from eastern cities to northern and central Illinois, while immigrants from Kentucky and other points south populated much of southern Illinois. Lincoln continued thinking about surveying after he was elected to the state legislature in 1834, passing bills authorizing further surveys like that of Mount Auburn as the population grew. He also dealt with surveyor appointments. The language of survey-ors stuck with him, as when he said he was planning to "set a few stakes" to claim his term for a congressional seat after a rival refused to follow the agreed upon succession plan.[67]

As his political ambitions grew, Lincoln sometimes found him-self at odds with his old boss, John Calhoun, whom he anonymously accused of corruption in a newspaper editorial. Calhoun, in fact, would later be appointed as surveyor-general of the Kansas territory by fraud-ulent proslavery forces.[68] Lincoln's surveyor background may also have played into his "spot" resolutions introduced during his term in Con-gress. The resolutions challenged President James K. Polk to specify "the particular spot of soil on which blood of our citizens was so shed," the spot at which Mexico supposedly invaded the United States in 1846, beginning the Mexican–American War, which resulted in the United States adding another third to its land area.[69] On his way to Washington for his own inauguration, Lincoln likely felt nostalgic as he passed "Point of Beginning," the stone obelisk marking the begin-ning of the U.S. Public Land Survey that opened up the Northwest Territory and became the starting point of almost all other lands to the west as far as the Pacific Ocean.[70] Even as president, Lincoln recalled his early days, noting that rather than a distinct separation of the two sides, there was nothing more than "surveyor's lines, over which people may walk back and forth without any consciousness of their presence." Using this philosophy, he encouraged Union men in the South to make their way North.[71]

So too grew his intellectual curiosity. Traveling around the area deliv-ering wayward mail, meeting townspeople, farmers, and merchants as he surveyed new and old properties, and watching as new technologi-cal breakthroughs entered the market, Lincoln expanded his appreciation of advancements in science and technology. Lincoln soon found himself a representative of the people in the Illinois state legislature. His new colleagues encouraged him to study the law and continue to enhance his education. After four terms in the legislature, he practiced law until elected to the U.S. Congress. Returning to Illinois between sessions, Lincoln experienced a wonder, and a calamity, that inspired his own scientific and technological achievement. He would get a patent.

CHAPTER 5

Calculating Niagara and the Only President with a Patent

LINCOLN BEGAN SERVING HIS SINGLE TERM IN THE U.S. CONGRESS WHEN he was thirty-eight years old. In the days of part-time politicians, congressmen returned home to resume their primary livelihoods between sessions. Lincoln was a prominent Whig, the only Whig in the Illinois delegation to Congress. Since 1848 was a presidential election year, he gladly accepted an invitation to travel through New England during the intersession to stump for Whig presidential candidate Zachary Taylor. Joined by Mary and their two young sons, Robert and Eddy, he made his way to Boston, which he used as a base to make day trips to various cities and towns in eastern Massachusetts. Lobbying for Taylor would later prove to be time well spent when it came to his own presidential aspirations, as would his second New England tour in 1860 following a much-celebrated Cooper Union speech.[1]

NIAGARA FALLS

After an exhausting eleven days in which he gave a dozen speeches in nine Massachusetts communities, Lincoln and family were ready to make the long trip home. Taking a train from Boston to New York City, then on to Albany, Lincoln found his way to upstate New York and the fabled Niagara Falls.[2] Formed during the last ice age, Niagara Falls consists of three separate cataracts: American and Bridal Veil Falls on the American side of the international border, and Horseshoe Falls on the Canadian side. The falls have a vertical drop of over 165 feet, while the incredible width of the combined falls creates an average flow of four million cubic feet per minute. The massive volume of water crossing the precipice into the gorge is something most visitors do not soon forget.

After seeing the falls, and taking time for a haircut and shave, Lincoln and his family continued their journey homeward by steamship through the Great Lakes to Chicago and back to Springfield. Sometime during the trip Lincoln wrote down his thoughts on Niagara, which seems to end midsentence and was never further developed.[3] This fragment provides an interesting look into Lincoln's scientific mind. He clearly had understood more science at this point than most frontier lawyers.

Lincoln fully appreciated the allure of the Falls. The fragment captures his first impression with the opening line: "Niagara-Falls! By what mysterious power is it that millions and millions, are drawn from all parts of the world, to gaze upon Niagara Falls?"[4] One modern historian notes that the simplicity of the opening exclamatory "establishes the hugeness of his subject." He further notes that "the exclamation point is both redundant and expressive," signs of someone moved by the splendor of the falls.[5] Lincoln's sensitivity is further shown as he recognizes that Niagara's "power to excite reflection, and emotion, is its great charm." Lincoln did admire the beauty of the falls, as well as the power of its attraction to people drawn from far and wide. But an astute systematic thinker like Lincoln would also be curious about the larger technical issues.

Whiling away the long days and nights on the steamship as it worked its way through the Great Lakes, Lincoln's mind was clearly on a future lecture about Niagara. He never completed his fragment, but he did mention Niagara Falls in a draft of his later lecture on discoveries and inventions before crossing it out.[6] With his analytical thinking, Lincoln did not believe there was any great mystery of the physics behind the falls itself.

"If the water moving onward in a great river, reaches a point where there is a perpendicular jog, of a hundred feet in descent, in the bottom of the river," Lincoln noted dryly, "it is plain the water will have a violent and continuous plunge at that point." Having dropped off the edge, "thus plunging, will foam, and roar, and send up a mist." If the sun is shining, it is only logical that "there will be perpetual rainbows."

Others may have been satisfied with the "mere physical" of Niagara Falls, or enthralled by the beauty without thinking too much about the science, but Lincoln's scientific mind took his observations much further. He thought of the phenomenon from multiple viewpoints, a characteristic that allowed him to make decisions with both deeper and broader understanding than many people. Examining his fragment gives us further insight into that mind.

"The geologist will demonstrate," Lincoln wrote, how the vast movement of water had caused the falls to wear "its way back to its present position." Niagara Falls had retreated about seven miles from its original location and was eroding at a rate of about five feet a year up through Lincoln's time.[7] Lincoln recognized that the water wears away the rock as it plunges over the falls, not just at the bottom but, more importantly, from the top. He speculated that geologists could "ascertain how *fast* it is wearing now, and so get a basis for determining how *long* it has been wearing back." From this, Lincoln said, the geologist could "finally demonstrate" that "this world is at least fourteen thousand years old." This estimate is remarkably close to the time of the Wisconsin glaciation that 10,000 to 15,000 years ago formed the Great Lakes and began the creation of Niagara Falls.[8] Given these insights, Lincoln may have been aware of Scottish geologist Charles Lyell's 1841 visit to Niagara and description of the uniformitarianism-based geological processes that created the falls and gorge.[9]

Lincoln's observations show an important awareness of geology most people would not have had. The bedrock underlying the lip of the falls is constantly attacked by the friction of the massive amounts of water and suspended particles flowing over it. The rock at the bottom of each of the individual falls is pummeled by tons of cascading water, which breaks it apart over time. Since the Niagara River flows north to Lake Ontario, the result is that the falls are slowly retreating upriver toward Lake Erie.[10] Repeated rock slides have broken up American Falls and created a significant talus field at its base. Engineers blocked the river flowing over American Falls in the 1960s in hopes of removing the fallen debris, only to determine that doing so might further undercut the stability of the falls. They decided to "allow the process of natural change to continue uninterrupted," and the river was unblocked.[11]

Lincoln also demonstrated a grasp of hydrological cycles, speculating that a natural philosopher "of a slightly different turn" would look at Niagara as the pouring of "all the surplus water which rains down on two or three hundred thousand square miles of the earth's surface." He was remarkably accurate in this estimate; today's scientists say the Niagara River and Lake Erie combined drain a watershed of 265,000 square miles. This same natural philosopher, according to Lincoln, might estimate "that five hundred thousand [to]ns of water, falls with its full weight, a distance of a hundred feet each minute—thus exerting a force equal to the lifting of the same weight, through the same space, in the same time." This was rather scientific stuff for a frontier lawyer with little formal education.

Lincoln was writing this as he steamed home from the East, meaning he was recalling all this from memory with no source material. But he did not stop there. Lincoln elaborated on this hydrology cycle by pulling in the role of the sun, which through the process of evaporation causes the water to be "constantly lifted up." He suggested that if enough water was raised from the watershed to feed the falls, his envisioned natural philosopher would be "overwhelmed in the contemplation of the vast power the sun is constantly exerting in quiet, noiseless operation of lifting water *up* to be rained *down* again." Lincoln sounds here more like a science geek than a future president. He would incorporate this view of solar power (as well as energy from the wind) in his later "Discoveries and Inventions" lecture.

"But still there is more," Lincoln exclaimed.

In the last paragraph he turns philosophical. He suggests that Niagara Falls "calls up the indefinite past," and "when Columbus first sought this continent—when Christ suffered on the cross—when Moses led Israel through the Red Sea—nay, even, when Adam first came from the hand of his Maker—then as now, Niagara was roaring here." In addition to the biblical references, Lincoln shows some familiarity with paleontology, noting that the "Mammoth and Mastodon" (two ancient elephant-like mammals), whose existence is demonstrated by "fragments of their monstrous bones," also "gazed on Niagara." Lincoln was blending the philosophical with the scientific.

At some later point, William Herndon went to New York and stopped at Niagara Falls. Upon his return, Herndon regaled Lincoln with an account of his trip. In describing the falls, he "indulged in a good deal of imagery." Herndon relates that "as I warmed up with the subject my descriptive powers expanded accordingly. The mad rush of water, the roar, the rapids, and the rainbow furnished me with an abundance of material for a stirring and impressive picture. The recollection of the gigantic and awe-inspiring scene stimulated my exuberant powers to the highest pitch."[12] Nearly exhausted with this description, Herndon then asked Lincoln of his opinion of Niagara Falls. "What made the deepest impression on you when you stood in the presence of the great natural wonder?" he queried Lincoln, expecting something equally imagery indulgent.

"The thing that struck me most forcibly when I saw the Falls," Lincoln said, "was, where in the world did all that water come from?"

Dumbfounded, the humorless Herndon could not believe his ears. The beauty! The splendor! Had the man not opened his eyes to the sight before him? Had he not opened his ears to the thundering roar of the water splashing into the mist below?

Herndon's explanation of Lincoln's answer was that "it in a very characteristic way illustrates how he looked at everything." Elaborating, Herndon added:

He had no eye for the magnificence and grandeur of the scene, for the rapids, the mist, the angry waters, and the roar of the whirlpool, but his mind, working in its accustomed channel, heedless of beauty or awe, followed irresistibly back to the first cause. It was in this light he viewed every question. However great the verbal foliage that concealed the nakedness of a good idea Lincoln stripped it all down till he could see clear the way between cause and effect. If there was any secret in his power this surely was it.[13]

Herndon was not giving Lincoln enough credit for imagination here. While clearly an analytical thinker, Lincoln was not so divorced from emotion that he would fail to be impressed with the majesty of Niagara Falls. But Lincoln was multidimensional in his thinking. While Herndon was enthralled by the beauty and power of the falls, Lincoln saw the falls as both beautiful and a learning experience. He appreciated not only its charm and power to excite emotion but also its hydrology, geology, and natural science aspects. Keeping in mind that the falls we see today are significantly lessened since the 1895 diversion of water into tunnels feeding the new hydroelectric plant, the site Lincoln saw must have been awe-inspiring indeed.[14]

With Herndon notoriously lacking a sense of humor, it is likely Lincoln was pulling his leg with his initial reply to his partner's "deepest impression" query about the falls. But the trip's events immediately following his brief visit to Niagara were important in securing the technical aspects of the falls in Lincoln's already scientifically primed mind, his "fascination from an early age with the human, the mechanical, and the natural, how things work in the world."[15]

Lincoln would view the falls one more time. During a July 1857 trip to New York, made ostensibly to collect an outstanding five-thousand-dollar fee for a railroad case, Lincoln stopped at Niagara for some sightseeing. Accompanied by Mary, nearly fourteen-year-old Robert, six-and-a-half-year-old Willie, and four-year-old Tad, Lincoln registered at Cataract House, signing the guest register on July 24 as "A. Lincoln & Family, Springfield, Illinois."[16] Cataract House had been built in 1825 and, following several rounds of expansion, had become the largest hotel in Niagara Falls, New York, with a commanding view of the Niagara River Rapids.[17] Mary Lincoln shortly after their return wrote to her half sister Emilie, noting that a portion of their summer was "spent most pleasantly traveling east," with stops in "Niagara, Canada, New York & other points of interest."[18] Given his analytical mind, it is highly likely, as husband and wife gazed romantically upon the grandeur of Niagara Falls, that Lincoln was secretly doing a little math in his head.

THE PATENT

Following his all-too-brief visit in 1848, Lincoln boarded the steamship *Globe* for the trip through the Great Lakes and on to Chicago, from whence he and his family traveled via the Illinois and Michigan Canal to LaSalle, then took a steamer to Peoria, before boarding a stagecoach for the final leg back to Springfield.[19] Tired and cranky from the long journey, Lincoln caught up with his law practice for several weeks before the next session of Congress would call him back to Washington. After finishing his sole term as congressman in 1849, Lincoln again returned to Springfield and threw himself into his law career full-time.

The 1848 trip provided him with one additional opportunity to put his analytical mind to work. As the *Globe* made its way through the narrow Detroit River, passing between Lakes Erie and Huron, it overtook another steamer, the *Canada*, which had run aground in the shallows passing Fighting Island. With his ship stuck fast, the captain ordered the crew to collect "all the loose planks, empty barrels, boxes, and the like which could be had" and force them under her hull to buoy the ship higher in the water.[20] This effort eventually allowed the *Canada* to escape her entrapment, but not until a few days after Lincoln and the *Globe* had passed into Lake Huron on their continuing voyage to Chicago. Ever the inquisitive one, and remembering his own experiences getting stuck on the New Salem dam back on the Sangamon, Lincoln was enthralled with the ongoing operation. The incident got him thinking seriously about how to solve this particular kind of problem.

As a young man first out on his own, Lincoln and his crewmates had gone only a short distance on the Sangamon River before getting their flatboat stuck on the Cameron and Rutledge mill dam, where it was hung up for a day and a night. Lincoln supervised the unloading of cargo from their flatboat to a boat borrowed from the townspeople of New Salem. Rather than offload the heaviest barrels, the crew rolled them forward to rebalance the boat. John Hanks claimed that Lincoln borrowed an auger and bored a hole over the bow hanging over the dam to drain the flooded boat. William Greene, a resident of New Salem, says the hole-boring story was "made up out of whole cloth—Offutt suggested it and Lincoln said he couldn't see it working." In any case, once the boat was light enough to float free, the crew poled both vessels below the dam and transferred the cargo back to the flatboat, which continued downriver to New Orleans.[21]

What the flatboat incident, the previous *Talisman* steamship grounding, and now the *Canada* all demonstrated was the difficulty of navigating the erratic rising and lowering waters of western rivers. Lincoln would promote improvements to navigation as he learned more about the basic physics of displacement and buoyancy.

Lincoln probably picked up the basic idea of displacement in his early studies of geometry when preparing to be a surveyor. Displacement in geometric terms is simply the straight-line distance from one position to another. When applied to ships, this translates into the distance a vessel sinks into the water before its weight equalizes with the pressure of the water pushing up.[22] A ship is said to have a certain degree of buoyancy, defined simply as the ability of something to float in a liquid, usually water.

To raise a ship that has run aground, or become hung up on a mill dam, another concept of physics is employed—the Archimedes principle. Archimedes was an ancient Greek mathematician and physicist who lived in the third century BCE. Among his many discoveries, besides deriving an accurate approximation of π (*pi*), was the principle of buoyancy that bears his name. In his treatise *On Floating Bodies*, Archimedes states: "Any object, totally or partially immersed in a fluid or liquid, is buoyed up by a force equal to the weight of the fluid displaced by the object." He supposedly discovered this principle after noticing that the level of water in his tub rose as he got in to take a bath, realizing this effect could be used to determine the volume of any irregularly shaped object. In practice, displacement is the occupation of a submerged body (like the hull of a ship) that would otherwise be occupied by a liquid, or the weight of fluid that would fill the volume displaced by a floating ship. This is measured in tons, which is why a ship's size is usually referred to in tonnage.[23]

According to Herndon, Lincoln had watched intently how the *Canada*'s captain used the power of displacement to buoy up the stranded vessel. Empty casks contain air, much lighter than the displacement of water. As additional lighter-than-water materials were placed under the hull, the ship gradually lifted until it was clear of the sandbar.[24] Lincoln recognized intuitively the application of the Archimedes principle, that the objective of underwater vehicle flotation systems was to counteract the weight of the vessel pushing down with some additional buoyancy pushing up. The wooden planks, boxes, barrels, and casks would provide that buoyancy. As the *Globe* continued on its way, Lincoln undoubtedly pondered deeply the problem of getting stranded vessels afloat. There had to be a better way. Obsessed with the idea, Lincoln decided to invent that better way.

Lincoln was no stranger to invention. New Salem's wool-carding mill owner, Hardin Bale, told Herndon that Lincoln had invented some sort of "water wheel—which ran under water," which Bale thought promised to be of some value, although apparently it was never further developed.[25] Lincoln also designed and constructed a small wooden wagon toy for his son Tad that Henry Ford later described as the "original forerunner of the steering system now developed to such a high efficiency in the modern motor car."[26]

For his design to lift stranded vessels, Lincoln decided on "expansible buoyant chambers placed at the sides of a vessel . . . in such a manner that . . . the buoyant chambers will be forced downwards into the water and at the same time expanded and filled with air for buoying up the vessel by the displacement of water."[27] Fleshing out his idea to get the design in line with the physics, Lincoln worked with a Springfield mechanic named Walter Davis to build a working model of the device. How much of the model Lincoln himself manufactured is uncertain, but at the very least he fashioned the central pillars.[28] When it was finished, Lincoln showed off the model in "the big water trough at the corner opposite" his office in downtown Springfield. One witness noted that the four-foot model was set afloat in the trough, then forced downward with bricks to simulate a grounding. Lincoln "then applied the air pumps modeled like the old fire bellows, four in number, two on each side that were beneath the lower or first deck and in a few moments, it slowly rose above the water about six inches." The gathered crowd, although much impressed, was not entirely convinced the device would help open up the Sangamon River for navigation, but they gave him three cheers for the entertainment value.[29]

When Lincoln returned to Washington for another session of Congress, he sought out Zenas C. Robbins, an experienced patent agent, to help navigate the cumbersome patent process. "He walked into my office one morning with a model of a western steamboat under his arm," reported Robbins. "After a friendly greeting he placed his model on my office-table and proceeded to explain the principles embodied therein and what he believed was his own invention, and which, if new, he desired to secure by letters patent." Robbins helped Lincoln create the necessary drawings and paperwork, and the patent application was submitted on March 10, 1849.[30]

While the theoretical concept of the invention was simple, the actual mechanism to achieve buoyancy was somewhat unwieldy, as was the ninety-six-word opening sentence of his application:

> *Be it known that I, Abraham Lincoln, of Springfield, in the county of Sangamon, in the state of Illinois, have invented a new and improved manner of combining adjustable buoyant air chambers with a steam boat or other vessel for the purpose of enabling their draught of water to be readily lessened to enable them to pass over bars, or through shallow water, without discharging their cargoes; and I do hereby declare the following to be a full, clear, and exact description thereof, reference being made to the accompanying drawings making a part of this specification.[31]*

His astounding grasp of both the necessary physics and the intricacies of the design is demonstrated in three accompanying figures—a side elevation, a transverse section, and a longitudinal vertical section—that show the placement of the buoyant chambers on the sides of the vessel. "Each buoyant chamber," he explains, "is composed of plank or metal, of suitable strength and stiffness, and the flexible sides and ends of the chambers, are composed of India-rubber cloth, or other suitable waterproof fabric, securely united to the edges and ends of the top and bottom of the chambers." These are in effect inflatable rubber bellows held in place within a strong collapsible frame that can be raised or lowered as needed. "A suitable number of vertical shafts or spars" would be secured to the bottom part of the bellows and to a main shaft passing horizontally through the center of the vessel. Ropes wound around the main shaft would, upon turning, raise or lower the vertical spars, thus inflating or deflating the chambers.

And on he went, describing in great detail every aspect of the system: how the bellows were to be operated, how the devices were attached to the vessel, how the system of ropes and pulleys was used to manipulate the positioning of the spars. Lincoln even considered the scalability of the design such that it could be operated by manpower on smaller vessels or by steam power on larger steamships. He incorporated enough flexibility in the design to cover a range of mechanical arrangements, thus providing broader protection for his patent. What he claimed as his patent was not to be limited by the specific design shown in the drawings, but the "combination of expansible buoyant chambers placed at the sides of the vessel" and a system to deploy them as needed. When finished, "the buoyant chambers will be contracted into a small space and secured against injury."[32]

Lincoln had used his still growing knowledge of hydraulics, hydrology, mechanics, and construction to successfully develop an application for "an improved method of lifting vessels over shoals." After submitting the application, Lincoln put his focus back on his responsibilities as U.S. congressman, which included drafting a bill that would have emancipated enslaved people in the District of Columbia if it had passed. A year earlier Congress had passed a new patent law that gave sole power of issuing patents to the commissioner of patents and increased the salaries of examiners to $2,500 per year, thus increasing the professionalism of the office. A law passed the following year moved the patent office from the State Department to the newly created Department of Interior (originally called the Home Department).[33]

On April 13, Robbins wrote excitedly to Lincoln: "It affords me great pleasure to inform you that I have obtained a favorable decision on your application.... The patent will be issued in about a month." On May 22, Abraham Lincoln received Patent Number 6469 from the U.S. Patent Office, the only president ever to receive a patent.[34] A few weeks later, Lincoln recommended his model creator, Walter Davis, be appointed receiver of the Land Office in Springfield.[35] While he had regaled Herndon with his belief of "the revolution it was destined to work in steamboat navigation," Lincoln made no attempt to commercialize the invention.[36] In truth, the apparatus was probably heavy enough in itself to weigh down the vessel, plus presented a potentially insurmountable array of ropes and pulleys on the deck that might limit room for cargo or crew movement. Still, the overall concept of inflatable chambers or pontoons has been employed in more recent times to raise sunken ships, so there is some merit to Lincoln's design even if he never promoted it.[37]

The original patent drawings, lost at some point, were rediscovered in 1997 in the patent office director's office.[38] The original model is stored in the Smithsonian Institution's vault. A second model, and possibly a third, may also exist. Clark Moulton Smith, who was married to Mary Lincoln's sister Ann, found the second model in the attic of Lincoln's Springfield home shortly after his assassination. The model was given to Shurtleff College in Alton but disappeared after the college closed in 1957.[39] In 1864, Adam S. Cameron requested Lincoln's consent to reproduce the model for the benefit of the Sanitary Commission. Given Lincoln's prominence, the model was sure to fetch considerably donations that the commission would use to support sick and wounded Union soldiers, according to Cameron. There is no evidence this third model was ever created.[40]

Newspapers and scientific magazines during the time of Lincoln's presidency revisited his patent and used it to make commentary on his current duties. "But it has fallen to his lot to be in command of a ship of uncommon burden on a voyage of uncommon danger," *Harper's Weekly* said soon after Lincoln's inauguration. They added, "It devolves upon him to navigate the ship of state through shallows of unprecedented peril, and over flats of unprecedented extent. The difficulty is how to prevent her grounding and becoming a wreck."[41] After giving the invention a somewhat tepid nod in December 1860, shortly after the assassination in 1865, *Scientific American* carried the *Harper's* theme with slightly more reverence: "The author's skill in buoying the great vessel of state over dangerous breakers has made his name honored throughout the civilized world."[42]

While he never visited Niagara again, the falls would come back into Lincoln's realm during the Civil War. Jean François Gravelet, a Frenchman who used the stage name Blondin, several times crossed Niagara on a tightrope 1,100 feet long and three inches thick about a mile downstream of Horseshoe Falls. He repeated the feat many times over the next few years, often making the passage more difficult by doing it blindfolded, on stilts, or carrying his manager on his back. On one occasion he dropped a bottle on a piece of twine and hauled up some Niagara River water to drink before resuming his journey.[43]

Lincoln was aware of Blondin's feats. One day when a group of visitors from the West dropped by the White House to complain of administrative omissions, Lincoln related a story. Suppose you had put all your wealth in gold in the hands of Blondin to carry across the Niagara River on a rope: "Would you shake the cable, or keep shouting to him, 'Blondin, stand up a little straighter—Blondin, stoop a little more,' etc.? No! you would hold your breath as well as your tongue, and keep your hands off until he was safe over." He then told them the government will "get you safe across" if you just leave us alone.[44]

Watching Blondin's tightrope crossing of the falls in the early summer of 1860, a young twenty-two-year-old Canadian, William Leonard Hunt, who styled himself "The Great Farini," felt he could do better.[45] On August 15, 1860, he did just that, not only walking a tightrope across the gorge but stopping in the middle to descend a hanging rope to sip a glass of wine on the *Maid of the Mist* tour boat before climbing back up to finish his walk to the other side.[46] Farini claimed that Lincoln watched a demonstration in 1863, remarking at the time, "Young man, don't be afraid, for if you should topple over and get in head down, I'm tall enough to wade you out." Since Lincoln never went to Niagara that year, Farini made the story up. Farini returned to Niagara again in 1864 to attempt wading to the lip wearing iron stilts, one of which broke and tossed him into the rapids not far from the Cataract Hotel. He hung onto a rock for several hours until he could be rescued.[47]

Niagara Falls was also featured in proposed peace talks during the Civil War. *New York Tribune* editor and political antagonist Horace Greeley claimed he had been approached in the summer of 1864 by Confederate negotiators interested in ending the war. Lincoln was incredulous of their actual power to negotiate but sent Greeley to Niagara, in part to get him out of the way. The expected failure of Greeley's mission caused some problems with the radical abolitionist wing of Congress but gave Lincoln time to discuss with Frederick Douglass a way to get more enslaved black men to escape to the North before the 1864 presidential election.[48]

His experiences on the waters and development of his patent enhanced Lincoln's appreciation for the importance of navigation and other public works projects. He would make internal improvements a lifelong goal, even when it was not politically expedient to do so.

PART III

LEGISLATIVE SCIENCE

CHAPTER 6

Internal Improvements and the Whig Way

ABRAHAM LINCOLN FIRST RAN FOR PUBLIC OFFICE AT THE AGE OF ONLY twenty-three. While the Whig Party did not formally exist until the mid-1830s, he claimed he was "always a Whig in politics."[1] The Whig Party conformed with Lincoln's growing understanding of the means for advancement, both personal and societal. To "better one's condition," one must be educated, self-driven, and immersed in an economic system that emphasized progressive fundamentals. Not content with advancing his skills in sequence, he chose to advance his education and become a politician at the same time.

The two major parties at the time were the Jacksonian Democrats, named after President Andrew Jackson, and the Anti-Jacksonians or the Democratic-Republican Party. As the Anti-Jacksonian leadership evolved from its founder, John Quincy Adams, to its major driver, Henry Clay, they became known as the Whig Party. Lincoln's relative Dennis Hanks and Little Pigeon Creek neighbor David Turnham both suggested Lincoln may have been a "Jackson man" in Indiana.[2] However he might have identified as a teenager in Indiana, by the time he moved to Illinois Lincoln had securely aligned with the Whig view of the world. Many farmers from eastern states left behind their Jacksonian roots as they moved westward into Ohio, Indiana, and Illinois, where more fertile land offered hopes of prosperity. Settling into new land with seemingly unlimited potential, these farmers voted with the Whigs beginning with the party's formation in the 1830s. Whig-leaning men like Lincoln migrated to the central part of Illinois. The rest of the state continued to lean toward the Jacksonian Democrats.[3]

85

The Whigs promoted Henry Clay's "American System" of economic development. They believed in modernizing the nation through government-supported "internal improvements," as well as the establishment of a national bank to help finance these improvements, and high tariffs to protect American investment from cheap foreign goods. Initially a national party, by the 1850s it had split into northern and southern Whigs, based primarily on sectional attitudes toward slavery. Whigs were modernist and reformist; Jacksonian Democrats were traditional and agrarian.[4]

Abraham Lincoln believed that internal improvements would be a catalyst for the economic development of the West.[5] Improvement projects included the building of roads, the widening and deepening of rivers to make them more navigable for the new steamships, the addition of canals to connect rivers, and eventually, the spread of railroads. For Lincoln, this was not a theoretical exercise; it was personal. As his family traveled from place to place, they lost many of their material possessions and livestock trying to ford flooded streams—that is, when they were not literally stuck in the muddy wagon ruts that served as roads. Later, he and his fellow lawyers would travel the Illinois eighth judicial circuit with Judge David Davis, who described the conditions as "bad roads, broken bridges, swimming of horses, and constant wetting" from "miniature swamps, miry and sticky, and extremely difficult to cross with teams and wagons." Improvements would ease transportation and expand potential market reach.[6]

The conflict between those who actively sought government-funded internal improvements and those who opposed them had been waging since the beginning of the nation. Economic thought fell into two broad groups, those who followed the beliefs of Alexander Hamilton and those who followed Thomas Jefferson. Hamiltonians favored a strong federal government that actively promoted industrial modernization. Jeffersonians preferred a weak federal government that allowed the states to independently develop a primarily agrarian, and slave-based, economy. Lincoln was solidly in the Hamiltonian camp, now associated with the Whig Party. Jacksonian Democrats carried on the Jeffersonian ideal.[7]

The Whig philosophy was not limited to industrialization; it was also about free-labor family farms. In the North, individual farmers tilled the land to support their families, selling or trading only the excess for goods they could not grow or make themselves. If additional labor was needed, they paid wages or provided room and board in exchange for services rendered. Whigs, and some northern Democrats, encouraged small-scale manufacturing, which could range from individual craftsmen to large investments in roads, canals, and navigable rivers. As economies shifted from barter to cash, the norm became economic mobility, class advancement, and the freedom to hire yourself out to better employers.[8] Lincoln explained the potential of Whiggish free labor succinctly: "The prudent, penniless beginner in the world, labors for wages awhile, saves a surplus with which to buy tools or land, for himself; then labors on his own account another while, and at length hires a new beginner to help him."[9] The Whigs saw progressive advancement as the future of America.

With its focus on infrastructure projects that would facilitate transportation and commerce, the Whigs believed they could unite the nation in common progressive goals. Improved navigation on inland waterways and expanding markets enabled by cross-state railways could more efficiently link raw cotton production in the South with milling and textile manufacturing in the North, thus eliminating sectionalism and providing for the common good of the growing nation.[10]

In stark contrast were the immense slave-labor cotton and sugar plantations of the South. Here an aristocratic ruling class controlled the vast majority of the wealth, relegating poorer white farmers to poverty or a life as hired hands. Competing with them were millions of black laborers maintained in chattel slavery by force of law and brutality. One prominent Southern slaveholder argued that these lower classes were the "mudsills" on which the edifice of civilized culture was built.[11] Southern society cultivated an honor system akin to European elites, in effect an artifact of station attained by birthright while others labored to put bread on the elites' tables. This economic structure was hierarchical and permanent, with virtually no chance of upward advancement for those not born into whiteness and privilege. While the North pushed for internal improvements to modernize America, the South discouraged such investment, arguing that it gave too much power to the federal government and shifted the nation away from its traditional agricultural nature.

Expansion of industry and commerce threatened the long-term stability of the plantation-slave labor economy. The slave-owning class rejected widespread education and modernization because it upset the existing hierarchical system. This contest between modernization, including its two versions of agrarianism—the free-labor family farm and the slave-labor plantation—created an irrepressible conflict that would lead to civil war.[12]

This was the climate when Lincoln threw his hat into the political arena. His first campaign announcement highlighted his commitment to the Whig philosophy. It also drew deeply from his own personal experience as a flatboatman. The announcement, published in the *Sangamo Journal* in March 1832, was verbose and convoluted in conformance with the writing style of the day. Only later would Lincoln learn from French philosopher Blaise Pascal's advice and take the time to write short. For all its length, Lincoln spent about two-thirds of it on internal improvements.

He began by acknowledging that "time and experience have verified to a demonstration, the public utility of internal improvements."[13] Barely living on his own for the first time, presumably he was talking about a collective historical experience rather than his own personal knowledge of economic theory. He intuitively used the Euclidean term "demonstration," although his exposure to geometry was still limited to his early study of Pike's *Arithmetick*. Lincoln did already seem to grasp how internal improvements could benefit the masses, not merely the wealthy class. "No person will deny," he wrote, "that the poorest and most thinly populated countries would be greatly benefitted by the opening of good roads, and in the clearing of navigable streams." Lincoln was not simply lip-synching political advice from mentors; he understood that "it is folly to undertake works of this or any other kind, without first knowing that we are able to finish them—as half-finished work generally proves to be labor lost." He declared that "there cannot be any objection to having railroads and canals" other than "the want of ability to pay." This latter observation would come back to haunt him several years later.

Even then Lincoln understood that railroads were the technology of the future. "No other improvement . . . can equal in utility the railroad," he told his potential constituents. He emphasized its advantages over other means of travel and commerce, for example, that it "is not interrupted by either high or low water, or freezing weather," which made water routes "precarious and uncertain." The problem was that the exorbitant financial burden was too overwhelming to undertake at this point in time. "There is a heart appalling shock" of its cost, Lincoln exclaimed, "estimated at $290,000" (over $8.2 million today). And so, Lincoln went on, "the improvement of Sangamo[n] river is an object much better to our infant resources."

This idea was self-serving given he had just moved to New Salem on the banks of the Sangamon River, which he admitted, acknowledging that he has spent the greater part of the last year on the waters, from his misadventure on the mill dam to his time working at the mill itself. These duties have made him much aware of the rise and fall of the river and its effect on transport and commerce. From these experiences he believed, "without fear of being contradicted," that navigation of the Sangamon River "may be rendered completely practicable, as high as the mouth of the South Fork, or probably higher, to vessels of from 25 to 30 tons burthen, for at least one half of all common years, and to vessels of much greater burthen a part of that time." To achieve this navigability would require only periodic clearing of drifted timber, which was easily removed.

Lincoln suggested an even grander scheme to make the Sangamon navigable. He calculated that New Salem was between twelve and eighteen miles "in something near a straight direction" above the river's confluence with the larger Illinois River at Beardstown, much shorter than its thirty- to thirty-five-mile meandering path. Perhaps recalling his own time working the Louisville and Portland Canal on the Ohio River, he noted that by "removing the turf" along the prairie land between the two points, a canal could be built to bypass much of the narrow and shallower curves of the river and provide for a shorter and more maneuverable flow for larger boats to travel. Even if this were done on a piecemeal basis where short canals were used to bypass the river's normal zigzag course, it would "lessen the distance" and improve navigability. Lincoln did not know the cost of this option, but he felt it probably less than the cost of railroads, the use of which could be revisited as finances became available. Either choice for internal improvements would provide a "more easy means of communication than we now possess, for the purpose of facilitating the task of exporting the surplus products of its fertile soil, and importing necessary articles from abroad."

"If elected," Lincoln wrote, any measure promoting such improvements "shall receive my support."

He then promptly enlisted to fight in the Black Hawk War and was away from Sangamon County for the next three months. When Lincoln returned in July, he gave his first official political speech to a large gathering in nearby Pappsville.[14] Like the speech itself, Lincoln noted, "My politics are short and sweet, like an old woman's dance." He reiterated what he had more verbosely written in March, that he was "in favor of the internal improvement system," a national bank, and a high protective tariff. "These are my sentiments and political principles. If elected I will be thankful. If not, it will be all the same."[15]

He lost. His inability to campaign during his Black Hawk War service had kept him from becoming known in the outlying county, but he garnered 277 of the 300 votes cast in the New Salem area, the people that knew him best. He had caught the political bug.

Two years later he ran again. His postmaster and surveying jobs allowed him to meet more people as he roamed the county delivering mail and platting out property. Plus he had gained some influential friends during his short time in the war. Lincoln's proposal for a canal from the Illinois River in Beardstown to the Sangamon River also gained him significant support. Since such a canal would allow year-round shipment of products from New Salem and the surrounding county, a large number of residents would see financial benefit. This time Lincoln was elected to his first term as an Illinois state legislator, for which he was paid three dollars a day, more than he had ever earned. He served three additional terms at four dollars a day.[16]

His study of grammar had helped him learn the virtue of brevity by the time he ran for reelection in 1836. He pledged unity, saying if elected he would "consider the whole people of Sangamon my constituents, as well those that oppose, as those who support me." He even suggested the rather progressive idea that voting rights might include females. He went on to declare his continued support for internal improvements, including using the proceeds from sales of federal public lands to enable Illinois to "dig canals and construct rail roads, without borrowing money and paying interest on it."[17] Lincoln received the highest vote of seventeen Sangamon County candidates and was joined by a contingent of fellow Whigs representing the county. Along with the two state senators elected, they formed the "Long Nine," reflecting their unusual six-foot-plus heights.[18]

Lincoln had been largely silent in his first term, but he did introduce a bill authorizing Samuel Musick to construct a toll bridge over Salt Creek in Sangamon County, his first infrastructure project.[19] He became more assertive in his second term and by the third had attained the primary leadership role for Whig priorities in the state, with internal improvements dominating. Lincoln became improvements' greatest champion, but early on it was the Democrats, led by a young Stephen A. Douglas, who developed the first all-inclusive bill for the development of roads, railroads, and canals and to expand river navigation throughout the state.[20] The Democrats would soon abandon the idea while Lincoln continued to support infrastructure development.

In 1837, an Act to Establish a General System of Internal Improvements gave a sense of the state's priorities. It specified the creation of a public works board to oversee a comprehensive slate of projects. One section allocated funds to improve navigation of the Wabash River, which because it served as a border line could be done in conjunction with the state of Indiana. Other river projects funded included dredging of the Illinois, Rock, Kaskaskia, and Little Wabash Rivers. The bill allocated funds to create a railroad from the city of Cairo in the far south of the state to a spot near the growing city of Chicago. Another railroad to be funded would go from Alton in the far west to Mount Carmel in the far east, with a spur south to Shawneetown. Yet another would run from Quincy in the west to the Indiana state line, including a bridge necessary to cross the Illinois River. About a dozen major railroad lines would crisscross the state. Leaving no detail unremarked, the bill specified that "habitually intemperate" engineers need not be employed—these railroads would not allow drunk drivers.[21]

Further bills also passed the Illinois legislature, amending the parameters somewhat as reality started to cause the rethinking of such ambitious projects. Later in 1837, the prosperous bubble of the preceding few years suddenly popped, sending all of the United States into a financial depression that dragged on into the mid-1840s. Having committed itself to significant capital outlay, Illinois was suddenly in substantial debt, as was most of the nation. Lincoln did what he could to salvage the program, which he noted, having been started, Illinoisans were "morally bound" to continue.[22] He argued that "we are now so far advanced in a general system of internal improvements that, if we would, we cannot retreat from it, without disgrace and great loss."[23]

As chair of the Finance Committee, Lincoln proposed a plan to finance the program by speculation on unsold land belonging to the federal government. He introduced a resolution asking permission for Illinois to purchase all the unsold government land in the state, about 20 million acres, at twenty-five cents an acre. The state would then sell it at a dollar and a quarter per acre. The resolution was passed in both the Illinois house and senate, but the federal government refused to accept the plan.[24] The few projects initiated randomly to encourage widespread district support resulted in a hodgepodge of disconnected rail lines, many of which ran only a few miles to nowhere in particular.[25] Most projects simply disappeared.

The one notable exception was the Illinois and Michigan Canal. Lincoln had earlier proposed a Beardstown and Sangamon Canal, which was authorized but later abandoned when an engineering survey determined the cost to be at least four times the initial estimate. Lincoln again was the one who proposed the Illinois and Michigan canal bill in the state legislature, which passed by a 40–12 vote.[26] As the financial crisis wiped out the possibility of more and more improvement projects, Lincoln narrowed in his focus to insist the Illinois and Michigan Canal be completed. He saw that canal as a vital cog in the machinery of commerce.

Lincoln realized much of the reason British industrialization was up to a century ahead of other western nations was their scientific tradition, a Protestant work ethic, a high degree of religious tolerance, ample supplies of coal, and efficient transportation networks of roads and canals.[27] He saw the same dynamic with the Erie Canal, which ran for 363 miles from the upper Hudson River in Albany, New York, to Lake Erie. Now goods from Europe and New England could enter New York Harbor, travel up the Hudson River, and be transported across New York by a navigable canal rather than having to offload goods into small wagons prone to weather-induced delays. This ease of transportation helped New York become a hub of domestic and international commerce. It also facilitated the growth of central and northern Illinois, in particular Chicago, which grew from a small hamlet of two thousand to a thriving metropolis.

The Erie Canal was completed in 1825 under the direction of New York Governor DeWitt Clinton. Lincoln later told his close friend Joshua Speed that it was "his highest ambition to be the DeWitt Clinton of Illinois."[28] The soon-to-be governor of New York, William Seward, also favored internal improvements for his state and engineered development of the Genesee Valley Canal.[29] Lincoln knew that the Erie Canal project had been ridiculed as "Clinton's Folly,"[30] but he understood the completed canal had been a huge success, carrying vast amounts of passenger and freight traffic and initiating an economic boom for the state. Lincoln saw the Illinois and Michigan Canal as accomplishing the same for Illinois.

The Illinois and Michigan Canal would run from Chicago to LaSalle, where it would connect via the Illinois River through to the Mississippi River.[31] With the Erie Canal already bringing East Coast commerce into the Great Lakes, the new canal would effectively open up all of the northeast trade down the Mississippi to New Orleans. Lincoln believed the canal would stimulate substantial economic growth in Illinois as businesses grew in townships along the route and more settlers moved into the improved western economy.

Lincoln approved the hiring of William Gooding, who had previously worked on the Erie Canal, to be chief engineer on the Illinois and Michigan. After his state legislative career ended, Lincoln went on to serve as a commissioner for the canal, from which perch he would deal with claims from businessmen and citizenry for many years.[32] Mismanagement almost killed the canal, just as it was derailing other internal improvements in the state, but unlike other projects, the Illinois and Michigan Canal became a Lincoln success story. Construction began in 1836 and, after a hiatus caused by the financial panic of 1837, was completed in 1848, just in time for Lincoln to travel the canal on his way home after visiting Niagara Falls. Eventually sixty feet wide with tow-paths on each edge for mules to pull barges through the canal, it provided a vital infrastructure for the economic growth of the region until it was replaced by the Illinois Waterway in 1933.[33]

Lincoln declined to run for reelection to the Illinois statehouse after his fourth term, and after 1842 he focused on his growing legal business, taking time out for a sudden wedding to Mary Todd. In 1846 he won election to the U.S. House of Representatives, taking office the following year. He also served as delegate to the River and Harbor Convention in Chicago. Secretary of War Jefferson Davis had convinced Democratic President Franklin Pierce to veto an internal improvements bill passed by Congress, except those projects that directly benefited the South. Slave-holders again were concerned that any increase in federal infrastructure in the North would shift political and economic power, thus threatening the long-term viability of slavery.[34] Chicago had been counting on improve-ments to its harbor to complement the expected opening of the Illinois and Michigan Canal a year later. The convention was essentially a protest against Polk's veto. Ships in the harbor lowered their flags to half-mast in mourning.[35] Newly elected congressman Lincoln gave a brief impromptu speech reported in the *Daily Missouri Republican*.[36] Mostly he called for harmony as the delegates debated the options for river and harbor improvements, in contrast to the interruptions, hisses, and jibes dishar-moniously being lobbed at delegates with opposing views. He acknowl-edged that "all agree that something in the way of internal improvement must be done. The difficulty is to discriminate, when to begin and where to stop." He admitted "there is great danger in going too far." To the con-cern that improvements are "sectional," he acknowledged that funding is often at the whim of members of Congress. Lincoln said that he did not support sectional improvements, but argued, "Is there any way to make improvements, except that some are benefitted more than others?" add-ing, "No improvement can be made that will benefit all alike."[37]

He so strongly believed in the long-term economic benefit of improvements that he used some of the limited time allotted to fresh-men congressmen to argue for internal improvements on the floor of the House. He began by rebutting the recent Democratic platform written for the 1848 nomination of Lewis Cass, which concluded the Constitution did not confer upon the federal government the power to carry on a system of internal improvements. Lincoln disagreed and systematically dismantled each of the positions offered to support that conclusion.

Lincoln provided concrete examples of the argument he previewed at the River and Harbor Convention. On the position that the burdens of improvements "would be *general*, while their benefits would be *local* and *partial*," Lincoln did not deny that there was some degree of truth. He then pointed out the logical axiom that "no commercial object of government patronage can be so exclusively *general*, as to not be of some peculiar *local* advantage; but on the other hand, nothing is so *local*, as to not be of some general advantage." As an example of the former, he reminded members that while a navy that protects shipping offers benefits to the nation as a whole, it also provides a specific local advantage to the port cities of Charleston, Baltimore, Philadelphia, New York, and Boston well beyond any benefit to interior towns in Illinois.[38]

Then he noted the converse is also true, that projects seemingly local can provide general benefit. Using the newly opened Illinois and Michigan Canal as an example, Lincoln acknowledged that "considered apart from its effects, it is perfectly local. Every inch of it is within the state of Illinois." But the effects are widespread. "In a very few days" after its opening, he explained, "sugar had been carried from New-Orleans through this canal to Buffalo in New-York." Having selected that route for its reduced cost of transport, a savings that seller and buyer presumably shared, "the result is, that the New Orleans merchant sold his sugar a little *dearer*, and the people of Buffalo sweetened their coffee a little *cheaper*." This benefit resulted "*from* the canal, not to Illinois where the canal *is*, but to Louisiana and New-York where it is not." This example "shows that the *benefits* of an improvement are by no means confined to the particular locality of the improvement itself."

Lincoln warned that if the nation refuses to make improvements of a general kind because it might provide benefits locally, then by using the same logic, states could refuse to make an improvement of a local kind because its benefits might be more general. In essence, the "if you do nothing for me, I will do nothing for you" mentality would inhibit both local and national economic development. He hoped instead that both the nation and the states would "in good faith" do what they could in the way of improvements such that inequality perceived in one place might be compensated in another, "and that the sum of the whole might not be very unequal."[39]

Lincoln was still fighting for internal improvements when he ran for president in 1860. Technological advancement had been rapid leading up to his nomination. The canal system had opened up the Midwest, and railroads were stringing themselves in all directions, creating towns and economies as they spread. Steamships were regular features on the Great Lakes and the great rivers like the Ohio and Mississippi. American reaping machines amazed visitors to the Paris World's Fair in 1855 with their ability to cut an acre of grain in a third of the time of European models. By 1860, the United States had become the fourth largest manufacturing country in the world. George Perkins Marsh, perhaps America's first environmentalist, approved of industrialization but also warned of the dangers of deforestation. Marsh began writing his now classic treatise *Man and Nature* as Lincoln accepted the nomination; once president, Lincoln appointed Marsh minister to Italy.[40] Long-standing Whig principles would become part of Lincoln's presidential platform.

The antislavery portion of the Whig Party evolved into the Republican Party in the 1850s, with the new party's central principle being opposition to the extension of slavery into the western territories. But the Republican Party also retained the Whig's progressivism when it came to economic development. The Republican platform of 1860 included seventeen declarations of principle, many dealing with slavery issues but five related to internal improvements. Principle 12 specifically supported American industry, stating that tariffs on foreign imports were needed "to encourage the development of the industrial interests of the whole country." It also called for reasonable wages for laborers, profitable pricing for farmers, and "adequate reward" for the skilled labor and enterprise of mechanics and manufacturers. Principle 13 specified passage of the Homestead Act, a policy of westward expansion by free-labor farmers and tradesmen that Democratic administrations had repeatedly vetoed. Principle 14 required "river and harbor improvements of a national character," arguing that such federal funding was authorized by the Constitution and "justified by the obligation of Government to protect the lives and property of its citizens." Principle 15 noted that "a railroad to the Pacific Ocean is imperatively demanded by the interests of the whole country." Lincoln fully supported the provisions of the Republican platform, many of which were enacted by Congress and implemented by Lincoln after his election, in particular the Homestead and Pacific Railroad (i.e., transcontinental railroad) provisions.[41]

As president, Lincoln understood the importance of improvements to protect against foreign dangers stimulated by the distraction of the Civil War. He pointed out in his first Annual Message to Congress in December 1861 that in addition to the obvious needs on the seacoasts, there was a need for harbor and navigation improvements on the Great Lakes and major rivers. He also called for intense railroad development to connect the loyal regions of East Tennessee and western North Carolina with the border state of Kentucky. The improvement, which he specified in detailed options, would be permanent and "worth its cost in all the future."[42]

His Annual Message the following year reiterated his emphasis on internal improvements. He reported on the substantial progress already being made on construction of the Pacific Railroad, which he had signed into law earlier in 1862. True to his Illinois roots, he pressed for congressional action to enlarge the capacities of the great canals in New York and Illinois, which were of "vital . . . importance to the whole nation." He promised to shortly provide Congress with "some interesting and valuable statistical information" regarding the military and commercial importance of enlarging the Illinois and Michigan Canal.[43]

Lincoln's view of a modernizing America was reflected in the Whig ideology and adopted by the emerging Republican Party. Progress was symbolized by the development of canals, steamships, railroads, and cities. He believed rivers and streams in the Midwest needed to be "widened, deepened, and made navigable."[44] Lincoln held that the federal government played a role in promoting scientific and technological advancement, arguing that the "legitimate object of government is 'to do for the people what needs to be done, but which they cannot, by individual effort, do at all, or do so well, for themselves.'"That included infrastructure projects and making available "common schools."[45] He also believed that government's "leading objective is, to elevate the condition of men—to lift artificial weights from all shoulders; to clear the paths of laudable pursuit for all; to afford all, an unfettered start, and a fair chance, in the race of life."[46]

But modernization created two Americas, with most industrialization occurring in the North while the South remained what historian James McPherson describes as "a labor-intensive, labor-repressive undiversified agricultural economy."[47] While the North saw improvements as a means to move forward, the South worried that "if Congress can make banks, roads, and canals under the Constitution, they can free any slave in the US."[48] So these economic conflicts exacerbated the other defining conflict of the time—slavery. And just as economics was driven in part by scientific and technological advancement, many proponents of slavery sought scientific support for their belief that white men were biologically, mentally, and creationally superior to black men.

CHAPTER 7

The Science of Slavery

THE ADVANCE OF TECHNOLOGY HAD ONE UNINTENDED EFFECT; IT PROlonged slavery. Whereas the Declaration of Independence declared it a self-evident truth that "all men are created equal," the U.S. Constitution subtly acknowledged the existence of slavery in many of the states. Allowing the continuation of slavery was a necessary compromise to entice the various states to accept the creation of a federal-level governance. The framers believed at that time that slavery was an antiquated institution, not only in opposition to the concept of a free country but also unsustainable as an economic system.

Two months before the Constitution was passed, the Continental Congress had enacted "An Ordinance for the Government of the United States, North-West of the River Ohio," commonly known as the Northwest Ordinance. Once the Constitution was in place, the new Congress quickly codified the ordinance. The law created the Northwest Territory, covering the area now consisting of Ohio, Indiana, Illinois, Michigan, Wisconsin, and part of Minnesota. Among the provisions was that the territory would be forever free; slavery would not be allowed. In addition, as of January 1, 1808, the international slave trade was abolished, at least in theory (in practice, the slave trade continued in the South up until the Civil War). The founders' belief was that slavery was on a path toward its ultimate extinction.

What they had not counted on was a new technology invented by Eli Whitney in 1794. Prior to the cotton gin, production of cotton was a laborious proposition. Workers, mostly enslaved, shuffled through the fields in the great heat and humidity of southern summers, handpicking cotton from the prickly plants. Enslaved women were expected to pick one hundred pounds a day, the men two or three times their weight, with four hundred pounds a day demanded of the most robust and experienced pickers. The work was backbreaking, with each worker stooped over to reach plant level. One hundred pounds meant pulling the cotton lint from seven thousand bolls, the small seed capsules containing the cotton fibers. Hands bled and cramped from the prickly pods and repetitive motion, hour after hour, day after day.[1]

Bags of over one hundred pounds were then compacted into bales of more than six hundred pounds. Prior to mechanization, the small sticky seeds had to be separated from the tangled fibers by hand, a process that was time-consuming, thus limiting the amount of cotton that would be planted. Once deseeded, the cotton had to be cleaned and carded (i.e., the fibers aligned) before being spun and woven into the cotton fabric used to make clothes.[2]

The laborious process of hand cleaning could produce up to a pound of cotton fiber a day per person. Whitney's simple device—essentially a wooden drum with hooks pulling cotton fibers through a mesh—increased that to about fifty-five pounds per day. This massive increase in productivity eliminated the seed-picking inefficiencies. Now rather than needing a large number of enslaved people spending many hours painstakingly pulling seeds out of the cotton fibers, the operation could be done in a tiny fraction of the time. Whitney himself made little money off the cotton gin because of patent-infringement issues, but another pursuit of his—the popularization of manufacturing with interchangeable parts—became a critical advantage to the North decades later during the Civil War.[3]

At first this technology might suggest the need for fewer enslaved workers, but as author Thomas Friedman notes, automating jobs can lead to more jobs being created. "At the beginning of the nineteenth century, many people had only one set of clothes," which were handmade. "By the end of that century, most people had multiple sets of clothing, drapes on their windows, rugs on their floors, and upholstery on their furniture." Because of automation, the production process was made more cost-effective, so it was easy for demand to grow.[4] Such was the case with the cotton gin. Suddenly the process of removing the seeds was tremendously faster, which resulted in vast cost savings and made the process of making clothes easier and more profitable. Increasing profits meant plantation owners could plant more acres, which meant acquiring more laborers to work the fields to feed the growing textile industry in New England and Great Britain.[5] Cotton exports exploded from less than half a million pounds in 1793 to over ninety-three million pounds less than twenty years later. By the 1850s, cotton had blossomed to more than half the total export value of the United States, supplying more than three-quarters of the cotton for the textile mills of England that employed as much as half of all English workingmen.[6]

Rather than on a path toward ultimate extinction, slavery rapidly became a growth industry because of the cotton gin. In the summer of 1858, Lincoln recalled the sentiments of South Carolina Representative Preston Brooks, at the time reveling in his recent attack on Senator Charles Sumner on the Senate floor. Lincoln paraphrased the hot-tempered plantation owner as acknowledging that "the invention of the cotton gin had made the perpetuity of slavery a necessity in this country."[7] Enslaved people were needed to tend the expanding cotton fields to meet the increasing need for clothing and other cotton-based products across the South, in the North, and overseas. In addition, not only were slaves valuable labor for cotton and sugar plantations, they became a "cash crop" in themselves, often encouraged by plantation owners to produce children for later forced labor or sale. Demand for slave labor more than tripled their value on the open market, and raising cotton became the primary means of achieving wealth in the South. Cotton was also the impetus for westward development in the Southern states.[8] Wade Hampton of South Carolina, for example, made more than $200,000 annually on his cotton plantation, equivalent to nearly seven million dollars today.[9] Cotton had become so ingrained in both the Southern and national economy that a trade magazine called the *American Cotton Planter* asserted it was the crop on which "the planter of the South, the farmer of the West and North-West, the manufacturer of the North, the merchants of the whole country, the Steamboat of the rivers, the coasting Vessel, the Rail Road and even the Telegraph" all depended.[10] As James Henry Hammond of South Carolina proclaimed in 1858, "Cotton is king."[11]

As with technology, science influenced the spread of slavery. When the Constitution was signed, the geography of the United States consisted of only the original thirteen colonies, now states, along the eastern seaboard. The western boundaries of the southernmost states were unclear but generally considered to be as far as the Mississippi River despite the presence of Indigenous peoples. The land just west of the Mississippi belonged ostensibly to the French, who again ignored the presence of native peoples. Further west was the property of Mexico and Spain.

Slavery had existed for over a century and a half prior to the nation's founding. One of the complaints written into the draft Declaration of Independence—removed from the final version for political expediency—was to chastise the British crown for forcing slavery on these shores. Lincoln recognized the "ultimate extinction" belief of the Founders by how they verbally hid the presence of slavery in the Constitution, which never uses the words *slave* or *slavery*, substituting euphemisms like "persons held in servitude." "Thus, the thing is hid away," Lincoln said in his Peoria speech, using medical terminology, "just as an afflicted man hides away a wen or a cancer, which he dares not cut out at once, lest he bleed to death; with the promise, nevertheless, that the cutting may begin at the end of a given time." He contended that the Founders compromised to get all parties to agree to the new form of government, believing that they could excise slavery over time. The Northwest Ordinance and banning of the international slave trade would speed up that process.[12]

Or so they thought. In 1803, President Thomas Jefferson finalized the Louisiana Purchase, which suddenly doubled the geographical extent of the country, adding Louisiana and points north to the present border with Canada and farther westward until reaching the land owned by Mexico. Later, in 1847, the United States gained another massive land grab, the spoils of a war with Mexico. Lincoln questioned President Polk's motives during his single term in Congress, asserting that the invasion was a pretense to expand slavery into the West. Southern leaders plotted to conquer the Caribbean, Central America, Panama, and Cuba to expand their empire.[13]

With the United States now sprawling coast to coast, and the status of slavery undefined in the new territories, politicians north and south battled for control. A first attempt to settle the issue in 1820 led to the Missouri Compromise. Missouri would enter the Union as a state, but all other lands of the Louisiana Purchase north of the southern border of the new state would be free from slavery. Slavery would be allowed in the limited lands below that border.[14] When the former Mexican lands were assumed, California was admitted as a free state while the rest of the area remained territory, status to be determined later.

This idea seemed satisfactory to most people because they thought the northern territories were unsuitable for growing cotton. Stephen A. Douglas argued that the climate and geography of the West and North were too dry and too mountainous, and thus assumed the South would not care.[15] He ignored the political power of having two senators and some number of representatives voting in favor of slaveholding interests even if those new states had few slaves.[16] He also missed the impact of new technological developments like the McCormick reaper and the John Deere stainless steel plow, both of which made agriculture on the northern plains more feasible and profitable.[17] Lincoln saw through Douglas's ruse. In his 1854 Peoria speech, Lincoln noted that there were five states—Delaware, Maryland, Virginia, Kentucky, and Missouri—plus the District of Columbia, all north of the Missouri Compromise line. These areas held more than a quarter of all the enslaved people in the nation. Climate would not prevent westward expansion of slavery.[18]

Lincoln understood both the technological and political implications of territorial expansion. As his political career grew, so did his concern that spreading slavery into the territories would eventually result in it becoming national. In his 1858 "House Divided" speech, he contended that the nation "will become all one thing or the other. Either the opponents of slavery will arrest the spread of it, and place it where the public mind shall rest in the belief that it is in the course of ultimate extinction, or its advocates will push it forward until it shall become alike lawful in all the States, North as well as South."[19] Passage of the Kansas-Nebraska Act and the Dred Scott decision in the 1850s made the possibility of slavery expanding throughout the country all too real.

Where geographical expansion of the boundaries of the United States provided more land to spread slavery, soil nutrition science played a role in creating the cotton belt and a craving for new lands. Most early plantations in Virginia and North Carolina, as well as smaller farms in New England, grew tobacco, which was especially hard on soil. Tobacco, cotton, and sugar beets all require substantial amounts of nitrogen and minerals. Repeated tobacco crops in the same field depleted nitrogen in soils so badly it led to infertility; the soil simply became unable to support new plants.[20] This was especially true in Virginia, where some of the more affluent early plantation owners such as George Washington, Thomas Jefferson, and James Madison began experimenting with crop rotation to deal with dead soils. In 1832, Edward Ruffin published *An Essay on Calcareous Manures*, perhaps the first to suggest using marl, a calcium carbonate clay, to neutralize acidic soils.[21] But neither of these nutrient-augmentation schemes was widely communicated until after the Civil War. Deforestation as settlers like the Lincolns swarmed across the Midwest also led to erosion of fertile topsoil in their wake.[22] By the 1850s, many Virginia planters were giving up on their plantations and selling enslaved people farther south to work on the expanding cotton acreage.[23]

Continuing soil depletion in the eastern states, fed by the improved profit enabled by the cotton gin, led to plantations spreading westward from tidewater Virginia, North Carolina, South Carolina, and Georgia into the territories that would become northern Florida, Alabama, Mississippi, Arkansas, Louisiana, and coastal Texas. These well-drained soils were initially rich in nitrogen, minerals, and other critical nutrients. The long hot summers were perfect for cotton production. Sugar beets and sugarcane also became huge growth crops in the Deep South, especially the wet fertile delta of Louisiana. But cotton burned out the nutrients in soil, so by necessity plantations continued to expand westward.[24]

Lincoln's family experienced some soil depletion issues in Kentucky and Indiana, which they handled by simply clearing and planting a new section of their land when yields decreased, or moving to a new farm. The problem likely never arose in the short time he lived on the farm with the rich soil of Illinois. But in his speeches Lincoln indicated he understood the importance of the "fertility of soil, and salubrity of climate" and the "variety of soil, climate and interest."[25] Indeed, soil in the South was so nutrient exhausted and eroded after decades of overfarming cotton that poor white and black farmers were often left hungry. Only in the twentieth century did an African American man by the name of George Washington Carver discover that legumes, including peanuts and soybeans, could enrich the soil with nitrogen and prevent erosion.

With a reliance on agriculture and disdain for internal improvements and industrialization, the South experienced many of the same productivity problems that later plagued Communism. Lincoln's future secretary of state, William Seward, grasped the lack of industrialization and failing plantations as he traveled through Virginia. "Exhausted soil, old and decaying towns, wretchedly-neglected roads, and in every respect, an absence of enterprise and improvement, distinguish the region." He blamed the degradation on the effect of slavery. Northerners believed that free-labor workers were naturally industrious, whereas the slave system provided little incentive for hard work and little motivation for innovative enterprise.[26] Lincoln too recognized the disadvantages of the slave-labor system and advantages of a paid labor force. "The hired laborer of yesterday," he noted, "labors on his account today; and will hire others to labor for him tomorrow." Improvement in condition "is the order of things in a society of equals," Lincoln said, adding that "free labor has the inspiration of hope; pure slavery has no hope."[27]

Some southerners acknowledged slave-labor limitations. In 1857, North Carolinian Hinton Rowan Helper published a book called *The Impending Crisis of the South*. He warned that slavery was forever hurting the Southern economy, which was why the South remained much less innovative and modernized than the North. Helper argued that the interests of a small number of wealthy slaveholders was adversely impacting the majority of small Southern farmers. "We are dependent on Northern capitalists for the means necessary to build our railroads, canals, and other public improvements," he wrote. Without the North, the South would collapse. Seeing imminent societal failure in the South, Helper lamented that "all the world sees, or ought to see, that in a commercial, mechanical, manufactural, financial, and literary point of view, we are as helpless as babes." All because of the rejection of scientific and technological advancement and reliance on a subjugated labor force.[28]

In tandem, the upward mobility of poorer whites stalled as wealth redistributed to fewer and fewer slaveholding planters. To prevent these poorer whites from joining forces with their fellow laboring black Americans, wealthy whites promoted racial hierarchies of value.[29] If poor whites were not so well off as the rich plantation owners, they were told, they were still white, hence superior to black people, whether the latter were free or enslaved.[30]

SCIENTIFIC RACISM

Charles Darwin, born on the same day as Abraham Lincoln, published *On the Origin of Species* in 1859. Lincoln was deep into his preliminary run for the presidency and most likely never read the book even if William Herndon had obtained a copy, but he was familiar with the general concepts of evolution that Darwin was documenting. In 1844, *Vestiges of the Natural History of Creation* by Scottish journalist Robert Chambers became a European and American bestseller. According to Herndon, Lincoln read it shortly after publication, "which interested him so much that he read it through."[31] *Vestiges* traced the history of creation from the planets, the Earth, rocks, sea plants, fish, land plants, and animals up to the origins of different tribes of humans. It promoted a somewhat undefined process of development from one level of complexity of life to the next. In many ways the views reflected the general concepts already developed, but as yet unpublished, by Darwin, although without the experimental scientific support. Darwin's ardent defender Thomas Huxley and many others attacked the book as unproven and rife with factual errors, probably because Huxley knew Darwin was still painstakingly documenting his more robust theories of evolutionary development. Other scientists at the time, for example, the influential Alexander von Humboldt, supported "in almost every particular its theories." Alfred Russel Wallace also had a more favorable opinion of *Vestiges*, which inspired him to carry out his own research to test the hypotheses presented, later sending his findings to Darwin.[32] Herndon noted that "Mr. Lincoln had always denied special creation, but from his want of education he did not know just what to believe. He adopted the progressive and development theory as taught more or less directly in that work."[33] By 1850, much of the scientific community had rejected the developmentalism of *Vestiges* in favor of special creation. This would change after Darwin's *Origin* was released at the end of the decade, but for now the theological factions dominated public thought.[34]

The perceived distinctions among the races had been actively debated for many years, from both theological and scientific perspectives. Much of this was an effort to rationalize the enslavement of other men. While not originally restricted to color of skin and with no biological meaning, the idea of race developed as an easy way to distinguish the majority white Europeans who settled in North America from nonwhites, including Indigenous peoples already present and black Africans brought against their will. But part of enslavement is the requirement of dominant parties to dehumanize those being enslaved. One way to do this was through polygenism, the theory that human races were of different origins. Influential scientists such as Louis Agassiz joined with other polygenists in promoting this concept of special creation. If different races of humans were created separately, they argued, then it was obvious that whites were created superior to blacks, and thus enslavement was the natural order.

A problem with the polygenism idea was that the Bible contradicted it. How could everyone descend from Adam and Eve as described in the Book of Genesis if God created multiple races of varying colors? And if races were static—and designed to be superior or inferior—why is it that color is a pliable characteristic, as the presence of mulatto, quadroon, octoroon, and other mixed-race individuals of different complexions so readily attested?

Monogenism, the traditional Adam and Eve concept of single creation, also had its inherent conflict. If all humans came into existence through a single creation, how is it that skin color varies so much? And how could one color be permanently superior to another? The answer, to those so inclined, was the Curse of Ham.

The Curse of Ham occurs in the Bible in Genesis 9:18–27. Technically, the curse was not directed at Ham but at his son Canaan, and possibly it was less a curse than a prophesy, depending on which interpretation of the various translations and adaptations of the biblical passages are cited. The story essentially is that the post-flood Noah drinks too much wine and falls asleep drunk and unclothed in his tent. His son Ham discovers him naked and tells the other two sons, Shem and Japheth, who modestly shuffle backward into the tent to throw a garment over their father. When Noah wakes up, he punishes Ham for the sin of seeing him in an inglorious state, cursing Ham's son Canaan to be forever a servant to Shem and Japheth. This convoluted story was interpreted by Southern slaveholders as justification for slavery, with blackness and racial hierarchy biblically defined. The fact that the Bible does not actually specify that Ham or Canaan, or any of Canaan's prodigy, were black is ignored. Blackness may have been introduced in the late sixteenth century by English travel writer George Best, who suggested all of Canaan's descendants would be "blacke and loathsome."[35] Using the Curse of Ham to justify slavery is less theological as it is ideologically expedient and, in Martin Luther King's later words, "blasphemy."[36] As confusing as the creationist rationale was, more worrying was the use of science to justify slavery.

The categorization of plants and animals had long been on scientists' minds, so in the mideighteenth century, and modified many times thereafter, a Swedish taxonomist named Carl Linnaeus constructed a classification scheme in a book called *Systema Naturae*. Linnaeus developed the formalized system of binomial nomenclature used today to describe all flora and fauna. Under that naming system, each organism is defined by a two-part genus + species terminology (e.g., humans are *Homo sapiens*). The system further creates a family tree of branching connected common ancestors, with the current hierarchy containing domain as its highest level, followed by kingdom, phylum, class, order, family, genus, species. Humans are thus: kingdom Eukarya, phylum Animalia, class Mammalia, order Primates, family Hominidae, genus *Homo*, and species *sapiens*. Linnaeus caused a stir because he placed humans with apes and monkeys under the order Anthropomorpha, roughly meaning "with human form" (now called Primates).[37]

But even Linnaeus struggled with the variability in human characteristics. Under *Homo sapiens* he listed five "varieties" of humans: Wild Man, American, European, Asiatic, and African, or roughly, caveman, red, white, yellow, and black. In later editions he added to these varieties an optional third element called subspecies to the normal two-part nomenclature, making the Wild Man into *Homo sapiens monstrosus*. The others became, in order, *Homo sapiens americanus, europaeus, asiaticus,* and *afer,* further assigning each to one of the four regions of the world and describing their characteristics. These were not neutral categories; he defined them by skin color and facial features, but also by value judgments reflecting the eurocentric white supremacist hierarchy that became the blueprint for racist stereotypes that continue today. Thus, Wild Man was a catchall category described as "four-footed, mute, hairy," originally defined as feral people, wolf boys, and wild girls. Americans were described as "copper-colored, choleric, erect" with thick, straight black hair, wide nostrils, and a "harsh face" who are "obstinate," paint themselves with fine red lines, and are "governed by customs." He described Europeans as "fair, sanguine, brawny" with yellow or brown flowing hair, blue eyes, gentle, and inventive," who wear clothes and are governed by laws. Asiatics were "sooty, melancholy, rigid" with black hair, dark eyes, "severe, haughty, and covetous," who are "covered in loose garments" and are "governed by opinions." His final variety was the Africans, with their black, frizzled hair, silky black skin, flat nose, and tumid lips, and were "crafty, indolent, and negligent," who "anoints himself with grease," while being "governed by caprice." Linnaeus and his followers eventually associated each of the four varieties (dropping the semifantastical *monstrosus*) with different personality types called choleric, sanguine, melancholic, and phlegmatic, again reflecting severe racial bias more than scientific analysis.[38]

Another race categorization scheme was developed a year before American independence by German anthropologist Johann Blumenbach. In his medical degree thesis, "On the Variety of Mankind," he analyzed the shapes and sizes of sixty human skulls as part of the relatively new science of craniometry. He placed humans into five taxonomic groups similar to those of Linnaeus: Caucasians (European, Middle Eastern, and North African origins), Mongolians (East Asians and some Central Asians), Malayan (Southeast Asians and Pacific Islanders), Ethiopian (Sub-Saharan Africans), and American (American Indian and other Indigenous peoples). He referred to these categories as White, Yellow, Brown, Black, and Red. Unlike Linnaeus, he did not conclude that any one variety was superior or inferior. Blumenbach may have been the first to suggest that climate and geography, in particular the amount of sun-light as a factor of distance from the equator, accounted for the different shades of men. He believed that all races had degenerated from an origi-nal Caucasian and would revert under controlled environmental condi-tions. No matter how many varieties subcategorized, all humans are one species. A colleague of Blumenbach went further, correctly noting that the idea of different racial categories was meaningless, that "the colors run together." Even Blumenbach noticed there was as much variation among individual Africans as there was between Africans and Europeans.[39]

Meanwhile, in the 1850s, Lincoln borrowed from fellow lawyer Clif-ton Moore a book that delved into the scientific evaluation of race. *The Types of Mankind* was coauthored by Alabama physician Josiah Nott and Egyptologist George Gliddon and included an essay by Louis Agassiz.[40] While polygenism had fallen out of favor by the time of Thomas Jefferson, it had seen a resurgence as slaveholders sought scientific support demon-strating that African black men were biologically inferior. *The Types of Mankind* promoted Nott's earlier argument for separate creation along with the more recent work of Samuel G. Morton. Morton was a respected physician and natural scientist at the time, but his reputation would ulti-mately be tarnished by his connection to the concept of scientific racism.[41]

Morton was best known for his collection of nearly one thousand human skulls obtained from various scientific expeditions around the globe, a collection so large and unique to have earned it the nickname "the American Golgotha." His detailed measurements of cranial capacity were published in a treatise called *Crania Americana*, dramatically enhanced with seventy-eight lithographs by artist John Collins that set a new stan-dard for accuracy in anatomical illustration.[42] Morton used his measure-ments to assess whether humans of different races were different species, something he claimed to have demonstrated by clear differences in cranial capacity, which he equated with brain size and intellectual superiority.[43] He asserted that brain size was greatest in Caucasians and smallest in Blacks, with Indians falling in the middle, conveniently matching the white supremacist attitudes of the time. From this he concluded that each race was separately created (polygenism) and placed in separate parts of the world.

Nott and Gliddon's *The Types of Mankind* and Morton's *Crania Americana* were eagerly promoted by Louis Agassiz, who declared that Morton's skull collection "alone had been worth the visit to America."[44] Agassiz was an accomplished and well-respected scientist, but his racial prejudices were so extreme that he could not bear to admit that black people could be remotely related to him.[45] Most scientists, however, rejected Morton's conclusions and questioned the veracity of his data. One German scientist, Frederick Teidemann, measured the weight of the brain of various Europeans, Africans, Asians, and Indigenous Indians. He concluded that "the brain of a Negro is upon the whole quite as large as that of the European and other human races." His research demonstrated "that neither anatomy nor physiology can justify placing [black people] beneath Europeans in a moral or intellectual point of view." Any inferiority of education, he said, was due to the oppression of slavery not innate inability.[46] More recently, work by Stephen J. Gould and later by Louis Menard has established that Morton's scientific study was flawed and the conclusions of him and like-minded proponents were swayed as much by bigotry as the robustness of the science.[47]

Other "scientific" rationalizations were routinely offered. In 1851, one Southern physician defined a new disease he called "drapetomania," derived from the Greek words for runaway (*drapetes*) and madness (*mania*), suggesting that only some acute disease could explain why a slave might run away from their supposedly benevolent master. Much earlier, Philadelphia physician Benjamin Rush proposed that black skin was the result of some form of leprosy. Skin color in itself was considered a pathology, although Rush was adamant that such a superficial condition had no implication for mental capacity, nor was it a basis for enslaving black men.[48] Attempts to rationalize slavery with science based on the works of Morton and the lobbying of Agassiz led Charles Darwin to specifically refute them in the opening pages of *On the Origin of Species*: "The view which most naturalists entertain, and which I formerly entertained," Darwin wrote, "namely, that each species has been independently created—is erroneous."[49] Darwin's theory of natural selection described incremental changes over long periods of time similar to the uniformitarianism view seen in such geological formations as Niagara Falls.

This inherent uncertainty in both the theological and scientific evaluations of "race" allowed those predisposed to finding a rationale for enslaving other humans plenty of room to do just that. This was the atmosphere in which Abraham Lincoln entered the fray to eliminate slavery in the United States.

LINCOLN'S EXAMINATION OF RACE

Slavery was immoral to Lincoln. While his flatboat trip to New Orleans gave him his first glimpse of slave auctions, it was not his first experience with the "peculiar institution." The Bardstown–Green River Turnpike passed adjacent to the family's Knob Creek farm in Kentucky. It commonly served as one of the overland routes slave traders used to move coffles of slaves to slave markets farther south. While young, the inquisitive Lincoln likely queried his parents about the stream of black men in chains. With their clear antislavery beliefs, his parents would have given him an honest reckoning of the evils of slavery.[50] "I am naturally antislavery. If slavery is not wrong, nothing is wrong. I cannot remember when I did not so think, and feel," he wrote to the editor of a Frankfurt, Kentucky, newspaper late in the Civil War.[51]

While his antislavery views were long-standing, Lincoln understood that most opponents of slavery did not necessarily equate freedom with full equality. Illinois' black laws were especially egregious in their treatment of blacks despite it being a free state. Most of the early settlers arrived from the South and thus held traditional beliefs about the relation between the races. During the series of debates between Lincoln and Stephen A. Douglas for the 1858 Senate seat, Douglas continually baited the largely racist audiences. He played to the fears of whites, both North and South, about what emancipation might mean with respect to competition for jobs, land, and wives. Douglas routinely used racist language—newspapers at the time substituted the less objectionable *Negro* for what he actually said—and repeatedly referred to Lincoln's party as the "Black Republicans," insisting that they were for full equality. Amalgamation, the intermarriage of black men with white women, was seen by most as an indefensible result of black equality.[52] The idea of amalgamation as an attack line was as effective as it was hypocritical, which Lincoln pointed out by reminding listeners that the vast majority of mixed-race Americans, over 405,000 by 1850, were the result of the rampant rape culture in which slaveholders routinely sexually exploited their female slaves.[53]

Douglas's attack strategy put Lincoln in an untenable position. If Lincoln had advocated for full equality, he would have ensured his overwhelming defeat in the election, if not a stoning from the often raucous, and overtly racist, crowds. He dealt with the dilemma by equivocating: "There is a physical difference between the white and black races which I believe will forever forbid the two races living together on terms of social and political equality." Given this difference, which he elsewhere identified simply as skin color, he said that if there must be the position of superior and inferior, he "as much as any other man" favored "having the superior position assigned" to the race to which he belonged. He added, however, that he "[did] not perceive that because the white man is to have the superior position the negro should be denied everything."[54] Earlier he had noted that the authors of the Declaration of Independence may not have intended to declare all men equal *in all respects*, but they did consider all men "equal in 'certain inalienable rights, among which are life, liberty, and the pursuit of happiness.'"[55]

These words may sound harsh to modern ears but were progressive for the time and place. Lincoln spoke and acted in much more egalitarian terms in other venues and also expressed the illogic of enslaving other men. Putting his Euclid studies to good use, he asked:

If A. can prove, however conclusively, that he may, of right, enslave B.—why may not B. snatch the same argument, and prove equally, that he may enslave A?

You say A. is white, and B. is black. It is color, *then; the lighter having the right to enslave the darker? Take care. By this rule, you are to be slave to the first man you meet, with a fairer skin than your own.*

You do not mean color *exactly?—You mean the whites are* intellectually *the superiors of blacks, and, therefore have the right to enslave them? Take care again. By this rule, you are to be slave to the first man you meet, with an intellect superior to your own.*

But, say you, it is a question of interest; *and, if you can make it your interest, you have the right to enslave another. Very well. And if he can make it his interest, he has the right to enslave you.*[56]

He went further in his Peoria speech, noting that "If the negro is a *man*, why then my ancient faith teaches me that 'all men are created equal'; and that there can be no moral right in connection with one man's making a slave of another."[57]

Theology and science might not provide reliable justification for slavery, but Lincoln understood that slavery was so entrenched in the economic and social system of both the North and the South that it would be difficult to rid it from the nation. His rail-splitting experience taught him that to achieve something difficult you need to start with the thin edge of the wedge and keep pounding it until you have forced the bonds to separate. He tried this with slavery, pushing for gradual compensated emancipation, sometimes with voluntary colonization. While he was flexible on the mechanisms, he was adamant about the one big thing: slavery could not spread into the territories. Some contend that Lincoln did not do enough, even after he issued the Emancipation Proclamation during the war, but he worked within the constitutional and legal frameworks and the realities of the time.

The premise that science demonstrated the superiority and inferiority of different races of humans had been contentious since the founding of the nation. Alexander Hamilton mocked Thomas Jefferson, perhaps our most scientific president, for Jefferson's belief that blacks were genetically inferior to whites, which Jefferson had written quite graphically, and inaccurately, in his *Notes on the State of Virginia*.[58] Pseudoscientific justifications for slavery continued up to and through the Civil War. Jefferson Davis maintained as Mississippi senator that blacks were more suited to hard labor. He claimed, "The European races now engaged in working the mines of California sink under the burning heat and sudden changes of climate, to which the African race are altogether better adapted. The production of rice, sugar, and cotton is no better adapted to slave labor than the digging, washing, and quarrying of the gold mines."[59]

This attitude existed even within Lincoln's own cabinet. Postmaster General Montgomery Blair, heir to the wealthy and influential Blair family of Maryland, recommended colonizing freed slaves outside the United States to some place hot and humid, where he thought they would be better suited to climatic conditions. Louis Agassiz had promoted the idea of "zoological provinces" for animal and plant life, a concept related to the current science of biomes. But Agassiz argued it applied equally well to humans, with white people better acclimated to temperate climes and black people to tropical climes, more or less equating skin color with climatic preference. Frederick Douglass, the leading African American abolitionist of the time, adamantly refuted this faulty theory in an 1862 letter to Blair. "If ever any people can be acclimatized, I think the Negro can claim to be so in this country" after nearly 250 years of black residence on American soil. This was mere ideology, not science, Douglass complained, and all discussion of "confining different varieties of men to different belts of the earth's surface" was "chimerical in the extreme."[60]

Southern leaders often cited "science" to justify slavery. In early 1861, newly appointed Confederate vice president Alexander Stephens laid out the "great physical, philosophical, and moral truths" of the new Confederacy. "This truth has been slow in the process of its development," he said, "like all other truths in the various departments of science" as espoused by Morton, Nott, and Agassiz. He even compared these "truths" to the heliocentric principles promoted by Galileo and William Harvey's theory of blood circulation. Stephens admitted that slavery "was the immediate cause of the late rupture and present revolution" (i.e., secession and the Civil War). He acknowledged that the Founders felt slavery was evil, that "the enslavement of the African was in violation of the laws of nature; that it was wrong in principle, socially, morally, and politically" and would eventually pass away. But the Founders were wrong to assume the equality of the races, Stephens claimed. Speaking of the Confederacy, he declared, "Our new government is founded upon exactly the opposite idea; its foundations are laid, its corner-stone rests, upon the great truth that the negro is not equal to the white man; that slavery subordination to the superior race is his natural and normal condition." Stephens recounted a colleague from one of the Northern states, perhaps Lincoln given their friendship, developed while serving together in the House of Representatives, who said the South would be compelled to yield on slavery because "it was as impossible to war successfully against a principle of politics, as it was in physics or mechanics."[61]

Stephens was not the only one who had promoted the "natural order" of slavery. John C. Calhoun of South Carolina had been the leading pro-slavery firebrand for decades until his death in 1850. He claimed the Founders were wrong in considering slavery a necessary evil that needed to be eradicated, instead promoting the idea that slavery was a "positive good" to those enslaved as well as to those who enslaved them.[62] In a note to himself after Calhoun's death, Lincoln identified the illogic of this "positive good" concept: "for although volume upon volume is written to prove slavery a very good thing, we never hear of the man who wishes to take the good of it, *by being a slave himself.*"[63] Falling back on his Euclid studies, he wrote to Boston manufacturer Henry L. Pierce to point out the problem with those who deny reality: "One would start with great confidence that he could convince any sane child that the simpler propositions of Euclid are true, but, nevertheless, he would fail, utterly, with one who should deny the definitions and axioms." Lincoln noted that "the principles of Jefferson are the definitions and axioms of free society. And yet they are denied, and evaded" and called "self-evident lies." He further wrote that "this is a world of compensations; and he who would *be* no slave, must consent to *have* no slave. Those who deny freedom to others, deserve it not for themselves; and, under a just God, cannot long retain it."[64]

In another note to himself, Lincoln put his scientific mind to challenging the logic behind slave owners who declared slavery was the "Will of God." He states that the Bible gives no answer to the question of whether a slave should be set free, which leaves the decision to the slave owner. "And while he considers it," Lincoln wrote, "he sits in the shade, with gloves on his hands, and subsists on the bread" that the slaves were "earning in the burning sun." If the slave owner decides that God wills the enslaved to stay that way, he retains his comfortable position; if he decides that God wills freedom for the enslaved, then the slave owner "has to walk out of the shade, throw off his gloves, and delve for his own bread." Lincoln noted this conflict of interest should be apparent to everyone.[65]

He went on to state that while most governments had been based on denial of equal rights of men, "*ours* began, by *affirming* those rights.

They said, some men are too *ignorant*, and *vicious*, to share in government. Possibly so, said we; and, by your system, you would always keep them ignorant, and vicious. We proposed to give *all* a chance; and we expected the weak to grow stronger, the ignorant, wiser; and all better, and happier together."[66]

Accepting the 1860 Republican nomination, Lincoln promised to adhere to the antislavery positions he helped guide into the party's platform. In the spring of 1862 he signed the Compensated Emancipation Act, freeing all enslaved people living in the District of Columbia. By fall he had issued the Emancipation Proclamation, declaring that all enslaved people in the states currently in rebellion would be "thenceforward and forever free."[67] These were wartime measures later supplanted by the Thirteenth Amendment, ending slavery forever. In his December 1862 Annual Message to Congress, Lincoln summed up his positions on slavery: "In giving freedom to the slave, we assure freedom to the free—honorable alike in what we give, and what we preserve. We shall nobly save, or meanly lose, the last, best, hope of earth. Other means may succeed; this could not fail. The way is plain, peaceful, generous, just—a way which, if followed, the world will forever applaud, and God must forever bless."[68]

PART IV

BECOMING A SCIENCE AND TECHNOLOGY LAWYER

CHAPTER 8

The Patent and Technology Cases

"I AM NOT AN ACCOMPLISHED LAWYER," LINCOLN WROTE IN NOTES FOR a law lecture, adding, "I find quite as much material for a lecture in those points wherein I have failed, as in those wherein I have been moderately successful."[1]

Lincoln was understating his expertise, as he did so often as a strategy to lower expectations, then exceed them. Like much of his education, Lincoln taught himself the law. Eastern elites benefited from classical educations and scholastic training in the law. Pioneer lawyers like Lincoln were largely self-taught by "reading" with an established lawyer.

Lincoln was elected to the Illinois state legislature on his second attempt and soon found his way for part of the year to the state capital in Vandalia. While there, he discovered how his lack of legal education inhibited his ability to pass laws governing his fellow Illinoisans. Bowling Green, the justice of the peace in New Salem, had encouraged Lincoln's natural curiosity by letting him attend sessions of his court. Lincoln also tagged along on the political trail with established lawyer John T. Stuart, whom he had met in the Black Hawk War and who was now a fellow state legislator. Stuart saw Lincoln's potential and lent him law books to study.[2]

The first law book Lincoln read was William Blackstone's *Commentaries on the Laws of England*, commonly known as Blackstone's *Commentaries*. In early nineteenth-century America there was little in the way of the established precedent that governs most modern legal proceedings. Trials were works of art as much as legally robust jurisprudence, especially in Lincoln's still largely frontier Illinois. Blackstone's *Commentaries* provided the bridge between the English law on which U.S. laws were largely based and the special circumstances inherent in the U.S. Constitution and common law. The book was divided into four sections or volumes based on the rights of persons (individuals and their relationships), of things (property), of private wrongs (civil liability), and of public wrongs (criminal liability).[3]

Blackstone tried to incorporate logical thought and scientific process into the application of common law in easy-to-understand language. Advocates and critics alike at the time noted that Blackstone gave polish to the "rugged science" of the law and "gave the law an air of a science."[4] Modern analysts note that Blackstone tried to balance the science of inquiry and human nature with an understanding of history and legal principles.[5] Some have criticized Blackstone's emphasis on a Whiggish use of history, which focuses on the rise of constitutional government, personal freedoms, and scientific progress as an inevitable march toward enlightenment.[6] Nevertheless, Blackstone's *Commentaries* were considered the Bible of the law at the time, and Lincoln studied it attentively. After Blackstone, Lincoln's self-study took him to Joseph Chitty's *A Practical Treatise on Pleadings*, Joseph Story's *Commentaries on Equity Jurisprudence*, Simon Greenleaf's *A Treatise on the Law of Evidence*, and James Kent's *Commentaries on American Law*. He also had access to the numerous law books of his two legal mentors and his third, now junior, partner. Based on their appellate case citations, Herndon and Lincoln likely subscribed to the *Law Library*, a 104-volume series of legal treatises, as well as many other law summary books. An avid book collector, Herndon also had many science and technology-oriented books on his shelves.[7]

Lincoln later counseled others to "get the books and read" as the best way to become a lawyer. Listing out the law books he read—Blackstone, Chitty, Story, Greenleaf, and others—he recommended budding lawyers read the books for themselves without an instructor, get a license, go to a practice, and keep reading. "Work, work, work, is the main thing," he told one novice.[8] As a U.S. congressman, Lincoln often assisted other Illinoisans to get patents for their inventions. He wrote to Amos Williams, for example, telling him to send a description and drawing of his invention, along with twenty dollars for the filing fee. Williams had sent a model, but Lincoln reminded him that "nothing can be done . . . without having a description of your invention. You perceive the reason for this."[9]

Passing the bar on the frontier required being quizzed on knowledge of the law and demonstrating "good character," which was duly vouched for by well-respected Springfield lawyer Stephen T. Logan. Lincoln had begun unofficially drafting legal documents while still living in New Salem, but once he formally had a law license he moved to Springfield and became junior partner with his mentor, John Todd Stuart. Stuart left much of the work to Lincoln while he pursued politics, which eventually took him from the state legislature to Washington as a U.S. congressman. When Stuart was reelected, the partnership dissolved and Lincoln joined with his other mentor, Stephen T. Logan. After several years as a junior partner, Lincoln decided to take on a junior partner of his own and formed a new law firm with William H. Herndon.[10]

Stuart had largely been absent, but Lincoln learned from Logan the importance of detailed case research and preparation. Lincoln was naturally logical in his thinking. Logan taught him to write more precise and succinct case readings. He now learned to break down the case into its critical components and watch for technical aspects that could be used in his clients' favor. According to Herndon, Lincoln did "love to dig up the question by the roots and hold it up and dry it before the fires of the mind."[11]

Lincoln rode the circuit three months every spring and three months every autumn. The backbone of Lincoln's legal career consisted of cases on the Eighth Judicial Circuit, spanning much of central Illinois and covering more than eleven thousand square miles.[12] A judge and several lawyers traveled from one county seat to another, spending a week or two at each stop, handling any cases in need of trials.[13] Prominent Bloomington jurist David Davis served as traveling judge for most of the years, while Lincoln was joined in the lawyer corps by Henry C. Whitney, Leonard Swett, Ward Hill Lamon, Lawrence Weldon, Usher Linder, and others. Lincoln often partnered with one of the other lawyers for more complex cases, but most of the time his fellow circuit riders were hired by his client's opponent. As soon as they arrived at the county seat, the lawyers would find a line of waiting business, which they handled in urgency, generally with only a perfunctory meeting with their client on the courthouse lawn before walking in to try the case in front of a jury that was already seated. The system required lawyers to think quickly and creatively, although most cases were routine, often involving liquor law violations or ownership of a litter of pigs.[14] Over time Lincoln became so respected by his fellow lawyers that he often sat in as judge, for as many as ninety-five cases in 1858 alone.[15]

Most of the early travel was done on horseback through the mud and swollen streams. Internal improvement programs helped solidify the roads in time with the growing rotundity of David Davis, thus accommodating the necessary switch to a horse-drawn carriage. Eventually, railroads would improve life on the circuit, although they failed to eliminate the summer dust and heat, winter biting cold and blizzards, or the monotonous stretches of prairie grass along the way.[16]

Most of Lincoln's early cases with Stuart and Logan were mundane—collections of promissory notes and debts. Trading notes was common in the largely cashless, barter-based pioneer economy, which resulted in ample work for frontier lawyers trying to untangle the often complicated passing of debt obligations. In one letter to his first law partner in 1840, for example, Lincoln said he had "secured our Truett debt by taking a new note with Myers," reminding Stuart that "the old note was in your individual name, and was sent to Gilbreath at Dixon's." After a few more exchanges of notes, Lincoln instructed his senior partner: "Don't neglect this, because Truett, as you will see by his letter, is very anxious about it." Lincoln did, however, take the time to append updates on pending legislation in his letters to Stuart, noting "Internal Improvements down. Canal down. Bank up."[17]

More than half of Lincoln's recorded 5,173 cases were on some form of debt collection or breach of contract, bringing in receipts of five to ten dollars a case. He sided with both creditors and debtors, winning most of the former because many defendants failed to appear and defaulted. He lost most of the cases in which he argued for the debtors.[18] All income was shared equally with Stuart, but Lincoln received only a third of the total when he was with Logan. When he took on Herndon as junior partner, Lincoln magnanimously shared the proceeds equally.[19] Lincoln also accepted divorce and other simple cases that required little preparation, especially while riding the circuit. He often discouraged litigation and served as a peacemaker in disputes. He despised what today might be called ambulance chasers, telling new lawyers to always "resolve to be honest."[20] As his career progressed, he undertook more complex work, shifting from community-based cases to more market-oriented litigation.[21] He tried over four hundred cases in the Illinois Supreme Court, although all were civil rather than criminal cases.[22] But to think only in terms of debt and corporate cases is to underestimate the breadth of Lincoln's law business. Over his twenty-five-year career as a litigator, his caseload included "a staggering variety of cases involving arbitration, assault and battery, bad debt, bankruptcy, bastardy, bestiality, breach of marriage, divorce, impeachment of an Illinois justice, insanity, land titles, libel, medical malpractice, murder, partnership dissolution, patent infringement, personal injuries, property damages, rape, railroad bonds, sexual slander, slave ownership, and wrongful dismissal."[23]

A Good Mechanical Mind

Lincoln may not have had the classical training of eastern lawyers, but he had a "good, mechanical mind and knowledge," according to Judge David Davis. While others belabored the past, Davis noted that Lincoln "looked far into the future and was philosophical, truly scientific in his inductions."[24] This was a time of profound growth in technology, spurred in part by the emphasis on internal improvements. Steam engines became more common in mills, replacing the horsepower and manpower that previously drove the saws, grain presses, and carding wheels. Increased cotton production in the South led to bigger textile mills in the North, with ready-made clothes replacing handmade apparel. Machinery like mechanical reapers and steel plows made farming life easier and expanded production.[25]

The increasingly complex society was ripe for savvy lawyers, and Lincoln quickly gained a reputation as a reliable attorney capable of taking on the growing number of technology, patent, and railroad cases sweeping the country. Named after its two biggest proponents, scientific thinking up to this point had been split between Newtonian, pursuing basic scientific knowledge for its own sake, and Baconian, applied science directed at solving specific needs or problems. Arguably there was a third way of thinking that blended the two, advocated by one of Lincoln's idols, Thomas Jefferson.[26] Lincoln's natural scientific curiosity led him to read intently in mathematics, astronomy, physics, and other sciences, but he also gravitated toward the practical applications of machinery, on which he gained substantial insights during his months on the circuit. Charles Zane, who traveled with Lincoln for ten years, recalls a time he saw Lincoln stop to examine a self-raking reaping machine on exhibition. It was the first self-raking reaper he had seen, yet he was able to describe clearly "how power and motion were communicated to the different appliances, especially to the sickle, the revolving rake, and the reel." Zane later saw Lincoln arguing a patent case in the federal court in Springfield. Models representing several machines had been introduced as evidence and were on the floor in front of the jury. Lincoln knelt down to better view the different parts of the machines, where he was joined by several members of the jury. Seeing this, the opposing attorney mumbled to his colleague, "I guess our case has gone to h—l; Lincoln and the jurors are on their knees together."[27]

Given his background, it was not surprising that Lincoln was often called on to handle patent cases related to farming and mill work. Several cases focused on plows, of which everyone seemed to have a new variation since John Deere invented his steel plow in 1837.[28] Lincoln was also involved in cases related to saw mills in which complaints revolved over improvements made to a portable circular saw mill or whether a new mill could achieve the promised capacity of three thousand board feet per day.[29] Combining both his saw mill and river navigation skills in another case, Lincoln represented Silas Deane against a suit brought by William Benson, a saw mill operator on the Sangamon River. Deane was upstream cutting logs, which he let float downstream until they struck and burst through Benson's mill dam, causing him great financial damage. Lincoln argued that the key question before the court was whether the Sangamon was considered navigable; if so, it would be deemed a "public highway" and his client was within his rights in floating the sawn logs. Should this be the case, Lincoln reasoned, Benson would be able to recover his damages by something called replevin, which means Deane could simply rebuild the broken dam without having to pay any further damages to Benson.[30]

Other cases entailed sale of patent rights, infringement of a method to manufacture bricks, and a new type of pump patent. In one contentious case, Lincoln and Herndon were asked to litigate disagreements between partners over an invention called an atmospheric churn. In a unique arrangement, the inventors had created a revolving device that would transfer a body of air from the top of a butter churn to the bottom, stimulating bubbles that would carry a quantity of cream to the top, thus allowing greater contact of the cream with oxygen, speeding up the butter-making process. The process did not work, but Lincoln was successful in settling the dispute between the partners. Unfortunately, he and Herndon were then forced to sue their own client to get paid.[31] Lincoln also was hired when a series of interrelated cases reached the Illinois Supreme Court based on a new technology intended to relieve the burdens of child-rearing. A suit was filed for fraud for what was called a horological cradle, a device with a mechanical function similar to a clock in which a baby's cradle was "rocked by machinery with a weight running on one or more pulleys; the cradle constituting the pendulum and which, being wound up, would rock itself, thus saving the continual labor to mother and nurses of rocking the cradle." The suit was settled because only the design patent had been sold, not the actual mechanical technology.[32] Lincoln won some technological cases and lost others, which was common for this type of work, as many cases were dismissed after the parties agreed to a settlement.

Lincoln's most famous patent infringement case was the Manny–McCormick reaper trial, which ironically, Lincoln never actually litigated. Prominent Chicago resident Cyrus McCormick and his father had patented a crude reaper machine in 1834, followed by several subsequent improvements over the years. Prior to its invention, it took six people an entire day to harvest two acres of wheat with a hand sickle. McCormick's reaper could bring in ten acres a day with only two people.[33] John Manny and others patented modified reapers, leading McCormick to sue him. Expecting the trial to be held in Chicago, the Manny legal team brought in Lincoln as the most qualified local patent lawyer and paid him four hundred dollars on retainer to begin preparing for the case.

Lincoln "went to Rockford," where Manny had his business, and "spent half a day, examining and studying Manny's machine" for comparison to McCormick's.[34] He told a friend that "he prepared himself as he thought thoroughly and flattered himself that he knew something of mechanics."[35] Seeking even more knowledge, he approached Springfield attorney Thomas Kidd as he was "explaining the Atkins Self-Raking Reaper" to an acquaintance. After listening for a while, Lincoln brought Kidd back to the state house, where pieces of both the Manny and McCormick reaping machines were present for examination. Reading his account recorded years later, it was apparent that the politically opposed Kidd was demeaning Lincoln's knowledge and heightening his own, but he did acknowledge Lincoln's fondness for the study of mechanics and that "he could very readily, with but little explanation, comprehend the uses of different parts and their relation to the other parts."[36]

Not long after this encounter, the case was relocated to Cincinnati, and Lincoln was dropped because a local Illinois presence was no longer needed, although the hiring attorney failed to inform him of the decision. Thinking he was still a member of the team, Lincoln went to Cincinnati expecting to be a significant part of the case, only to find himself ostracized by the new attorneys, Edwin Stanton and George Harding. Lincoln was angry and embarrassed, yet he stayed on to watch the trial and pick up some tips. The circuit court found no infringement, but McCormick appealed it to the U.S. Supreme Court, where the judgment was affirmed along the lines of the brief Lincoln had prepared but which had been ignored.[37] A few years later, now president, Lincoln apparently held no grudge for his treatment, later appointing Stanton his secretary of war and offering Harding the commissioner of patents, which he declined.[38]

MEDICAL CASES AND ASTRONOMY

A small number, less than 1 percent, of Lincoln's cases required management of medical expert witnesses. He participated in at least thirty-nine medical-related cases, and many of his forty-four murder cases needed such expertise.[39] Lincoln creatively used chicken bones in one medical malpractice suit. Samuel Fleming suffered two broken legs when the chimney of a house fell on him during a raging fire in Bloomington. Physicians Thomas Rogers and Eli Crothers set the severely damaged bones, saving both legs against the odds. Unfortunately, the right leg healed crooked and slightly shorter than the left. Rogers and Crothers agreed to reset the crooked right leg, but Fleming stopped them midway, complaining of unendurable pain. He then sued the doctors for malpractice. Defending the doctors, Lincoln demonstrated the difference in pliability between young and old bones using chicken bones. He argued that the doctors could have used the normal remedy for such damage by amputating both legs, but Fleming insisted on saving them. As with so many cases, this one eventually resulted in a settlement, but Lincoln showed that he understood basic medical principles and could be creative in communicating them to a jury.[40]

In one intriguing murder case, Lincoln advised the prosecution of Isaac Wyant, who had his arm amputated after being shot in a border dispute with Anson Rusk. Following his recovery, Wyant sought out and shot Rusk four times, then pleaded not guilty by reason of temporary insanity. This was one of the first such "insanity defense" cases ever tried. Lincoln thought Wyant was faking the mental illness, but the jury found Wyant persuasive and sent him to the state mental hospital for treatment.[41] The temporary insanity defense would later be used successfully by Congressman Daniel Sickles after he shot his wife's lover in front of witnesses across the street from the White House.[42]

A more substantive murder case, nicknamed the Almanac Trial, hit closer to home. William "Duff" Armstrong and James Norris had been arrested for murdering James Preston Metzker in a drunken brawl. Norris was quickly tried and convicted for his role. Armstrong was the son of Hannah Armstrong, whom Lincoln had known back in his New Salem days, so Lincoln offered to defend him without charge. During the trial, Lincoln cross-examined a witness who claimed to have seen Armstrong strike Metzker from a distance of 150 feet "under a bright moon." Questioning the accuracy of his testimony, Lincoln produced an 1857 almanac showing the moon on that night was too low in the sky at the time of the fight for the witness to see anything.[43]

This understanding of celestial timing was not new to Lincoln. His earlier studies of astronomy had kept him aware of happenings in the sky. The year before, gazing up at the stars while strolling along Lake Michigan in Chicago, he offered a spontaneous discourse on astronomical science to Adeline Judd, the wife of his close colleague Norman Judd. Adeline recalled that Lincoln began to speak of the mysteries, poetry, and beauty of the stars. He talked "of the discoveries since the invention of the telescope, which had thrown a flood of light and knowledge on what before was incomprehensible and mysterious; of the wonderful computations of scientists who had measured the miles of seemingly endless space which separated the planets in our solar system from our central sun, and our sun from other suns, which were now gemming the heavens above us with their resplendent beauty." He even speculated on what "increased power of the lens" might help astronomers discover in the centuries to come.[44]

Lincoln was building off his previous sightings, having witnessed an exceptional display of the Leonid meteor showers in 1833 while living in New Salem.[45] He may also have seen Miss Mitchell's Comet, discovered in the night skies by Maria Mitchell in 1847. Mitchell would become the first female professor astronomy at newly founded Vassar College during the Civil War.[46] The night before his Jonesboro debate with Stephen A. Douglas in 1858, Lincoln observed Donati's Comet streak across the sky with its long, easily visible dust and gas tail. Horace White, a reporter for the *Chicago Press & Tribune*, was with him and reported that "Mr. Lincoln greatly admired this strange visitor, and he and I sat for an hour or more in front of the hotel looking at it."[47]

With this background and fascination with astronomy, Lincoln knew exactly how to counter the witness's testimony with the actual state of moonlight the night of the murder. Some have suggested that Lincoln may have tampered with the almanac to get his desired conditions, but recent studies have definitively shown that on August 29, 1857, the moon was indeed very low in the sky by the time of the fatal fight.[48] Lincoln successfully created enough uncertainty around the credibility of the witness, and the jury found Armstrong not guilty.

Rising Waters

Lincoln's past experience getting stuck on the mill dam came in handy when he took on one of his most informative cases, commonly called the Sand Bar Case. The case was revealing because, in an age where trial transcripts were almost never kept, journalist Robert Hitt was paid to sit through the entire trial and create a comprehensive 482-page trial transcript, although he omitted the closing arguments.

The case revolved around the accretion of new land created by various efforts to turn Lake Michigan's shoreline at Chicago into a practical harbor, something nature had not designed it to do. Channels were dug, piers were built, and a great deal of sand was dredged. Eventually, Chicago had a harbor. In 1833, the government cut a channel across lakefront lots owned separately by William Johnston and William Jones. A newly erected pier caused the accretion of nearly 1,200 feet of new land, roughly six acres, which both Johnston and Jones claimed as their own. After four trials, the last of which found for Johnston, Jones appealed to the Supreme Court, which reversed the judgment and sent it back to the lower courts. At this point, Jones retained Lincoln, and after an eleven-day trial, the jury sided with Jones.[49]

The case highlighted Lincoln's knowledge of natural environments and his clear, logical communication to jurors. A legal colleague, while not specifically talking about the Sand Bar Case, seemed to capture the flavor of it when he called Lincoln "an admirable tactician" who "steered this jury from the bayous and eddies of side issues and kept them clear of the snags and sand bars, if any were put in the real channel of his case."[50] Fellow lawyer Leonard Swett also suggested Lincoln had a knack for focusing the juror on the key question while minimizing the rest. "By giving away six points and carrying the seventh, he carried the case."[51] Lincoln demonstrated this Euclidean logic and technical expertise in a letter to Johnson's attorney Robert Kinzie before the trial, querying him on such technical matters as the intersection of the pier, the accreted new lakeshore, and the properties in question, as well as the timing of the land formation and any changes since the initial pier was erected.[52] During the trial, Lincoln's background in surveying helped him cross-examine the surveyor George Snow, catching that there were two maps created, each one alternatively benefiting the claims of the two litigants. Lincoln's questioning of the land surveys was key to winning the case. He was paid $350 for his services (about $11,600 today).[53]

Lincoln and his partners handled at least forty-nine cases involving rivers, navigation, and bridges.[54] While still living in New Salem, Lincoln had gained experience navigating a variety of boats along rivers, from small skiffs to flatboats to piloting the *Talisman* and other steamships through local waters. The Columbus Insurance Company naturally turned to Lincoln when they needed legal expertise following an accident in which the steamship *Falcon* collided with a bridge over the Illinois River at Peoria. The *Falcon* had been towing several boats at the time, and one of them, the *Troy*, sank after striking the pier, destroying its cargo of wheat. The insurance company covering the cargo paid out the claim but then hired Lincoln to sue the Peoria Bridge Company on the claim that the bridge was an obstruction. The bridge company argued that the state legislature had authorized construction of the bridge and therefore the company was not liable. The case resulted in a hung jury, and the parties settled.[55]

What made the Columbus Insurance case so interesting was that Lincoln took the opposite position to that in his more famous *Effie Afton* Case a few years later. That case, more formally known as *Hurd et al. v. Rock Island Bridge Company*, involved a 430-ton, 230-foot-long side-wheeler steamship, the *Effie Afton*, traveling up the Mississippi from St. Louis on its way to St. Paul, Minnesota, a regular route for the ship. At Rock Island, Illinois, the *Effie Afton*, carrying more than $115,000 in goods and two hundred people, struck the long pier of a newly constructed railroad bridge, twisted over to hit the opposite short pier, then burst into flames and sank. A portion of the bridge also caught fire and sustained substantial damage. The captain and owner of the ship, John Hurd, with financial support from the steamship company, sued the bridge company, arguing that the bridge was an obstruction. Lincoln was hired by the bridge company to refute the obstruction charge. Contrary to his earlier case, Lincoln argued that the bridge was not the problem, that "gross negligence" of the steamship operators caused the destruction.[56]

Unlike the much broader lower Mississippi River, the upper Mississippi beginning at Rock Island was narrower and prone to occasional rapids that limited steamboat access. But traffic continued to grow, in part to service the growing area around Galena, Illinois, where the mining of lead had increased the population.[57] The U.S. Army had sent a young engineer by the name of Robert E. Lee to survey the Rock Island rapids, although no improvements were ever made. Later, the bridge project itself was opposed by Secretary of War Jefferson Davis, who actively worked to thwart construction because he did not want a potential transcontinental railroad to follow a northern route, thus inhibiting Southern state expansion of slavery to the western territories.[58] The new railroad bridge quickly became a pawn in the competing interests of steamboats versus railroads, north–south versus east–west commerce, and St. Louis as the hub of riverboat traffic versus Chicago as the growing hub of rail traffic.[59]

The *Effie Afton* Case had a nearly verbatim transcript of Lincoln's closing arguments, which gives us a look at his expertise handling a highly technical and complicated case. Scholars David Hirsch and Dan Van Haften maintain that Lincoln employed the six elements of Euclid's geometric propositions to structure his logical closing argument to the jury.[60] Lincoln prepared for the trial by spending a week at the site of the incident on Rock Island. He hired an engineer to measure the speed of the current and determine any eddies that may have been caused by construction of the bridge piers. He then set himself to debunk the plaintiff's argument that the design of the bridge abutments necessarily created unsafe conditions. The trial included expert testimony from riverboat pilots, bridge engineers, civil engineers, and other scientific experts. A model of the steamboat, another of the bridge, maps of the area, and engineering reports were all presented as evidence.[61]

Lincoln insisted he had no prejudice against steamboats or the city of St. Louis, yet also slyly convinced the jury that steamship companies and St. Louis would both benefit from inability of the railroads to build bridges across the Mississippi. He noted that the demands for travel from east to west were no less important than that of the river. He then got technical. Using the *Effie Afton* model, Lincoln showed the errors in the plaintiff's contention that the starboard (right) paddle wheel of the steamship was at full speed when the boat hit the long pier, then somehow swung around to hit the short pier without moving forward. "The fact is undisputed that she did not move one inch ahead while she was moving this thirty-one-feet sideways," Lincoln explained. He noted that the plaintiff "says that the current and the swell coming from the long pier drove her against the long pier. In other words, drove her toward the very pier from which the current came! It is an absurdity, an impossibility." Gaining momentum, Lincoln told the jurors that "I shall try to prove that the average velocity of the current through the draw with the boat in it should be five and a half miles an hour; that it is slowest at the head of the pier and swiftest at the foot of the pier." He then went on to describe in detail the speed of the current at different points, the depth of the river, and the effect of the steamship's presence on the speed of water moving between the piers. Digging into even more detail, he described measurements of any potential cross-currents and eddies formed by the bridge piers, the river flow, and the steamship movement. He carefully demonstrated with logic and science that the cause of the incident was more likely the faulty piloting of the vessel than the construction of the bridge. This closing argument took him through the afternoon and continued the next morning, with the jury held in rapt attention for its entirety.[62]

Knowing that the jurors would be unlikely to follow every detail of his technical argument, Lincoln summed up the case succinctly: "The plaintiffs have to establish that the bridge is a material obstruction and that they have managed their boat with reasonable care and skill.... They must show due skill and care." Further, "it is unreasonable for [the pilot] to dash on heedless of this structure that has been legally put there."

As with so many other complicated cases, the jury failed to reach a unanimous verdict. But Lincoln's deft cross-examination and persuasive closing argument convinced nine of the twelve men on the panel that the bridge was not an obstruction and that the steamship operator was at fault. Officially, the trial ended in the hung jury, but in practice it guaranteed that railroad companies could build bridges across the Mississippi and other rivers without fear of being sued as obstructions. Lincoln had set a critical precedent. Railroads were being built at a rapid pace, and this was the first railroad bridge built across the Mississippi River. It represented the ability to quickly ship commercial wares east to west rather than transport goods down the Mississippi River, across the Caribbean, transported by land travel across the Central American isthmus, reloaded on ships in the Pacific Ocean, and transported up the coast to California. A direct land route by railroad was a major threat to the steamship business, but it was also a means to open up the West, modernize transportation, and stimulate the continental economy. The bridge was rebuilt and operational within a few weeks after the incident even though litigation continued. The U.S. Supreme Court in its December 1862 term finally settled the matter when it found in favor of the railroad, although by that time the point was moot as the new railroad economy had quickly grown, with Lincoln heavily involved in the push to transform the modern transportation economy. Lincoln had seen New Salem fade away as the Sangamon River showed its lack of navigability. Railroads were the wave of the future.[63]

CHAPTER 9

Working For, and Against, the Railroads

IN HIS ROCK ISLAND BRIDGE SUMMATION, LINCOLN EMPATHIZED WITH the steamship companies, recalling his own days on the Ohio, Mississippi, and Sangamon Rivers. "The last thing that would be pleasing to him would be to have one of these great channels, extending almost from where it never freezes to where it never thaws, blocked up." But, he noted, as important as the river was to transportation, "there is travel from East to West, whose demands are not less important than that of the river." Illinois was growing with "a rapidity never before seen in the history of the world," and that growth was moving westward. Only the railroad could sustain the transport and commerce to Iowa, the Northwest, and beyond.[1]

Railroading had grown on Lincoln. In his first campaign announcement, he said the cost of railroads was prohibitive. Later, when railroads enabled his fellow circuit-riding lawyers to return home to Springfield on weekends, Lincoln more often chose to remain on the road, exploring the latest advancements and political connections.[2] Years of promoting internal improvements and technological development of steam engines had decreased the overall costs of railroads and significantly broadened their reach.

Railroad development had come a long way since Lincoln's first foray into politics. The first locomotive in the United States was the *Best Friend of Charleston*, beginning in its namesake South Carolina city. Passengers noted that it was as fast as a rocket. Briefly the longest railroad in the world, it quickly fell behind as Southern sensibilities inhibited cross-boundary connections, and there was always the fear that the enslaved would use the railroad for a quick escape.[3] No such concerns impeded the North. The Baltimore & Ohio Railroad, born on the Fourth of July in 1828, swiftly became the first important railroad line in the United States. A year later, Peter Cooper built a small steam engine he called *Tom Thumb*, named after the diminutive English folklore character who was "no bigger than his father's thumb." The anthracite-coal-fueled engine barely pulled a railway car but was sufficient to convince the Baltimore & Ohio to develop more suitable steam engines, an advancement over the horse-pulled railcars that preceded it.[4] The first railroad in Illinois was the Northern Cross Railroad, running from Meredosia along the Illinois River through Springfield about sixty miles away, eventually extending east to the Indiana border and west to the Mississippi River. Lincoln saw such development as "a link in a great chain of railroad communication which shall unite Boston and New York with the Mississippi."[5]

Expansion of railroad service proceeded at meteoric pace in Illinois. During the 1850s, spurred on by the internal improvement program Lincoln championed, the state's rail network grew from a mere 111 miles to nearly 2,800 miles. Statutes like the Illinois Central Railroad Tax Act helped expand total railroad mileage in the United States from nine thousand miles to over thirty thousand miles in only a decade. Chicago became a major rail hub, with fifteen different rail systems converging to connect the eastern market to the Gulf via the Erie Canal, Great Lakes, Illinois and Michigan Canal, and Mississippi River. Travel time between Chicago and Springfield was reduced from three days to half a day, which led to enormous population growth in both cities. Most notable was creation of the Illinois Central Railroad, which when completed in 1856 was the world's longest railroad at over seven hundred miles.[6] The railroad even led to the first town named after Lincoln. Lincoln, Illinois, was created as a water stop and passenger depot for the Illinois Central's line between Bloomington and Springfield. Abraham Lincoln had laid out the town and filed the paperwork, inspiring the town fathers to name it after him, although perhaps it was also a public relations stunt to get in the railroad's good graces. A consummate teetotaler, Lincoln christened the new town using the juice of a watermelon.[7]

About two-thirds of railroad growth was in the North, facilitated by, and helping to advance, its rapidly developing industrial capability. While fewer miles of track were laid in the South, the railways that did run in the South provided additional technological impetus for the expansion of slavery. Built primarily using slave labor, railroads in the South created the transportation network needed to interlace cotton-growing plantations with hubs expediting shipment north. These networks linked raw cotton with the textile mills of New England and the financiers of New York, thus ensuring virtually all states had some stake in the cotton industry. Southern plantations supplied more than 75 percent of the cotton used in northern mills, while cotton became the nation's biggest export, feeding British and other industrial nations' textile manufacturing. Technology linked much of the North and much of Europe to slavery.[8]

One railway problem plagued both North and South. All trains required two parallel rails separated by a gauge—the distance between the two rails. Many of the early internal improvement projects Lincoln supported went to a myriad of newly incorporated railroad companies that built short lengths of track at different gauges. Most lines were less than ninety miles long. This ownership patchwork resulted in track gauges ranging from three feet to as much as five feet, plus even narrower gauges for various mining operations. Much later, a width of four feet, eight and a half inches would become the "standard gauge," with the North much quicker in moving to the standard. By 1861, about 53 percent of northern railways used the standard gauge, with standardization proceeding quickly once the military started driving railroad expansion. Southern states refused to coordinate on track gauge, which resulted in a wide range of gauges that became one of several limitations to Southern supply movements during the Civil War.[9] Lincoln later insisted that the transcontinental railroad be all of one gauge. He understood the necessity of an interconnected, more advanced technological world for the future.

Railroads followed the patterns established with inventions and patents. Interstate squabbles and the aristocratic social structure hampered Southern innovation. Nearly 95 percent of all successful applications for patents in the twenty years preceding the Civil War were received in Northern states, many tied to the proximity of railroad developments.[10] Telegraph lines were strung up alongside railroad tracks, which led a pre-teen Thomas Edison to become a railroad "butch," then by his teen years an experimental chemist and telegraph operator. He began his inventing career improving telegraph designs, all by the time of the Civil War.[11] As with the tracks themselves, fewer telegraph lines could be found in the South as the slavery-dominant economy required tighter control of communication.[12]

Another railroad-inspired technological advance was standard time. Most middle-class families had at least one cheap clock in their house by the 1830s,[13] and according to William Herndon, Lincoln was fascinated by them (along with omnibuses, language, paddle wheels, and idioms). These things "never escaped his observation and analysis."[14] With his frequent railroad travel, Lincoln became aware that time was what the local community said the time was, with no synchronization and virtually no coordination. "Counties, provinces, even neighboring villages used different means of telling time," with some communities using midnight as the base hour, some using noon . . . or sunrise . . . or sunset. As late as the 1860s, there were about seventy different time zones in the United States. Travelers had to reset their watches as they passed from one zone to another, something that became increasingly necessary as the spreading railroad network encouraged more routine travel to distant locations.[15] This lack of standardized time thwarted any attempt of the railroad companies to coordinate efficient transport schedules. Time standards could change from one station to the next, and even between the station and the local town it served. It was the railroads, and later weather forecasting agencies, that pushed for an agreed upon set of standard times and time zones. The demands of technology and industrialization drove the standardization of time.[16] Lincoln followed along closely.

WORKING FOR THE RAILROADS

The spiderwebbed westward sprawl of railroad networks created a number of logistical and legal issues that bolstered the Lincoln and Herndon law practice. Railroad cases made up only 4 percent of Lincoln's caseload overall, about 160 cases, but they were some of the most lucrative of his career. He tried cases for or against fourteen separate railroad companies, with some railroad names changing as lines merged or were replaced. The original Northern Cross Railroad, for example, later became the

Sangamon and Morgan, and still later the Great Western Railroad, from whose station Lincoln gave his farewell address to Springfield when he left to attend his first presidential inauguration. By far his most frequent, and lucrative, client was the Illinois Central Railroad, which was the only one to put him on retainer for a significant period of time.[17] It was Lincoln's rival Stephen A. Douglas who had greased the wheels of Congress to authorize construction of the Illinois Central from Chicago, conveniently going through land Douglas had surreptitiously acquired in shady land dealings.[18]

Lincoln's first important railroad case was highly influential and routinely cited in legal arguments for many decades. The Alton & Sangamon Railroad retained Lincoln to sue James A. Barret, a subscriber who refused to pay the balance of his account. Railroad company charters required them to issue stock to finance the project. In this case, each share cost one hundred dollars, for which subscribers paid 5 percent down with the balance in installments called for periodically by the railroad's board of directors. Barret had purchased thirty shares but refused to pay the balance, claiming that the legislature changed the railroad's route, thus no longer passing land Barret owned, whose market value he had hoped would increase. Barret contended that the changed route voided the subscription agreement. Lincoln countered that the change was necessary because of unforeseen construction limitations along the originally proposed route. After Barret lost in the lower court, he appealed to the Illinois Supreme Court, who again concurred with Lincoln's position, concluding that "a few obstinate stockholders should not be permitted to deprive the public and the company of the advantages that will result from a superior and less expensive route."[19] The Barret case pitted public policy against the rights of individuals. The case found that stockholders were not released from their subscription obligations even when charter amendments altered the original purpose of the company, setting an important precedent for railroad law adhered to throughout the rest of the nineteenth century. Public and corporate interests would often prevail over individual convenience and profit. Lincoln later argued that "legislation and adjudication must follow, and conform to, the progress of society."[20]

Lincoln demonstrated that he was not afraid to challenge those who had hired him. In February he had informed one of the railroad's stock commissioners that various documents including the subscription book were necessary to win the case. When that same commissioner complained to Lincoln six months later that he had not been informed of such a need, Lincoln replied that "you & I, by our correspondence, had it distinctly settled that I should need this book . . . and you had distinctly promised me you would send them up." Lincoln forcibly added, "Now, send them at once."[21] The case also established Lincoln as a logic-based attorney adept at reducing complex legal issues to their most fundamental parts. He was equally skillful understanding contract law, a growing area of business as subscription-based railroads expanded across the nation.

Overall, Lincoln and his partners were hired by the Alton & Sangamon Railroad twelve times in his career.[22] Further precedents were set when Lincoln defended the Alton & Sangamon in several lawsuits related to the taking of land for a railroad's right-of-way through privately owned property. In one case, the railroad obtained the right to lay tracks across two plots owned by George Baugh, and the two parties subsequently argued over fencing to keep cattle off the tracks. The Illinois Supreme Court found that no law compelled one person or corporation to fence the land of another, nor could Baugh obstruct the passing of the railroad. In another case, the same court found that the legislative statutes never contemplated paying damages to a landowner "for the privilege of having a railroad constructed through his lands when the value added to the land by the construction was equal to the injury." While the landowner lost the use of the land the government seized by eminent domain and then handed over to the railroad, the law concluded that adjoining land would increase in value enough to compensate for that loss. This decision presumes the intangible value gained equally offset the much more tangible value lost. Worse, adjoining lands owned by others whose land had not been seized would also gain value at the expense of land lost to someone else. This concept was controversial, and many landowners felt cheated by the process, a displeasure leading to increasing dissatisfaction with the new supremacy of corporate rights over individuals.[23]

As Lincoln's reputation grew, so did the scope of his railroad cases. Railroads were America's first big businesses, which raised legal questions not previously imagined. Lincoln helped set those precedents, often while working for one of the biggest of those big businesses, the Illinois Central Railroad. In October 1851, the Illinois Central put Lincoln on a standard legal retainer in exchange for being available to assist company lawyers on railroad-related legal matters. As part of the agreement, Lincoln was barred from representing individuals or companies suing the railroad. He continued to work for the Illinois Central throughout the 1850s, representing them in forty-seven cases, including at least a dozen before the Illinois Supreme Court.[24]

One person who was a constant thorn in the railroad's legal business was a landowner named Wilson Allen. Allen sued the Illinois Central seven times on various issues and was a witness on three law suits filed by others. Usually, his complaints related to property infringement or damage, such as the time he argued the railroad had excavated fifty thousand cubic feet of soil from his property and left "unfilled mines and pits." He sued for five thousand dollars in damages and won, but the jury awarded only $762.50. In another case, Allen sued for two thousand dollars, claiming the railroad obstructed a creek's flow during construction, leaving a large pond that caused illness in his family. Again, the jury found in his favor but awarded him only $286 in damages. In another case involving holes, the jury gave Allen only fifteen dollars. Allen also sued several times regarding commitments to build fences and cattle guards. Beginning in 1855, the state imposed a duty on railroads to "erect and thereafter maintain fences" to "prevent cattle, horses, sheep and hogs from getting on to such railroad." Allen and others still often sued, complaining of inadequate fencing.[25]

One issue Lincoln worked on in several cases was that of railroad liability for goods damaged in transport. Before railroads, cargo transport was limited to what could fit in saddlebags on a horse or on a flatboat or, later, on a stagecoach or steamboat. These were treated as public carriers and were strictly liable for loss or damage to goods transported no matter what the reason. Any losses were generally minimal. Railroads opened up the option for substantial cargo transport on a more frequent schedule, and thus were more likely to incur substantial losses over time. Railroads sought to limit their liability. Since much of their transport were livestock, several of Lincoln's cases attempted to insulate the Illinois Central from losses of hogs, cattle, and other animals. Livestock posed unique problems not seen in dry or liquid goods transport. They required adequate feed, space, and temperature conditions that were hard to maintain in a railway car open enough to allow sufficient fresh air.

In one case, Morrison and Crabtree contracted with the Illinois Central to ship four hundred cattle from Urbana to Chicago, but at a reduced rate that released the railroad from liability except for gross negligence. Delays and equipment malfunction led to the death of one steer and weight loss to several other cattle. Illinois Central lost in a jury trial, then hired Lincoln to argue the appeal in the Illinois Supreme Court. Unlike an earlier case in which they rejected Lincoln's arguments about the death of five hundred hogs in transit, here the justices agreed with Lincoln, that the railroad had a right to modify contracts to reduce their liability for especially difficult cargo such as live animals. The company was not completely off without responsibility as it could still be liable if there had been gross negligence, but the contract specifically provided the reduced fare benefit in return for limits on strict liability. This and similar cases again set important precedents for the fast-growing railroad industry, as it has for other large corporate liability issues ever since.[26]

Other cases Lincoln worked on for the Illinois Central focused on establishing how railroads were taxed. As with today, many counties and states exempted railroads from taxation as a way to promote development, based on the belief that future economic growth would more than offset the initial tax losses. The Illinois Central railroad charter had given it tax exemption for a period of six years, the time expected for its construction. After that time, the railroad would pay 5 percent of its gross receipts along with a property tax, all of which went to the state, which promised no other state and local tax assessments. This was actually a greater burden on the railroad than other railroad lines in the nation, but then McLean County issued its own tax requirement since it gained nothing from what was being paid to the state. McLean County won the lower court decision, but Lincoln's arguments convinced the state Supreme Court to rule for the railroad, concluding that the state legislature was within its authority to exempt property from taxation. The case protected the Illinois Central from being taxed by every county in Illinois where it owned property, thus saving it untold amounts of money.[27]

Or maybe not. The original agreement with the state stipulated that if the 5 percent tax on receipts plus property tax did not amount to "seven percent of the gross receipts," then the rate would be 7 percent, in essence ensuring that the actual tax rate was higher. Except that the railroad considered 7 percent the cap on taxes while the state auditor believed the upper limit was open-ended if the amount of property tax was high. After being hired by the railroad, Lincoln sent a letter to the state auditor, Jesse Dubois, a longtime friend, asking him to accept ninety thousand dollars in settlement of the suit because "they can pay no more." He went on to tell Dubois that he wrote not "as a lawyer seeking an advantage for a client; but only as a friend, only urging you to do, what I think I would do if I were in your situation."[28]

Lincoln's track record for the railroad was mixed. Most cases were settled out of court. Of the fourteen that went to jury, Lincoln won only two. More important was that he reduced the cost to the railroad substantially despite the railroad's growing unpopularity.[29] Based on their personal experience, the Illinois Central respected Lincoln's skills as a lawyer, but they also realized he was "the most prominent of his political party," with connections that made him invaluable, as his correspondence with Jesse Dubois demonstrated.[30]

WORKING AGAINST THE RAILROADS

Each of these cases helped build the legal framework that governed how railroads were legally managed for decades to come. But Lincoln was not always working for the railroads. He brought cases against the railroads almost as much as he worked for them. Sixty-two of the 133 cases (47%) he and his partners were involved in were brought against railroads; seventy-one were working for railroads (53%).[31] While he worked on behalf of the Illinois Central 90 percent of the time, he did oppose them on occasion. With the exception of the Illinois Central and the

Alton & Sangamon Railroads, which were about 88 percent of his railroad cases, Lincoln and Herndon opposed railroads more often than they represented them.[32]

Most notably, he was forced to sue the Illinois Central for his fee after successfully representing them in the above McLean County tax case. Lincoln had served the railroad well over many years, often taking limited fees; for example, he had drawn only $150 for a year's worth of work encompassing "at least fifteen cases (I believe one or two more) and I have concluded to lump them off at ten dollars a case."[33] This time he wanted to get paid the value of the work.

After jockeying around to ensure Lincoln was free to represent them, the railroad had paid him a retainer to get him started.[34] The case was complicated, involved several trials, including the Illinois Supreme Court. Lincoln won the case and submitted his bill for five thousand dollars, an amount more than the annual salary of the Illinois governor. After a week, he wrote to the railroad's counsel requesting status, who indicated it had been sent to the company president and attorney, who refused to pay it. Lincoln sued. Knowing he needed to justify such a large amount, Lincoln included an affidavit providing for the depositions of other prominent lawyers, all of them his friends—Norman Judd, Isaac Arnold, Grant Goodrich, Archibald Williams, and his former law partner, Stephen T. Logan—each of whom vouched for the appropriateness of the fee.[35] When the case came up for trial, no representative for the railroad was present, and the judge awarded Lincoln the five thousand dollars. John Douglass, the Illinois Central Railroad's attorney, did show up the next day and begged for a new trial, which Lincoln did not resist. Setting aside the earlier verdict, they retried the case and the jury again decided for Lincoln. This time they awarded him $4,800 because Lincoln had received $200 as a retainer (in fact, the records show he had received $250). As with all fees received by the firm, Lincoln shared this fee equally with William Herndon.[36]

Lincoln was one of the first attorneys to actively protect the well-being of railroad workers. In 1854, he sued the Great Western Railroad on behalf of brakeman Jasper Harris. An engineer named George Armstrong began moving the train while Harris was boarding a tanker car.

Harris was "thrown down, and his right foot, ankle, leg and thigh [was] greatly torn, crushed, and broken." The damage was severe enough that they amputated his right leg above the knee. The suit sought ten thousand dollars in damages, citing the negligence of the engineer for moving the train without authorization and signal from the conductor. The case apparently settled out of court as Harris later dismissed it.[37] The case was important because Lincoln argued that employers were liable for providing safe work environments and were responsible for injuries caused by negligence. The precedent was short-lived as, soon after the case ended, legislators passed a "fellow-servant rule," preventing employees from suing their employers. Given the danger of early railroad work, injuries were common. While Lincoln argued the concept in 1854, only in 1908 was the Federal Employers' Liability Act (FELA) passed to provide injury protection for railroad workers.[38]

Many of Lincoln's cases against the railroads mirrored his cases for them, representing subscribers who felt disenfranchised by the actions of the railroads. Ironically, his earlier success in the Barret case came back to haunt him when he sued the Illinois River Railroad on behalf of Charles Sprague.[39] Sprague had committed Cass County to pay fifty thousand dollars in stock subscriptions to the Illinois River Railroad. Changes in the original route led Sprague, who was also president of the Rock Island & Alton Railroad, to believe the charter alteration was a breach of contract and hired Lincoln to prove his case. When Illinois Supreme Court Chief Justice Caton found for the railroad, he invoked the doctrine of public necessity and cited the precedent Lincoln had set in *Barret v. Alton & Sangamon Railroad* six years earlier. Judges for a similar case also cited the Barret precedent against another of Lincoln's clients.[40]

Lincoln was also not successful on another case he took to the Illinois Supreme Court against the railroads. A landowner hired Lincoln to oppose attempts by the Chicago, Burlington & Quincy Railroad to take land to build depots and workshops. After the court ruled against him, Lincoln wrote the client, Charles Hoyt, pleading that "I do not think I could ever have argued the case better than I did." He added, "Very sorry for the result, but I do not think it could have been prevented."[41]

Overall, Lincoln was a successful attorney in his work for the railroads. Many of his cases were settled out of court, and in almost all cases where the railroads lost, the penalties paid were substantially lower than that requested. His work for the Illinois Central Railroad was especially challenging. As the railroad expanded, it received increasing hostility from citizens who had their land and livestock taken, damaged, or otherwise inhibited from normal operations. Lincoln learned to mediate disputes and negotiate settlements to keep the railroad in operation while trying to protect the rights of landowners and workers.[42] His work was so well respected that a story circulated saying that after giving his Cooper Union speech in New York City in February 1860, Erastus Corning, president of the New York Central Railroad, offered Lincoln a salary of ten thousand dollars a year to become the railroad's general counsel. Corning had approached his cousin and a friend of Lincoln, James B. Merwin, who introduced the two in the lobby of the Astor House hotel in New York. Shocking both Merwin and Lincoln, Corning presented the offer abruptly, then told Lincoln not to make a decision until he received a letter from him. No letter had been found, but historian John Starr reached out to the railroad in the early twentieth century to determine its veracity and was told that it would have been common for informal discussions to be had before a formal offer was made. Lincoln immediately made clear that he would not accept the offer, having already begun planning for the soon-to-be-decided Republican nomination for president. The fact that Lincoln was often called into cases by eastern elites whenever there was a western angle demonstrates that respect for his legal work extended beyond Illinois.[43]

Even without the impressive salary proposed by Corning, Lincoln received some of his most lucrative fees for railroad work, allowing him to become financially comfortable, although not wealthy. More significantly, Lincoln helped set important precedents for the growing railroad industry that would facilitate its expansion, the growth of technology and industrialization, and westward movement of the enlarging American population, especially in the North.

The railroads played a sizeable role in Lincoln's political career as well. During his 1858 campaign for Senate, Lincoln and Stephen A. Douglas relied on the railroads to move around the state for their famous debates. Douglas traveled 5,227 miles in one hundred days, with Lincoln covering a similar distance via a variety of conveyances, including 350 miles by boat, 600 by carriage, and 3,400 by the railroads.[44] Douglas's travel was aided by his good friend and benefactor, George B. McClellan, then vice president of the Illinois Central Railroad, who provided a luxurious private railcar for Douglas's use.[45] McClellan, who had earlier served in the military and considered himself a protégé of then secretary of war Jefferson Davis, was picked to assess a Southern railroad route to the Pacific.

Samuel Clemens, known to the world by his pseudonym Mark Twain, was a player by association in the transcontinental railroad saga. Clemens was born in Hannibal, Missouri, shortly after Halley's Comet had made its regular but rare pass by the Earth.[46] At that time in 1835, the twenty-six-year-old amateur astronomy buff Lincoln, who two years earlier had marveled at the Leonid meteor showers, may very well have been gazing at the skies when Mark Twain came into this world. Lincoln was living in New Salem, Illinois, just a stone's throw across the Mississippi River from Hannibal. Later, in 1859, Lincoln rode the Hannibal & St. Joseph Railroad to give a speech in Council Bluffs, Iowa.[47] The railroad just happened to be chartered in the office of Mark Twain's father thirteen years before. While in Iowa, Lincoln met with Grenville Dodge, a railroad engineer and surveyor. During the Civil War, Dodge worked as Ulysses S. Grant's chief of intelligence before being tasked by Lincoln to determine the best location for an eastern terminus of the transcontinental railroad. Lincoln accepted Dodge's advice and decided the railroad would be built along a northern route. Lincoln then picked its starting point—Council Bluffs, Iowa.[48]

On February 11, 1861, Abraham Lincoln gave his farewell-to-Springfield speech at the Great Western Railroad Depot. Over the next twelve days he would travel over 1,900 miles, along eighteen different railway lines, and through eight states to Washington for his first inauguration. He was not finished with the railroads, which would become critical to the war effort during his presidency and carry him one more time over the rails back home. But that was still in the future. Before then he would continue to explore the scientific and technological advances in society. He would go out on the lecture tour.

CHAPTER 10

The Science Lectures

IN HIS YOUTH, ABRAHAM LINCOLN CLIMBED ONTO A TREE STUMP MANY times to mimic the fiery oratory of traveling preachers, the most common public speakers in frontier Kentucky and Illinois. He learned storytelling from his father and often held the attention of his playmates with his humorous stories and anecdotes. After reaching adulthood, Lincoln eagerly embraced and delivered numerous speeches, giving over one hundred alone during his 1858 Senate campaign against longtime rival Stephen A. Douglas. As the leading Whig in Illinois, he was called on to give eulogies for grand political figures like Henry Clay and President Zachary Taylor.[1] All of these were inherently political.

A growing lecture circuit movement opened up the potential for significant honorariums to those who could fill the void with intellectual and entertaining lectures on a variety of topics. In some cases, lectures were given as charity, with some of the proceeds going to building libraries, churches, or other community pursuits, but even here the lecturer could make a good sum to supplement other activities. While constantly busy balancing his legal obligations and his political ambitions, Lincoln considered putting together a series of lectures to help earn extra money.

The lyceum system and the lecture circuit in general were "in full flower" immediately after the Civil War, according to one of its biggest stars—Mark Twain. The average lecturer could make $100 a night (minus 10 percent to their agent), with the most famous names making $250 in smaller towns and $400 in big cities. Other than Twain, lecturers on the circuit included the Reverend Henry Ward Beecher, abolitionist and women's rights advocate Anna Dickinson, newspaperman Horace

Greeley, abolitionist Wendell Phillips, political commentator David Ross Locke (playing one of Lincoln's favorite characters, Petroleum V. Nasby), Arctic explorer Isaac Israel Hayes, and eminent scientist Louis Agassiz.[2] Agassiz was an outlier among the famous scientists of the time. Others, including James Hall, James Dana, Charles Wilkes, John Torrey, and Asa Gray, preferred writing for other scientists only, believing the general public incapable of understanding at the level they wished to teach.[3] Global travelers and naturalists often filled lecture seats. Lincoln's colleague and friend Orville H. Browning recalled in his diary that he saw Herman Melville lecture on his travels in the South Sea islands, which he found "erratic but interesting." Melville had written several short stories and novels reflecting his experiences, most notably *Moby Dick*. He would later visit Lincoln in the White House to ask for employment.[4]

Lincoln gave his first lecture in early 1838 before the members of the Young Men's Lyceum in Springfield. "The Perpetuation of Our Political Institutions" was more about the dangers to established government than partisan political positions. Lincoln warned against the outrages of mob law, like those that two months before had resulted in the murder of abolitionist editor Elijah Lovejoy. "At what point then is the approach of danger to be expected?" Lincoln asked, then "I answer, if it ever reach us, it must spring up amongst us. . . . If destruction be our lot, we must ourselves be its author and finisher. As a nation of freemen, we must live through all time, or die by suicide." Emphasizing the importance of rational political institutions to the concept of self-governance, he previewed the fight over slavery that would dominate his later years.[5]

Four years later, he gave an address to Springfield's Washington Temperance Society on what would have been its namesake president's 110th birthday.[6] Temperance societies had arisen to combat one of the frontier's biggest problems—excessive drinking. With little else to do besides work and no entertainment other than the occasional traveling revival shows, alcoholism was commonplace. Whiskey became the libation of choice, and taken in excess led to spousal abuse, family neglect, and chronic unemployment. Focused originally on allowing temperate, that is, moderate, drinking, the later temperance movement often took on the aura of religious fervor, where drinking was a sin reflecting severe moral failing and constituted a train ride to destruction. Full prohibition from drinking became the goal, with zealous moral outrage often used to castigate alcohol abusers.[7]

Lincoln rarely judged anyone on their moral differences. Instead, he tried to understand the position of others before offering his views. This had served him well in his legal career, where convincing a jury of the merits of the case was less about right or wrong and more about helping each juror relate to the circumstances of the client. Likewise, Lincoln despised slavery as an institution but did not consider Southerners to be of lesser moral stock; rather, they were trapped by their circumstances. "I have no prejudice against the Southern people," Lincoln said in Ottawa, Illinois. "They are just as we would be in their situation. If slavery did not now exist amongst them, they would not introduce it. If it did now exist among us, we should not instantly give it up."[8] Avoiding demonization, Lincoln did not moralize against those he deemed to be suffering from alcoholism even though he was not a drinker himself. He carefully counseled temperance leaders to offer compassion and support to those inflicted rather than reprimand and reproach. He had to walk a logical tightrope since temperance followers were commonly slavery abolitionists, whose political support he needed to advance his career.[9]

Two other topics for lectures apparently never made it past the initial concept. Around 1848 Lincoln wrote a set of notes for a lecture on Niagara Falls and the scientific and philosophical ramifications of such a wondrous spectacle.[10] He wrote another fragment expecting to turn it into a law lecture. Both of these preliminary written thoughts offered up memorable Lincoln quotes despite never having been delivered in actual lectures. To young men choosing the law for a profession, for example, he advised, "Resolve to be honest at all events; and if in your own judgment you cannot be an honest lawyer, resolve to be honest without being a lawyer."[11]

Lincoln always kept an eye on technological advancement and spent much of his political career advocating for internal improvements that would expand economic opportunities for all Americans. He believed that education was the most important subject people could be engaged in. Following his own advice, he continued his self-study of new topics his entire life. With this in mind, a scientific theme for a public lecture seemed logical.

Lecture on Discoveries and Inventions

Where the specific idea for a lecture on discoveries and inventions came from is a bit murky. Henry C. Whitney claimed that he and Lincoln were riding the legal circuit in the fall of 1855, with Whitney reading from celebrated lecturer George Bancroft's treatise on the promise and progress of the human race. Lincoln informed him that he "had for some time been contemplating the writing of a lecture on *man*" and that he "proposed to review man from his earliest primeval state to his present high development."[12] The widow of Lincoln's colleague Norman Judd told a story in which Lincoln was visiting her and her husband in 1856 on the shores of Lake Michigan. After contemplating the constellation Orion and the red giant star Arcturus "as they wheeled, seeming around the earth," Lincoln went on to speak of "other discoveries, and also of the inventions which had been made during the long cycles of time between the present and those early days when the sons of Adam began to make use of the material things about them, and invent instruments of various kinds in brass and gold and silver." Mrs. Judd claimed that Lincoln gave a "succinct account of all the inventions referred to in the Garden of Eden until the Bible record ended, 600. B.C."[13]

Another possible influence was poet Walt Whitman, whom Lincoln never met but often nodded to in greeting during his daily summer commute between the White House and the Old Soldiers Home. Whitman had written the line, "The latest news, discoveries, and inventions . . ." in an early edition of his epic poetry collection *Leaves of Grass*, which Herndon said Lincoln had eagerly read. In another poem published in 1856, Whitman referred repeatedly to the types of discoveries and inventions Lincoln celebrated in his lecture.[14]

Analyzing the "Lecture on Discoveries and Inventions" is complicated by the fact that only partial transcripts appear to remain. John Nicolay in a *Century Magazine* article on "Lincoln's Literary Experiments," and later in Nicolay and Hay's *Abraham Lincoln: A History*, discusses only the second half of the lecture.[15] Basler's multivolume *Collected Works* has both parts but lists them in different volumes as if they were two separate lectures. The confusion arose because the two handwritten parts of the lecture were left with the only surviving daughter of Mary Lincoln's uncle, who passed them to Dr. Samuel Melvin after Lincoln's assassination. Believing they were separate lectures, Melvin kept one part and sold the other part to Charles Gunther, who later sold it to renowned Lincoln collector Oliver Barrett. In the 1990s, historian Wayne Temple demonstrated that the two parts were indeed from the same lecture.[16] A prominent newspaper in Bloomington, Illinois, the site of his first presentation of the lecture, carried a significant account referencing both parts of the lecture, as well as two subjects—laughter and music—that are not in either existing part.[17] The lecture most likely included another written piece in the middle, now lost. The two pieces have some overlap and seeming repetition, for example, mentioning Adam's fig leaf and steam power in both, which suggests both parts are early drafts that Lincoln revised and consolidated into a final lecture.

More recently, Robert Lincoln historian Jason Emerson discovered letters between Robert and John Nicolay revealing that the two pieces, perhaps additional missing segments, and maybe some revisions were contained in "a [manuscript] book, thin, in black cover, evidently got for the purpose of copying the Lecture into it, as was done by my father in his own hand."[18] Robert concluded the book was "evidently the one used in delivery." Unfortunately, Robert lost the book and it has never been found.

Whatever the final construct, Lincoln gave the lecture on six different occasions in central Illinois between April 1858 and April 1860. The first was in Bloomington on April 6, 1858. Ten months later, he repeated the lecture in Jacksonville and again in Springfield on February 21, 1859. After giving it in Decatur in January 1860, his planned repeat in Bloomington in April was canceled due to poor turnout. He did present the lecture late in January in Pontiac to "a very large audience." His return engagement in Springfield two months after rising to national prominence with his Cooper Union speech was given before a "large and intelligent audience."[19] Many more requests for Lincoln to present the lecture were made by prominent community leaders across the state, but Lincoln declined. With all his earlier lectures, he had limited himself to places and times that coincided with legal and political business so as not to inconvenience himself. His nomination as the Republican candidate for president in May eliminated any spare time available for the scientific lecture circuit.

Many contemporaries were not impressed with the lecture. Herndon thought the lecture was "commonplace" and was "met with disapproval from his friends." Herndon went so far as to claim that Lincoln "himself was filled with disgust."[20] Robert Lincoln and John Nicolay both dismissed it as nothing more than a literary experiment, a "mere recreation to satisfy the craving for a change from the monotony of law and politics." They considered leaving the lecture out of the Nicolay and Hay's compendium of letters and documents. What they did include was the second half only.[21]

But these views miss the important blending of science, technology, and economic improvement that were the focal point for the Whig political philosophy, and for Lincoln personally. It was common for lecturers to embed political themes in academic topics, and Lincoln was no stranger to this idea.[22] The lecture reflected Lincoln's curiosity about science and its applications.[23] Taken in broad strokes, the discoveries and inventions lecture promoted Lincoln's belief that society was best served by encouraging advancement and bettering one's condition. Mindful of the literacy levels of the masses in the still-growing Illinois, Lincoln wove this thread in the first section through a biblical framework that most people would find familiar. In the second section he turned to "Young America," a political concept that, again, most people at the time would have been familiar with.

"All creation is a mine, and every man, a miner."[24] Lincoln had developed a belief that mining was one key to economic development. On the last day of his life, he told Speaker of the House Schuyler Colfax that he had "very large ideas of the mineral wealth of our nation. I believe it practically inexhaustible."[25] In beginning with a reference to mining, Lincoln was priming the audience to understand the extractive nature of resources, and like digging energy and economy out of the land, man "was to dig out his destiny." He considered learning a way of mining existing knowledge for new uses.

Channeling its first clause, Lincoln dove straight into biblical references comfortable to the audience. "In the beginning, the mine was unopened, and the miner stood naked, and knowledgeless, upon it." Lincoln was quick to add, "fishes, birds, beasts, and creeping things" are mere "feeders and lodgers," continuing their struggle for survival instinctively, in the same way they have done for ages. In contrast, he separated out what makes humans different: "Man is not the only animal who labors, but he is the only one who *improves* his workmanship." This improvement, Lincoln revealed, was accomplished "by Discoveries and Inventions." Man can better his condition, both personally and by improving society around him. Innovation happens when man applies his intellect to solving problems, and those solutions lead to other innovations.[26]

At first these solutions were simple. After the fall from grace, Adam and Eve discover their nakedness, and their first invention was "the fig-leaf-apron." This became the origin of clothing, "the one thing for which nearly half of the toil and care of the human race has ever since been expended."

Making more references to Genesis in the Bible, Lincoln remarked on how the fig leaf was replaced by "coats of skins" that "clothed them," not dissimilar to what Lincoln wore in his earliest years growing up in Kentucky. But innovations continued to build on this early framework: "The most important improvement ever made in connection with clothing, was the invention of spinning and weaving." The ability to create clothing not just by skinning an animal but by producing thread from the fibers of animals and plants provided a leap in human clothing. Wool and "the hair from several species of animals" could be woven into pants and shirts and coats. Fibrous extracts from plants could be similarly spun and woven, including hemp, flax, silk, and especially cotton. While he did not mention it directly in the lecture, Lincoln understood the importance of cotton and another invention, the cotton gin, to the growth and spread of slavery.

From clothing, Lincoln jumped to "the discovery of the properties of *iron*, and the making of *iron tools*." "We can scarcely conceive the possibility of making much of anything else," Lincoln told his listeners, "without the use of iron tools." He even speculated, "how could the 'gopher wood' for the Ark, have been gotten out without an axe?" Referring to Genesis again, Lincoln noted the many instances of iron mentioned in the Bible, from tools to instruments, to bedsteads, to furnaces. His focus on iron as "among the earliest of important discoveries and inventions" foreshadowed the importance of iron cladding in the coming Civil War.

Lincoln next turned to transportation. As with clothing, he stressed the advantages of inventive, productive labor that improves the human condition.[27] Here the goal was to advance beyond human motive power to get from place to place. Inventive thought led to development of the wheel, then wagons on land and boats on water. These were powered by animals such as horses, mules, and oxen on land, or wind and paddles on the water.

Here Lincoln thought back to his own invention for a system to float boats over obstructions. He reminded his audience of "the philosophical principle upon which the use of the boat primarily depends—to wit, the *principle*, that anything will float, which cannot sink without displacing more than its own *weight* of water," although he admitted it was unlikely that principle of physics was known when the first boats were made. Rather, it was by observation of floating objects that the self-evident principle was discovered where objects heavier than water could remain on the surface of water.

Lincoln explored another topic on which he was eminently conversive—agriculture. Describing food as man's "first necessity," he explained that after the fall, "labor was imposed on the race, as a penalty—a curse." He lamented that while agriculture was perhaps the most important science, it had derived less direct advantage from discovery and invention than almost any other. The plow was one example of invention put to work in the field, but only after man had conceived of substituting other forces for man's muscular power. These forces, Lincoln indicated, were "the strength of animals, and the power of the wind, of running streams, and of steam." Lincoln would revisit agriculture as president, but his foresight in seeing the advantages of wind showed that he was ahead of scientists of the time. "Of all the forces of nature, I should think the *wind* contains the largest amount of *motive power*—that is, power to move things."

"Take any given space on the earth's surface," Lincoln said, and all the power exerted by men, beasts, running water, and steam "shall not equal the one hundredth part of what is exerted by the blowing of the wind over and upon the same space." Here was the man who opened with man's digging out his destiny in an extractive economy now turning to renewable energy innovations. He acknowledged that the intermittent nature of wind had so far limited controlling and directing it, which was why it was yet "an untamed, and unharnessed force," but argued that one of the greatest discoveries to be made was how to put the unsurpassed energy of the wind to work for man.[28]

Lincoln also spoke of running streams as a motive power, in particular its application to mills and other machinery by means of the waterwheel. Again, referring to its use in the Bible, Lincoln reflected on his own personal experience working the grist and saw mills in New Salem. He introduced the idea of steam power, which was a modern discovery but not yet fully put toward useful work.

In the second part of the lecture, Lincoln demonstrated a far-ranging knowledge of the world that went beyond expectations for someone who had seen so little of it.[29] In describing "Young America," Lincoln showed his understanding of the sourcing of various commodities, including "cotton fabrics from Manchester [England] and Lowell [Massachusetts]; furs from the Arctic regions ... [and] buffalo-robe from the Rocky Mountains." He knew sugar production was a mainstay of Louisiana, "coffee and fruits from the tropics; salt from Turk's Island [now Turks and Caicos]; fish from Newfoundland [Atlantic Canada]; tea from China, and spices from the Indies." He understood that the Pacific Ocean was the main source of whales and the whale oil that fueled lamps. He knew that diamonds were prevalent in Brazil, gold in California, and Spanish cigars could be gotten in Havana, Cuba. His long history of promoting internal improvements and working for the railroads led him to suggest that "the iron horse is panting and impatient" to carry Young America from place to place.

Young America had its heyday in the early 1850s when younger members of the Democratic party attempted to wrest control from the party's "old fogy wire-pullers" and hand the presidential nomination to

Douglas.[30] Young America, according to Lincoln with Douglas in mind, was "conceited, and arrogant." Suggesting cosmopolitan wealth, Lincoln defined Young America as owning a large part of the world "by possessing it; and all the rest by right of wanting it, and intending to have it." Young America's main invention was "Manifest Destiny," the belief that the nation should conquer the continent from coast to coast. The new disdains the old, which included the first man, Adam.

"The great difference between Young America and Old Fogy, is the result of *Discoveries, Inventions*, and *Improvements*. These, in turn, are the result of *observation, reflection* and *experiment*."

Lincoln chastised flaws in the nation's new character, including arrogance, desire for mastery and limitless acquisition, moral duplicity, and contempt for everything old.[31] Old Fogy was the one who took the time to reflect on what he observed. Lincoln circled around to give credit to Adam for being "the first to invent the art of invention," which led him to invent the fig-leaf apron. This reminded Lincoln that Eve, given that sewing had since become "woman's work," probably took the leading part as mother of all fig-leaf sewing societies, while, Lincoln perhaps added with an evocative wink, Adam did no more than to "stand by and thread the needle."

Over time, man developed the habit of observation and reflection akin to the scientific method established by Francis Bacon, which led to discoveries, inventions, and improvements.[32] Among the observations was the lifting of a pot lid as water heats up, which generated the invention of using steam to produce power for boats, locomotives, and machinery. This required no special genius, Lincoln told us, but rather contemplating what you see and how it might be applied to useful work. It was the old fogies who did this; Young America wants it, but had not done the work nor appreciated the work done by his predecessors.[33]

In his opening paragraph to this second section of the lecture, Lincoln alluded to the telegraph, the "lightning" that stands ready to be harnessed to meet Young America's every whim. This "inclination to exchange thoughts with one another" led to discoveries and inventions in communication. After again crediting Adam with articulating speech and naming the animals, Lincoln went on to show his understanding of basic human anatomy, with the capacity of the tongue to "count from one to one hundred" using "two hundred and eighty-three distinct sounds or syllables ... seven each second." The ability to talk enabled us to spread ideas, which promoted further reflection, discoveries, and inventions. Likely here was where Lincoln interjected the subjects of laughter and music reported by attendees and newspapers.[34]

"But speech alone, valuable as it ever has been, and is, has not advanced the condition of the world much." With his overarching theme of bettering the condition of man threaded throughout the lecture, Lincoln pointed out that as important as speech was, it was limited to those who can hear and understand the particular language being spoken. To effectively communicate to a wider audience, man invented writing. "Writing—the art of communicating thoughts to the mind, through the eye—is the great invention of the world."

The anatomy of the eye seems to have been of special interest to Lincoln. He mentioned the eye several times in this part of the lecture. Lincoln said that "it may be of some passing interest to notice the wonderful powers of the eye, in conveying ideas to the mind from writing." Putting to use his mathematical proficiency, he calculates the speed at which the eye can read the written numbers one to one hundred faster than the tongue can speak them, and "determine whether every word is spelled correctly."

Lincoln also discoursed on the eye as president according to David Homer Bates, manager of the U.S. Military Telegraph Corps during the war. On one of his daily visits to the telegraph office, Lincoln "began to talk of the functions of the eye and brain when one is reading aloud from a printed page." Lincoln notoriously liked to read out loud, a habit that annoyed his law partner Herndon immensely. He had come across a book in his youth, Lincoln told Bates, stating that as each letter and word and sentence appeared before the eye, "it was pictured upon the retina so that each particular word could be spoken aloud at the exact moment when its printed form in the volume was reflected upon the eye." Bates records that Lincoln "discoursed at some length upon this marvel, remarking upon the curious fact that the eye is capable of receiving simultaneously several distinct impressions or a series of impressions constantly changing as one continues to read across the page, and that these numerous and some-times radically different impressions are communicated from eye to brain and then back to the vocal organs by means of the most delicate nerves." These impressions were translated by the brain into thought and sent back to the organs of speech. Lincoln "likened this mysterious, instantaneous and two-fold operation to the telegraph."[35]

Further elaborating on writing, Lincoln noted one great benefit is that it allowed us to "converse with the dead, the absent, and the unborn, at all distances of time and of space; and great, not only in its direct benefits, but greatest help, to all other inventions." He explored the wonder of turning sounds into marks recognizable to others by sight, with those sounds being divided into parts that could be combined to create new sounds—the phonetic alphabet turned into words and sentences. "All history, all science, all government, all commerce, and nearly all social intercourse" are made possible by writing.

Given the illegibility of some handwriting, the invention of the printing press was both necessary and allowed ideas to be transmitted to a vastly larger number of people, something that hand copying of text could not achieve. The "art of artificial writing" started off slow with its reliance on wooden blocks, but the invention of movable metal type provided the ability to quickly and cheaply produce newspapers.[36] Lincoln had been an avid newspaper reader growing up, and printing presses that could spin out newspapers on a daily basis helped bring news of the world to the masses. Newspapers became the cutting-edge pioneers of the industrial revolution.[37]

Communicating ideas to both distant readers and those less privileged helped democratize America. Lincoln also turned it into a rallying call for the rights of enslaved men and women. "It is very probably—almost certain," Lincoln lectured, "that the great mass of men, at that time, were utterly unconscious, that their conditions, or their minds, were capable of improvement." The masses "not only looked upon the educated few as superior beings," they saw themselves incapable of rising to equality. While cleverly using language directed at white audiences, Lincoln subtly flowed from a lecture on discoveries and inventions to a social commentary on slavery.

The great task that printing came into the world to perform was "to emancipate the mind from this false and underestimate of itself," Lincoln argued. It was difficult to now "conceive how strong this slavery of the mind was; and how long it did, of necessity, take, to break its shackles, and to get a habit of freedom of thought, established." He argues that this "emancipation of thought" was what made America such an innovative nation, that freedom encouraged invention.[38]

Among the discoveries playing a role in development was what Lincoln called "the invention of negroes, or, of the present mode of using them." With this he was deploring how the invention of race-based slavery had "advanced" the production of goods. In the past, forced labor produced goods used by the household to which they belonged. Plantation slavery in the United States used enslaved labor "mainly to produce commodities for trade on a world market." Historian Miller suggests that plantation owners were happy to use technological advancements such as steam-powered machinery, telegraph communication, and railroad transportation, even as they were less available than in the North, to expand their slave-labor-based empires. They also "invented" new ways of organizing work (gang systems) and management (overseers). Even the few industrial factories in the South used enslaved labor to produce commodities.[39] Lincoln was warning that technology cannot always be assumed to be good for all.

"Next came the patent laws." Lincoln brought his scientific lecture to a close by speaking on how critical the invention of patent law was to innovation. Prior to the patent system, begun in England in 1624 and later adopted in the United States, "any man might instantly use what another had invented; so that the inventor had no special advantage from his own invention." What incentive did anyone have to develop something new if anyone else could simply copy it and benefit? Lincoln answers: "The patent system changed this; secured to the inventor, for a limited time, the exclusive use of his invention; and thereby added the fuel of *interest* to the *fire* of genius, in the discovery and production of new and useful things."

WISCONSIN STATE AGRICULTURAL SOCIETY ADDRESS

"Discoveries and Inventions" was a lecture that Lincoln "had gotten up" and took on the circuit. In contrast, his address before the Wisconsin State Agricultural Society in Milwaukee on September 30, 1859, was by request. Much of Lincoln's address focused on refuting the dubious "mud-sill theory" promoted by South Carolina Senator James H. Hammond. Hammond had argued that for society to have an upper class, which was necessary for "progress, civilization, and refinement," a lower class was required to "do the menial duties." He likened this lower class to the bottom timber of a house, the mud-sill, which supports a building. Hammond believed that slavery provided this service more efficiently than the free-labor system of the North, which he averred was worse than slavery because workers were "fatally fixed in that condition for life." They would labor forever without even receiving the "free" housing provided by slave owners. Lincoln refuted this, using his own experience as a laborer risen to high station in life as an example of the progress any laborer could achieve.[40]

Lincoln also took on science and technology in this lecture. He reminded his audience that the chief use of agricultural fairs was to "make mutual exchange of agricultural discovery, information, and knowledge," the dissemination of what one may know to everyone. By sharing information on new inventions and techniques, all may benefit.

Avoiding the kind of pandering most audiences might expect, Lincoln offered some blunt guidance on the future of agriculture. His first suggestion was to expect "greater thoroughness" in farming. Crop yields were much lower than capacity, he thought, noting that while a reasonable potential was fifty bushels of wheat per acre, the average crop in the wheat-growing regions was only eighteen bushels. To counter this, he pled for more intensive cultivation, not only as a means to increase food production but also for the psychological benefit of the farmer. "Every man is proud of what he does well; and no man is proud of what he does not do well." Those with their heart in their work "will do twice as much of it with less fatigue." Lincoln was encouraging farmers to work harder, but also smarter. He argued that while it would take more labor to "push the soil up to something near its full capacity," efficiency increases such that crop yields quickly outpaced the cost of additional labor. "Deeper plowing, analysis of soils, experiments with manures and varieties of seeds, observance of seasons and the like" would enhance profits because "the same product would be got from . . . half the quantity of land." Falling back on Euclidian language, he stated that "this proposition is self-evident." The statistical detail that Lincoln provided in the address with respect to crop yields reflected his avid study of agriculture.[41] He advised farmers to abandon their old habits and employ new methods of plowing, crop rotation, and machinery while seeking to bring more science into agriculture.[42]

Lincoln also expands on his promotion of steam power begun in the "Discoveries and Inventions" lecture. "The successful application of steam power, to farm work is a *desideratum*," he says, "especially a Steam Plow." Such a plow must do all the work cheaper and more rapidly than plowing with animals. The trouble was that he had never seen such a thing. Indeed, the first steam plow was not invented until 1863 in England, four years after Lincoln's address.[43] But Lincoln had already "thought a good deal, in an abstract way, about a Steam Plow." It would need to be designed "to apply the larger proportion of its power to the cutting and turning of the soil, and the smallest, to the moving itself over the field." As he proceeded, Lincoln dug further into the power consumption and mechanical efficiency logistics of such a plow, fully understanding that most of the energy from the steam needed to be put toward the actual plowing rather than simply moving the plow. After expounding on the technological details for several minutes, he said that he had "not point[ed] out difficulties, in order to discourage, but in order that being seen, they may be the more readily overcome." Lincoln's mechanical mind had worked out the basic principles to be met by a successful plow, and he challenged those present to set to accomplishing it.

Meeting this challenge required free labor and "its natural companion, education." Lincoln had championed universal education as far back as his first political campaign in New Salem. "No other human occupation opens so wide a field for the profitable and agreeable combination of labor with cultivated thought, as agriculture." Perhaps again channeling Walt Whitman, Lincoln noted "every blade of grass is a study." Showing his command of farming life, he said that soils, seeds, hedges, fences, drainage, mowing, threshing, irrigation, pest and disease control, livestock, trees, fruits, flowers—"the thousand things of which these are specimens"—are each a world of study within itself. "In all this, book-learning is available. A capacity, and taste, for reading, gives access to whatever has already been discovered by others. It is the key, or one of the keys, to the already solved problems."

In essence, Lincoln was capturing a microcosm of his own life in his scientific lectures. Tracing discoveries and inventions through biblical references made sense, as technological advances have existed as long as human beings have and most listeners would have read the Bible in their homes. Tools of increasing complexity arose early, and agriculture was the predominant profession of most early Americans, and therefore a source of great potential improvement through invention. While graduation to inventive innovation from basic observations took a long time to occur, once man invented the art of invention, the process increased rapidly, as it continues to do today. Lincoln alluded to the major component that was missing as man slowly discovered writing, printing, steam power, wind energy, and eventually the weapons of war that defined Lincoln's presidency. Scientific and technological improvements had tended to be individual activities. What was needed was a system of improvement. That was the basis for Lincoln's support for internal improvements, canals, and railroads. The scientific method needed to be institutionalized into government action.

PART V

MODERNIZING AMERICA

CHAPTER 11

Institutionalizing Science

JOSEPH HENRY WAS NOT INITIALLY IMPRESSED WITH ABRAHAM LINcoln. The first secretary of the Smithsonian Institution had shared many dinners with the sophisticated former senator and Smithsonian regent Jefferson Davis and was unsure of this self-taught frontier lawyer. Yet Henry felt obliged to visit the new president soon after Lincoln had settled into "that big white house."[1] Henry's misgivings were reinforced as he waited impatiently in the anteroom while a steady stream of riffraff filed in and out of the president's office. When finally allowed to see him, Henry thought Lincoln appeared careworn, withdrawn, and ill at ease.[2] After routine pleasantries, Henry explained the role of the Smithsonian and invited Lincoln to attend the next regents' meeting. The conversation was uncomfortable and brief; the president seemed disinterested. Was Lincoln the uneducated, uncultured boor rumors made him out to be, one who could never understand the high intellectual ambitions of the Smithsonian Institution?[3] Perhaps the open dislike by Henry's family was justified for the man General McClellan would call an uncouth "gorilla"?[4]

No, Henry thought, Lincoln was simply preoccupied with more urgent matters. Fort Sumter had fallen only three weeks before and, as longtime friend Captain Montgomery Meigs informed Henry, Lincoln was weighing options in the hopes of quickly ending the rebellion.[5] Perhaps he should not be so hasty to judge. Indeed, over time Henry would appreciate Lincoln's folksy intellect. Lincoln himself would rapidly see the importance of science to the war effort . . . and to the future of the Union.

RAISING THE CASTLE

Lincoln got his first taste of the famed red sandstone building known as "The Castle" a dozen years earlier while serving as a U.S. congressman. His inherent interest in science and technology likely drew him to the odd building being erected on the marshy edge of what later became the National Mall, then nothing more than a stinking, pestilence-filled plot of barren swampland. The inquisitive Lincoln also likely glanced at the first volume of the Smithsonian's *Contributions to Knowledge*, published during his congressional term.[6]

The history of the Smithsonian is an odd one. To this day no one understands why James Smithson, an Englishman who had never visited the United States, left a half-million-dollar bequest to start the institution that bears his name.[7] In spite of the stigma of an illegitimate birth—the by-product of a dalliance between Sir Hugh Percy (née Smithson), the first duke of Northumberland, and wealthy widow Elizabeth Hungerford Keate Macie—Smithson was no slouch when it came to science.[8] He had studied chemistry and mineralogy at the prestigious Oxford University, researched a variety of eclectic topics, and published more than two dozen scientific papers.[9]

Smithson, never marrying, died in 1829 with a will stipulating his entire accumulated wealth be given to his nephew, Henry James Hungerford. Should Hungerford leave no heirs, the inheritance would transfer in its entirety "to the United States of America, to found at Washington, under the name of the Smithsonian Institution, an establishment for the increase and diffusion of knowledge among men."[10] Hungerford conveniently died in 1835 with no wife or children and, suddenly, the United States had the Smithson money.

As it turned out, not so suddenly. Major disagreements over whether the United States should accept money from an often-belligerent foreign nation dragged out the deliberations. President Andrew Jackson could not be bothered, and many Southerners in Congress saw the money as another attempt by Northerners to expand the power and reach of the federal government. Even many Northerners saw it as "beneath the dignity" of the United States to accept money from the dreaded English.[11] Regardless of this animosity, and with elder statesman John Quincy

Adams throwing his considerable influence behind the proposal, Congress officially accepted the legacy in 1836. Even then it would be another eight years before Congress could agree on how to use it.[12]

Part of the problem was how to define "the increase and diffusion of knowledge." While politicians dithered, the scientific community itself was divided on how best to use the funds. Some prominent scientists wanted the money distributed as research grants; others wanted a public museum cataloging the scientific wealth of the expanding country. All agreed that the United States was sorely lacking in organized scientific knowledge and the Smithsonian should in some way develop American exceptionalism. At the time, the nation's scientific genius was loosely collected in local institutions comprising a small number of professional scientists and their many amateur, yet wealthy, collaborators. Boston was the main center of intellectual enterprise, followed closely by Philadelphia and New York. Like its cohorts elsewhere, the Academy of Natural Sciences of Philadelphia was a small, exclusive group of elitist naturalists who had attempted to build on the more theoretical Junto and American Philosophical Society, both started by Benjamin Franklin.

In 1848, the academy would spawn the American Association for the Advancement of Science (AAAS), now a paragon of scientific intellect. AAAS's mission was "to promote scientific dialogue in order to allow for greater scientific collaboration." More often than not, however, early meetings became mired in bickering among the various factions rather than promoting science.[13] Its first president was Joseph Henry. In February 1861, Henry wrote to Frederick Augustus Porter Barnard, who although born in Massachusetts, was president of the University of Mississippi and the incoming president of AAAS. Given the secession of several Southern states that winter, they agreed the annual meeting scheduled for April in Nashville should be postponed. The AAAS did not meet again until 1866, a year after the war ended, so it could provide no useful advice to President Lincoln.[14]

Another group of influential men before the war was the informal network of scientists who called themselves the "Scientific Lazzaroni." Led by Alexander Dallas Bache, great-grandson of Benjamin Franklin, the group's self-mocking name—*Lazzaroni* was slang for homeless beggars in Naples, Italy—belied the highly regarded scientists mostly based in Cambridge, Massachusetts. Bache along with Joseph Henry, geologist Louis Agassiz, mathematician Benjamin Peirce, chemist Oliver Wolcott Gibbs, and others used their influence to encourage greater scientific development in the United States. Yet even this group of impressive minds had limited influence as the Civil War approached.[15]

Notwithstanding these groups, the Smithson bequest reached a United States with nothing comparable to the great European scientific institutions. Louis XIV of France had established an Academy of Sciences in the late 1660s, following on the heels of the Royal Society in the United Kingdom a few years earlier. By 1831 the UK also had its British Association for the Advancement of Science. While science in Europe was booming, the United States lagged severely behind in intellectual prowess. One prominent scientist summed up the state of U.S. scientific knowledge as "puffs of quackery," noting that "every man who can burn phosphorus in oxygen and exhibit a few experiments to a class of Young Ladies is called a man of science." That scientist was Joseph Henry.[16]

Henry resigned his professorship at Princeton University soon after and accepted the challenge of turning a vague idea into the international jewel that is today's Smithsonian Institution. Over the next decade he supervised the building of the Castle, developed scientific research programs, and fought with politicians about whether the institution would be research oriented, a national library, or a museum. Henry pushed the former and abhorred the two latter. He preferred to fund scientific studies and their publication under the Smithsonian's name. Henry envisioned America as a world leader in science despite ongoing political tensions between the sections. Henry lost the museum battle, and now the Smithsonian consists of a dozen museums on the National Mall and elsewhere, a far cry from the single red sandstone Castle that housed Henry's office. Henry and his family had lived in a large boarding house across the street from the Patent Office on Eighth and G Streets, NW, another building dear to Lincoln's heart.[17] Once the Castle was built, the family moved into the new living quarters in the east wing.

Less than a month after their first meeting, Joseph Henry and Smithsonian regent Cornelius Felton paid another visit to the president.[18]

Lincoln had taken Henry's advice and appointed Captain James Melville Gilliss superintendent of the U.S. Naval Observatory, left without a leader after the departure of peevish oceanographer Matthew Fontaine Maury to the Confederacy.[19] This time the two got along well and Henry believed Lincoln to be much improved in manner and appearance.

Scientists were often treated with disdain and suspicion by both the general populace and the politically connected. European and American scientific organizations comprised largely an aristocratic elite, those who could afford the leisure time to pursue science.[20] Thomas Jefferson is often considered our most scientific president, inventing a myriad of devices for use on his Virginia plantation. While Lincoln struggled with farm chores, Jefferson and other eastern elites received classical educations at preparatory schools and colleges, benefiting from the enslaved people they forced to perform manual labor.

Lincoln was concerned that much of the knowledge gained by elites never trickled down to workers, frontier farmers, and tradesmen. He anticipated the potential benefits of science and technology for the masses and firmly believed that the government should assist men to rise up and better their condition. Education and broad practical dissemination of scientific knowledge to the public was one way to make that happen.

As the war proceeded, Lincoln repeatedly relied on Henry as an informal science adviser, although the closeness of the relationship remains uncertain. Historian Marc Rothenberg suggests they had the kind of professional relationship one might expect between a president and key adviser. Lincoln probably enjoyed Henry's company and they did talk about issues, but Henry more often dealt directly with key cabinet members: Secretaries of the Navy Welles, State Seward, and War Stanton, in that order.[21] Contemporaries who knew both men gave them credit for a deeper relationship, firmly believing that the two men genuinely respected each other's intellect and capabilities. According to Civil War correspondent Charles Carleton Coffin, Henry occasionally spent evenings with the president, chatting over issues of the day in the family quarters.[22] Contrary to his first impression, Henry discovered that Lincoln showed "a comprehensive grasp of every subject on which he has conversed." He was impressed with the many books Lincoln had read, and even more impressed that he "remembers their contents better than I do." Henry acknowledged that Lincoln had many great men around him but he seems "their equal, if not their superior." Henry also detected Lincoln's habit of deprecating his own level of knowledge. One time, Henry recalled, "I desired to induce him to understand, and look favorably upon, a change which I wish to make in the policy of the Light-House Board in a matter requiring some scientific knowledge. He professed his ignorance, or rather, he ridiculed his knowledge of it, and yet he discussed it as intelligently" as anyone in the field.[23]

Others suggested Lincoln found Henry a breath of fresh air, quite different from the stream of office seekers, grieving widows, complaining generals, and demanding secretaries who gave him not a moment's peace. Lucius Chittenden, the register of the Treasury and one of the rainmakers that kept the government financially afloat during these trying years, extolled the value of the Smithsonian to Lincoln. Lincoln admitted his first impression was "that the Smithsonian was printing a great amount of useless information," but "Professor Henry has convinced me of my error. It must be a grand school if it produces such thinkers as he is. He is one of the pleasantest men I have ever met; so unassuming, simple, and sincere. I wish we had a few thousand more such men!"[24]

Not that Henry and Lincoln always saw eye to eye. As party leader, Lincoln supported the use of the Smithsonian's auditorium for a series of antislavery lectures. Lincoln attended, and especially admired, the one by Horace Greeley in late 1861.[25] When told that Greeley would be speaking, Lincoln said, "In print every one of his words seems to weigh about a ton; I want to see what he has to say about us." Lincoln told antislavery Congressman George W. Julian of Indiana, "That address is full of good thoughts, and I would like to take the manuscript home with me and carefully read it over."[26] Henry, on the other hand, was not happy. He was a Union man, but he was not an abolitionist.[27] He had worked hard to keep the Smithsonian about science, not politics—even to the point of refusing to fly the Union flag over the Castle or to house Union soldiers—and here he was being compelled to open the meeting room to abolitionist lecturers.[28] Henry preferred to sponsor scientific lectures like the January 1862 lecture by Dr. Hayes on Arctic explorations that was given to a packed house. Pressured, Henry grudgingly surrendered the room to Greeley, Wendell Phillips, Henry Ward Beecher, and others but refused to allow Frederick Douglass's scheduled appearance as the final speaker in the series, writing, "I would not let the lecture of the coloured man to be given in the room of the Institution."[29]

Henry had been friends with Jefferson Davis, who had actively supported the Smithsonian mission.[30] On the day Lincoln first arrived in Washington, Henry mentioned to friends he was "pleased Jefferson Davis has been appointed President of the southern confederacy for I put confidence in his talents and integrity."[31] His former friendships with Davis and other now Confederate leaders would put a strain on his relationship with many in Congress holding the purse strings of the institution's funding. It led some in Washington to question his patriotism.

Thus, it was no surprise when reports of Henry's suspected Southern sympathies reached the president. One occasion made these suspicions clear while demonstrating how difficult it was to get reliable reporting. In a November 21, 1864, entry in his diary, Henry admitted that an Englishman "who calls himself Professor Anderson" had accused him of being a traitor.[32] He did not elaborate on the incident, but Quartermaster Montgomery Meigs, in a letter written soon after, noted that he was in the White House with the president and Henry when Anderson and his supporters arrived frantically accusing Meigs of "exhibiting lights to the enemy from the Capitol," while Henry was charged with the "same treason."[33] A version told years later by Lincoln confidant Noah Brooks dropped Meigs and Anderson from the story and included himself along with Henry and Lincoln. In his version, "a modest shopkeeper whose home was not far from the Smithsonian Institution" warned Lincoln of the lights shining frequently from one of the Smithsonian towers around midnight. Without realizing that Henry was one of the two men sitting in the room, the shopkeeper asserted that he had heard "that Professor Henry is a Southern man and a rebel sympathizer" and thus assumed the lights were signals directed to nearby Confederate troops. Lincoln, feeling confident in his science advisor, introduced the gentleman to Professor Henry and asked Henry to respond. While Lincoln chuckled at "the look of dismay on the countenance" of the shopkeeper, Henry explained that the lights were from a lantern used to read the Smithsonian's meteorological instruments at night.[34] An even more pulsating version by twentieth-century poet and biographer Carl Sandburg has Henry being delivered as a prisoner into the White House by an army officer. After asking Henry "why sentence of death should not immediately be pronounced" upon him, Lincoln mirthfully admitted he had joined Henry in the tower the night before during the testing of new army signals. Henry was released and the army officer slunk away in embarrassment.[35]

Whichever version you might choose to believe, Lincoln clearly relied on Henry's expertise and made every effort to protect the Smithsonian during the war. Funding was always a problem, and in a November 11, 1862, letter to William Seward, Henry anxiously begged for Lincoln to grant power of attorney to a London law firm attempting to recover a part of the original bequest of James Smithson not yet received. Lincoln granted Henry's request, and the remaining funds, approximately $25,000 in gold, were transferred.[36] The Smithsonian would continue to exist.

PERMANENT COMMISSION

Lincoln's enthusiasm for mathematics, science, and technology made him a national sounding board for innovations, but he simply could not handle all the inventors pouring letters into his mailbox or showing up at the White House expecting a stamp of approval for their miraculous "war-ending invention."[37] Unlike today, there was no military-industrial complex developing new weapons during the Civil War. When it came to innovation, the government relied on "the chance, unreliable labors of inventors and amateurs of science" who "literally besieged official Washington after the outbreak of the war."[38]

Probably with Lincoln's knowledge, Joseph Henry proposed to Secretary Welles an advisory board to serve as a more efficient mechanism for evaluating new ideas to aid the war effort. The navy had earlier tried a similar idea with its Naval Examining Board, but it failed in six months due to insufficient funding.[39] By early 1863 Welles was willing to implement Henry's idea, in part because any experimental research would be conducted by the originator, not the navy. With Lincoln's approval, Welles created the Permanent Commission of the Navy Department "to which all subjects of a scientific character on which the Government may require information may be referred."[40] The three-member commission—Henry was joined by equally ubiquitous Alexander Dallas Bache (superintendent of the Coast Survey) and Charles Henry Davis (chief of the Bureau of Navigation)—met several times a week to evaluate the stream of proposals.[41] After more than three dozen meetings in the first few months, Henry grumbled to Harvard botanist Asa Gray that his duties on the commission were overwhelming; the commission "occupied nearly all my time" other than that devoted to Smithsonian business.[42]

In one meeting alone they reported on a variety of inventions including Mr. G. Dettloff's "submarine galvano-electric battery within the interior of a torpedo," which, unfortunately, the commission felt was "too complicated in arrangement, and too defective in detail, to be available in practice." They also issued unfavorable opinions on various devices to explode torpedoes (i.e., underwater mines). One inventor, a Thomas Taylor of Massachusetts, proposed the use of "suffocating missiles," a technology actually centuries old. Taylor showed two letters in support, one noting that he had exhibited his shell in 1862 to President Lincoln and Senator O. H. Browning. Lincoln had apparently taken no substantive action. While Taylor was vouched for as "a gentleman of high scientific attainments," here again the decision of the commission was unfavorable, noting that "this particular mixture of chemical ingredients would be more dangerous to friends than foes."[43]

In one intriguing letter to his daughter Mary, Henry told her of a commissioner meeting held high atop the tower of the Smithsonian, "for observing a new method of signals" designed by Lt. George H. Felt, "founded on the projection from rockets, of stars of different colors in different orders of succession. Thus, a blue star might signify number one—a red and then a white star, number 35." He would then check the number against the corresponding word in the signal book. After writing this in a personal letter, Henry perhaps belatedly cautioned his daughter to keep this top-secret information from being made public.[44]

From its creation in early 1863, the commission evaluated over three hundred proposals ranging from warship designs to underwater guns to torpedoes, all of which their originators claimed would immediately end the war in the Union's favor. Despite the optimism of the inventors, mostly these ideas were oversold and underperforming.[45] After the war, Henry bragged that the Permanent Commission kept the government "from rushing into many schemes which, under guise of patriotism, were intended to advance individual interest."[46]

The commission relieved Lincoln of the steady stream of inventors that had besieged him since the beginning of the war, but it did not stop all of them. Lincoln continued to receive letters and visits for the remainder of the war, and the always curious commander-in-chief continued to personally test some of the weapons that came his way. As the burdens of war became overwhelming, more and more often Lincoln would refer inventors to the Permanent Commission or directly to the military personnel most likely capable of evaluating the proposal.

And yet inventors still badgered Lincoln even after their proposal had been evaluated by the commission, either because the commission had refused their self-professed miraculous discovery or because a decision was bogged down in endless bureaucratic delay. John H. Schenk angrily wrote to Lincoln in early 1864 complaining he had been waiting a year to get approvals, yet the evaluation "is still throttled nearly to death with Red tape."[47] A few months later, John D. Hall wrote to Lincoln about his idea to lay cable across waterways to cut enemy obstructions lower than the keel of Union ironclads. He had originally written to Gideon Welles, who forwarded it to the Permanent Commission, and now impatiently was writing Lincoln. He complained that "notwithstanding these devices are so simple that any mechanical mind may easily comprehend them in the space of ten minutes of time," he had yet to receive any report after thirty days. He asked Lincoln to speed up the acceptance. He received a reply that his invention was under consideration.[48] Sometimes even Lincoln's positive intervention had no effect. Inventor Peter Yates had proposed an "Improvement on Steam Engines" that was the subject of several letters between Yates, Lincoln, Welles, and the members of the commission. In the end, Charles Henry Davis grumbled to Welles that the "invention has not been described with sufficient clearness to be perfectly understood," but based on what he could infer, "the loss of power which this invention is intended to prevent does not exist."[49]

On the other hand, Thomas Schuebly wrote Lincoln in late 1863 enthusiastically thanking him for supporting development of his new "impregnable" ironclad steamer, which the Permanent Commission told him to build at his own expense. Testing of this new ironclad, Schuebly cautioned in his letter, would be delayed slightly. It apparently was never built.[50]

Despite its name, the Permanent Commission petered into nonexistence midway into 1865 as new weaponry became less important than mass manufacture of conventional rifles for the postwar occupation.[51] The idea has been resurrected over the years as new wars required evaluation of new technology. One such board, the Naval Consulting Board, was chaired by Thomas Edison during World War I and led to the creation of the internally integrated Naval Research Laboratory, which still exists in Washington, DC.[52]

NATIONAL ACADEMY OF SCIENCES

Eying an opportunity to showcase American science, Lincoln appointed Henry to yet another commission, this one organizing American participation in the International Exhibition scheduled for London in 1862. Lincoln approved the commission's recommendations in December 1861, and the House Ways and Means Committee endorsed an appropriation of thirty-five thousand dollars for expenses. Yet neither the full House nor the Senate could pass a bill, and the lack of political and financial support discouraged many companies from participating. The lost opportunity probably hackled Lincoln as the exhibition showcased such industrial advances as the electrical telegraph, submarine cables, and a new thermoplastic called Parkesine, later renamed Celluloid, which became the basis of Thomas Edison's motion picture film.[53]

While Henry was involved in a variety of activities, other Lazzaroni were pushing for a much broader scientific body. The seeds of the National Academy of Sciences had been planted in 1851 when Alexander Bache called for a federal "institution of science ... to guide public action in reference to scientific matters."[54] By 1858, Louis Agassiz had outlined a basic structure and organization of such an academy, but President Buchanan and the antebellum Congress refused to act.

Agassiz, however, had not given up on the idea. Sensing an opportunity with the more science-friendly Lincoln at the helm, Agassiz enlisted the support of Massachusetts Senator Henry Wilson to prepare a bill.[55] Wilson had close ties with Lincoln and had worked with him on a law to emancipate the slaves in the District of Columbia, so he likely discussed the academy idea with the president. Indeed, a cryptic note from Lincoln during this time asked, "Will Senator Wilson please call and see me." Another enigmatic note from Charles H. Davis suggests he may also have directly lobbied Lincoln midway between the bill's introduction and passing.[56]

After originally introducing the bill in committee on February 20, Wilson cleverly queried the chair just before session adjournment late on March 3 for the right "to take up a bill, which, I think, will consume no time, and to which I hope there will be no opposition. . . . It will take but a moment, I think, and I should like to have it passed." With senators eager to head home, and because it required no funding appropriation, the short bill establishing the National Academy of Sciences (NAS) was hurriedly read, then passed on a voice vote. Immediately, it was sent over to the House to receive similar rubber-stamping, then rushed up to President Lincoln, who signed it that night.[57]

The function of the NAS was stipulated in six lines of the brief chartering document. When called upon by the government, members were to "investigate, examine, experiment, and report upon any subject of science or art." Appropriate expenses for conducting and reporting this work would be borne by the government, but neither the academy nor the individual scientists were to receive any form of compensation—the NAS would be a volunteer organization.[58]

The NAS created a charter membership of fifty specifically named scientists, which not surprisingly included Joseph Henry as well as Louis Agassiz, mathematician Frederick Barnard, Naval Observatory Director James Gilliss, Admiral John Dahlgren, geologist James D. Dana, Admiral Charles H. Davis, botanist Asa Gray, mathematician Benjamin Peirce, chemist Benjamin Silliman, and its first president, Alexander Dallas Bache. Shortly after the initial meeting, Henry reported to his daughter Mary that the "affairs of the Academy have gone off very favorably and the establishment bids fair to do good service in the way of advancing science."[59]

Creation of the NAS was not without controversy, even seen as ill-conceived by many entrenched forces. The selection of the fifty charter members seemed haphazard. Some men named were startled by their inclusion, while other prominent scientists were befuddled by their exclusion. Joseph Henry claimed to have been left out of the selection process and told Princeton astronomer (and brother-in-law) Stephen Alexander he was "not well pleased" with the list of charter members, nor "the manner in which it was made." Bache rebuffed Henry, claiming he had indeed had an opportunity to object to the members listed. More than a year later Henry quietly admitted he had not objected because he thought Congress would never pass the bill.[60]

The fifty charter members did appear to reflect Bache's preferences rather than a balanced representation of the various scientific fields, as Bache included his friends and excluded his enemies. Henry believed certain qualified scientists should have been on the initial list; Smithsonian curator Spencer Baird, for example, was arbitrarily excluded. Henry and Agassiz had a major falling out because of this omission, but with the support of Asa Gray and other influential scientists, Baird was eventually elected an academy member to replace one who had died.[61]

To this day, the NAS remains an informal resource where unpaid advisers evaluate scientific questions. Greatly expanded by President Woodrow Wilson during World War I, there are now over 2,300 members plus almost five hundred foreign associates available to the White House, Congress, and government agencies for advice related to a variety of technical questions, including man-made climate change, agriculture, and science communication. The NAS now has a broad mission that includes "validating scientific excellence, enhancing the vitality of the scientific enterprise, guiding public policy with science, and communicating the nature, values, and judgments of science to government and the public." Increasingly, the NAS has taken on coordination with other science academies around the globe. If it remains dormant, it is only because a particular administration chooses not to take advantage of the combined expertise of NAS scientists.[62]

DEPARTMENT OF AGRICULTURE

As much as he disliked farmwork—he complained his father treated him like a slave—Lincoln never forgot his farming roots and desperately wanted to improve the farming life. Although a shift toward greater industrialization and manufacturing was already underway in the North, agriculture remained the major economic driver nationwide. More than half of the labor force in 1860 were farmers.[63] Most had little or no formal education and had been largely ignored by the federal government. In his 1859 lecture to the Wisconsin State Agricultural Society, Lincoln had pleaded with farmers to modernize. As president, Lincoln favored government intervention to help people better their condition and looked for ways to bring science to agriculture.

In his first Annual Message to Congress on December 3, 1861, Lincoln wrote:

> *Agriculture, confessedly the largest interest of the nation, has not a department nor a bureau, but a clerkship only, assigned to it in the Government. While it is fortunate that this great interest is so independent in its nature as to not have demanded and extorted more from the Government, I respectfully ask Congress to consider whether something more cannot be given voluntarily with general advantage.... While I make no suggestions as to details, I venture the opinion that an agricultural and statistical bureau might profitably be organized.[64]*

Congress took the hint. With his Republican Party in control and uncooperative Southern representatives no longer an impediment to action, Congress passed a bill creating the Department of Agriculture, which Lincoln signed into law on May 15, 1862. Its goal was to institutionalize science in agriculture and thus put farming on the path to the future.[65]

The bill, sent to the president by the aptly named Galusha Grow, Speaker of the House of Representatives, and Solomon Foot, president pro tem of the Senate, stipulated that the role of the new independent Department of Agriculture was "to acquire and to diffuse among the people of the United States useful information on subjects connected with agriculture in the most general and comprehensive sense of that word, and to procure, propagate, and distribute among the people new and valuable seeds and plants."[66]

In his next Annual Message to Congress, Lincoln eagerly reported that he had "caused the Department of Agriculture of the United States to be organized."[67] The new department would develop scientific experiments, collect statistics, test new seeds and plants, and disseminate any knowledge gained to agriculturists. As innovative variations were developed, seeds, cereals, and cuttings would be distributed to farmers for widespread propagation. New knowledge on nutrition, soil management, tilling strategies, and crop rotation would also be relayed to farmers so they could improve crop yields. Lincoln's vision of bringing scientific benefits to the people would begin.

Some of these activities were already being conducted within the Department of State by the commissioner of patents, Henry Leavitt Ellsworth. Ellsworth was a Yale-educated attorney with a preoccupation with agriculture, so on his own initiative he started collecting and dispensing new varieties of seeds. By 1839 Congress had established an Agricultural Division within the Patent Office, later transferred to the new Department of the Interior, and Ellsworth's annual reports called for the application of chemistry to agriculture. For this, Ellsworth has been called the "Father of the Department of Agriculture."[68]

Ellsworth had died in 1858. Lincoln named Isaac Newton as his first commissioner of the Department of Agriculture, which the president called his "people's department." Newton—no relation to the famed English astronomer, mathematician, and physicist—was an agriculturist who had made acquaintance with Lincoln while selling farm products to the White House.[69] Though Newton was derided early on for his lack of formal education, Lincoln took a liking to him, perhaps because he could relate to his initiative and self-schooling. Newton turned out to be well suited for the job.

Near the end of 1862, Newton sent a fifty-four-page handwritten account to Lincoln, the first annual report from the department. After describing the history of agriculture through the ages, Newton reported excellent harvests of crops across the Northern states even with the loss of many men serving the war effort. He noted that the North, with its free labor, was faring better than the South, whose slave-labor system harmed fertility and agricultural yield.[70]

Newton went on to tout agricultural science advancements made by inventor Jethro Tull (horse-drawn hoe, mechanical seed drill, improved plow), chemist Sir Humphrey Davy (*Elements of Agricultural Chemistry*), agricultural writer Arthur Young (*Annals of Agriculture*), and the reapers of John Henry Manny and Cyrus McCormick, with which Lincoln was already familiar from his legal career. Reiterating Lincoln's Wisconsin speech, Newton noted that agricultural progress requires "a more thorough Knowledge and practice ... as a Science and an Art." Further objectives of the department included collecting and using statistics to demonstrate which methods work best, farmer outreach, soil analysis, establishing professorships, and constructing an agricultural library and museum. Newton even laid out a plan for increasing cotton cultivation in free states, reporting that an experiment the previous summer yielded up to one thousand pounds of cotton per acre in Illinois, a Northern state not known for its cotton production. Plans were to actively induce farmers in Kentucky, Missouri, southern Illinois, Indiana, and Kansas to produce cotton in an effort to replace cotton crops no longer available from the South.[71]

All of this would eventually lead to a more thorough education of the farmer in physical science and political economy.[72] In too much of the nation, Newton wrote, farmers continued to cultivate depleted soil, thus necessitating the application of manure as fertilizer in an unwinnable battle against soil nutrient exhaustion. Using science, including proper tilling practices, crop rotation, and nutrient preservation, he argued, agriculture could provide greater consistency and magnitude of production for decades to come.[73] Lincoln had successfully turned his much-maligned farming drudgery into a department that would transform American agriculture.

INSTITUTIONALIZED SCIENCE

The institutionalization of science within the federal government continued to proceed at a rapid pace during the Lincoln administration. In a spurt of substantive congressional activity and presidential signatures that might boggle the modern mind, Lincoln signed several laws that expanded the nation's ability to integrate science into public activity.

Five days after creating the Department of Agriculture, Lincoln signed the Homestead Act, deeding to westward settlers one-fourth-square-mile tracts of free land. Taking effect on January 1, 1863, the same day he issued the final Emancipation Proclamation, the Homestead Act had a tremendous effect on the expansion of the United States and remained in effect for more than a century.[74]

Not surprisingly, the question of populating newly acquired federal lands became entangled in the greater disagreement over slavery. As a western pioneer, Lincoln and other Northerners sought to spread free labor into the lands acquired by the Louisiana Purchase and Mexican War. Southerners saw the chance to spread slavery. While much western land was unsuitable for slave-labor crops like cotton, the political power of slave state representation in Congress was immense. Homesteading had been an issue from the time of the Revolution up until the Civil War; the two sections of the country simply could not agree on the terms. With slaveholding states no longer part of Congress, the Republican-dominated members were able to push through "free labor" policies Southerners had previously obstructed.

The Homestead Act was relatively simple despite its enormous contribution to the modernization of America. Qualified settlers could select a tract of up to 160 acres of public land for a minimal administrative fee. To obtain permanent title, they needed only to take up residence within six months, place at least ten acres under cultivation, and remain on the property for five consecutive years. The result was immediate and enthusiastic. Westward movement began even before the war ended and accelerated in the immediate postwar period. Over the next fifteen years, nearly 130 million acres were added to the nation's farmland, about fifty million between the Mississippi River and the Rocky Mountains. The act, along with other progressive bills signed by Lincoln, was largely responsible for settlement of the West to the exclusion of slavery.[75]

The act was even more progressive than it appeared. Women were free to claim homestead lands in the territories even though they were barred from owning land in their own names in most of the existing states. Homesteads were also open to African Americans, many of whom were experiencing freedom for the first time, taking advantage of the opportunity to own and manage their own lands. The same was true for most immigrants, who likewise fled discrimination in the East to begin self-sufficient lives homesteading.[76] While farming remained the dominant occupation, the Homestead Act helped shift the nation from the subsistence farming Lincoln knew well to a market-based agricultural system, thus propelling the United States to become one of the world's largest producers of food and commodities.

The blistering rate of modernization continued. In early July, Lincoln signed the Land-Grant College Act. James Buchanan had vetoed the idea in 1859, but with Lincoln's encouragement, Senator Justin Morrill reintroduced it for easy passage and Lincoln's welcome signature. The act donated federal land to the states, which could sell parcels to establish a permanent endowment to fund public colleges. The act required these colleges to teach "scientific and classical studies" and to "promote the liberal and practical education of the industrial classes" in agricultural and the mechanic arts. Iowa quickly accepted the provisions of the act and designated its existing Iowa State Agricultural College (now Iowa State University) as the first official land-grant college. The first new institution created under the act was Kansas State University. Isaac Funk, a close friend of Lincoln's, founded the first land-grant college in Illinois.[77] Others soon followed, including many in the South to aid its postwar rejuvenation. Because of discrimination against African Americans in the former slave-owning states, a second Morrill Land-Grant Act was passed in 1890 requiring the state either to demonstrate race was not an admissions criterion or to designate a separate land-grant institution for persons of color. Many states chose the latter, which while discriminatory did result in the creation of several historically black colleges and universities (HBCUs). In 1994 the land-grant status was extended to tribal colleges and universities, and today there are 106 land-grant colleges.[78]

The importance of these land-grant colleges cannot be overstated. Only 5 percent of American males (and no females) went to college by the beginning of the war. While all colleges taught fundamental science at the undergraduate level, the courses were intended to stimulate the logical thought necessary to succeed in the student's field of choice (e.g., law, medicine, business). Science was designed to teach students problem solving, not prepare them for careers in science. No laboratory work was done; at best, the professor would do demonstrations if he or the facility could afford the equipment. While the first Ph.D. in North America was awarded in 1861 by Yale, only later did graduate degrees become more common. Prior to the war, if you wanted to become an actual scientist, you directly paid a professor to study with, often in Europe. With his signature, Lincoln created colleges that taught science and technology degrees, which served as a basis for the expansion of science training for the rest of the nineteenth century and beyond.[79]

Some historians argue that these acts of modernization were undertaken by Congress with little if any role by Lincoln.[80] This severely undervalues Lincoln's influence. Both the Homestead Act and Land-Grant Act had been on the congressional agenda for fifteen years, only to be stymied by Southern Democrats who saw modernization as a threat to their slavery-driven aristocracy.[81] Lincoln's lifelong obsession with internal improvements as a means of economic and personal growth demonstrated his support for progressive legislation, the inclusion of which he encouraged in the 1860 Republican platform. On his way to Washington for the inauguration, Lincoln stated his position to a committee representing eighteen German industrial associations: "An allusion has been made to the Homestead Law. I think it worthy of consideration, and that the wild lands of the country should be distributed so that every man should have the means and opportunity of benefitting his condition."[82] Lincoln also met "several times a week" with Galusha Grow, primary champion of homesteading in the House of Representatives, and undoubtedly indicated his eagerness to pass such bills while the opportunity existed.[83] Lincoln assigned Secretary of War Stanton and Secretary of the Navy Welles as key liaisons with Congress to ensure passage of the Pacific railroad bill. The Homestead, Land-Grant, and Pacific Railroad Acts were critical to making the West hospitable to settlement.[84] The Land-Grant Act also was the federal government's first involvement in education; it succeeded in democratizing higher education and expanded Lincoln's belief, stated in his first political speech: "I view [education] as the most important subject which we as a people can be engaged in."[85] Lincoln clearly influenced the passage and principles of these groundbreaking legislative acts.

For one of his more intriguing contributions to the institutionalizing of science, Lincoln may have been responding to the exploits of Clarence King, dubbed by many as "The Explorer King." John Hay would later refer to King as "the best and brightest man of his generation," who as a twenty-one-year-old in 1862 traveled across the United States to the relatively unexplored state of California to work for the state geological survey. King was the first man to climb many of the highest peaks in the Sierra Nevada mountains. He also conducted the first official survey of Yosemite Valley.[86]

Inspired by King and the spectacular photographs of Carleton Watkins, Lincoln was also acting on the request of Senator John Conness, who introduced the legislation not long after presenting a commemorative cane to the president.[87] On June 30, 1864, Lincoln signed into law the Yosemite Grant Act. The act states "That there shall be, and is hereby, granted to the State of California, the ... [area] known as Yosemite Valley ... [and] the 'Mariposa Big Tree Grove.' ... The State shall accept this grant upon the express conditions that the premises should be held for public use, resort, and recreation."[88]

Lincoln had never been to California, yet he understood its great importance to the cohesion of the Union. He felt California was critical to the future of the United States and sought ways to encourage westward development. Three weeks before his assassination, Lincoln told his friend Charles Maltby, superintendent of Indian affairs for California, that he had long desired to see the state and marveled at "the production of her gold mines." He also told Maltby that "I have it now in purpose when the railroad is finished, to visit your wonderful state," a visit that would never come to fruition.[89]

Originally, the beauty of Yosemite Valley and the grandeur of the Giant Sequoia trees in Mariposa Grove was ceded to caretaking by the state of California. Much later, John Muir came on the scene. Having lived in and explored the Yosemite and nearby Hetch Hetchy Valleys, Muir teamed up with influential *Century Magazine* editor Robert Underwood

Johnson to recapture Yosemite from state park status to federal. Through their efforts, on October 1, 1890, Yosemite became the nation's third national park.[90]

The Yosemite grant signed by Lincoln was nothing short of miraculous given the circumstances. To have set aside a protected environmental area while the country was tearing itself apart was a testament to Lincoln's and Congress's foresight. Lincoln's signature set precedent for establishing Yellowstone as the first national park in 1872, to be followed by protection for the other pristine, and irreplaceable, vistas we enjoy today.

One scientific institution that Lincoln had protected and advanced during the war took a major hit on the frigid winter's afternoon of January 24, 1865. Joseph Henry sat in his third-floor office in the Smithsonian Castle, alternatively updating his notebook and staring out the great rose window squeezed between the two front towers. Stirring, he noticed a sooty burning odor. Likewise, his daughter Mary was reading in the library until she noticed the room darkening, a thick cloud of smoke obscuring the view. The Castle was on fire![91]

Rushing to save whatever they could, father and daughter managed to grab a few books, some papers, and a bit of clothing. Others arrived to help pull out furniture items. Flames poured out the tower windows and scorched the ornamental stonework. Mary described it as "a beautiful friend tasting to the utmost the pleasure of destruction."[92] Her poetical observation was interrupted as the flames reached the top of the tower, where Henry's papers were kept, destroying a historical and scientific record that had taken a lifetime to build.

Investigations showed that the fire was accidental, a result of negligence. Men renovating the building had vented a stove exhaust pipe into an air chamber inside the wall rather than to an external vent. After smoldering for days, the heated wood had finally erupted into flames. Destroyed was the apparatus room, the picture gallery, the regents room, and the lecture hall. Among the treasures lost were all James Smithson's personal effects, including the manuscripts, meteorites, and minerals that had seeded the new institution.[93] Also lost were an extensive collection of scientific instruments and nearly a hundred thousand letters and reports documenting the founding of the institution and a decade of scientific research from all over the world. All of James Smithson's unpublished scientific research was lost forever.[94] It would take twelve years and $125,000 to repair the building and correct faulty construction.[95] Indirectly lost was James Melville Gillis, chief astronomer and director of the Naval Observatory, who succumbed to exhaustion during the building evacuation and suffered a fatal stroke two weeks later.[96] Saved was Smithson's small personal collection of books. Only 115 volumes and never bound in leather covers, they at least provide some surviving connection to the man who made the Smithsonian possible.[97]

Two days after the fire, Henry shambled to the White House. Lincoln "expressed much sympathy" and ordered the War Department to raise a temporary roof over the scorched portions of the Castle.[98] Montgomery Meigs, a longtime friend of Henry and one of Lincoln's favorite engineers, pulled together the needed materials and carpenters to build a roof designed by architect Edward Clark. Henry would spend the next several months organizing renovations, taking time out to attend Lincoln's second inaugural on March 4. At his side was Mary Henry, who made a passing reference to seeing the famous actor John Wilkes Booth in the balcony above them.

Lincoln's lifelong enthusiasm for science and technology, combined with his belief that the federal government should help the populace better their condition, made him an amenable partner of congressional efforts to institutionalize science. Once suspicious of scientists because of their overall elitism and the preponderance of con men, the national attitude toward science had begun to change. No longer the sole realm of a wealthy elite, technological advances were more and more affecting the masses, in part due to a refocusing on practical science rather than less publicly relatable theoretical research.

Lincoln's influence institutionalizing science was not finished. In his 1862 Annual Message to Congress he indicated a preference for connecting the United States with Europe by an Atlantic telegraph, as well as a similar project to extend the Pacific telegraph between San Francisco and the Russian empire. He also argued for development of "the immense mineral resources" of some of the territories, most notably the silver lode in Nevada, a western territory that would become a state just in time to give its electoral votes to Lincoln in the 1864 election. Lincoln specifically argued for a scientific exploration of the mineral regions and publication of the findings as a means of raising cash for the war effort as well as diminishing the burdens of the people.[99]

Lincoln also understood the importance of transportation for economic development. Throughout his career he had championed improvements to navigable rivers, canals, roads, and railroads. Now as president he urged Congress to take action on the long-suffering development of the transcontinental railroad. Stuck in sectional infighting for years, the Pacific Railroad Act of 1862 was encouraged and signed by Lincoln, who stipulated a starting location in Council Bluffs, Iowa. Lincoln pleaded with Congress to act forcefully on the project.[100] Lincoln also stressed to Congress the "military and commercial importance of enlarging the Illinois and Michigan Canal" and the need for improvements to the Illinois River and enlarging the Erie Canal of New York. Such projects continued the internal improvement theme Lincoln had promoted since his first campaign.

While he was busy institutionalizing science within the federal government, the war continued. Lincoln and technically savvy people like Joseph Henry, Alexander Bache, an itinerant balloonist, and an irascible Swedish American inventor would be on the front lines facilitating the development of new technology.

CHAPTER 12

The Technology of War

LINCOLN RELIED ON SCIENCE AND TECHNOLOGY TO ADVANCE THE MILI-
tary effort in several fundamental ways: weaponry, transportation, communication, and in the broader sense of strategy. With respect to weapons,
he personally tested some inventions and improvements, entertained
innovators, charged the Permanent Commission with evaluating new
weapons, pressured ordnance officers, and ensured that ironclads would
keep the military ahead of the technological curve. For transportation, he
facilitated the strategic deployment of railroads and balloons to aid the
war effort and encouraged the capture and control of rivers and coastlines.
For communication, he nationalized the telegraph and deftly used public
letters to clarify policy and shape public sentiment. All of these built on
his lifelong interest in technology, his time on the waters, his working for
the railroads, and his promotion of internal improvements.

Despite the creation of the Permanent Commission, inventors continued to besiege Lincoln with new ideas for weaponry. How many of
the hundreds of letters addressed to him actually reached his desk is
unknown, but some clearly did. Lincoln endorsed many letters, directing
a particular cabinet secretary—most often Secretary of War Stanton or
Secretary of the Navy Welles—to take whatever action specified. Usually these were suggestions to give some attention to the invention in
question, often phrased as "Respectfully submitted" to Stanton or Welles
for consideration.[1] Occasionally, Lincoln directed his guidance to specific
technical experts like his request to venerable engineer Joseph G. Totten. Asked to give his opinion on an invention by Reverend Paul Franklin Jones purported to improve operation of heavy gun batteries, Totten

advised not proceeding. Indignant, Jones wrote Lincoln to complain that Totten had done him a "great injustice," pleading with Lincoln to overrule him. Lincoln stuck with Totten's assessment.[2]

The Civil War has often been referred to as the first "high-tech" or "modern" war. This is misleading. Every war uses the latest technology, moving from swords for close up fighting, as one example, to bows and arrows that expand the range of attack. Changes in tactics can also be considered modernization. Improved technology did gain more usage over the course of the four years of battle. Lincoln contributed to all aspects of this transformation.

Always eager to learn, Lincoln borrowed from the Library of Congress Henry Halleck's treatise *Elements of Military Art and Science*, which had become the standard instruction on strategy, fortification, and tactics in battle. By this time, Lincoln had become impatient with the lack of military movement by his general-in-chief, George B. McClellan, whom he had known since McClellan had aided Stephen A. Douglas in the 1858 debates. McClellan had substantial military experience while Lincoln had virtually none, but Lincoln was intent on learning military strategy to prod his frustratingly slow generals into action.[3] While he likely never read Carl von Clausewitz's *On War*, Lincoln's strategic decision making suggests he had an instinctive understanding of Clausewitzian theories of war. Clausewitz, like Lincoln, relied on rational and reasoned thought common during the Enlightenment. Clausewitz argued that military attack should focus on the center of gravity of any enemy, which Lincoln correctly identified as its army rather than ground to be captured and held. Lincoln also understood Clausewitz's concept of trinity, the interlinking of the general populace, the army, and the government. By managing all three aspects, Lincoln was able to integrate logical arguments with logistical military movement. While he lacked substantive military training, Lincoln's strength was strategic intelligence, the grasp that the North's advantage in numbers was best used by simultaneously pressing the attack on Southern armies in different places. This strategic sense was thwarted early in the war by generals lacking either the commanding ability or the inclination to follow this thinking.[4] Once he found a general with a like-minded military philosophy in Ulysses S. Grant, Lincoln returned Halleck's treatise to the Library of Congress.

Overwhelming manpower and strategic thinking were not enough; one must have weapons. Lincoln pressed his army and navy to employ the latest technical weapons available and was instrumental in getting several of them into production. Standing in his way was Chief of Ordnance James Wolfe Ripley. Sixty-six years old at the beginning of the war, Ripley had risen through the ranks since his service in the War of 1812 and under Andrew Jackson's command during the Seminole War. Employing a combination of firmness and tact while in command of Fort Moultrie during the 1833 nullification crisis brought him to the attention of General Winfield Scott. While superintendent of the Springfield Armory, Ripley was instrumental in developing the new .58 caliber rifled musket, which later became the primary weapon for infantrymen during the Civil War. Throughout his Civil War service, he retained his sometimes-unpopular insistence on strict adherence to procurement regulations. Ripley strongly believed that it was more essential to get sufficient numbers of standard weapons to troops in the field than to integrate a broad range of technologically advanced, and usually unproven, weaponry. This put Ripley at odds with Lincoln, who continued to support the latest inventions.[5]

Among the new weaponry that Lincoln supported were some that Ripley attempted to avoid. Early in the war, Walter Sherwin was invited to the White House to demonstrate his breech-loading cannon. Setting a model on the table in Lincoln's office, he instructed Lincoln and his cabinet on its operation. Lincoln was impressed enough to send a letter to Ripley asking him to give it a test. Ripley rejected the cannon outright, citing its excessive weight and cost, and told Sherwin that the department was too busy to be bothered.[6] Perhaps thinking back to his days contemplating the blacksmith trade, Lincoln later ordered the testing of a wrought-iron seven-caliber cannon constructed by Horatio Ames. He specifically ordered that a board of officers be assigned to make trials of the cannon, and "the ordnance bureaus of the War and Navy Departments shall provide suitable shot, shells, and ammunition" for making the tests. These guns were to provide "great power and penetration" for use against Confederate ironclads.[7]

Lincoln took an interest in small arms as well. A few weeks into the war, he pressed Captain John Dahlgren on a new gun presented by Orison Blunt. After encouraging Dahlgren to "please see Mr. Blunt," Lincoln wrote, "What do you think of it? Would the government do well to purchase some of them?" When Dahlgren replied positively the same day, Lincoln endorsed the envelope with another prod for action: "I saw the gun myself, and witnessed some experiments with it," Lincoln wrote, adding, "I really think it worthy the attention of the government." Presumably, these were the Enfield-patterned rifles Blunt made for the army a year later.[8]

Pursuing another promising new rifle, Lincoln wrote to Ripley "to introduce you to Mr. Strong who has what appears to be an ingenious and useful Carbine" and asked Ripley to give it a service test.[9] Strong was an unlikable man with dubious ethics, but his breech-loading carbine provided the advantage of faster loading at the base of the shorter barrel compared to the longer-barreled, muzzle-loading muskets most commonly in use. Ripley was unimpressed. While admitting that the new system was "novel and ingenious," he told Lincoln that it was no better than any of the other breech-loading rifles available, which Ripley found to be too complicated to employ in service. Keep it simple was Ripley's motto, and he preferred old muskets to simplify supply of guns and ammunition to thousands of green troops.[10]

Ripley had a point. Much of the Union's production capacity and its existing stocks of weapons were lost to the Confederacy, in part through the treasonous actions of former secretary of war John Floyd.[11] The lack of a significant standing army prior to the war necessitated the enlistment of hundreds of thousands of former farmers, tradesmen, and vagrants into the military, most with no experience with weapons of war. Adding a hodgepodge of small arms of different calibers and degree of complication created a no-win situation in Ripley's view. Faster-firing guns in the hands of untested soldiers often led to wasted ammunition, which was heavy and expensive. Inexperienced soldiers in the heat of battle were likely to fire as fast as they could, often dropping weapons, ammunition, and gear before running away in panic. Ripley understood that more advanced weaponry was not self-evidently better in the field, and his conservatism was the norm in military circles.[12]

Lincoln did understand this concept and rarely overruled Ripley and officers in the field if they felt they knew better. John Hay acknowledged that "Lincoln had a quick comprehension of mechanical principles and often detected a flaw in an invention which the contriver had overlooked."[13] But just as keenly he understood how some mechanics could be useful, so Lincoln continued to push the idea of advancing weaponry as much as was practical. When something of particular value in his mind came along, he was more assertive in telling Ripley and others to put it into circulation. One example was the Spencer repeating rifle.

Most breech-loading rifles were still single-shot weapons. The Spencer had a seven-round tube magazine that loaded from the butt of the rifle, feeding each shell into the breech with a lever that expelled the spent shell. Experienced users could fire twenty rounds per minute, compared to only two or three with a muzzleloader. The short barrel made it perfect for cavalry, which was its main use both during and after the Civil War. Lincoln personally tested the rifle. Spencer had a private meeting with the president, who found the mechanism fascinating. Spencer later suggested, perhaps a bit hyperbolically, that Lincoln put the rifle back together after watching Spencer take it apart and lay the parts on the table. The next day, Lincoln and Spencer went out to the field behind the White House, set up a board "about six inches wide and three feet high, with a black spot on either end, about forty yards away." Six of Lincoln's seven shots hit close to the bull's-eye. John Hay, Lincoln's secretary, admitted that "the President made some pretty good shots."[14]

Finding the Spencer repeating rifle to be a sufficient advancement, Lincoln overruled Ripley's reticence and ordered the military to purchase ten thousand units for distribution. By the end of the war, nearly one hundred thousand Spencer rifles and carbines were in service.[15] Various breechloaders, rifles, carbines, and repeaters by Spencer, Enfield, Sharps, Whitworth, Springfield, and others played important roles in the war, including Berdan's sharpshooters at Gettysburg and the critical Battle of Chickamauga.

Another type of advanced weapon that Lincoln promoted was the multishot guns we might refer to as "machine guns." Technically called the "Union Repeating Gun" by its salesman, J. D. Mills, one was dubbed by Lincoln the "coffee-mill" gun due to its resemblance to that faithful brewer of morning sustenance. A single barrel was fed by bullets dropped into a hopper, then fired using a hand crank mounted on the rear. In August 1861, Lincoln wrote Ripley: "If ten of the repeating guns, of the pattern exhibited to me this morning, by Mr. Mills, near the Washington Monument in this City, shall be well made, and furnished to the government of the U.S. within, or about thirty days from this date, I advise that the government pay for them double the sum which good mechanics of that class shall say the material, and labor of making and delivering here are worth."[16] Getting further concurrence of General McClellan on the potential usefulness in battle, in December Lincoln told Ripley to "let the fifty guns be ordered."[17]

Lincoln never stopped looking for better versions of weapons he had pushed. In the middle of 1862 Lincoln showed he understood the mechanics of repeating weapons in a letter to Stanton: "I have examined and seen tried the 'Raphael Repeater' and consider it a decided improvement upon what was called the 'Coffee Mill Gun' in . . . that it is better arranged to prevent the escape of gas."[18] Later in the war, another repeating weapon was introduced by Dr. Richard Gatling. He claimed that "it is regarded, by all who have seen it operate, as the most effective implement of warfare invented during the war, and it is just the thing needed to aid in crushing the present rebellion" (underlining in original). To ensure no confusion with what he saw an inferior product, "I assure you my invention is no 'coffee mill gun.'"[19] Rather than a single barrel, the Gatling had six barrels capable of firing up to 350 rounds a minute. Repeating weapons of varying types were employed occasionally during the war, for example, at Middleburg in 1862, but typically these pieces were limited to guarding locations such as bridges, being too unwieldy for infantry movements.[20]

Lincoln was perhaps too closely involved in one weapons test. He frequently visited the Washington Navy Yard to discuss weapons and strategy with Captain Dahlgren, a like-minded acolyte of technology. In late 1862, Lincoln, Secretary of State William Seward, and Secretary of Treasury Salmon P. Chase went down to the banks of the Anacostia River to witness testing of the Hyde rocket. Instead of shooting off across the river, the rocket exploded, nearly sending shrapnel into the group of distinguished leaders, all of whom escaped unharmed. Lincoln skipped the next trial two days later when the rocket flew out of control and landed on the roof of a nearby blacksmith shop.[21]

BEYOND WEAPONRY—RAILROADING THE WINNING STRATEGY

Railroads probably contributed more to the North winning the Civil War than advanced weaponry. Lincoln understood the importance of the railroad to overall strategy and quickly moved to shift control of railways from private companies to the military. He saw how the Manassas Gap Railroad had carried many of Confederate General Joseph Johnston's men to the front, thereby providing the reinforcements that turned an apparent Union victory at the First Battle of Bull Run into a Confederate rout. The Baltimore & Ohio Railroad later accomplished a similar feat, transporting nearly twenty-five thousand men from Virginia to Chattanooga to keep that city under Union control.[22]

The North was better positioned to take advantage of the railroads than the South. Not only did they have more than twice as many miles of track at the beginning of the war, the North's rail lines were connected in a network while the South's were predominantly built from cotton fields to seaports with limited interconnections.[23] Lincoln had watched railroads grow from an expensive afterthought in the early days of internal improvements to the dominant mode of travel and commerce. His legal work for the railroads had made him many connections at executive levels, whose favors he called upon to facilitate railroad traffic and expansion when the war started. Samuel Felton, president of the Philadelphia, Wilmington & Baltimore Railroad, had been instrumental in discovering the plot to assassinate Lincoln in Baltimore on his way to Washington for the inauguration.[24]

Lincoln also had a habit of collecting acquaintances with other technically minded people. There was Joseph Henry and Louis Agassiz for science, and there was John Dahlgren, Montgomery Meigs, and the highly skilled, if somewhat irascible, railroad engineer Herman Haupt for technology. Lincoln and Stanton had given Haupt almost total control over the railroad system, and Haupt's efforts to transport troops and supplies to Gettysburg dramatically assisted the Union success. Early in 1862, when Lincoln was visiting General Irwin McDowell's army in Fredericksburg, Haupt accompanied him to a new bridge across Potomac Creek. After returning to Washington, Lincoln mentioned that he had "seen the most remarkable structure that human eyes ever rested upon. That man Haupt has built a bridge across Potomac Creek, about 400 feet long and nearly 100 feet high, over which loaded trains are running every hour, and, upon my word, gentlemen, there is nothing in it but beanpoles and cornstalks."[25]

While pressing his generals to be more aggressive—he complained McClellan had the "slows"—Lincoln continued to consider the strategic value of railroads in wartime. He encouraged the destruction of the South's railroad hubs and supply lines in hopes it would speed the end of the war. Haupt was adept at rebuilding tracks and bridges, facilitated by the more advanced industrial capacity of the North. The South was limited in such capacity, making it harder for them to repair tracks and keep locomotives running.[26] Several inventors wrote to Lincoln with methods for "making torn up rails useless by twisting them out of shape," since simply bending them could be reversed. Another claimed he had a machine that would either curl or straighten rails as needed.[27] Lincoln was finally happy with his generals when they started following his suggestions. General William Sherman, for example, left a three-hundred-mile trail of destruction on his late 1864 March to the Sea, including burning "railroads and telegraph lines."[28] Sherman's use of railroad-track-twisting technology, contorting rails into unredeemable tangles, gained them the nickname "Sherman's Neck Ties."[29]

Lincoln had assumed sweeping power to nationalize the North's privately owned railroad system when Congress passed the Railways and Telegraph Act, which created the United States Military Railroad (USMRR). The government could take for military use any railway line as needed, and could impress any railroad employee into service in a war zone. Lincoln rarely had to force companies into compliance though, as they quickly saw the benefit of supporting the Union effort. During the war, the USMRR cooperated with private companies to buy, build, or capture 419 locomotives and 6,330 cars. The railroad was crucial to moving the infantry to the front. Railcars also transported heavy gun batteries and mortars, as well as served as movable command cars.[30]

AN IRONCLAD FUTURE

Lincoln also played a vital role in the development of ironclad warships. His life on the waters had impressed upon him the great importance of the Mississippi River, then for transport and commerce, now as a military strategy. If the North could get control of the lower river, they could effectively cut the South in two, separating the three western states from the eastern states of the Confederacy. Lincoln discussed this overarching goal with General Winfield Scott, who devised what became known as the Anaconda Plan of coastal blockades in tandem with troop movements to snake down the Mississippi River. Some of the earliest ironclads in the North were river gunships designed to accomplish this plan.[31]

Most of the limited number of warships available to the North at the beginning of the war were large wooden sailing vessels, the backbone of all previous navies. The ships in the Gosport Navy Yard in Norfolk had been scuttled and set afire by the Union when Virginia seceded to keep them away from the Confederacy. Among several wooden ships burned was the USS *Merrimack*, sunk down to its hull. But the job had not been done thoroughly enough; Southern forces recovered the ship and encased its newly rebuilt decks with iron sheets. Renamed the CSS *Virginia* (but still called the *Merrimack* by many, both then and today), the new ironclad ship became the South's biggest threat to the Union navy. Secretary of Navy Gideon Welles immediately advertised for designs for a Union ironclad vessel. Swedish American inventor John Ericsson answered the call.[32]

Ericsson was no stranger to the navy, but not in a good way. The navy had scapegoated Ericsson for a cannon mishap on board the USS *Princeton* in 1844, which resulted in the deaths of two cabinet members and nearly injuring then-president John Tyler. Ericsson was coaxed to present his plans for an ironclad he had designed several years before, one that had impressed Napoleon III, although the French leader had passed on purchasing any. Ericsson wrote to Lincoln in August 1861 telling him that, despite his previous mistreatment by the navy, "attachment to the Union alone impels me to offer my services at this fearful crisis—my life if need be—in the great cause which Providence has called you to defend."[33] At a preliminary demonstration of the model presented by Ericsson promoter Cornelius Bushnell, Lincoln "made a careful study of what was said to resemble a cheese-box on a raft," after which he effectively became a salesman for the design before the Ironclad Board.[34] Shortly thereafter, despite the lingering mutual displeasure between the old-guard navy men constituting the Ironclad Board and a disgruntled Ericsson, but with Lincoln's support ("it seems to me there is something in it"), Ericsson received a contract to build the USS *Monitor*. Soon after the *Monitor* had been built, but before the normal training cruises, it was Lincoln pressing the case to get the *Monitor* down to Hampton Roads as the *Virginia* was about to begin its short, but destructive, reign of terror.

Lincoln featured in another significant event in ironclad warfare. On March 8, 1862, the *Virginia* (*Merrimack*) destroyed two Union wooden-hulled ships in Hampton Roads. The *Monitor* arrived the next day and fought the *Virginia* to a draw, successfully preventing further damage. Both vessels retreated for repairs. The next day Lincoln visited *Monitor*'s commander Lieutenant John Worden, recuperating after receiving wounds to his eyes during the battle. Lincoln wrote Gideon Welles to express his concerns after speaking with Worden. Demonstrating his inherent understanding of mechanical devices, Lincoln warned that the *Monitor* "could be boarded and captured very easily—first, after boarding, by wedging the turret, so that it would not turn, and then by pouring water in her & drowning her machinery." He warned Welles to "not go sky-larking up to Norfolk."[35] But skylarking to Norfolk was exactly what Lincoln did two months later. On May 5, 1862, Lincoln, Secretary of War Edwin Stanton, Secretary of the Treasury Salmon Chase, and other dignitaries set sail on the revenue cutter *Miami* for Fort Monroe. With driving rain and stormy seas, even Lincoln felt sick and unable to eat, according to Chase, who suffered the same fate. During their trip, they stopped off to tour the eponymously named ocean steamer provided to the navy by wealthy magnate Cornelius Vanderbilt. After arriving at Fort Monroe, they sailed out into Hampton Roads and toured the *Monitor*, now improved with a new steam pump and engines in preparation for their next encounter with the *Virginia*. The *Monitor*'s paymaster, William Keeler, reported that Lincoln "examined these vessels with much care, making the most detailed inquiries as to their construction and operation." He would have seen the dented turret made by the *Virginia*'s cannonballs, along with the rebuilt and modified pilothouse where Lt. Worden had been injured.[36]

As the week progressed, Lincoln would get close enough to see the *Virginia* sitting off Craney Island. The stage was set for another *Monitor–Virginia* battle, a battle that would never take place, in part due to Lincoln's actions. Frustrated by his military's slow movement, Lincoln served as his own commanding general in Hampton Roads, directing and pushing for the taking of Norfolk and the Gosport Navy Yard in nearby Portsmouth. Lincoln "had been listening to a Pilot & studying a chart," according to Chase, "and wished to go see" a "nearer landing" he had identified. He even guided the landing party onto Confederate-held soil for a place where the Union Army to make their trek into the city as it was being abandoned by the Confederates.[37]

Meanwhile, all this activity being directed by Lincoln created problems for the CSS *Virginia*. Unwilling to take on the *Monitor* and its supporting ships, the *Virginia*'s commander began preparations to run his ship up the James River. Unfortunately, removing ballast to reduce how low the ship drafted was not sufficient for the *Virginia* to move into shallower water. Having now lightened the load, the ship was no longer stable in deeper water, so not in a position to fight its way out to the sea. Facing an unfathomable situation, commander Josiah Tattnall opted to save his crew for the future and destroy the *Virginia* to keep it out of Union hands. Lincoln and others could see the burning hulk from the *Monitor* and Fort Monroe. The Confederacy's first ironclad was no more.

As they made their way back to Washington on the USS *Baltimore*, Secretary Chase wrote his daughter. "So ended a brilliant week's campaign of the President," Chase wrote. He was "quite certain that if [Lincoln] had not come down, Norfolk would still have been in the possession of the enemy & the *Merrimac* as grim & defiant & as much a terror as ever."[38]

This was the only case of a sitting president taking active command of troops in the field during a time of war. By the time Lincoln returned to the Washington Navy Yard on May 12, news of the capture of Norfolk and the destruction of the *Virginia* had already reached the city. Lincoln was greeted as a conquering hero. The *Monitor* never did get its second encounter with the *Virginia*, and it too would find a watery grave not long after in a storm. But the age of wooden sailing ships was over. The age of iron ships had begun.

And submarines. Because the Confederacy had fewer men, less extensive rail lines, and limited manufacturing capacity, they had to be innovative.[39] The South developed ironclads, torpedoes (what we now call underwater mines), and other inventive ways to counter their deficiencies while the North had less need for new weaponry, as James Ripley was keen to reiterate at every opportunity. The Confederate *Hunley* was the first submarine to sink an enemy's warship when it sunk the USS *Housatonic* in February 1864. Unfortunately for the Confederacy, the *Hunley*'s two unsuccessful test trials and one successful mission, after which it sunk and was lost for 150 years, killed more of its own crew than it did Union seamen. The Union also had a submarine, although it too had little impact on the success of the war. Within a few months after the attack on Fort Sumter, a French engineer by the name of Brutus de Villeroi wrote to Lincoln offering his submersible vessel dubbed the *Alligator*. As with other inventions he thought could be useful, Lincoln "Respectfully submitted" the idea to the Navy Department. A contract was signed and the twenty-crew-member, fifty-foot-long iron submarine was accepted by the navy. Lincoln observed the *Alligator* in operation in the spring of 1863. Soon after, the submarine sank in bad weather before it had seen combat action. Submarines would have to wait for future wars to be useful.[40]

BALLOONING WARFARE
Lincoln also looked to the skies to give every advantage to Union troops. Researcher Charles M. Evans notes that Pennsylvanian John Wise is often credited with being the first American to make significant contributions to the science of ballooning, including atmospheric conditions and construction.[41] He was joined early in the war by James Allen. But it was Thaddeus Lowe who had the most success engaging Lincoln and getting a contract to form an air corps. Lowe hooked up with Smithsonian

Secretary Joseph Henry, and together they impressed Lincoln enough to gain his support. Lincoln repeatedly tried to get his first secretary of war, Simon Cameron, and General-in-Chief Winfield Scott to employ Lowe. Lincoln wrote General Scott on July 25, 1861, saying, "Will Lieut. Genl. Scott please see Professor Lowe, once more about his balloon."[42] When Scott still failed to act, Lincoln reportedly became more assertive, ordering Scott to "facilitate his work in every way."[43] Lowe eventually fielded a dozen balloons and made over three thousand ascensions using tethered balloons inflated by portable hydrogen gas generators.[44] Lincoln gave Lowe the civilian title of chief aeronaut of the Union Army.

Lowe was an effective self-promoter who knew whose favors to garner. Joseph Henry had gotten him in the front door, Lincoln had gotten him a contract with General Scott, and his greatest use of balloons for reconnaissance was during General McClellan's Peninsula campaign. To ingratiate himself with McClellan, Lowe put a picture of the general on the back of one of his biggest balloons, the *Intrepid*.[45] But Lowe used another gimmick—he ran a telegraph line to the tethered balloon to report back in real time enemy troop numbers and movements. To ensure he maintained connection with the highest authority, on June 16, 1861, Lowe lifted his balloon *Enterprise* up near the White House and sent a telegraph to Lincoln: "This point of observation commands an area near fifty miles in diameter. . . . I have the pleasure of sending you this first dispatch ever telegraphed from an aerial station and in acknowledging indebtedness to your encouragement for the opportunity of demonstrating the availability of the science of aeronautics in the military service of the country."[46]

There were others who promoted balloons to Lincoln, although he quickly realized that some of them were cranks. Beginning early in 1861 and continuing throughout the Civil War, the prolific Edward L. Tippett sent many letters to Lincoln touting every possible invention, including balloons for warfare. One letter seemed to have caught Lincoln at a bad time in February 1865. In a long rambling letter, Tippett wanted the opportunity to demonstrate to Lincoln "the practicability; by a mathematical problem, easy to understand; of the absolute existence, of a self-moving machine, yet to be developed for the glory of God, and the happiness of the human family." Unimpressed, Lincoln endorsed the outside of the envelope: "Tippett: Crazy Man."[47]

TELEGRAPHING THE FUTURE

Contrary to telegraph operator David Homer Bates's claim that Lincoln had seen his first telegraph by watching Charles Tinker only a few years before the war, Lincoln had encountered "lightning messages" shortly after its first arrival in Springfield in 1848. His actual first use was a telegram to Simeon Francis dated June 9, 1848, reporting that Zachary Taylor had been nominated for president at the Whig convention. The telegram had been reprinted in the *Illinois Daily Journal* newspaper. Lincoln regularly used the telegraph in both legal and political capacities for the next decade.[48]

The first telegraph message—"What Hath God Wrought?"—was sent by Samuel F. B. Morse from Washington, DC, to Baltimore in 1844. Morse had used technology developed by Joseph Henry to commercialize "instant messaging," but it had never been used strategically in wartime.[49] Telegraphy had grown rapidly, literally alongside the railroads as most early telegraph lines followed the railroad gradings being built.[50] This communication helped the railroad companies grow into huge corporations, aided the standardization of timetables, and facilitated the westward migration of people and commerce. Lincoln used the telegraph to direct battle plans.

But first he needed access. When the war started there was no telegraph line running to the War Department offices next to the White House, never mind into the president's mansion itself.

As the First Battle at Bull Run raged, aging and largely immobile General-in-Chief Winfield Scott took a nap, accustomed to the traditional lack of communication during battles. Lincoln was more intent for news, spending hours in the War Department while army engineers like Andrew Carnegie strung telegraph wires into northern Virginia, never quite reaching the front as men on horseback rushed to deliver information.[51] A year later, at the second battle near Bull Run Creek, Lincoln was actively monitoring telegraph messages as the battle ensued. According to Bates, "when in the telegraph office, Lincoln was most at ease of access. He often talked with the cipher-operators (all messages were put into codes), asking questions about the dispatches which were translating from or into cipher."[52]

Lincoln was aided by the fact that he appointed Thomas A. Scott, vice president of the Pennsylvania Railroad, as assistant secretary of war, along with Edward S. Sanford, president of the American Telegraph Company, whom he put in charge of military telegraphs.[53] Similar to what he did with railroads using the power of congressional acts, Lincoln effectively nationalized the country's telegraph network and put it under control of the military.[54] Lincoln used the telegraph sparingly early in the war, sending no more than twenty telegrams throughout 1861. But after taking control in early 1862, Lincoln became an avid reader and sender of telegrams to more actively manage generals in the field, in particular those like McClellan who seemed eager to train troops but not to use them in combat.[55]

But use the telegraph Lincoln did. The value of the telegraph was reinforced daily. Lincoln received many messages over the new Pacific and Atlantic telegraph that began operation in October of 1861, including one from Governor-Elect Leland Stanford noting, "Today California is but a second's distance from the national Capital." Stanford went on to become president of the Central Pacific Railroad, the western leg of the transcontinental railroad system Lincoln signed into existence in 1862.[56] The first transcontinental telegraph message was sent from California Chief Justice Stephen Field in San Francisco to Lincoln in Washington over the Western Union telegraph lines. Lincoln would appoint Field as the newly created tenth U.S. Supreme Court justice.

Lincoln occasionally used telegrams to vent his frustration, most often at General McClellan. In early October 1862, a month after the Battle of Antietam, with little or no movement on the part of McClellan's army, Lincoln wrote a long letter that included: "You know I desired ... you to cross the Potomac below, instead of above the Shenandoah and Blue Ridge. My idea was that this would at once menace the enemies' communications, which I would seize if he would permit." He laid out specific goals and strategies regarding cutting off communications, and then should the opportunity exist, "try to beat him to Richmond on the inside track." All too familiar with McClellan's tendency not to fight, Lincoln added, "I say 'try'; if we never try, we shall never succeed." When McClellan complained about tired horses, Lincoln shot back by telegraph: "I have just read your dispatch about sore tongued and fatigued horses. Will you pardon me for asking what the horses of your army have done since the battle of Antietam that fatigue anything?"[57] Lincoln removed McClellan from command a few weeks later.

The lack of urgency from his generals meant Lincoln often became his own general-in-chief, much of which he accomplished by telegraph. In May 1862, Lincoln sent a flurry of telegrams directing his generals in an attempt to trap Confederate General Stonewall Jackson in the Shenandoah Valley of western Virginia. Telling Union General John C. Fremont to "put the utmost speed in it," Lincoln implored, "Do not lose a minute." Lincoln continued to press his military to action in the valley, but despite these efforts, Jackson still outmaneuvered the Union generals and escaped.[58] Later in the war, Lincoln was able to back away from direct management of war strategy because he had growing confidence in Generals Ulysses S. Grant, William T. Sherman, and Philip Sheridan. He still spent much of his day in the telegraph office, but mostly to get news of the war, not personally micromanage it.

Telegraph lines helped the North communicate better than the South even with the constant need to lay new lines as the battlefront moved and to repair lines cut by enemy raiders. They were also used by the new "wire services" like the Associated Press to fill newspapers with war news.[59] One further use of the telegraph was paramount to both the war effort and Lincoln's political fortunes. In the summer of 1864, Lincoln thought he was going to lose his reelection bid. He wrote what has become known as the "blind memorandum," which stated that if he should lose the election, "it will be my duty to so co-operate with the President elect, as to save the Union between the election and the inauguration; as he will have secured his election on such ground that he cannot possibly save it afterwards."[60] Soon after everyone in his cabinet signed the back of the folded memo without reading it, military successes by Sherman and Sheridan changed the tide of public sentiment. But Lincoln also got a boost from Nevada, which became a state just a few days before the November election. The timing was so close that the 175 handwritten pages of the state constitution were telegraphed. Since there was no single direct line to Washington, the process took twelve hours to tap out the document from Carson City, Nevada, to Salt Lake City, Utah. The process was then repeated from Salt Lake to Chicago, and again to Philadelphia, and finally to Washington, DC. Without the telegraph, the constitution would not have arrived in time for it to be voted on in Congress so Nevada could give its three electoral votes to Lincoln for his second term. Total cost? About sixty thousand dollars in today's currency.[61]

Nevada was important for another reason. Its gold and silver mines contributed hundreds of millions to the war effort, helping relieve the vast financial burden of the ongoing war. Lincoln identified Nevada as the approximate location where the transcontinental railroad might connect (it ended up in Utah).[62] Lincoln had used a mining metaphor to open up his lecture on discoveries and inventions and was cognizant of mining as a significant resource in the West. This awareness of the natural resource and scientific aspects of economic growth helped him understand that many of the challenges of war were scientific, not just technological.

CHAPTER 13

The Science of War

LINCOLN TOOK A SCIENTIFIC APPROACH TO MILITARY STRATEGY. THE Anaconda Plan's focus was on securing the coastlines and the Mississippi River. Recognizing New Orleans as the hub of the cotton trade and commerce, Lincoln saw it as the first port to be targeted for blockade. He also hoped to block Southern ship traffic from Charleston, South Carolina, to cut off Confederate attempts to woo Great Britain and France to their side. Helping him make this happen was Alexander Dallas Bache and the Coast Survey. The Coast Survey had been authorized by Thomas Jefferson, and Bache, who was Benjamin Franklin's great-grandson, was quick to send nautical charts of the Chesapeake Bay to Lincoln. He also forwarded two terrestrial maps produced by the survey that had far-reaching influence on Lincoln's decisions on emancipation and military strategy.[1]

The first map was of the state of Virginia. A relatively new technique of color-coded shading was used to show the percentage of enslaved population in each county based on the 1860 census. The darker-shaded counties reflecting higher percentages of enslaved persons were primarily in the tidewater region and toward the southern part of the state. The mountainous western counties held only small percentages of enslaved. That told Lincoln the western counties were less likely to support the insurrection, and indeed, those counties rejoined the Union as the new state of West Virginia.

The second map showed the entire slaveholding portion of the country. Lincoln quickly recognized that the four "border" states—Missouri, Kentucky, Maryland, and Delaware—had relatively few slaves in most of their counties. That fact helped inform Lincoln's strategies to retain the border states in the Union, including proposals for gradual compensated emancipation in an effort to stimulate the process of freeing the enslaved.[2] The map also clearly showed that eastern Tennessee had relatively few slaves, which again allowed him to target that region for initial military and diplomatic forays in the hope many of the residents would retain their Union sentiments. Also clear was that the highest densities of enslaved populations were in the cotton belt of the Deep South and along the Mississippi River borders of Louisiana, Mississippi, and Arkansas, where over 90 percent of the populations of some counties were enslaved. The map reinforced the importance of capturing New Orleans to cut off the main supply and transport line for the Confederate economy. Controlling the Mississippi was the key to the war, which "could never be brought to a close until that key is in our pocket."[3] It also reinforced the belief that the Deep South was so dependent on slavery it would never willingly give it up. Lincoln found this second map especially fascinating, according to Francis Carpenter, who spent six months at the White House preparing his famous painting *First Reading of the Emancipation Proclamation by President Lincoln*. Carpenter added the Southern slavery map to the lower right corner of his painting, reflecting its significance to the decision-making process.[4]

A LITTLE ELECTROMAGNETISM

Bache and Joseph Henry assisted Lincoln with another scientific problem that arose with the shift from wooden vessels to ironclads—all that iron siding confused the ship's compasses, which meant navigation became a nightmare. The basic physics of magnetism was stymieing this technological advance.[5]

Henry had significant experience with magnetism. He had developed a powerful electromagnet at Princeton prior to taking over the Smithsonian. The magnet was a precursor to the modern direct current motor, further commercialized by others, including Thomas Edison and Nikola Tesla. Henry's discoveries also made the telegraph feasible, a fact that Samuel F. B. Morse later refused to acknowledge when he expanded on Henry's ideas.[6] Lincoln was no stranger to compasses either, having used a brass-encased compass during his surveying days. He also had a rudimentary understanding of electricity. Back when he was traveling between debates as an Illinois state legislator, Lincoln passed the home of George Forquer, the man he was about to debate. Forquer had been a Whig but switched to the Democratic Party and, suspiciously, was immediately appointed to the lucrative political position of register of the Land Office. Many questioned his motives and integrity, including Lincoln in the *Sangamo Journal*. Soon after his appointment, Forquer built a wooden-frame house, the best house in Springfield, and erected a lightning rod to protect it. It was the only such rod in the county and the first time Lincoln ever came across one.

Lincoln, of course, queried about how the rod worked. None of his companions knew, so Lincoln rode into town and, according to his close friend Joshua Speed, bought a book on the properties of lightning so as to inform his knowledge. His later law partner, William Herndon, said that Lincoln told him the incident led him to study the properties of electricity and the utility of the rod as a conductor.[7]

But in 1836 the lightning rod was a novelty. After Lincoln gave his speech in Springfield, Forquer stood up to give a rebuttal, saying, "This young man will have to be taken down; and I'm truly sorry that the task devolves to me." He then responded to Lincoln's speech with a great deal of condescension and moral superiority. Lincoln watched silently, then retook the stage and began, "Mr. Forquer commenced his speech by announcing that the young man would have to be taken down. It is for you, fellow citizens, not for me to say whether I am up or down." Suggesting that he is not up on the tricks and trades of politicians, and referring to his recent discovery, he continued: "I desire place and distinction; but I would rather die now than, like the gentleman, live to see the day that I would change my politics for an office worth three thousand dollars a year, and then feel compelled to erect a lightning rod to protect a guilty conscience from an offended God."[8]

Lincoln had become conversant enough in the concepts of electricity and magnetism that in an 1858 Chicago speech just prior to his debates with Stephen A. Douglas he spoke of the "electric cord" in the Declaration of Independence "that links the hearts of patriotic and liberty-loving men together."[9]

When Bache and Henry and the National Academy of Sciences took on the compass problem, Lincoln comprehended the issue even if he was not knowledgeable enough to devise a solution. The Navy Department called for the formation of Committee No. 3, generally referred to as the Compass Committee, to "investigate and report upon the subject of magnetic deviation in iron ships." Compasses are necessary to ensure ships steer in the right direction, especially on dark nights and in stormy seas. They worked fine with the wood-hulled ships that made up the majority of all warships until that time. But now both North and South were hurriedly covering the decks and hulls above the waterline with plates of iron, which presented a unique problem—the iron-clad hulls attracted the magnetism of the compass and made them useless. The large masses of iron a few feet from the compasses caused a large and variable amount of deviation of the magnetized needle.

Various solutions were attempted, some of which seemed counterintuitive, such as placing the compasses on thick iron pots or putting them in zinc cases packed with charcoal. The Compass Committee eliminated these ineffective methods and settled on a method invented by an English astronomer that consisted of placing bar magnets in locations around the compass to counteract the local attraction. To test this solution, the committee supervised the correction of compasses on twenty-seven vessels of all kinds—sloops, monitors, gunboats, propellers, side-wheel steamers, tugs, and transports. Alexander Bache provided two staff to work full-time for six months making magnetic observations on a standard ironclad in the Brooklyn Navy Yard, as well as additional experiments on an ironclad at Charlestown Navy Yard in Boston. Without the NAS, the Union navy may have been hamstrung by its compasses failing when they were most needed.[10]

The government also asked the NAS to investigate how to solve another recurring problem associated with the new ironclads—rust. All that iron plating hanging in salt water oxidized over time and became fragile and heavy. After about eight months of research, the evaluation committee issued a report saying that, while many plans to protect iron hulls had been devised, none were sufficiently effective to warrant recommendations. They were working at a disadvantage. Only in modern days did scientific investigation start looking at the compositions of paints and the effectiveness of different mixtures against corrosion or a second problem—fouling by barnacles and other sea creatures who found the iron plating perfect for attachment. The committee did recommend experiments to be tried, but they never happened.[11]

Other NAS committees active during the Civil War looked at the uniformity of weights and measures, the veracity of Saxton's alcoholometer, the reliability of previous wind and current charts, and surprisingly, tests to determine the purity of whiskey, the expansion of steam, and the manufacture of cent coins. Another committee conducted an investigation into an explosion on the steamer *Chenango*, a double-bowed ship with a bow and rudder at each end.[12]

A CLIMATE OF CHANGE

Lincoln was acutely aware of the natural world around him. He had learned some forest ecology, agronomy, and hydrology while growing up on the farm, and he spent many weeks sleeping under the stars while riding the legal circuit. Somehow, despite a life in landlocked states, he learned about ocean species. In a political speech in 1852, he mentioned codfish, found only in the Atlantic and Pacific Oceans.[13] He mentioned whales in his lecture on discoveries and inventions.[14] In his debates with Stephen A. Douglas he accused his opponent of trying to distract from a failed argument by "playing cuttlefish," which Lincoln explained was "a small species of fish that has no mode of defending itself when pursued except by throwing out a black fluid, which makes the water so dark the enemy cannot see it and thus it escapes."[15] Interestingly, when it came to his Anaconda Plan (named after a snake endemic only to South America), there was some debate as to whether the snake was the most appropriate analogy. Lucius Chittenden, who served as Lincoln's register of the Treasury, wrote that some in the Potomac Naturalists Club active in Washington during and after the war believed a giant octopus was a better fit. The octopus, cuttlefish, or squid had long arms and suckers that reach into all areas of enemy territory, overpowering it in many places at the same time. That fit Lincoln's military strategy exactly; he repeatedly advocated for his generals "to move at once upon the enemy's whole line so as to bring into action to our advantage our great superiority in numbers." He informed Henry Halleck and General Don Buell in January 1862 that his "general idea of this war [is] to be that we have the *greater* numbers, and the enemy has the *greater* facility of concentrating forces upon points of collision; that we must fail, unless we can find some way of making *our* advantage an over-match of *his*; and this can only be done by menacing him with superior forces at *different* points, at the *same* time." A multiarmed cuttlefish would do nicely, in Lincoln's mathematical estimation.[16]

Environmental factors played an important role in troop movements. Lincoln knew well from his days on the circuit about trying to travel during the snows of winter or rains of spring. Weather was as much a factor in battle plans as troop strength. Cold and rain and mud made military movements nearly impossible much of the time, and woolen uniforms became unbearable in the heat of the summer. Joseph Henry in the 1850s had arranged for a system of weather reporters sending telegraph reports each morning from all over the country. The information was posted at the Smithsonian and published, although no attempt was made to forecast future weather. Henry's weather system was disrupted when the Civil War began.[17] Without even this rudimentary information, unexpected bad weather could lead to armies mired in mud, epitomized by General Burnside's "Mud March" in early 1863 at Rappahannock and General McClellan's failures in the Peninsula Campaign.[18]

A talented weatherman would be invaluable. Since Abraham Lincoln was a magnet for every self-avowed inventor and expert, one man claiming to be a "Certified Practical Meteorologist & Expert in Computing the Changes of the Weather" reached out to "His Excellency, The President."

Francis L. Capen wrote to Lincoln on April 25, 1863. "It would give me great pleasure," Capen wrote, "to assure you of the fine weather suitable for a visit to the front or for starting an Expedition fraught with momentous interests to the Country." Offering his services, Capen added, "Please refer me, favorably to the War Department. I will guarantee to furnish Meteorological information that will save many a serious sacrifice." To nail down his point further, Capen enclosed his calling card, on which he wrote: "Thousands of lives & millions of dollars may be saved by the application of Science to the War." Lincoln was intrigued. Having access to a professional meteorologist could provide a much-needed advantage to the floundering war effort. Lincoln invited Capen to visit the White House for what effectively was a job interview. After the meeting, however, Lincoln was less than impressed.

On the back of Capen's original letter Lincoln vented: "It seems to me Mr. Capen knows nothing about the weather, in advance. He told me three days ago that it would not rain again till the 30th of April or 1st of May. It is raining now & has been for ten hours—I cannot spare any more time to Mr. Capen. A. Lincoln."

So much for having a professional meteorologist helping the war effort.[19] After the war, Henry was able to reconstitute his nationwide weather collection system, which became the precursor to today's national weather service.

Another weather-related phenomenon that affected conduct of the war was something neither Lincoln nor many others had heard of at the time—acoustic shadows. Communication during battle was difficult under the best conditions. Telegraph lines could be rigged from command post to headquarters but were not possible in the actual battlefield. A clear sight line from a nearby hill gave the best feedback, but often by exposing commanders to great risk, and would become useless after clouds of cannon and musket smoke saturated the field. Signaling with semaphore flags or at night with torches or calcium lights had similar visual limitations. Therefore, sound was commonly used to provide generals with information about the course of the battle. Commanders would often tell their subordinate generals to listen for signals to attack. But what if you could not hear any sound?

Henry, who among his many other duties was a member of the Light-House Board, had experienced similar acoustic lapses leading to nautical misfortunes. He had transformed the board into a center for applied research in optics, thermodynamics, and acoustics.[20] He likely helped Lincoln understand the experiences his generals were reporting at several important battles, although Henry disagreed on its cause with Irish scientist John Tyndall, who was simultaneously studying the anomaly using data from Henry's own Light-House Board.

Sound waves spread in a similar way as the concentric circles made after dropping a small object into a still pond. They are affected by their own frequency as well as by absorption and redirection by the atmosphere, ground, obstructions, refraction, temperature, and wind. Very low- or very high-frequency sounds become harder to hear than more moderate sounds, so the sound of cannon fire may not carry as far as that of a rifle. Sound may be absorbed by foliage or be refracted upward due to temperature differences in the air or wind shear. Sometimes those close by cannot hear the sound of battle while those far away can hear it clearly. This phenomenon can have dire consequences in battles where sound signals are key to military strategy.

In Iuka, Mississippi, for example, Ulysses S. Grant had planned a simultaneous pincer attack on Confederate soldiers. He ordered General Ord to hold his engagement until he heard the sounds of General Rosecrans attacking from the south. Apparently neither Ord nor Grant heard the sound of Rosecrans's guns despite battle raging for hours just out of sight, and Ord never attacked. Had Ord engaged, significant injury to the Confederate army of Major Sterling Price would have occurred. Similar complications were experienced during battles at Fort Donelson, Seven Pines, Perryville, Chancellorsville, and Five Forks. The occurrence was also noted by a Confederate soldier watching the battle of the ironclads at Hampton Roads; he could not hear any sound even though he could see fierce cannonades ahead of him.[21]

Recalling his surveying days, Lincoln often thought in mathematical terms when discussing military strategy with his generals. Besides being frustrated by McClellan's "slows," Lincoln thought that McClellan was lacking in strategic judgment. Pushing him to move, Lincoln pointed out that "a circle whose circumference shall pass through Harper's Ferry, Front-Royal, and Strasburg, and whose center shall be a little North East of Winchester, almost certainly has within it this morning, the forces of Jackson, Ewell, and Edward Johnson." He added that General Shields "retook Front Royal . . . one hundred and fifty of the enemy, two locomotives and eleven cars, some other property and stores, and saved the bridge," showing he understood the technological and strategic importance of the area. If he expected his logic to get McClellan moving, he was mistaken.[22]

Lincoln's self-study of Euclid's geometry was evident in his use of geometry terms in the Gettysburg Address. Researchers Hirsch and Van Haften have delineated the address and other Lincoln writings and demonstrated that both Lincoln and Thomas Jefferson in his Declaration of Independence employed Euclid's six elements in constructing speeches and writings.[23] But whereas Jefferson considered "all men are created equal" as a self-evident axiom, Lincoln referred to it as a proposition, that is, something to be proven by action over time. Democracy, Lincoln sought to demonstrate, took continual work to maintain, and the Civil War was a test to determine if it "could long endure."[24]

OF SALTPETER AND COAL—NATURAL RESOURCES IN WARTIME

Two other scientific issues plagued Lincoln during the war—the availability of niter and coal. One of them affected the infamous *Trent* Affair, the other the possible colonization of freed slaves.

Niter is the mineral form of potassium nitrate, also called saltpeter, and has been used for meat processing, as a thickening agent in some soups and stews, and in fertilizers. By far its most important use in wartime was as an oxidizer for black powder or gunpowder, which was 75 percent potassium nitrate, 12 percent sulfur, and 13 percent charcoal. The United States had been getting saltpeter from India, through Britain, but when it became clear the war would last for some time, the government quickly used up the established stocks. Chemist Lammot du Pont, whose family business had been purchasing saltpeter for decades, arranged through Assistant Navy Secretary Gustavus Fox to have Lincoln assign du Pont to a secret mission to sail to Britain and obtain new contracts.

About three days into the trip, Union Captain Charles Wilkes on the USS *San Jacinto* stopped the British ship *Trent* off the coast of Cuba and removed James Mason and John Slidell, two Confederate diplomats bound for Britain and France. Wilkes had commanded the South Seas Exploring Expedition in the South Pacific, which was critical to the advancement of science in the United States.[25] The *Trent* Affair almost instigated a war with Britain until Lincoln released Mason and Slidell, noting that he could handle only "one war at a time." Beyond that, the *Trent* incident led the British to halt the saltpeter sale to du Pont on behalf of the Union. They reversed their position after the two Confederate diplomats were on a ship to Britain, which almost absurdly was the same ship du Pont was on with a letter facilitating the purchase of additional saltpeter. Du Pont was able to return with promises of substantial supplies of saltpeter, but hoarding and demand still created a significant shortage that doubled and then tripled the price.[26]

Lincoln's concerns with saltpeter did not end with du Pont's secret mission. Resolution of the *Trent* Affair and the British agreement to allow saltpeter shipments should have reinforced British support for the Union. But Lincoln had to report to Congress on another incident involving saltpeter—the British ship *Lilla* had been seized in the summer of 1862 for carrying saltpeter destined for the Confederacy. Tensions with Britain continued throughout the war, but Lincoln successfully avoided the nightmarish scenario of multiple wars at a time.[27]

Meanwhile, Lincoln had been engaged in correspondence with Isaac R. Diller, an old friend who proposed "a new and secret art of making gunpowder."[28] Diller was acting as an agent for a German developer of a chlorate-based gunpowder as an alternative to that based on saltpeter (potassium nitrate). After consulting with his favorite weapons expert, Captain John Dahlgren at the Washington Navy Yard, Lincoln entered into an agreement with Diller authorizing additional secret testing in a rented building on Timber Creek in New Jersey.[29] Lincoln took an active role in the process, scoping a detailed memorandum of instructions for the testing and asking a series of questions demonstrating his knowledge and inquisitiveness. Among his questions were the following: Did the powder contained any saltpeter or sulfur? Could the ingredients be obtained in sufficient quantities in the United States? Could manufacture be achieved more efficiently and with less danger than ordinary gunpowder? Would it ignite under 300° Celsius? Would it explode with as little pressure as ordinary gunpowder? Would it deteriorate in storage? And more. Diller never solved the challenges of cheap manufacture or safe transport, and since the Union managed to stockpile sufficient stores of saltpeter-based gunpowder for the remainder of the war, the project was eventually abandoned.[30] Meanwhile, the South was resorting to extracting nitrogen from women's urine to make the potassium nitrate needed for gunpowder.[31]

Emancipation had the potential to end slavery, but the underlying racism of white supremacy remained an ongoing factor. Most white Americans, even those favoring abolition of slavery, were hostile to the idea of full equality for formerly enslaved people. Some proposed colonization to Africa or the Caribbean as a way for black people to set up a more equitable society. Lincoln supported this idea, although only as a voluntary option for those who chose to do so. He also felt presentation of that option might assuage the fears of whites. One scientific issue that also impacted emancipation and colonization decisions was the need for coal.

In early 1865, Lincoln wrote to John Garrett, president of the Baltimore & Ohio Railroad, begging him to bring coal to make gas. "It is very important to us," Lincoln said, or else "we shall soon all be in the dark here."[32] Coal gas still dominated the exterior and interior lighting market at the time, predating the late nineteenth-century shift to methane-based natural gas. Coal was also used as a more efficient fuel over wood for steamships and railroad locomotives. Early coal sources were soft bituminous coal because it often could be found close to the surface, but technological advancements in the decade before the Civil War enabled the mining of anthracite coal, found much deeper in the earth. Anthracite was much harder than bituminous, had less sulfur, burned hotter, produced less smoke, and resulted in less waste. Anthracite could also be mined in Pennsylvania, well behind Union lines.[33] It was coal miners from Pennsylvania who constructed the cutting-edge tunnel and set off explosives under Confederate lines in what has become known as the Battle of the Crater.[34] But coal-fueled ships enforcing the blockade of Southern ports spent much of their time far away from Northern coal supplies, so some local option would greatly improve naval strategy.

Two days before the Confederacy opened fire on Fort Sumter, Ambrose W. Thompson met with Lincoln to gain support for a coal-mining project in the Chiriquí region of the Granadine Confederation (now Panama near the border with Costa Rica).[35] Thompson headed a corporation that had been created to provide coal to the U.S. Navy. Lincoln again relied on Smithsonian Secretary Joseph Henry for scientific advice. Henry wrote to John Peter Lesley, one of the leading geologists in the United States and an expert on coal. In his confidential letter he said he was writing on behalf of President Lincoln and Secretary of State Seward to get Lesley's opinion on the value of the coal deposit in the Chiriquí district. Interest in the coal was twofold. It was needed for coal-fired boilers for steamships and railroad locomotives, but it also offered itself as a possible solution to the likely emancipation of enslaved people. Lincoln and others had hoped that freed slaves (and other free blacks) could be relocated to avoid the problems of a racially mixed society. Should the Chiriquí coal be viable, it could serve as an economic basis for such a colony. Henry asked Lesley to give him "in addition to your opinion derived from general scientific principles any reliable information you may possess relative to this matter." In his reply, Lesley gave the worst possible news to Henry's and Lincoln's ears. The coal was tertiary coal, also known as lignite or brown coal (as opposed to bituminous black coal), consisting of only 30 to 60 percent carbon (anthracite hard coal is 80 to 90 percent carbon). Thus, Lesley noted, the Chiriquí coal was "as nearly worthless as any 'fuel' can be." He further opined that "the property will always be of little or no value to its owners" and warned that the government would likely regret any plan to enter into contract for the land. "If I have any influence on the government," Lesley wrote to Henry, "I should decidedly use it to dissuade from touching Chiriqui coal."[36]

Lincoln was not immediately convinced by Lesley's report as he was still looking for a solution to the problem that would be created by the end of slavery. On August 14, 1862 (after he had already drafted but not yet released the Emancipation Proclamation), Lincoln met with a delegation of freemen and advocated for the establishment of a black colony in Central America, most likely in Chiriquí. According to a report in the *National Intelligencer* (August 16, 1862), Lincoln stated that he found the physical differences between the two races "a great disadvantage to us both, as I think. Your race suffers very greatly, many of them, by living among us, while ours suffer from your presence." He admitted that slavery was, in his judgment, "the greatest wrong inflicted on any people," but he did not see how even freedom from slavery would improve their lot "on a continent [where] not a single man of your race is made the equal of a single man of ours."[37] While Lincoln had wanted to pursue Chiriquí further, the Central

American nations of Honduras, Nicaragua, and Costa Rica all made it clear they were opposed to any such colony. Eventually, Lincoln dropped the idea on Seward's recommendation.[38] Whether it was because the coal was of no value or because of the local opposition to the project is uncertain. Later Lincoln dropped the misconceived idea of colonization altogether.

Other scientific issues also crossed Lincoln's desk during the war. In early 1863 he requested Stanton and Welles each appoint an officer to test an incendiary shell and fluid devised by New Jersey chemist Alfred Berney.[39] Lincoln was also being kept up to date on Thaddeus Lowe's continuing struggles to manufacture gas to fill his reconnaissance balloons. Lowe had experimented with a variety of gases, with varying degrees of success: hydrogen gas lifted the most weight, coal gas worked well only with lighter loads, and ammonia gas accidentally froze the brass tubing from which it was made. Eventually, he successfully designed and built portable hydrogen gas generators that could be used in the field. He even launched a balloon from a converted coal barge renamed the *George Washington Park Custis*, making it the world's first dedicated aircraft carrier. The North also had to deal with the South's innovative land and sea explosive devices. One was shaped like a lump of coal but filled with powder, which would explode when crews tossed them into their ship's steam boiler. There were also horological torpedoes, what we call time bombs, and an electrically triggered explosive used to severely damage Union vessels at City Point. Lincoln also had to make decisions on some of the weapons options proposed that carried ethical complications. Among them were Short's and Berney's incendiary and Greek fire devices, the use of chloroform and chlorine gas, and various poisonous and noxious chemicals to disable or severely injure opposing armies. Lincoln chose not to use these options and issued General Order No. 100, also known as the Lieber Code, which prohibited the use of poison, stating, "The use of poison in any manner, be it to poison well, or food, or arms, is wholly excluded from modern warfare. He that uses it puts himself out of the pale of the law and usages of war." The Lieber Code also stipulated the ethical and humane treatment of civilians, captured soldiers, and black prisoners of war. The code was a basis for the later Hague and Geneva Conventions in international law.[40]

Science and technology issues often merged with military strategy issues and economic development. One set of volumes available in the White House contained scientific information related to the ongoing transcontinental railroad progress, and one volume falls open easily to charts of the Pacific stars, suggesting Lincoln or his heirs may have spent time studying them.[41] Lincoln had observed the Leonid meteor storm in 1833, which he recalled to visitors in the White House years later. The local deacon feared that the judgment day had come after seeing the sky filled with shooting stars. Lincoln told the White House visitors, fearful of the outcome of the war, that "Gentlemen, the world did not come to an end then, nor will the Union now." Lincoln probably was aware of the Carrington solar flare event in 1859 that created an extended auroral storm causing severe interruption of telegraph transmissions in the United States for several days.[42]

War weary and worn out from the constant pressure, Lincoln occasionally made his way to the U.S. Naval Observatory to humor his interest in astronomy. In May 1863 he stopped by the observatory with Major General Daniel Butterfield.[43] Three months later, Lincoln traveled to the observatory to look at the stars through the newly upgraded 9.6-inch telescope recently installed. He was met there by astronomer Asaph Hall, who helped Lincoln locate the bright star Arcturus. Lincoln visited the observatory on other occasions as well, often inviting others to join him. Longtime friend Joseph Gillespie told Herndon that Lincoln "invited me one day at Washington City to call upon him in the evening when he said we would go to the observatory and take a look at the Moon through the large telescope." The night was cloudy and the excursion was called off.[44] When not at the observatory, Lincoln peered through his own small telescope at the White House, searching alternatively for stars, sailing ships on the Potomac, or the red sandstone Castle of the Smithsonian Institution.[45]

On March 4, 1865, all of those present at Lincoln's second inaugural address would have been privy to a rare daytime viewing of the planet Venus. Weeks later, Lincoln traveled by steamboat to City Point to confer with Ulysses S. Grant and get some time away from the stress of Washington. He walked the streets of Richmond after it fell, then heard about

Robert E. Lee's surrender as he returned to Washington a few days later. Lincoln's war-weariness was about to end, and he planned for a cheerier second term. On April 14 he took a leisurely carriage ride with Mrs. Lincoln. "We must be more cheerful, Mother," he told her. They planned to travel to the Holy Land after his time in Washington was complete. Those plans were never to come to fruition.

CHAPTER 14

Assassination Science

DR. CHARLES LEALE EXAMINED THE FALLEN PRESIDENT AND KNEW immediately the wound was mortal. Twenty-three years old and only six weeks after receiving his medical degree from Bellevue Hospital Medical College, Leale found himself in charge of the shocking murder scene. He had been sitting in the dress circle at Ford's Theatre when "about half past ten . . . the report of a pistol was distinctly heard and about a minute after a man of low stature with black hair and eyes was seen leaping to the stage beneath, holding in his hand a drawn dagger." Rushing to the Presidential Box, Leale observed Lincoln "in a state of general paralysis." Lincoln's labored breath was intermittent, no pulse could be detected, and he was "profoundly comatose."[1]

But where was the wound? Initially, Leale searched for a knife wound because Major Henry Rathbone, who had been accompanying the president and Mrs. Lincoln with his fiancée Clara Harris, was bleeding profusely from a slash along his left arm.[2] Finding none, and noticing Lincoln had stopped breathing and his pupils were dilated, Leale probed for a head wound and "found clotted blood on the head about an inch and a half behind the left ear." After clearing the clot, there was "a sudden spasmodic gasp of breath," after which Lincoln again breathed intermittently and noisily.[3] Lincoln's autonomic nervous system was keeping him alive for the time being, but the clock was already ticking.

April 14, 1865, had been a busy day for Abraham Lincoln. The previous week he had walked through Richmond, arriving back in Washington to a telegram saying the South's main army would fight no more. On this Good Friday, Lincoln felt rejuvenated, relieved that the war would soon end and he could focus his second term on reconstructing the Union. The day started with a welcome visit. Captain Robert Lincoln, the president's son, returned to the city in time to join Lincoln for breakfast. Robert brought firsthand witness to the recent surrender of Confederate General Robert E. Lee to Union General Ulysses S. Grant at Appomattox Courthouse. Many formal interviews later (including with former New Hampshire senator John P. Hale, whose daughter Lucy was later discovered to be secretly engaged to John Wilkes Booth), Lincoln held a cabinet meeting in which he related a recurring dream of a ship "moving with great rapidity toward a dark and indefinite shore."[4]

Perhaps inspired by the dream or simply his interest in technology, Lincoln and Mary went out for a carriage ride and found their way to the Washington Navy Yard. Lincoln had frequented the Navy Yard to talk strategy with John A. Dahlgren, who by that time had risen to the rank of admiral. Lincoln went on this day to see three ironclad ships recently damaged in action at Fort Fisher, North Carolina, including the Passaic-class monitor USS *Montauk*. After touring the vessels and talking with Navy Yard staff, the Lincolns returned to the White House and shortly thereafter set out again for what they had hoped would be a relaxing night at the theater. *Our American Cousin*, a comedy, should lift their spirits as this long grueling Civil War appeared to be coming to an end.

Instead, Lincoln's life ended. John Wilkes Booth had slipped into the president's box at Ford's Theatre and fired a single shot into the back of Lincoln's head. Booth then slashed Rathbone before leaping from the box to the stage, yelled *Sic Semper Tyrannus*, "Thus Ever to Tyrants," and ran out the stage door into the alley, where he escaped on horseback. In contrast to the advanced repeating weapons that Lincoln so often advocated, Booth's gun was a Deringer, made to fire one lead ball. A Deringer (the original design, as opposed to a derringer, which is any similar gun by other manufacturers) is a single-shot, muzzle-loading, seven-groove rifled, percussion pocket pistol. Most Deringers were .41 caliber, but the one used by Booth was .44 caliber, a remarkably large ball for such a small gun. Prior to entering the theater, Booth loaded the Deringer by pouring ten grains by weight of black powder into the muzzle before ramming in one lead ball wrapped in a tiny cloth patch. A percussion cap was put in place and the hammer rested gently up until the time Booth pulled the trigger.[5]

Leale's description of his actions that night grew more detailed and extravagant in repeated telling over the years, but the basic facts remained the same. He was joined in the box by surgeons Doctors Charles F. Taft and Albert F. A. King. They agreed that Lincoln would not survive the rugged trip back to the White House yet were concerned that the president should not die in a theater—still considered a dubious location, especially on Good Friday. He was carried out the front door and across the street to be placed in the small rear room of Petersen's boarding house, where he was laid out diagonally on a bed too short for his elongated body.[6] These doctors were joined at the Petersen house by several other surgeons, including Surgeon General Joseph K. Barnes and Lincoln's personal physician, Robert K. Stone. Stone noted that the wound was plugged by coagulating blood, bone debris, and brain tissue, causing a buildup of cranial pressure and "stertorous" (noisy and labored) breathing. "On cleaning this away," wrote Stone lyrically, "the wound bled steadily . . . and respiration became instantly as sweet and regular as an infant." Lincoln never regained consciousness. A long metal Nélaton's probe was inserted into the wound several times to determine the path of the ball. Nothing more could be done except to monitor the president's pulse and breathing over a night of waiting for the inevitable.[7]

PRESIDENTIAL AUTOPSY

When the surgeons removed Lincoln's clothes to search for additional wounds, they found him to be remarkably fit. Lincoln was worn out from the pressures of a four-year war but retained his overall athleticism. Reminiscent of his rail-splitting days, Lincoln used an axe to chop wood for the soldier's campfire at Depot Field Hospital at City Point a week before his assassination. He had spent the day shaking hands, chopped up a twenty-foot log of white oak, then held the axe by the handle out at a ninety-degree angle from his body to the amazement and delight of the troops.[8]

Lincoln's health was not always so robust. He contracted a form of malaria called ague at least twice in his lifetime. He periodically suffered from melancholy, and on at least two occasions his friends worried he might become suicidal. He likely took blue mass pills for his melancholy for a time. Blue mass contains finely dispersed elemental mercury, which has the potential to cause neurobehavioral problems. Indeed, Lincoln reported he had stopped taking the pills long before his presidency because they made him "feel cross." During his presidency, he used the services of Issachar Zacharie, a self-styled chiropodist. "Dr. Zacharie," Lincoln endorsed, "has operated on my feet with great success, and considerable addition to my comfort." Lincoln was so pleased with the relief for his "troublesome corns" that he sent Zacharie to General Nathaniel P. Banks in New Orleans, where he not only soothed the sore feet of thousands of soldiers but acted as Lincoln's contact and informant with the Jewish community.[9]

One major medical incident coincided with his address at Gettysburg in late 1863. Lincoln was weak and dizzy as he rose to speak, with the symptoms intensifying on the train back to Washington. Back pains developed, and by the fourth day of being bedridden he experienced a scarlet rash, which soon became vesicular. Lincoln had virus-induced smallpox, or at least a less virulent form called variola. Over the next three weeks, lesions appeared and worsened, finally drying and peeling. Lincoln likely had never received a vaccination for smallpox. The vaccine had limited availability and effectiveness at that time but was given to the Army of the Potomac to protect them from the epidemic that was plaguing major cities in the United States. Lincoln recovered, and to this day there is speculation that his case was more severe than his staff admitted. His free African American valet, William Johnson, was not so lucky. Contracting smallpox soon after Lincoln, Johnson passed away in late January. He had come with Lincoln from Springfield to Washington, and Lincoln had found him jobs in the White House and the Treasury Department. Lincoln arranged for Johnson's family to receive his pay and for his burial at Arlington National Cemetery.[10]

Lincoln gained some basic medical familiarity because of his malpractice case experience. He also made some executive decisions during the war that affected medical care of the troops. Medical capabilities in general remained limited at the beginning of the Civil War.

Most practitioners in the field had no understanding of the role of microbes in infection. Techniques such as bloodletting via cutting veins or sucking leeches were on their way out of favor but still occasionally practiced. As with Lincoln's blue mass pills, toxins like mercury, lead acetate, and even turpentine were still commonly used to treat illness, often with worse results than doing nothing. Diseases like dysentery, typhoid, ague, yellow fever, malaria, scurvy, pneumonia, smallpox, and even mumps, measles, and tuberculosis were as dangerous as battles. Poor hygiene, improper separation of latrines and drinking water sources, bad weather, spoiled food and water, and the presence of myriad disease-carrying flies, mosquitoes, ticks, maggots, and fleas meant that at least 10 percent of any army division was incapacitated by disease. About two-thirds of the estimated 750,000 deaths during the Civil War were due to disease.[11]

Bureaucracy was also a problem. Like Chief of Ordnance Ripley, the head of the medical corps, Clement Finley, was more interested in saving money than adequately provisioning army physicians and surgeons with supplies to take care of the wounded. One solution was a civilian organization called the United States Sanitary Commission. While reluctant at first—he worried it might be "a fifth wheel on a coach," that is, unnecessary—Lincoln did approve creation of the commission in June 1861 and supported its work thereafter.[12] Another public health legacy of the Civil War was expansion of the Office of the Surgeon General, the forerunner of today's National Library of Medicine, now housed at the National Institutes of Health outside Washington, DC. These logistical improvements and the record number of deaths and traumatic injuries incurred during the war resulted in improving medical care as the war progressed.[13] Beginning in 1862, field medics were trained in basic first aid, which saved thousands of lives. Around the same time, a three-step system for evacuating wounded soldiers using a new Ambulance Corps was instituted. First, a field dressing station applied tourniquets and dressed wounds. Second, the wounded were moved to a field hospital for emergency medical intervention and surgery. Finally, ambulances transported soldiers to hospitals away from the battlefield for long-term treatment. This is the basis for today's triage, transport, and care system.[14]

Most of the surgical procedures during the war were amputations, the removal of limbs shattered by bullets, shells, or cannonballs. Good surgeons could remove a limb in less than three minutes. These surgeries were brutal but often saved the lives of those soldiers hit, although not always. Many of the wounded died later as infection spread throughout the body, often introduced by the dirty hands and equipment of the surgeons themselves. The sheer number of amputations did help surgeons gain awareness of ways to combat infection even if they did not understand the microbial biology at the time. Contrary to myth, most surgeries were performed using ether or chloroform as anesthesia, so most men were asleep during amputations. Disinfection using alcohol or chemicals such as lead nitrate, zinc chloride, or carbolic acid helped reduce disease and gangrene. With so many amputations, a robust business in prosthetics—artificial arms and legs—gained traction during and after the war. No longer the proverbial peg leg of pirates, prosthetics became more flexible, many intricately designed with movable joints and extremities.[15] Plastic surgery, in particular the repair of massive facial disfigurement, also grew rapidly after the Civil War. Overall, around 95 percent of those sick and injured men who reached general hospitals survived their trauma.[16]

Another Civil War scientific oddity is worth mentioning even though Lincoln was not directly involved. In April 1862, the Battle of Shiloh left almost 3,500 Union and Confederate soldiers dead and around 16,000 wounded. The number of wounded meant many of them lay in muddy fields for two frigid days and nights waiting for medical personnel to reach them. Some of them observed a strange greenish-blue glow in their wounds, and doctors noticed that those who glowed had a better survival rate than those who did not. The phenomenon came to be known as "Angel's Glow." The cause remained a mystery until almost 140 years later. Tiny parasitic roundworms called nematodes hold the symbiotic bacteria species *Photorhabdus luminescens* in their guts. The nematodes burrow into insects found in mud and live in their blood vessels, where they vomit up the bacteria, which release enzymes to digest the insect and other bacteria, providing nutrients for both nematodes and their symbiont bacteria. As this happens, the bacteria glow, which may also attract new insects for the nematode/bacteria combination. Normally, the human body is too warm for the bacteria, but the unusual cold April in Tennessee during the Battle of Shiloh caused wounded soldiers to suffer from hypothermia, significantly lowering their body temperature—enough to allow the nematodes and bacteria to attack the insects attracted to open wounds. Because the glowing bacteria also killed off competing pathogenic bacteria that might cause infection, those with glowing wounds survived more often.[17]

Leale remained at Lincoln's side during the night as Surgeon General Barnes oversaw the president's final hours. Death was recorded at 7:22 a.m. on April 15, 1865. Lincoln's pastor, Phineas Gurley, offered a prayer for the family and the nation. Secretary of War Edwin Stanton sobbingly uttered, "Now he belongs to the Ages."

Lincoln's body was transferred to the White House, where army surgeons Joseph Woodward and Edward Curtis performed an autopsy under Barnes's supervision. Other physicians attended as observers, including Assistant Surgeon General Crane, Charles Taft, and William Notson. General Christopher Augur and newly sworn-in president Andrew Johnson may have attended in part.[18] Dr. Stone, Lincoln's personal physician, was present both at the Petersen house and the autopsy. His report is handwritten on pages stained with human blood, although whether it was Lincoln's or Rathbone's is impossible to determine.[19]

"The eyelids and surrounding parts of the face were greatly ecchymosed," Woodward wrote, noting that ruptured blood vessels under the skin were causing discoloration. He added that Lincoln's eyes were protruding from built up pressure. The Deringer ball had "entered the occipital bone about an inch to the left of the median line and just above the left lateral sinus, which it opened. It then penetrated the dura mater passed through the left posterior lobe of the cerebrum, entered the left later lateral ventricle and lodged in the white matter of the cerebrum just above the anterior portion of the left corpus striatum, where it was found." All this medical terminology means is that the lead ball entered the back of the head low on the left side, passed upward and almost all the way through the brain, and rested behind the eye. The surgeons disagreed on which eye. Woodward and Stone both indicated the left eye, but Barnes and Taft wrote that it was the right eye.[20] Secretary of the Navy Welles wrote in his diary that Lincoln's right eye had begun to swell about an hour after being shot, giving more credence to the right-eye view.[21] Deficiencies in recordkeeping standards from Lincoln's autopsy were in part the reason for much more robust standards in future years.

In any case, besides the obvious damage produced by the track of the ball, the increasing pressure of congealing blood caused severe clotting, instigating Lincoln's general paralysis and comatose state. The brain stem was undamaged, hence the continued automatic function and breathing for some time.[22] At one point early in the autopsy, assistant surgeon Curtis lifted a piece of shattered bone at the back of Lincoln's head "when suddenly, from out a cruel rent that traverses it from end to end, through these very fingers there slips something hard—slips and falls with a metal's mocking clatter into a basin set beneath. The search is satisfied; a little pellet of lead!"[23] Writing to his mother later, Curtis captured the overwhelming sense of the tragedy: "There it lay upon the white china, a little black mass no bigger than the end of my finger—dull, motionless and harmless, yet the cause of such mighty changes in the world's history as we may perhaps never realize."[24]

Days after Lincoln's last visit to the *Montauk*, the ironclad became the temporary prison for six of the accused assassin's coconspirators. All but Doctor Samuel Mudd and Mary Surratt were kept on board before being transferred to the Old Arsenal Penitentiary for trial. Eight conspirators were convicted. Four were sentenced to prison; four were hanged for their roles in the assassination of President Lincoln, the attempted assassination of William Seward, and the planned assassination of Vice President Andrew Johnson.[25]

The *Montauk* had one more role to play in this American tragedy. The assassin, John Wilkes Booth, had passed over the Navy Yard Bridge during his escape out of Washington, but twelve days later the body of Booth was brought back to the Navy Yard and onto the deck of the *Montauk* for examination and autopsy.[26] He had been killed in the Garrett barn by a soldier named Thomas "Boston" Corbett, whose history of odd behavior (he once castrated himself to curb a desire for prostitutes) has been linked to his many years employed as a hatter, a job that required working around a great deal of mercury, the inspiration for Lewis Carroll's Hatter in *Alice in Wonderland* and of the phrase "mad as a hatter."[27]

On the *Montauk*, Barnes and Woodward again did the postmortem examination. They noted the fracture of Booth's fibula (small bone of the lower leg) three inches above the ankle joint. Like Lincoln, the cause of death was a gunshot wound, this time slightly lower in the neck that cut through the fourth and fifth cervical vertebrae, severing the spinal cord. Barnes reported that "paralysis of the entire body was immediate," although unlike his victim, Booth experienced "all the horrors of consciousness of suffering and death" for "the two hours he lingered" before he died.[28]

As the Union army searched for Booth and chased the escaping Confederate President Jefferson Davis, Lincoln began his long trip back to Springfield.[29] Lincoln had ridden many a railroad on the legal circuit and political campaigns. He had traveled a circuitous route from Illinois to Washington for his inauguration, zigzagging to touch base in as many Northern cities as could be arranged.[30] Now he would retrace that circuitous route on the way back to the city that had been his home for twenty-five years prior to his presidency. His body traveled in a specially built railroad car named the *United States*, complete with the newest technology—quadruple trucks and broad tread wheels to enable it to run over nearly all railroads in the nation. For eleven days he would unknowingly ride the rails he had come to know so well. At times he would revisit his time on the waters as the car carrying his casket was rolled onto a barge and ferried across the Hudson and other rivers along the route. Lincoln's funeral train would cover 1,700 miles across seven states, with mourners lining the tracks for almost the entire way, alerted by the "lightning messages" of the telegraph Lincoln had so often employed during the war. Traveling at a pace of up to twenty miles per hour, the train slowed to about five miles per hour when passing through crowds so the people could at least see the special car carrying their martyred leader. It stopped in large cities to put his body on display for hundreds of thousands to see. More than seven million people witnessed some part of the funeral trip.[31]

Embalming Sciences

Lincoln helped advance science even in death. Embalming was in its infancy at the beginning of the Civil War. Like so many other sciences and technologies, the enormous number of fatalities during the war provided ample opportunity to develop new methodologies. War was good for business, with embalmers charging twice as much for officers as for privates.[32]

For the Lincolns, it started with Willie. William Wallace "Willie" Lincoln was twelve years old when he died of typhoid fever in the White House in February 1862. The president and Mary Lincoln were devastated. Willie's younger brother Tad was also afflicted but would live. This personal tragedy on top of the ongoing Civil War was almost too much to bear for both of them, and Mary would never completely recover. But Willie's death, and those of 700,000 soldiers during the Civil War, also ushered in advances in the embalming sciences and launched the funeral industry, in part because Abraham Lincoln chose to have Willie embalmed.[33]

Called in to care for the body, the Charles D. Brown and Joseph B. Alexander undertaking firm embalmed Willie Lincoln using a new process. Their senior employee, Henry Platt Cattell, did the actual embalming, as well as that for President Lincoln three years later. Even as the surgeons did Lincoln's autopsy, Dr. Stone expressed his "great surprise" that the embalmer had already arrived, insisting that "the embalmment of the body . . . would immediately follow our necropsy."[34]

The process of embalming was complex. Generally, the blood was drained from the body, although it was not necessary in all cases to do so. In Willie's and Abraham's cases, blood was drained through the jugular vein in the neck, while the embalming fluid was pumped into the body via the femoral artery in the thigh. There were several recipes for the embalming fluid. Zinc chloride was the most common preservative, often made by dissolving strips of zinc sheets in hydrochloric acid. The fluid slowed down the degradation process and hardened the remains to a marblelike state, thus preserving the appearance of the body for a longer period of time.[35]

Prior to the Civil War, those who died were buried quickly to avoid the nastiness of decomposing bodies. Because of advances made in the art and science of embalming during the Civil War and after, led by the work of Dr. Thomas Holmes, it became standard practice to preserve the dead so that they may make the long trips home for proper burial by their families. After Lincoln himself was embalmed, Dr. Brown remained with the funeral train through its winding route from Washington to Springfield. At each major stop, Lincoln's body was solemnly transported into town to rest in state. But as the days passed, the body deteriorated faster than the attendants could do the necessary touch-ups. Black splotches had begun to appear on Lincoln's face and neck. The *New York Times* reported "the color is leaden, almost brown; the forehead recedes sharp and clearly marked; the eyes deep sunk and closely held upon the sockets; the cheek bones, always high are unusually prominent; the cheeks hollowed and deep pitted; the unnaturally thin lips shut tight and firm as if glued together; and the small chin, covered with a slight beard, seemed pointed and sharp." Brown and the other undertakers preserved Lincoln as best as possible for the grieving populace.[36]

Embalming did have its drawbacks. While zinc chloride became the most often used chemical, arsenic-laced compounds were also common, as were various types of alcohol, creosote, mercury, turpentine, and lead and aluminum salts. Arsenic contamination is often found near Civil War–era cemeteries. The presence of embalmers could also have a negative effect on soldier morale. In January 1865, Ulysses S. Grant had issued an order requiring embalmers to be licensed and to remain behind the lines out of sight. About forty thousand soldiers were embalmed during the war.[37]

Because of the ongoing Civil War in 1862, Willie Lincoln was initially interred in Oak Hill Cemetery in the Georgetown neighborhood of Washington, D.C. He remained in the Carroll family mausoleum until Lincoln's assassination, after which Willie's body accompanied that of the fallen president on the train back to Springfield, Illinois, where both were interred in Oak Ridge Cemetery. Eventually, all the Lincolns except Robert were laid to rest in the Lincoln Tomb. Because of his brief Civil War military service and his long service to subsequent presidents, Robert's tomb is in Arlington National Cemetery, across the river from the Lincoln Memorial.

CONTINUING INQUISITION

When Lincoln related his ship dream to his cabinet the morning of his assassination, he said its earlier occurrences had presaged Union victories. When General Grant pointed out that at least one of the battles Lincoln listed was certainly not a victory, Lincoln noted that he still felt it an omen of something important to occur. That part was true; his days on earth would come to an end.[38]

But medical inquisitiveness into Lincoln's death did not end. There remains a seemingly unlimited fascination with our sixteenth president, and that fascination extends to queries about his health and his family. Much of this inquiry relies on the modern science of DNA analysis, something unheard of in Lincoln's time, although Lincoln may have had an intuitive sense of its existence. In Herndon's biography of his former law partner, he says that Lincoln thought his maternal grandmother, Lucey Hanks, had been taken advantage of by a wealthy Virginia planter, resulting in the birth of Lincoln's mother, Nancy Hanks Lincoln. Given the lack of education of both his parents, Lincoln believed he inherited from this unknown planter "his power of analysis, his logic, his mental activity, his ambition, and all the qualities that distinguished him from the other members and descendants of the Hanks family." The laws of genetics and inherited traits would not be discovered until the early twentieth century (based on work done in Europe by Gregor Mendel around the time of the Civil War), but Lincoln seemed to sense the inheritability of intellect much earlier.[39] Lincoln's genetic lineage has recently been confirmed in the Nancy Hanks Lincoln mtDNA Study. Using mitochondrial DNA, they conclude that Nancy Hanks Lincoln was indeed the daughter of Lucey Hanks, whose parents were simple farmers, Joseph and Anna Lee Hanks. Identity of Nancy, Hanks Lincoln's father remains unknown given the lack of a patrilineal DNA chain, meaning the possibility exists that Lincoln inherited his mental acuity from this mysterious Virginia planter.[40]

The scientific inquiries expand to Lincoln's wife, Mary. Unquestionably prone to emotional outbursts directed at her husband and others, Mary has been the subject of unending speculation as to the cause of her erratic behavior. She could be "nervous and excitable," explosively violent at times, and yet loving and supportive of Lincoln and their sons. No records exist of her medical condition or treatment other than for the four months her oldest son Robert had her institutionalized years after the assassination. While modern psychologists decry diagnosing a patient they have never met, many believe the evidence strongly suggests Mary suffered from bipolar disorder, a condition that was unlabeled but surely present in her time. Biographers of Abraham Lincoln, as well as Mary Lincoln biographer Jason Emerson, seem to lean toward bipolar, while most Mary Lincoln biographers tend to be more sympathetic. Other researchers trying to explain Mary's behavior speculate on anything from Lyme disease to diabetes, and most recently "pernicious anemia," based on nothing more than letters and photographs. An exhibit at President Lincoln's Cottage, where the Lincoln family spent the summers during his presidency to get away from the pestilent-plagued swamp around the White House, claimed that Mary was not insane (a broad term formerly applied to a wide range of psychological conditions); she was merely experiencing extreme bereavement from the early deaths of three of her four children and her husband. We will never know for sure, but that will not end the speculation.[41]

Lincoln himself is a never-ending target of medical speculation. In the 1960s, two researchers independently published in medical journals their claims that Lincoln suffered from a rare disease called Marfan syndrome. The disease is a genetic disorder of the connective tissue present throughout the body, tissue that essentially holds the organs and tissues together. Lincoln did epitomize some of the noted characteristics of Marfan, including being very tall and thin, with disproportionately long arms, legs, fingers, and toes. But the syndrome also includes characteristics that did not fit Lincoln: scoliosis (a sideways curve of the spine); heart, lung, and eye problems; and chest pains. Lincoln throughout his life was lanky, but he was also athletic and strong despite the weight of war in his final years. In Lincoln's day, Marfan's would likely have led to a relatively early death, long before the time his life was taken by an assassin. The two researchers who claimed Lincoln had the syndrome disagreed with each other on the lineage—Dr. Abraham Gordon argued in 1962 that the disease was passed to Lincoln through his mother's side, while Dr. Harold Schwartz in 1964 claimed it came through a paternal route. Both arguments were weakened by lack of, and misrepresented, familial descriptions. The often contentious debate continued into the 1990s, when research panels were convened to discuss whether DNA analysis would provide significant enough information to settle the issue. They concluded that "the diagnosis of Marfan syndrome is established by detailed family history and physical examination, along with other medical tests, not by DNA analysis." They further noted that "DNA could only be used for investigating the molecular basis for Marfan syndrome, not yet for diagnostic purposes." Today's consensus is that Lincoln did not suffer from Marfan syndrome. Yet the idea refuses to die.[42]

Another disease that some modern physicians attribute to Lincoln is multiple endocrine neoplasia 2B (MEN 2B). Dr. John G. Sotos was struck by the same Marfan syndrome characteristics previously described and came up with the MEN 2B diagnosis based entirely on photographs of Lincoln in his final years. Like Marfan syndrome, MEN 2B is a rare genetic disease whose traits include a marfanoid appearance as well as a variety of oddball characteristics Sotos claimed were embodied in Lincoln: constipation, the mole on his cheek, a drooping eyelid, pseudodepression, and most definingly, what Sotos saw as lumps on Lincoln's lips. The disease can cause benign tumors around the nerves of the lips, tongue, and eyelids, which Sotos claimed photographs "unmistakably show." Others are more skeptical.

One of the results of MEN 2B is thyroid cancer, and some experts do feel that the final photographs of the living Abraham Lincoln in 1865 may indicate the disease. Problematic is that MEN 2B most often was fatal early in life, with the average life expectancy only twenty-one years. A definitive assessment is possible as there is an identifiable MEN 2B gene. Actual samples of Lincoln's DNA are limited, however, and those that Sotos has tested are not proven to be from Lincoln. Tests undertaken to date have not found the relevant gene. Whether Lincoln had MEN 2B, or any other diseases, may never be demonstrably known given the lack of actual medical evidence and the difficulty or impossibility of obtaining any.[43]

What is undeniable is that Lincoln continues to be a source of scientific fascination all these years after his death.

Epilogue

PAINTED ONTO THE DOME INSIDE THE THOMAS JEFFERSON BUILDING OF the Library of Congress is a circular mural by Edwin Howland Blashfield. Twelve seated figures in turn reflect the twelve countries, or epochs, which Blashfield felt contributed most to American civilization. To the immediate right of each figure is a tablet on which is inscribed the name of the country typified. Below is the "outstanding contribution of that country to human progress." The figures follow in chronological order beginning with Egypt, which represents written records. The twelfth figure, representing America, signifies the field of science and is modeled after Abraham Lincoln. As described in *On These Walls: Inscriptions and Quotations in the Library of Congress*: "The figure, an engineer whose face was modeled from Abraham Lincoln's, sits in his machine shop pondering a problem of mechanics. In front of him is an electric dynamo, representing the American contribution to the advancement of electricity."[1] Immediately before Lincoln on the mural is France, whose contribution is emancipation because of *The Declaration of the Rights of Man* (*Les Droits de l'Homme*), adopted by the French Assembly in 1789.

The depiction of Lincoln as a representative of American science reflects the significance he placed on it during his lifetime. The juxtaposition of a Lincoln figure bracketed by "Emancipation" and "Science" is both intentional and a summation of his contributions to the modernization of America. Lincoln was no engineer, of course, but Blashfield's use of Lincoln's visage and a posture reminiscent of Rodin's *Le Penseur* (*The Thinker*) to reflect a mechanically minded thinker does Lincoln justice. The view among several of Lincoln's contemporaries is summarized by his cocounsel on the *Parker v. Hoyt* waterwheel patent case: Lincoln "had a great mechanical genius," Grant Goodrich wrote to William Herndon, and "could understand readily the principles & mechanical action of machinery, & had the power, in his clear, simple illustrations & style to make the jury comprehend them."[2]

Even the use of an electrical dynamo to represent science captures an aspect of Lincoln. He once described the Declaration of Independence as the "electric cord" that links liberty-loving men here and abroad.[3] Another electrical link is through his relationship with Joseph Henry, the secretary of the Smithsonian. Like Lincoln, Henry was largely self-taught. Early in his career, he helped define the nascent field of electricity. His improvements to the weak electromagnet design then existing gave rise to the powerful electromagnets now today's standard. Henry's innovations included the first machine to use electromagnetism for motion, the precursor to the modern direct current motor, also called a dynamo, so fittingly depicted in Blashfield's mural. Henry's experiments also made possible development of the telegraph, and it was Henry's initial designs that were appropriated, then further developed, by Samuel F. B. Morse and used strategically by Lincoln in the Civil War. Michael Faraday, often credited as the father of electromagnetic self-inductance, actually got his ideas from Henry, who was notoriously slow to publish. As Lincoln's informal science adviser, Henry no doubt expounded on these principles to the ever-curious Lincoln during their many conversations.[4]

The references to Lincoln in the Library of Congress continue with a painting above the central door entering the reading room. This painting is titled *Government* and represents the ideal state. The figure of Good Government holds a plaque on which is inscribed Lincoln's pivotal line from the Gettysburg Address, "A government of the people, by the people, and for the people."[5]

Lincoln has another connection to the Jefferson Building of the Library of Congress. The current building sits on top of the land that once held Mrs. Sprigg's boarding house, where Lincoln lived as a member of Congress. Directly behind the Capitol, it was a perfect location for Lincoln and his fellow boarders—mostly other Whigs and abolitionists—to discuss the issues of the day while close enough to rush over for last-minute votes.

Lincoln as president was a regular borrower of books from the library's shelves, at that time still housed within the Capitol building. Topics of books loaned to Lincoln ranged from the strategy of war to the plays of Shakespeare, and of course, keeping up on science and technology.[6]

An unsatisfying life of subsistence farming like his ancestors was anathema to Abraham Lincoln. Always curious, Lincoln dedicated himself to a life of personal improvement. Even on the farm he paid attention to the basic sciences of agronomy, forest ecology, hydrology, weather, climate, and disease. When not plowing the fields, taking the grain to the mill, or splitting rails, Lincoln was reading every book he could borrow from friends and neighbors near and far away. When his mathematical and linguistic knowledge outpaced his peers and his teachers, he continued to study on his own. Lincoln's layering of independent study and life experience enabled him to engage in trades ranging from merchant to surveyor. He studied grammar to improve his writing and speech capabilities. Becoming a state-level politician at an early age revealed his lack of legal training, so he read Blackstone and other books to become a lawyer. He studied Euclid's geometry to improve his logic after meeting established political leaders during his single term in Congress. Lincoln had a thirst for knowledge that rivaled the eastern elites, without the privileges of formal education, wealth, or political access that aided the Founding Fathers and their descendants. Through this internal drive, this autodidacticism, Lincoln sought to better his condition.

As Lincoln matured, he began to connect this personal self-improvement goal with broader socioeconomic and political improvement. The nation was undergoing a dramatic shift from a predominantly agricultural economy to an integrated industrial economy spreading westward. Illinois became a literal crossroads between the expanding eastern civilization and the unincorporated western territories, which gave it a geographically and politically central role in the two overarching issues of the times: technological advancement and the expansion of slavery. Lincoln came to recognize the critical conflicts in both areas, and in both, he saw how they affected the lives of the common man.

Lincoln initially focused on economic issues. He promoted an expansive system of internal improvements, what we today call infrastructure projects. Internal improvements were the main focus in his first run for office, embracing the Whig philosophy of technological and transportation advancement even before he officially became a Whig. He saw how the Erie Canal had grown the New York and New England economy exponentially, so he proposed and lobbied for an Illinois and Michigan Canal to connect the Great Lakes (and points eastward) with the Mississippi River (and points southward). When railroads began to spread westward to Illinois, he included them in his internal improvement plans. He pushed to deepen and widen the Sangamon River to improve the navigability of rivers to expanding steamship traffic. His own patent stemmed from his experience stranded on the New Salem mill dam when flatboating down the Sangamon River, and on the action taken to free a grounded steamship in the Great Lakes after he visited Niagara Falls. He increasingly recognized the importance of scientific and technological advancement to transportation, to economic development, and to the freedom of all men everywhere.

He was able to implement these beliefs as his legal career expanded from simple debt and divorce cases to technology and patent cases. As Lincoln traveled the circuit, he routinely stopped to learn about any new mechanical equipment he encountered. This interest led to involvement in seminal cases helping to transform society. While he was left out of the Manny–McCormick reaper case after it was moved to Cincinnati, he had analyzed the technological differences between the two inventions, knowledge that he relied on for other patent cases. Lincoln's summation in the *Effie Afton* Case ensured the railroads would supplant steamships for transportation and commerce, ushering in a new era in economic and westward expansion that made the whole country into a single market. Cases he argued for, and against, the railroads established legal precedents that defined corporate and labor rights for decades to come. He even integrated his fascination with astronomy, strategically employing an almanac to win acquittal for the son of an old friend accused of murder.

Lincoln embraced science and technology to present a lecture on "discoveries and inventions." Tracing the inventiveness of humanity from the biblical Adam and Eve through modern printing and the patent system, which "added the fuel of interest to the fire of genius" with its protection of inventors' rights for a period of time, he was able to show the common man a pathway to success. Recalling his days on the farm, Lincoln encouraged farmers in Wisconsin to employ more science in their fields to improve yields. These lectures provided the background for his presidential program of national improvement.

The study of Euclid's geometry prepared Lincoln for a logical and analytical view of slavery. Carefully researching the votes cast by the Founders following their enactment of the Constitution, at Cooper Union Lincoln built a logical case for their belief that slavery was put onto a path toward its ultimate extinction.[7] That belief proved to be premature as they could not have anticipated the role technology would play in the exponential growth of slavery. Eli Whitney's cotton gin made growing cotton profitable for the first time. With expanding federal territory resulting from the Louisiana Purchase and Mexican War, more and more land was put into cotton production. Lincoln foresaw this expansion for what it was, an opportunity for slaveholding states to spread slavery westward and northward, threatening a time where slavery engulfed the nation. "I do not expect the Union to be dissolved ... but I do expect it will cease to be divided. It will become *all* one thing or *all* the other."[8]

But Lincoln recognized that slavery could not simply be abolished by unilateral act of Congress, as such a law would certainly be found unconstitutional by the proslavery Supreme Court. Beyond this major legal aspect, Lincoln understood that scientific and theological arguments were being made to rationalize the domination of "inferior" black men by "superior" white ones. No less than respected scientist Louis Agassiz promoted scientific "proof" of racial superiority of the white race. Even Joseph Henry had white supremacist leanings despite his strong pro-Union convictions. Lincoln sought to find a pathway through these controversies. He read papers and books promoting and refuting these "proofs" so he could better position his response. He came to believe that the Declaration's "all men are created equal" applied to everyone, notwithstanding race, at least as far as the "natural right to eat the bread she earns with her own hands without asking leave of anyone else." In this regard, he added, "she is my equal, and the equal of all others."[9]

Lincoln's disapproval of slavery tied in with his personal belief in self-improvement and his political view on the role of government. In contrast to chattel slavery, in which a person's social and economic position, and that of his descendants, cannot change, free society offered the opportunity for upward mobility. He told Congress soon after the start of the war that the goals of both sides were clear. The Southern states wanted to maintain a system in which some people could hold other people in bondage. "On the side of the Union," however, Lincoln explained, "it is a struggle for maintaining in the world, that form, and substance of government, whose leading object is, to elevate the condition of men—to lift artificial weights from all shoulders—to clear the paths of laudable pursuit for all—to afford all, an unfettered start, and a fair chance, in the race of life." That opportunity for a fair chance applied to all men.[10]

Later, when pressed to rescind his Emancipation Proclamation, he forcefully argued that the proclamation promises freedom, "and the promise being made, must be kept."[11] Lincoln was a strategic thinker. Always the logician, Lincoln knew the racist society of the time could not accept full equality for African Americans, but he also knew that once a domino was toppled, others were sure to follow. In his final speech, he called for voting rights for black men, that suffrage be conferred "on the very intelligent, and on those who serve our cause as soldiers."[12] He knew, once started, progress was hard to rescind and would gain momentum. The Fourteenth Amendment, passed three years later, guaranteed citizenship and equal protection under the law for all Americans. Then the Fifteenth Amendment in 1870 protected everyone's right to vote.

His commitment to science and technology played a major role in winning the Civil War. Lincoln personally encouraged the development of innovations, from more effective weapons to balloon reconnaissance to ironclad warships. He was the first president to strategically use the telegraph in wartime. He grappled with scientific issues related to saltpeter for gunpowder and the ethics of poisonous weapons. To relax, he visited the Naval Observatory to gaze at the stars.

Most importantly, Lincoln institutionalized science within the federal government. He relied on Joseph Henry not just for the expertise of the Smithsonian Institution, but also to lead the Permanent Commission of the navy to evaluate new weapons designs. The commission in its various iterations was the forerunner of today's Naval Research Laboratory. Lincoln's signature creating the National Academy of Sciences helped put the United States onto a path to build scientific and technological expertise rivaling that of Europe. He instigated creation of the Department of Agriculture to bring science to farming. Today the department runs extensive research programs, funds agronomic investigations, and disseminates new knowledge to farmers big and small. The department also provides an infrastructure framework to smooth the devastating swings of crop yields affected by floods, droughts, and other climatic extremes. And it was Lincoln who set aside the first land for federally funded protection; Yosemite was the precursor to the national park system we enjoy today.

All of these efforts were premised on the idea of an active federal government that could "do for a community of people, whatever they need to have done, but cannot do, at *all*, or cannot, so *well* do, for themselves— in their separate, and individual capacities."[13] As historian Richard Striner described it, Lincoln "provided the basis for national modernization, long-term planning, and national cohesiveness that turned our nation into a global superpower by the middle of the twentieth century."[14]

This concept was the basis for federal action by future presidents. Franklin Delano Roosevelt's New Deal created the Works Progress Administration and other programs to put Great Depression–era Americans to work building and repairing roads, bridges, railroads, and parks. It was the internal improvements program of his time. Harry S. Truman's Fair Deal continued this philosophy, seeking to turn the wartime economy into a peacetime economy. Dwight D. Eisenhower created a national network of interstate highways. Lyndon Johnson's Great Society sought to finish the work Lincoln's Emancipation Proclamation and the three Reconstruction Amendments had started, to eliminate poverty and racial injustice. Barack Obama's Affordable Care Act and similar legislation brought access to health care to those for whom it had been unobtainable. In 2013, Obama addressed the National Academy of Sciences on the 150th anniversary of its creation by Abraham Lincoln. He noted, "President Lincoln had the wisdom to look forward, and he recognized that finding a way to harness the highest caliber scientific advice for the government would serve a whole range of long-term goals for the nation."[15] Lincoln continues to inspire politicians on both sides of the aisle, as both parties claim the mantle of the "Party of Lincoln."

Lincoln's inspiration reaches scientists as well as politicians. Thomas Edison was fourteen years old when the Civil War began but already adept with telegraph transmission, blazing a trail to "send our news by lightning, on the telegraphic wire," as a popular song of the era intoned. Four years later he would tap out the message that Lincoln had been assassinated. Still later Edison would demonstrate his phonograph at the National Academy of Sciences and meet with Joseph Henry, and after inventing the film projector, one of his first silent films was *The Life of Abraham Lincoln*. Edison was so enamored that he placed Lincoln's profile on his own letterhead, writing out a testimonial that Lincoln's "life and character" would "stand as a monument" forever.[16] Lincoln's reputation reached across the Atlantic Ocean to another scientist named Michael Pupin. A Serbian immigrant arriving in the United States a decade after Lincoln's passing, Pupin named Abraham Lincoln one of his only two friends in America. Later enrolling in night school at Cooper Union because of Lincoln's 1860 speech, Pupin went on to compete in developing electrical dynamos with another Serbian immigrant, Nikola Tesla.[17] More recently, astrophysicist and recipient of the Abraham Lincoln Presidential Library Foundation Leadership Prize Neil deGrasse Tyson argued that Lincoln was a science champion. Tyson noted that "while most remember Honest Abe for war and peace, and slavery and freedom, the time has come to remember him for setting our Nation on a course of scientifically enlightened governance, without which we all may perish from this Earth."

As Americans continue the journey into an uncertain national future, we can heed Lincoln's advice to Congress at the end of 1862: "The dogmas of the quiet past, are inadequate to the stormy present. The occasion is piled high with difficulty, and we must rise with the occasion. As our case is new, so we must think anew, and act anew. We must disenthrall ourselves, and then we shall save our country."[18]

The dome of the Capitol serves as a metaphor of the principal role of government to elevate the condition of men. Unfinished at the beginning of the war, the old copper-clad wooden dome was being replaced with a new cast-iron one, its skeletal ribs incomplete above Lincoln as he gave his first inaugural address. Lincoln insisted that construction must go on during the Civil War to show the people that its government continued to operate. By his second inaugural address, a twenty-foot-tall bronze Statue of Freedom towered atop the completed dome. Technology had helped build the huge new structure. Lincoln recognized that science and technology would help build the new United States.

Acknowledgments

As with any book of this nature, the author stands on the shoulders of every researcher who paved the way so that others may follow, especially those who have painstakingly compiled and edited many of the letters, documents, and primary materials that are the basis for all Lincoln research. I have been privileged to meet many of the most highly respected Lincoln scholars still living. From them I have gained insights, guidance, and encouragement for this and my previous books.

I begin by thanking Sidney Blumenthal for writing the foreword for this book. I first met Sidney at a symposium shortly before the first of his planned five-volume series on the political life of Abraham Lincoln was published. In the years since then, he has remained a giving and gracious source of information and support. And as readers can see in his foreword, he is a wonderful and insightful writer.

As I write this, I am president of the Lincoln Group of the District of Columbia, founded in the 1930s and perhaps the most active multi-faceted Lincoln organization in existence. Through monthly lectures and study forums, I have been privileged to know numerous colleagues and friends. While too many to list, here are a few who have been especially supportive: John O'Brien, Jon Willen, Susan and Bernie Dennis, Wendy Swanson, Buzz Carnahan, Elizabeth Smith Brownstein, Catherine Lincoln, Rod Ross, Craig Howell, Debbie Jackson, Janet Saros, Rachel Riley, John Swallow, Jon Blackman, Diane Putney, Ted Beal, Dick Meyer, Ed Epstein, Richard Margolies, Carolyn Landry, Carl Adams, Scott Schroeder, Caroline Van Deusen, Carol Johnston, John Cooper, Matt Fink, Marida Amodio Mancino, Charlie Doty, Bob Willard, Dorothy D'Antoni, and many others. I am forever indebted to the mentorship of the late John Elliff and the late Paul Pascal. Special thanks to Rod Ross for providing so many opportunities to help reach a greater audience.

I have also worked with a stellar group of scholars as a member of the board and current treasurer of the Abraham Lincoln Institute. I have gained insights from Michelle Krowl, Edna Greene Medford, Lucas Morel, Ron Soodalter, Terry Alford, Michael Burlingame, Stacy Pratt McDermott (Stacy Lynn), Jason Emerson, Tom Horrocks, Gordon Leidner, James Swanson, Paul Tetreault, and Jonathan White. Another group in which I am active, the Lincoln Forum, has provided access to and deep discussions with some of the leading Abraham Lincoln scholars in the world, including Harold Holzer, Frank Williams, Craig Symonds, Wendy Allen, Dan Weinberg, David Hirsch, and Dan Van Haften. On my trips to "The Land of Lincoln" (aka Illinois), I have been privileged to meet with some of the finest minds of the Abraham Lincoln Association, including Wayne Temple, Kathryn Harris, Bob Lenz, Guy Fraker, Richard Hart, Sarah Watson, Bob Willard, and Christian McWhirter.

Research libraries, museums, and papers collections are the backbone of historical research, and it would be criminal not to acknowledge the assistance of so many people over the years of research needed to prepare this book. Michelle Krowl at the Library of Congress and James Cornelius, formerly of the Abraham Lincoln Presidential Library and Museum, were especially helpful. Thanks to Emily Rapoza for giving me a tour of the vault and so much help finding pertinent files in their outstanding Lincoln Collection at the Allen County Public Library. My thanks also to Michael Lynch and Steven Wilson of the Abraham Lincoln Library and Museum in Harrogate, Tennessee, for hosting me on a visit, showing me some of the coolest parts of their collection, and giving me access to many Lincoln-related papers, especially those of John Worden, commander of the Union ironclad USS *Monitor*. Frank Smith at the African American Civil War Memorial and Museum in Washington, D.C., has provided stellar information on the United States Colored Troops.

The friendship and assistance given to me by a variety of smaller venues helped me immensely, so thank you to the four delightful women at the Rockport, Indiana, public library who helped me find the Lincoln Landing site memorial, and especially the Genealogy Department for giving me access to their Lincoln collection; the gentleman at the Lincoln Pioneer Village in Rockport for his attention during my visit; the Henry Ford Museum and Greenfield Village, especially the docent of the Logan County Court House and the many people who helped explain the mills;

the reenactors in the Living Historical Farm at the Lincoln Boyhood National Memorial in Lincoln City, Indiana, who diligently explained everything from how to make candles from rendered hog fat to Thomas Lincoln's skills as a carpenter; and the park rangers at the Abraham Lincoln Birthplace National Park, especially Park Ranger William Ozment for explaining how the log cabin was made.

It takes a lot of expertise to cover such a far-ranging book. I am grateful to all the experts who graciously gave me the benefit of their knowledge. I thank Marc Rothenberg, longtime director of the Papers of Joseph Henry project at the Smithsonian Institution, for our long discussion of the relationship between Joseph Henry and Abraham Lincoln and for reviewing an excerpt of that chapter. Douglas L. Wilson helped steer me to Herndon's papers for the *Vestiges of Creation* book, not to mention his work with Rodney O. Davis to organize and annotate all the letters and interviews compiled by William Herndon shortly after Lincoln's assassination. Thank you Dr. Jon Willen, a prolific reenactor of Civil War surgery, for his friendship and extensive medical knowledge of the time period; Larry West for his help in tracking down information on the history of photography during the period; Melissa Winn for her photography expertise; former congressman Jerry Weller and Howard Marks, the past and current presidents of the Illinois State Society, for their encouragement and insights; Steven Wilson for providing me with copies of Wayne Temple's two-part "Lincoln the Lecturer" papers from the *Lincoln Herald*; Erin Carlson Mast and Curtis Harris for their support and tour at President Lincoln Cottage. I also thank Anna Gibson Holloway for insights on the *Monitor* and giving me contacts at the Hunley project; Narciso Gomez, who portrayed Gustav, John Ericsson's assistant, at the Monitor Center at the Mariners' Museum during my visit (along with additional information beyond the displays he sent me); and Karen Needles for her Lincoln Archives Digital Project documents and other resources. Thanks to Amanda Kirby and all the people of the Shenandoah Valley Agricultural Research and Extension Center who maintain the Cyrus McCormick Farm in Raphine, Virginia. After my visit, Amanda took the time to provide me with follow-up information that was useful for my research. Thank you to funeral director Jeffrey Jones for his insights into the art and science of embalming, past and present. Thank you to George Mason University Professor Christopher Hamner, who provided substantial insights into the technology of the Civil War and Lincoln's strategic thinking.

I am deeply indebted to Ed Steers for answering my questions about milk sickness and brucellosis, in addition to many other scientific issues. Both Ed and I had long careers as scientists before turning to Lincoln studies. He has single-handedly demonstrated that being both a scientist and a Lincoln historian is not an oxymoron.

Many others have provided specific expertise used in this book. Jason Emerson provided guidance on Lincoln as an inventor and steered me toward how Robert Lincoln's interest in astronomy was rooted in his father's lifelong curiosity. David Hirsch and Dan Van Haften helped me understand Lincoln's use of Euclid's six elements for his political speeches and writings. David Wiegers guided me to even more Lincoln statues during my long road trips around Kentucky, Indiana, Illinois, and overseas. Journalist and author Robert O'Harrow Jr. sent me files on Lincoln's Civil War quartermaster, Montgomery Meigs. Kathryn Canavan provided advice on Dupont's inventions library, as well as a document on Niagara Falls. Thank you to Michael Burlingame for his magnificent "green monster," the two-volume *Abraham Lincoln: A Life* with its incredible depth of sourcing, as well as for suggestions and leads to additional material; Harold Holzer for his incalculable insight, knowledge, and tips; Jonathan W. White for his support and insights. Stacy Pratt McDermott (Stacy Lynn) provided information on Mary Lincoln's visit to Niagara Falls. James Green, division director at NASA, took time to discuss Lincoln and Civil War balloons with me, plus provided two papers on the 1859 astral event.

I have also gained from conversations and correspondence with James Swanson, Thomas Mackie, Carole Adrienne Murphy, Will Fenton, David Gerleman, Brent Wielt, and Melody Arnold, and thank you to Mike Hardy, who runs the Learning About Lincoln Facebook page, for his friendship and support. I thank also Mary, Jeremy, and Nick at the *Railsplitter* podcast for three episodes reviewing my previous book, *Lincoln: The Man Who Saved America* and for having me on their podcast again during the heart of the COVID pandemic to talk about Lincoln and viruses. A special thanks to independent filmmaker and activist Annabel Park for helping me see the value of bringing Lincoln scholarship to a broader public audience.

Many thanks to my literary agent, Marilyn Allen, for her work finding a stellar publisher for this book. Thank you to my editor, Gene Brissie, and Rowman & Littlefield for having confidence in the viability of the topic in the marketplace. I appreciate the opportunity to bring Lincoln's lesser-known commitments to science and technology to the public.

As with all long-term endeavors, there are many who must exhibit supreme patience and forbearance during the time needed for an author's obsessions to turn ideas into a book. Extra special thanks and affection go out to Ru Sun for her constant encouragement, constructive criticism, and exceptional attention to detail, and for the patience of Job. This book and I are much better because of her presence.

Notes

Introduction

1. Bruce, Robert V. 1987. *The Launching of Modern American Science, 1846–1876*. Alfred A. Knopf, 115–16.
2. Brookhiser, Richard. 2014. *Founders' Son: A Life of Abraham Lincoln*. Basic Books, 2–3.
3. Wulf, Andrea. 2015. *The Invention of Nature: Alexander Von Humboldt's New World*. Alfred A. Knopf, 105; Bedini, Silvio A. 2002. *Jefferson and Science*. Thomas Jefferson Foundation, 15–29; Holton, Gerald, and Gerhard Sonnert. 1999. "A Vision of Jeffersonian Science." *Issues in Science and Technology* 16(1):61–65.
4. Bedini, *Jefferson and Science*, 12.
5. Speech at Independence Hall, February 22, 1861, in Basler, Roy P., ed. 1953. *The Collected Works of Abraham Lincoln*. Rutgers University Press, 4:240; speech at Springfield, Illinois, June 26, 1857, in ibid., 2:407.
6. Vernon Burton lecture to the Lincoln Group of DC, April 16, 2013.
7. The territories were populated by Native Americans, of course, but the rights of these peoples were largely ignored by the battling North and South as white settlers pressed westward.
8. Autobiography written for John L. Scripps, June 1860, in *Collected Works*, 4:67.
9. For a full transcription of the U.S. Constitution, see https://www.archives.gov/founding-docs/constitution-transcript.

Chapter 1: Farming Science

1. Jordan, Philip D. 1944. "The Death of Nancy Hanks Lincoln." *Indiana Magazine of History* 40(2):103–10.
2. Burlingame, Michael. 2008. *Abraham Lincoln: A Life*. Johns Hopkins University Press, chap. 2, p. 89. (Page numbers from online manuscript version.)
3. Angier, Natalie. 2007. *The Canon: A Whirligig Tour of the Beautiful Basics of Science*. Houghton Mifflin, 21–22.
4. Herndon, William H., and Jesse W. Weik. 2006. *Herndon's Lincoln*. Ed. Douglas L. Wilson and Rodney O. Davis. University of Illinois Press, 15; John L. Scripps letter to William H. Herndon, June 24, 1865, in Wilson, Douglas L., and Rodney O. Davis, eds. 1998. *Herndon's Informants*. University of Illinois Press, 57.
5. Holzer, Harold, and Norton Garfinkle. 2015. *A Just and Generous Nation*. Basic Books, 174.
6. Vernon Burton, personal correspondence, April 16, 2013; Tackach, James. 2019. *Lincoln and the Natural Environment*. Southern Illinois University Press, 9.

7. Marx, Leo. 1964. *The Machine in the Garden: Technology and the Pastoral Ideal in America*. Oxford University Press, 115.

8. Shaw, Robert, and Michael Burlingame. 2012. *Abraham Lincoln Traveled This Way*. Firelight, 15.

9. Autobiography written for John L. Scripps in June 1860, in *Collected Works*, 4:61–62.

10. Bartelt, William E. 2008. *There I Grew Up: Remembering Abraham Lincoln's Indiana Youth*. Indiana Historical Society Press, 11; Skeen, C. Edward. 2003. *1816: America Rising*. University Press of Kentucky, 6.

11. Klingaman, William K., and Nicholas P. Klingaman. 2013. *The Year without Summer: 1816 and the Volcano That Darkened the World and Changed History*. St. Martin's Press, 88, 238.

12. Ibid., 201.

13. Skeen, C. Edward. 1981. "The Year Without a Summer: A Historical Review." *Journal of the Early Republic* 1(1):51–67; Wood, Gillen D'Arcy. 2014. "The Volcano That Changed the Course of History." *Slate*, April 09. https://slate.com/technology/2014/04/tambora-eruption-caused-the-year-without-a-summer-cholera-opium-famine-and-arctic-exploration.html.

14. Klingaman and Klingaman, *Year without Summer*, 166.

15. Ibid., 282.

16. Ibid., 16.

17. Oppenheimer, Clive. 2003. "Climatic, Environmental and Human Consequences of the Largest Known Historic Eruption: Tambora Volcano (Indonesia) 1815." *Progress in Physical Geography* 27(2):230–59; Klingaman and Klingaman, *Year without Summer*, 12; Stothers, Richard B. 1984. "The Great Tambora Eruption in 1815 and Its Aftermath." *Science* 224(4654):1191–98; Evans, Robert. 2002. "Blast from the Past." *Smithsonian*, July. https://www.smithsonianmag.com/history/blast-from-the-past-65102374/; "1816: The Year without a Summer," New England Historical Society, http://newenglandhistoricalsociety.com/1816-year-without-a-summer/. Some at the time pointed to unusual sunspot activity, while even more outlandish suggestions included the melting of icy mountains by wind, cooling of the earth's core, sudden changes to "electrical fluids" that supposedly moved between the planet's surface and the atmosphere, and even earthquakes or lightning rods. Another idea was that the summer was related to a mini ice age that covered portions of the northern hemisphere from 1400 to around 1860. This is highly unlikely given that no other year during the 460-year period seems to have elicited such a noteworthy series of weather events.

18. Bartelt, *There I Grew Up*, 11; Skeen, *America Rising*, 1; Klingaman and Klingaman, *Year without Summer*; Harrington, C. R., ed. 1992. *The Year without a Summer? World Climate in 1816*. Canadian Museum of Nature, Ottawa, Canada. https://www.biodiversitylibrary.org/bibliography/81797#/summary.

19. Brinkman, Marilyn Salzl. 2015. "First Job for Pioneers—Clear Stumps." *SC Times*, February 14, 2015. https://www.sctimes.com/story/life/2015/02/14/pioneers-farming-started-stump-clearing/23418141/.

20. *Collected Works*, 4:62.

21. Ibid., 4:62.

22. Warren, Louis A. 1959. *Lincoln's Youth: Indiana Years, Seven to Twenty-One, 1816–1830*. Appleton Century Crofts, 26, citing J. S. Duss. 1914. *George Rapp and His Associates (The Harmony Society)*. Hollenbeck Press, 11–12.

23. Dirck, Brian R. 2017. *Lincoln in Indiana*. Southern Illinois University Press, 5, 30.

24. Bartelt, *There I Grew Up*, 14; Bearss, Edwin. 1967. *Lincoln Boyhood—as a Living Historical Farm*. National Park Service, National Technical Information Service Report PB 200500, Springfield, VA, pp. 43–48; Dennis Hanks to William H. Herndon, January 6, 1866, in Wilson and Davis, *Herndon's Informants*, 153–54.

25. Brinkman, "First Job for Pioneers."

26. Dodge, Daniel Kilham. 1900/2000. *Abraham Lincoln: The Evolution of His Literary Style*. University of Illinois Press, 29; Carpenter, F. B. 1869. *The Inner Life of Abraham Lincoln: Six Months at the White House*. Hurd and Houghton, 224–25.

27. William Wood, interview with William H. Herndon, September 15, 1865, in Wilson and Davis, *Herndon's Informants*, 124.

28. Cornelius, James M., and Carla Knorowski. 2016. *Under Lincoln's Hat: 100 Objects That Tell the Story of His life and Legacy*. LP Books, 143.

29. Heiligmann, Randall B., "Controlling Undesirable Trees, Shrubs, and Vines in Your Woodland," Ohio State University Fact Sheet, https://web.archive.org/web/20010320060728/http://ohioline.osu.edu/for-fact/0045.html; Dirck, *Lincoln in Indiana*, 31.

30. Ranger William Ozment, personal communication, Abraham Lincoln Birthplace National Historical Park, Hodgenville, Kentucky, May 8, 2018.

31. "Log Home Logs: All You Need to Know." Lag Cabin Hub, January 31, 2017. https://www.logcabinhub.com/log-home-logs-all-you-need-to-know/; Shelley, Patrick. "How to Build a Log Cabin, Just Like the Pioneers Did." https://www.offthegridnews.com/how-to-2/how-to-build-a-log-cabin-just-like-the-pioneers-did/.

32. Septima Collis, cited in Burlingame, *Abraham Lincoln*, chap. 35, p. 3954.

33. Ranger William Ozment, personal communication, May 8, 2018; Ewbank, Lewis B. 1942. "Building a Pioneer Home." *Indiana Magazine of History* 37:121; McCutcheon, Marc. 1993. *The Writer's Guide to Everyday Life in the 1800s*. Writer's Digest Books, 91; Augustus H. Chapman statement, in Wilson and Davis, *Herndon's Informants*, 99.

34. Interview with Jack Peck, 1888, in Smith, *Lincoln and the Lincolns*, 179–71, cited in Burlingame, *Abraham Lincoln*, chap. 1, p. 53.

35. Dirck, *Lincoln in Indiana*, 33; Schreeder, C. C. "The Lincolns and Their Home in Spencer County, Indiana." *Southwestern Indiana Historical Society Annuals* 4:157–69, cited in Bartelt, William E., and Joshua A. Claybourn, eds. 2019. *Abe's Youth: Shaping the Future President*. Indiana University Press, 144.

36. Dirck, *Lincoln in Indiana*, 33.

37. Varhola, Michael J. 1999. *Everyday Life during the Civil War*. Writer's Digest Books, 82–83; McCutcheon, *Writer's Guide to Everyday Life*, 173–87; Lee, Hilde Gabriel. 1992. *Taste of the States: A Food History of America*. Howell Press, 72–73; Ewbank, "Building a Pioneer Home," 115; Temple, Wayne C. 2004. *"The Taste Is in My Mouth a Little . . .": Lincoln's Victuals and Potables*. Mayhaven.

38. Czajka, Christopher W. "'Without Peas and Things Put into It': Food on the Frontier." Frontier House. https://www.thirteen.org/wnet/frontierhouse/frontierlife/essay6.html. John Hanks was Lincoln's mother's cousin (i.e., his first cousin once removed).

39. Waltmann, Henry G. 1975. *Pioneer Farming in Indiana: Thomas Lincoln's Major Crops, 1816–1830*. Association for Living Historical Farms and Agricultural Museums, Smithsonian Institution, 6–26, cited in Dirck, *Lincoln in Indiana*, 34; Lee, *Taste of the States*, 72–73; Temple, *"Taste Is in My Mouth a Little"*; "Kentucky," in "Traditional State Foods & Recipes." Food Timeline. http://www.foodtimeline.org/statefoods.html#kentucky; Czajka, "'Without Peas and Things Put into It.'"

40. Dennis Hanks, interview with Erastus Wright, in Wilson and Davis, *Herdon's Informants*, 27.

41. *Collected Works*, 4:62.

42. Ewbank, "Building a Pioneer Home," 111–28.

43. Autobiography written for Jesse Fell, December 20, 1859, in *Collected Works*, 3:511.

44. Chen, Sandie Angulo. 2015. "What Did People Eat in the 1800s?" Ancestry.com blog, April 29. https://blogs.ancestry.com/cm/what-was-life-like-200-years-ago/.

45. Excerpt from "The Bear Hunt," September 6, 1846, in *Collected Works*, 1:386.

46. Edwards, Everett E. 1933. "Lincoln's Attitude toward Farm Problems." Address given December 15, 1933. Bureau of Agricultural Economics (originally published in *Agricultural Library Notes* 6 [February 1931]: 29–33); "What Is Karst?" University of Texas at Austin. https://web.archive.org/web/20060516002856/http://www.esi.utexas.edu/outreach/caves/karst.php; "Sinking Spring." Abraham Lincoln Birthplace. https://www.nps.gov/abli/learn/historyculture/sinking-spring.htm.

47. Lincoln to Samuel Haycraft, June 4, 1960, in *Collected Works*, 4:70; Edwards, "Lincoln's Attitude toward Farm Problems."

48. A. H. Chapman, written statement, September 8, 1865, in Wilson and Davis, *Herndon's Informants*, 98; Dennis Hanks, interview with William H. Herndon, in ibid., 105.

49. Matilda Johnston Moore, interview with William H. Herndon, in ibid., 109.

50. Atwood, T. C., and H. P. Weeks. 2003. "Sex-Specific Patterns of Mineral Lick Preference in White-Tailed Deer." *Northeastern Naturalist* 10(4):409–14; Time Staff. 1982. "A Brief History of Salt." *Time*, March 15. https://time.com/3957460/a-brief-history-of-salt/.

51. Ewbank, "Building a Pioneer Home," 111–28; Editorial Staff. 2014. "The Science of Salting: How to Preserve Food with Salt." *Fine Dining Lovers*, October 28. https://www.finedininglovers.com/article/science-salting-how-preserve-food-salt.

52. Courtwright, David T. 1991. "Disease, Death, and Disorder on the American Frontier." *Journal of the History of Medicine and Allied Sciences* 46(4):457–92; Dirck, Brian. 2019. *The Black Heavens: Abraham Lincoln and Death*. Southern Illinois University Press.

53. McCutcheon, *Writer's Guide to Everyday Life*, 157, 163, 164; Bartelt and Claybourn, *Abe's Youth*, 173.

54. Muller-Schwartz, Dietland, and Lixing Sun. 2003. *The Beaver: Natural History of a Wetlands Engineer*. Comstock, 43.

55. Scripps, John Locke. 2010. *Vote Lincoln! The Presidential Campaign Biography of Abraham Lincoln, 1860*. Boston Hill Press, 33; autobiography for Scripps, in *Collected*

Works, 4:62; Stewart, Amy. 2009. *Wicked Plants: The Weed That Killed Lincoln's Mother and Other Botanical Atrocities*. Algonquin Books of Chapel Hill, 213–15; Jordan, "Death of Nancy Hanks Lincoln," 103–10.

56. Herndon and Weik, *Herndon's Lincoln*, 30; Lamon, Ward Hill. 1872/2013. *The Life of Abraham Lincoln*. Rep. ed. including letter from Theo. Lemon. Echo Library, 30–31; Stewart, *Wicked Plants*, 213–15.

57. Stewart, *Wicked Plants*, 213–15.

58. Ibid.; Bartelt, *There I Grew Up*, 20; Snively, William D. 1966. "Discoverer of the Cause of Milk Sickness." *Journal of the American Medical Association* 196:1058–60.

59. Tabler, Dave. 2019. "The Curse of the Milk Sickness." *Appalachian History*, February 18. http://www.appalachianhistory.net/2019/02/the-curse-of-milk-sickness-part-1-of-2.html and http://www.appalachianhistory.net/2019/02/the-curse-of-milk-sickness-part-2-of-2.html; Jordan, "Death of Nancy Hanks Lincoln," 103–10.

60. Daly, Walter J. 2006. "The 'Slows': The Torment of Milk Sickness on the Midwest Frontier." *Indiana Magazine of History* 102(1):29–40; Davis, T. Zane, et al. 2018. "Effect of Grinding and Long-Term Storage on the Toxicity of White Snakeroot (*Ageratina altissima*) in Goats." *Research in Veterinary Science* 118:419–22. Biomedical researcher and Lincoln historian Edward Steers Jr. argues that tremetone is the actual toxic chemical. Tremetone is one of many components of tremetol, which most historians report as the toxic chemical. Steers also suggests that Nancy Lincoln may have died of brucellosis, a bacterial disease that more logically fits the circumstances (e.g., only a few people died despite all of them drinking the milk of infected cows) (personal communication, 2019; Steers, Edward, Jr. 2021. *Getting Right with Lincoln*. University Press of Kentucky, 146–47).

61. Jordan, "Death of Nancy Hanks Lincoln," 103–10; Herndon and Weik, *Herndon's Lincoln*, 30; Lamon, *Life of Abraham Lincoln*, 213–15.

62. Bartelt, *There I Grew Up*, 20; Snively, "Discoverer of the Cause of Milk Sickness," 1058.

63. Burlingame, *Abraham Lincoln*, chap. 2, p. 169.

64. Klingaman and Klingaman, *Year without Summer*, 87, 90. Planting clover or scattering manure or gypsum could reinvigorate soil nutrients. Pioneers often plowed only shallow furrows, so when cold weather struck in the summer, moisture on the surface froze and dislodged seedlings.

65. Shaw and Burlingame, *Abraham Lincoln Traveled This Way*, 29–30; autobiography for Scripps, in *Collected Works*, 4:63; Howells, William D. 1938. *Life of Abraham Lincoln*. Abraham Lincoln Association, 23.

66. Shaw and Burlingame, *Abraham Lincoln Traveled This Way*, 29; Burlingame, *Abraham Lincoln*, chap. 2, p. 173.

67. Hoekstra, J. M., et al. 2010. *The Atlas of Global Conservation: Changes, Challenges, and Opportunities to Make a Difference*. University of California Press; "Central Forest-Grasslands Transition." World Wildlife Federation. https://www.worldwildlife.org/ecoregions/na0804.

68. "Illinois." Netstate. http://www.netstate.com/states/geography/il_geography.htm.

69. "Prairie Soils." Soil Science Society of America. https://www.soils4teachers.org/prairies/.

70. "Prairie Grasses." FermiLab. https://ed.fnal.gov/entry_exhibits/grass/grass_title.html; Shaw and Burlingame, *Abraham Lincoln Traveled This Way*, 136ff.

71. Friedman, Thomas. 2016. *Thank You for Being Late*. Farrar, Straus and Giroux, 319–20.

72. Harlan, Becky. 2015. "Digging Deep Reveals the Intricate World of Roots." *National Geographic*, October 15. https://www.nationalgeographic.com/photography/proof/2015/10/15/digging-deep-reveals-the-intricate-world-of-roots/.

73. Lincoln to John Hanks, August 24, 1860, in *Collected Works*, 4:100.

74. Dirck, *Lincoln in Indiana*, 106; Waltmann, *Pioneer Farming in Indiana*, 23; "The Cast Iron Plow." Today in Sci. https://todayinsci.com/Events/Plow/Plow_CastIron.htm.

75. Landers, Jackson. 2015. "Did John Deere's Best Invention Spark a Revolution or an Environmental Disaster?" *Smithsonian*, December 17. https://www.smithsonianmag.com/smithsonian-institution/did-john-deeres-best-invention-spark-revolution-or-environmental-disaster-180957080/; "The Original Steel Plow." John Deere. https://www.deere.com/en/our-company/history/john-deere-plow/.

76. Steinbacher-Kemp, Bill. 2007. "Pictures from Our Past." *Pantagraph*, March 18. https://www.pantagraph.com/news/pictures-from-our-past/article_c48d46c6-cc39-54a3-8cc7-de8f3d99a831.html.

77. Miller, Richard Lawrence. 2006. *Lincoln and His World: The Early Years, Birth to Illinois Legislature*. Stackpole Books, 99; Burlingame, *Abraham Lincoln*, chap. 2, pp. 176–77; Abraham Lincoln National Heritage Area, Looking for Lincoln wayside sign, "Winter of the Deep Snow," in Decatur, Illinois.

78. Edwards, "Lincoln's Attitude toward Farm Problems."

79. Friedman, *Thank You for Being Late*, 319–20.

80. Chen, "What Did People Eat in the 1800s?"

81. Everett, Griff, Stepanie H. Hitchcock, Jane Middleton, and Rosemary H. Timms. 2006. *"Samuel Slater—Hero or Traitor?"* Maypole Promotions.

82. *Collected Works*, 3:472–73; Burlingame, *Abraham Lincoln*, chap. 2, p. 179; Edwards, "Lincoln's Attitude toward Farm Problems."

83. Dirck, *Lincoln in Indiana*, 66.

Chapter 2: Educating Lincoln: From Readin' to Euclid

1. *Sangamo Journal*, March 15, 1832, in *Collected Works*, 1:8.

2. Dodge, *Abraham Lincoln*, 4.

3. Autobiography for Scripps, in *Collected Works*, 4:62.

4. Bowers, Claude. 1945. *The Young Jefferson, 1743–1789*. Houghton Mifflin, cited in Bedini, Silvio A. 1990. *Thomas Jefferson: Statesman of Science*. Macmillan, 254.

5. Warren, Louis. 1941. "Lincoln's Formal Education." *Lincoln Lore* 647:1.

6. Autobiography for Fell, in *Collected Works*, 3:511.

7. Dennis Hanks, interview with William Herndon, June 13, 1865, in Wilson and Davis, *Herndon's Informants*, 37; Dennis Hanks, interview with Jesse Weik, 1886, in ibid., 598.

8. Autobiography for Scripps, in *Collected Works*, 4:61; Sarah Bush Lincoln, interview with Herndon, in Wilson and Davis, *Herndon's Informants*, 107–8; Herndon and Weik, *Herndon's Lincoln*, 35n.

9. Leonard Swett in Rice, Allen Thorndike. 1886. *Reminiscences of Abraham Lincoln*. North American Publishing, 458.

10. Marty, Myron. 2008. "Schooling in Lincoln's America and Lincoln's Extraordinary Self-Schooling." In Fornieri, Joseph R., and Sara Vaughn Gabbard. *Lincoln's America, 1809–1865*. Southern Illinois University Press, 57.

11. Dirck, *Lincoln in Indiana*, 72.

12. Autobiography for Fell, in *Collected Works*, 3:511.

13. Burlingame, *Abraham Lincoln*, chap. 1, 64–65.

14. Thayer, William M. 1863. *The Pioneer Boy and How He Became President*. Walker, Wise and Company, 22.

15. Coffin, Charles Carleton. 1892. *Abraham Lincoln*. Harper & Brothers, 23.

16. Autobiography for Scripps, in *Collected Works*, 4:62.

17. Herndon and Weik, *Herndon's Lincoln*, 207.

18. Autobiography for Fell, in *Collected Works*, 3:511.

19. Dilworth, Thomas. 1796. *Dilworth's Spelling Book, Improved: A New Guide to the English Tongue*. John McCulluch; Bray, Robert. 2007. "What Abraham Lincoln Read: An Evaluative and Annotated List." *Journal of the Abraham Lincoln Association* (henceforth *JALA*) 28(2):48; Fraker, Guy C. 2020. "Kirkham's Grammar: English Grammar in Familiar Lectures." *For the People* 22(1):8.

20. Warren, Louis. 1939. "Scott's Lessons in Elocution." *Lincoln Lore* 512 (January 30).

21. Bartelt, *There I Grew Up*, 194–95; Bray, "What Abraham Lincoln Read," 78.

22. Wilson and Davis, *Herndon's Informants*, 25–27.

23. Burlingame, *Abraham Lincoln*, chap. 2, 122.

24. Duncan, Kunigunde, and D. F. Nichols. 1944. *Mentor Graham: The Man Who Taught Lincoln*. University of Chicago Press, 250 (Graham, letter to Herndon, July 15, 1865).

25. Kirkham, Samuel. 1999. *Kirkham's Grammar: The Book That Shaped Lincoln's Prose*. Octavo Press, 12, 17.

26. William Greene, letter to James Q. Howard, in Mearns, David C. 1948. *The Lincoln Papers*. Doubleday, 1:153.

27. Swett in Rice, *Reminiscences*, 458.

28. Nathaniel Grigsby, interview with Herndon, September 12, 1865, in Wilson and Davis, *Herndon's Informants*, 112; Warren, Louis. 1930. "Pike's Arithmetic." *Lincoln Lore* 67; Warren, Louis. 1940. "Book of Examples of Arithmetic." *Lincoln Lore* 596; Houser, M. L. 1943. *Young Abraham Lincoln Mathematician*. Lester O. Schriver, 14.

29. Clements, McKenzie A., and Nerida F. Ellerton. 2015. "Abraham Lincoln's Cyphering Book and the *Abbaco* Tradition." *JALA* 36(1):1; PDF copies are available at the Abraham Lincoln Presidential Library and Museum (henceforth ALPLM), Document #200001.

30. Sarma, S. R. "Rule of Three and Its Variations in India." In Dold-Samplonius, Y., J. W. Dauben, M. Folkerts, and B. Van Dalen, eds. *From China to Paris: 2000 Years*

Transmission of Mathematical Ideas. Franz Steiner Verlag, 133–56; Kent, David J. 2014. "Lincoln and the Rule of Three." *Lincolnian* 32:4–6.

31. ALPLM, Document #200001; Warren, *Lincoln's Youth*; Houser, *Young Abraham Lincoln Mathematician*; Warren, "Book of Examples of Arithmetic."

32. Leavitt, Dudley. 1826. *Pike's System of Arithmetick, Abridged*. Jacob B. Moore; Daboll, Nathan. 1817. *Daboll's Schoolmaster's Assistant (Daboll's Arithmetic)*. E & E Hosford.

33. Silverman, Jason. 2018. "Finding Lincoln in the Most Unusual Places." *Lincoln Herald* 120(3–4):136.

34. Fortune, William. "Lincoln in Indiana." In Bartelt and Claybourn, *Abe's Youth*, 39; Atkinson, Eleanor. 1908. *The Boyhood of Lincoln*. McClure, 31.

35. Hirsch, David, and Dan Van Haften. 2010. *Abraham Lincoln and the Structure of Reason*. Savas Beatie, 23.

36. Struik, Dirk J. 1967. *A Concise History of Mathematics*. Dover, 51; Casey, John. 1885. *The First Six Books of the Elements of Euclid*. 3rd ed. Hodges, Figgis & Company.

37. McCoy, Drew R. 2002. "An Old-Fashioned Nationalism: Lincoln, Jefferson, and the American Tradition." *JALA* 23(1):58; Jefferson, Thomas. 2002. *Notes on the State of Virginia*. Bedford/St. Martins, 177.

38. Herndon and Weik, *Herndon's Lincoln*, 194.

39. Casey, *First Six Books*, 1, 6; Hirsch and Van Haften, *Abraham Lincoln and the Structure of Reason*, 24.

40. Signified by the Greek letter *phi* and equal to the irrational number 1.61803. . . . For an accessible discussion of the golden ration, see Livio, Mario. 2002. *The Golden Ratio*. Broadway Books.

41. Casey, *First Six Books*.

42. Fourth debate with Stephen A. Douglas, Charleston, Illinois, September 18, 1858, in *Collected Works*, 3:186.

43. Hirsch and Van Haften, *Abraham Lincoln and the Structure of Reason*.

44. Bray, "What Abraham Lincoln Read."

45. Sarah Lincoln to Herndon, September 8, 1865, in Wilson and Davis, *Herndon's Informants*, 107; Hertz, Emanuel. 1938. *The Hidden Lincoln*. Viking.

46. Gulliver, J. P. "Reminiscences." *New York Independent*, September 1, 1864, cited in Carpenter, Francis B. 1867. *Six Months in the White House: The Story of a Picture*. Hurd and Houghton, 312–13.

47. Joshua Speed, letter to Herndon, December 6, 1866, in Wilson and Davis, *Herndon's Informants*, 498.

48. Burlingame, *Abraham Lincoln*, chap. 26, 2804–5.

49. Graham, letter to Herndon, July 15, 1865, in Duncan and Nichols, *Mentor Graham*, 250.

50. Washington correspondence, February 23, 1861, *Philadelphia Inquirer*, February 25, 1861.

51. Graham, letter to Herndon, July 15, 1865, in Duncan and Nichols, *Mentor Graham*, 250.

52. Rutledge to Herndon, November 1, 1866, in Wilson and Davis, *Herndon's Informants*, 384; Rutledge to Herndon, November 30, 1866, in ibid., 426.

53. Herndon and Weik, *Herndon's Lincoln*, 37; Anna Caroline Roby Gentry, interview with Herndon, September 17, 1865, in Wilson and Davis, *Herndon's Informants*, 132.

54. Bray, "What Abraham Lincoln Read," 68; Houser, M. L. 1942. *Young Abraham Lincoln and Log College*. Lester O. Shriver, 33; Houser, M. L. 1957. *Lincoln's Education and Other Essays*. Bookman Associates, 318.

55. Swett in Rice, *Reminiscences*, 467.

56. Vosmeier, Sarah McNair. 1988. "Robert V. Bruce and the Launching of Modern American Science, 1846–1876." *Lincoln Lore* 1792: 3.

57. Bray, "What Abraham Lincoln Read," 68; Houser, *Lincoln's Education*, 318.

58. Robert Rutledge, letter to Herndon, November 1, 1866, in Wilson and Davis, *Herndon's Informants*, 384–85.

59. Dr. John Allen, interview with James Q. Howard, "Notes of James Q. Howard about Abraham Lincoln," May 1860, Library of Congress, 1 http://memory.loc.gov/mss/mal/mal1/029/0297401/010.jpg.

60. Bruce, *Launching of Modern American Science*, 116; Burlingame, *Abraham Lincoln*, chap. 3, 230–31; Marty, "Schooling in Lincoln's America," 63–64.

61. Bray, "What Abraham Lincoln Read," 35; Blumenthal, Sidney. 2019. *All The Powers of Earth 1856–1860: The Political Life of Abraham Lincoln*. Simon & Schuster, 194–95.

62. Bray, "What Abraham Lincoln Read," 39; Brewster, George. 1943. *A New Philosophy of Matter Showing the Identity of All the Imponderables and the Influence Which Electricity Exerts over Matter in Producing All Chemical Changes and All Motion*. A. W. Maddocks, 216.

63. Bray, "What Abraham Lincoln Read," 52; Temple, Wayne C. 2005. "Herndon on Lincoln: An Unknown Interview with a List of Books in the Lincoln & Herndon Law Office." *Journal of the Illinois State Historical Society* 98:34–50.

64. Bruce, Robert V. 1956. *Lincoln and the Tools of War*. Bobbs-Merrill, 12; Wells, David A., ed. 1850. *The Annual of Scientific Discovery, or, Year-Book of Facts in Science and Art*. Gould, Kendall, and Lincoln.

65. Bruce, *Lincoln and the Tools of War*, 12.

66. Herndon, letter to Weik, December 16, 1885, in Wilson, Douglas L., and Rodney O. Davis. 2016. *Herndon on Lincoln: Letters*. University of Illinois Press, 175.

67. Herndon, letter to Weik, February 27, 1891, in Wilson and Davis, *Herndon on Lincoln*, 342.

68. Bruce, *Lincoln and the Tools of War*, 12; Lander, James. 2011. "Herndon's 'Auction List' and Lincoln's Interest in Science." *JALA* 32(2):21.

69. Townsend, George Alfred. 1867. *The Real Life of Abraham Lincoln: A Talk with Mr. Herndon, His Late Law Partner*. Publication Office, Bible House, 4–5; Burlingame, *Abraham Lincoln*, chap. 18, 2060.

70. Donald, David Herbert. 1948. *Lincoln's Herndon*. Alfred A. Knopf, 15.

71. Newton, Joseph Fort. 1910. *Lincoln and Herndon*. Torch Press, 254.

72. Lander, "Herndon's 'Auction List,'" 17.

73. Gillespie, letter to Herndon, December 8, 1866, in Wilson and Davis, *Herndon's Informants*, 505–6.

74. Davis, interview with Herndon, September 20, 1866, in Wilson and Davis, *Herndon's Informants*, 350; Gillespie, letter to Herndon, December 8, 1866, in ibid., 505–6.
75. *Sangamo Journal*, March 15, 1832, in *Collected Works*, 1:8.
76. Autobiography for Scripps, in ibid., 4:62.
77. Eulogy to Henry Clay, July 6, 1852, in ibid., 2:124.
78. Resolution introduced in Illinois legislature, December 2, 1840, in ibid., 1:213–14.

Chapter 3: Life on the Waters

1. Warren, Louis. 1946. "Lincoln Homes on the Water Courses." *Lincoln Lore* 922 (December 9).
2. Autobiography for Scripps, in *Collected Works*, 4:61.
3. McMurtry, R. 1937. "The Lincoln Migration from Kentucky to Indiana." *Indiana Magazine of History* 33(4):421.
4. Warren, Louis. 1932. "The Lincolns Crossing the Ohio." *Lincoln Lore* 177 (August 29); McMurtry, "Lincoln Migration," 413–14.
5. Green B. Taylor, interview with Herndon, September 16, 1865, in Wilson and Davis, *Herndon's Informants*, 129–30; Joseph C. Richardson, interview with Herndon, September 14, 1866, in ibid., 119.
6. Warren, Louis. 1947. "Lincoln: A Hoosier Trojan Youth." *Lincoln Lore* 951 (June 30).
7. Taylor interview, in Wilson and Davis, *Herndon's Informants*, 129–30; Burlingame, *Abraham Lincoln*, chap. 2, 148, citing correspondence "down the Ohio and round about," dated September 21, 1890, *Chicago Tribune*, 25.
8. Warren, *Lincoln's Youth*, 145.
9. William D. Kelley in Rice, *Reminiscences*, 279–80.
10. Warren, *Lincoln's Youth*, 146–47. A slightly different story is given in Murr, J. Edward. 1918. "Lincoln's Ambition to Become a River Pilot." *Indiana Magazine of History* 14(2):151–52, in which Lincoln admitted to carrying passengers across the river. By either version, the case was dismissed.
11. McCutcheon, *Writer's Guide to Everyday Life*, 78.
12. Augustus H. Chapman, statement to Herndon, September 8, 1865, in Wilson and Davis, *Herndon's Informants*, 100–101.
13. William Wood, interview with Herndon, September 15, 1865, in Wilson and Davis, *Herndon's Informants*, 124.
14. Murr, "Lincoln's Ambition," 148.
15. Records, T. W. 1946. "Flatboats." *Indiana Magazine of History* 42:327; Mackie, Thomas. 2018. "The Ambitious River Man: Lincoln's Attachment to Rivers and Internal Improvements." *Lincoln Herald* 120(2):60.
16. Campenalla, Richard. 2010. *Lincoln in New Orleans: The 1828–1831 Flatboat Voyages and Their Place in History*. University of Louisiana at Lafayette Press, 12.
17. Taylor, Daniel Cravens. 2019. *Thomas Lincoln, Abraham's Father*. Beacon, 51; Malone, Thomas J. 1939. "Stepmothered to Greatness." *American Legion Magazine* 26(2):4; Warren, *Lincoln's Youth*, 5, 61; A. H. Chapman, statement to Herndon, September 8, 1865, in Wilson and Davis, *Herndon's Informants*, 100, 102.

18. Campenalla, *Lincoln in New Orleans*, 10.

19. Taylor, *Thomas Lincoln*, 51; Malone, "Stepmothered to Greatness," 4; Warren, *Lincoln's Youth*, 5, 61; Chapman, in Wilson and Davis, *Herndon's Informants*, 100, 102.

20. Meyer, Balthasar H. 1917. *History of Transportation in the United States before 1860*. Carnegie Institution, 110.

21. Records, "Flatboats," 330–31.

22. Joseph Gillespie, letter to Herndon, January 31, 1866, in Wilson and Davis, *Herndon's Informants*, 181.

23. Whitney, Henry C. 1907. *Lincoln the Citizen*. Current Literature Publishing, 49–50.

24. Campanella, *Lincoln in New Orleans*, 35–38; Records, "Flatboats," 331–32.

25. Campanella, *Lincoln in New Orleans*, 35.

26. Ibid., 54, citing an affidavit by E. Grant Gentry, September 5, 1936, Van Natter Papers.

27. Ibid., 54, citing Jacquess, A. C. 2006. "The Journals of Davy Crockett commencing December 28th 1834." *Indiana Magazine of History* 102(1):22.

28. Whitney, *Lincoln the Citizen*, 52.

29. Campanella, *Lincoln in New Orleans*, 143.

30. John Hanks, interview with Herndon, in Wilson and Davis, *Herndon's Informants*, 457.

31. Burlingame, *Abraham Lincoln*, 182–83.

32. William G. Greene, interview with Herndon, May 30, 1865, in Wilson and Davis, *Herndon's Informants*, 17.

33. Burlingame, *Abraham Lincoln*, 191, citing Springfield correspondence, 4 September, *New York Evening Post*, September 8, 1860.

34. McCutcheon, *Writer's Guide to Everyday Life*, 86.

35. Campanella, *Lincoln in New Orleans*, 264.

36. Twain, Mark. 1883. *Life on the Mississippi*. James R. Osgood & Company, 62.

37. Campanella, *Lincoln in New Orleans*, 264; Twain, *Life on the Mississippi*, 162; Wert, Jeffry D. 2018. *Civil War Barons: The Tycoons, Entrepreneurs, Inventors, and Visionaries Who Forged Victory and Shaped a Nation*. De Capo Press, 56–57.

38. Crump, Thomas. 2009. *Abraham Lincoln's World: How Riverboats, Railroads, and Republicans Transformed America*. Continuum Books, 21–22.

39. Ibid.; Bartelt, William E. 2017. "Young Lincoln and the Ohio." *Lincoln Lore* 1916:22–24.

40. Campanella, *Lincoln in New Orleans*, 86–87, 96.

41. Ibid., 217; John Hanks, interviews with Herndon, in Wilson and Davis, *Herndon's Informants*, 454; Herndon and Weik, *Herndon's Lincoln*, 1:76. Herndon reports that Hanks claimed he heard Lincoln say in New Orleans that he would "hit it hard" (meaning slavery), but Lincoln says in his Scripps autobiography that Hanks had turned back in St. Louis so would not have been present in New Orleans.

42. Campanella, *Lincoln in New Orleans*, 120, citing Flint, Timothy. 1826. *Recollections of the Last Ten Years*. Cummings, Hilliard, and Company, 308; Bartelt, "Young Lincoln and the Ohio," 22–24.

43. Warren, *Lincoln's Youth*, 144, citing *Evansville Daily Journal*, July 2, 1860.

44. McCutcheon, *Writer's Guide to Everyday Life*, 86; Trollope, Frances. 1832. *Domestic Manners of the Americans*. Dodd, Mead, 13, as cited in Burlingame, *Abraham Lincoln*.

45. Twain, *Life on the Mississippi*, 77.

46. Crump, *Abraham Lincoln's World*, 21.

47. Blumenthal, Sidney. 2016. *A Self-Made Man, 1809–1849: The Political Life of Abraham Lincoln*. Simon & Schuster, 57; Burlingame, *Abraham Lincoln*, 232–33; Power, John Carroll, and Sarah A. Power. 1876. *History of the Early Settlers of Sangamon County*. Edwin A. Wilson, 42–44.

48. Herndon and Weik, *Herndon's Lincoln*, 66–68; *Sangamo Journal*, March 29, 1832, 3:1; J. Rowan Herndon, letter to Herndon, June 11, 1865, in Wilson and Davis, *Herndon's Informants*, 34; Pratt, Harry E. 1943. "Lincoln Pilots the Talisman." *Abraham Lincoln Quarterly* 2:319–29.

Chapter 4: The Technical Trades

1. Hart, Richard E. 2019. *The Collected Works of Thomas Lincoln: Carpenter and Cabinetmaker*. Pigeon Creek Series, xvii.

2. Ewbank, "Building a Pioneer Home," 114; Elizabeth Crawford, interview with Herndon, September 16, 1865, Wilson and Davis, *Herndon's Informants*, 126.

3. Burlingame, *Abraham Lincoln*, chap. 3, 257, citing "Reminiscences" of Robert H. Osborne, quoting Lincoln's words in January 1861, *Lerna (IL) Eagle*, Lincoln anniversary issue, 1928.

4. Klingamann and Klingamann, *Year without Summer*, 23.

5. Murr, J. Edward. 1918. "Lincoln a Hoosier." *Indiana Magazine of History* 14(1):71.

6. McCullough, David. 2019. *The Pioneers: The Heroic Story of the Settlers Who Brought the American Ideal West*. Simon & Schuster, 71.

7. A good basic source is "Wrought Iron—Properties, Applications," AZO Materials, April 12, 2013, https://www.azom.com/article.aspx?ArticleID=9555.

8. Burlingame, *Abraham Lincoln*, chap. 29, 3157–58, citing Horace Porter. 1897. *Campaigning with Grant*. Century, 415.

9. Dirck, *Lincoln in Indiana*, 58.

10. John Hanks, interview with Herndon, 1865–1866, in Wilson and Davis, *Herndon's Informants*, 454; E. R. Burba, letter to Herndon, March 31, 1866, in ibid., 240; A. H. Chapman, statement to Herndon, September 8, 1865, in ibid., 98.

11. Warren, *Lincoln's Youth*, 139–40; John Romine, interview with Herndon, September 14, 1865, in Wilson and Davis, *Herndon's Informants*, 118; William Wood, interview with Herndon, September 15, 1865, in ibid., 123; David Turnham, interview with Herndon, September 15, 1865, in ibid., 122; McMurtry, R. Gerald. 1943. "Thomas Lincoln's Corner Cupboard: An Adventure in Historical Research." *Lincoln Herald* 45(1):19–22; McMurtry, R. Gerald. 1943. "Thomas Lincoln's Corner Cupboard: A Further Adventure in Historical Research." *Lincoln Herald* 45(2):32–33.

12. Steers, Edward, Jr. 2021. *Getting Right with Lincoln: Correcting Misconceptions about Our Greatest President*. University Press of Kentucky, 11.

13. Warren, *Lincoln's Youth*, 26, citing Duss, *George Rapp*, 11–12.

14. Hart, *Collected Works of Thomas Lincoln*, xvi, 64; Elizabeth Crawford, in Wilson and Davis, *Herndon's Informants*, 125; J. W. Wartmann, letter to Herndon, July 21, 1865, in ibid., 79; Cohen, I. Bernard. 1995. *Science and the Founding Fathers: Science in the Political Thought of Thomas Jefferson, Benjamin Franklin, John Adams, and James Madison*. W. W. Norton, 288.

15. Crump, *Abraham Lincoln's World*, 2.

16. Denny, Mark. 2007. *Ingenium: Five Machines That Changed the World*. Johns Hopkins University Press, 36–38.

17. Blumenthal, *Self-Made Man*, 24.

18. Oliver C. Terry, letter to Jesse Weik, July 1888, in Wilson and Davis, *Herndon's Informants*, 662–63.

19. David Turnham, letter to Herndon, February 21, 1866, in ibid., 216–17.

20. Herndon and Weik, *Herndon's Lincoln*, 29.

21. Ibid., 51.

22. Ibid. Herndon told Ward Hill Lamon in a March 6, 1870, letter that the phrase was "Get up—you old lazy divil" and that Lincoln awoke about midnight, not the next morning. See Wilson and Davis, *Herndon on Lincoln*, 100. Also, in a letter to Andrew Boyd on December 29, 1869, he says the phrase was "Get up you old devil." Ibid., 76.

23. Autobiography for Scripps, in *Collected Works*, 4:62. For asymmetrical facial structure, see Johnson, Carla K. 2007. "Abe Lincoln Diagnosed with Facial Defect." NBC News, August 13. https://www.nbcnews.com/id/wbna20250871.

24. Herndon and Weik, *Herndon's Lincoln*, 51.

25. Silvestri, Vito N., and Alfred P. Lairo. 2013. *Abraham Lincoln's Intellectual Development, 1809–1837*. Wasteland Press, 64.

26. Jason Duncan, letter to Herndon, late 1866–early 1867, in Wilson and Davis, *Herndon's Informants*, 539.

27. Herndon and Weik, *Herndon's Lincoln*, 87. This incident was reported by several of Herndon's informants, and the weights lifted ranged from 1,000 to 1,300 pounds.

28. Abner Y. Ellis, letter to Herndon, January 23, 1866, in Wilson and Davis, *Herndon's Informants*, 170.

29. Czajka, "'Without Peas and Things to Put into It.'"

30. James Short, letter to Herndon, July 7, 1865, in Wilson and Davis, *Herndon's Informants*, 73; Mentor Graham, interview with Herndon, May 29, 1865, in ibid., 9; William G. Greene, interview with James Q. Howard, "Notes of James Q. Howard about Abraham Lincoln," May 1860, Library of Congress, p. 32.

31. Mortgage drawn for William Green Jr. to Reuben Radford, January 15, 1833, in *Collected Works*, 1:15–16; Thomas, Benjamin P. 1934. *Lincoln's New Salem*. Abraham Lincoln Association, 70; autobiography for Scripps, in *Collected Works*, 4:65.

32. ALPLM, Document #200001; Warren, *Lincoln's Youth*; Houser, *Young Abraham Lincoln Mathematician*; Warren, "Book of Examples of Arithmetic."

33. William G. Greene, interview with Herndon, in Wilson and Davis, *Herndon's Informants*, 20. For the dispute, see Spears, Zarel C., and Robert S. Barton. 1947. *Berry and Lincoln: Frontier Merchants, the Store That "Winked Out."* Stratford House.

34. Burlingame, *Abraham Lincoln*, chap. 3, 262.

35. Autobiography for Scripps, in *Collected Works*, 4:65.

36. Pratt, Harry E. 1943. *The Personal Finances of Abraham Lincoln*. Abraham Lincoln Association, 14; Leonard Swett in Rice, *Reminiscences*, 465–66.

37. Autobiography for Scripps, in *Collected Works*, 4:65.

38. Dr. John Allen, interview with James Q. Howard, "Notes of James Q. Howard about Abraham Lincoln," May 1860, Library of Congress, p. 1.

39. Kaplan, Fred. 2008. *Lincoln: The Biography of a Writer*. HarperCollins, 18–19.

40. Letter to Francis P. Blair Sr. and John C. Rives, November 3, 1835, in *Collected Works*, 1:38.

41. Kaplan, Fred. 2017. *Lincoln and the Abolitionists: John Quincy Adams, Slavery, and the Civil War*. HarperCollins, 18–19; Holzer, Harold. 2014. *Lincoln and the Power of the Press*. Simon & Schuster.

42. Thomas, Benjamin P. 1933. "Lincoln the Postmaster." *Bulletin of the Abraham Lincoln Association* 31:5–6; Bruce, *Launching of Modern American Science*, 241; Peck, W. Emerson. 1898. "Lincoln's Stint in the Postal Service." *Lincolnian* 7(3):2–3.

43. Thomas, "Lincoln the Postmaster," 6.

44. Ibid., 7–8; Shaw and Burlingame, *Abraham Lincoln Traveled This Way*, 56.

45. Bruce, *Launching of Modern American Science*, 241; Burlingame, *Abraham Lincoln*, chap. 8, 765. The House chambers during Lincoln's time are now Statuary Hall in the U.S. Capitol. The small post office room was officially named the Lincoln Room by bipartisan resolution in 2019.

46. Graham, letter to Herndon, in Duncan and Nichols, *Mentor Graham*, 252. There is some question as to whether Mentor Graham tutored Lincoln in surveying, e.g., see Temple, Wayne C. 1970. *Lincoln Herald*, Summer, 70; Herndon and Weik, *Herndon's Lincoln*, 111; Baber, Adin. 2002. *A. Lincoln with Compass and Chain*. Illinois Professional Land Surveyors Association, 8.

47. Houser, *Young Abraham Lincoln Mathematician*, 20; autobiography for Scripps, in *Collected Works*, 4:65; Bedini, *Jefferson and Science*, 15–20; Dirck, *Lincoln in Indiana*, 8; Scripps, *Vote Lincoln!*, 69.

48. Autobiography for Scripps, in *Collected Works*, 4:65.

49. Sandburg, Carl. 1926. *Abraham Lincoln: The Prairie Years*. Harcourt, Brace, and Co., 1:169.

50. Flint, Abel. 1830. *A System of Geometry and Trigonometry with a Treatise on Surveying*. 6th ed. Cooke and Company, 9ff.

51. Ibid., 24ff.

52. Baber, *A. Lincoln with Compass and Chain*, 3.

53. Rayner, William H., and Milton O. Schmidt. 1955. *Elementary Surveying*. D. Van Nostrand, 157.

54. Baber, *A. Lincoln with Compass and Chain*, 11.

55. Ibid., 12–14. Lincoln's surveying equipment now resides at the New Salem State Historic Site.

56. Elizabeth Herndon Graham Bell, interview with Herndon, March 1887, in Wilson and Davis, *Herndon's Informants*, 606.

57. Baber, *A. Lincoln with Compass and Chain*, 30.

58. Blumenthal, *Self-Made Man*, 79.
59. Baber, *A. Lincoln with Compass and Chain*, 119; Dooley, Raymond N. 1959. "Lincoln and His Namesake Town." *Journal of the Illinois State Historical Society* 52:130–45.
60. Baber, *A. Lincoln with Compass and Chain*, xxii, 71.
61. Herndon and Weik, *Herndon's Lincoln*, 214–15.
62. Baber, *A. Lincoln with Compass and Chain*, 11.
63. Van Bergen, interview with John G. Nicolay, July 7, 1875, in Burlingame, Michael, ed. 2006. *An Oral History of Abraham Lincoln: John G. Nicolay's Interviews and Essays*. Southern Illinois University Press, 33.
64. Burlingame, *Abraham Lincoln*, chap. 3, 277.
65. Robert L. Wilson, letter to Herndon, February 10, 1866, in Wilson and Davis, *Herndon's Informants*, 201; Henry McHenry, interview with Herndon, May 28, 1865, in ibid., 14–15.
66. Burlingame, *Abraham Lincoln*, chap. 3, 281; Hardin Bale, interview with Herndon, May 29, 1865, in Wilson and Davis, *Herndon's Informants*, 13; James Short, letter to Herndon, July 7, 1865, in ibid., 74.
67. Fraker, Guy. 2017. *A Guide to Lincoln's Eighth Judicial Circuit*. Southern Illinois University Press, 108; *Collected Works*, 1:31; *Sangamo Journal*, January 17, 1835, 3:1; Temple, Wayne C. 1986. *Lincoln's Connections with the Illinois & Michigan Canal, His Return from Congress in '48, and His Invention*. Illinois Bell, 20; *Collected Works*, 1:350.
68. Blumenthal, *Self-Made Man*, 164; Blumenthal, Sidney. 2017. *Wrestling with His Angel, 1849–1856: The Political Life of Abraham Lincoln*. Simon & Schuster, 344; *Collected Works*, 2:230.
69. Crump, *Abraham Lincoln's World*, 167.
70. Widmer, Ted. 2020. *Lincoln on the Verge: Thirteen Days to Washington*. Simon & Schuster, 206.
71. Annual Message to Congress, December 1, 1862, in *Collected Works*, 5:528.

Chapter 5: Calculating Niagara and the Only President with a Patent
1. Hanna, William F. 1983. *Abraham among the Yankees: Abraham Lincoln's 1848 Visit to Massachusetts*. Old Colony Historical Society. The Lincoln Tomb in Springfield, Illinois, refers to Edward Baker Lincoln as "Eddie," but Lincoln and Mary always used "Eddy" in their letters. See Wheeler, Samuel P. 2012. "Solving a Lincoln Literary Mystery: 'Little Eddie.'" *JALA* 33(2):34–46.
2. Starr, John W., Jr. 1927. *Lincoln and the Railroads*. Dodd, Mead & Company, 52.
3. For haircut and shave, see "Niagara Wax Museum of History: Lincoln's Haircut Chair," RoadsideAmerica.com, https://www.roadsideamerica.com/story/32732, and "'Then as Now, Niagara Was Roaring Here': Abraham Lincoln (1809–1865)," Niagara Falls Museums, https://niagarafallsmuseums.ca/discover-our-history/history-notes/AbrahamLincoln.aspx.
4. Fragment on Niagara Falls, in *Collected Works*, 2:10–11. All quotations from here to end are from this fragment unless otherwise noted. Spelling errors are corrected.
5. Kaplan, *Lincoln: Biography of a Writer*, 193.
6. See *Collected Works*, 2:442n3.

7. Remedial efforts ongoing since 1942 have reduced erosion to about one foot per year. See "Rate of Erosion of Niagara Falls," *Niagara Falls Travel Blog*, February 6, 2015, https://www.niagarafallshotels.com/blog/rate-erosion-niagara-falls/.

8. Harris, Ann G., Esther Tuttle, and Sherwood D. Tuttle. 1997. *Geology of National Parks*. 5th ed. Kendall Hunt.

9. Described in Lyell, Charles. 1830. *Principles of Geology*. John Murray, 167. http://darwin-online.org.uk/content/frameset?viewtype=text&itemID=A505.1&pageseq=1.

10. Berton, Pierre. 1992. *Niagara: A History of the Falls*. Excelsior Editions, 13.

11. Ibid., 406–12.

12. Herndon and Weik, *Herndon's Lincoln*, 187.

13. Ibid., 188.

14. Kent, David J. 2013. *Tesla: The Wizard of Electricity*. Fall River Press, 101–3.

15. Kaplan, *Lincoln: Biography of a Writer*, 195.

16. Warren, Louis. 1935. *Lincoln Lore* 319:1.

17. See "Cataract House Hotel," Niagara Falls Hotels & Campgrounds: A History, http://www.niagarafrontier.com/earlyhotels.html#CataractHouse.

18. Mary Lincoln, letter to Emilie Todd Helm, September 20, 1857, in Turner, Justin G., and Linda Levitt Turner. 1987. *Mary Todd Lincoln: Her Life and Letters*. Fromm International, 50. Mary also visited without her husband in August 1861. See ibid., 93.

19. Starr, *Lincoln and the Railroads*, 52; Temple, *Lincoln's Connections*, 43–54; *Illinois Gazette*, October 14, 1848, 2, col. 2.

20. Temple, *Lincoln's Connections*, 35. Herndon incorrectly states that it was the *Globe* that got stuck.

21. John Hanks, interview with Herndon, June 13, 1865, in Wilson and Davis, *Herndon's Informants*, 44, 457; William G. Greene, interview with Herndon, May 30, 1865, in ibid., 17.

22. For a simple explanation, see "Distance and Displacement," Physics Hypertextbook, https://physics.info/displacement/.

23. "Archimedes Principle," Science Direct, https://www.sciencedirect.com/topics/engineering/archimedes-principle.

24. Herndon and Weik, *Herndon's Lincoln*, 188.

25. Hardin Bale, interview with Herndon, May 29, 1865, in Wilson and Davis, *Herndon's Informants*, 13.

26. Brownstein, Elizabeth Smith. 2005. *Lincoln's Other White House: The Untold Story of the Man and His Presidency*. John Wiley & Sons, 151.

27. *Senate Report of the Commissioner of Patents for the Year 1849: Part 1. Arts and Manufactures*, 1850, Office of Printers to the Senate, 262.

28. Herndon and Weik, *Herndon's Lincoln*, 188; Weik, Jesse W. 1922. *The Real Lincoln: A Portrait*. Houghton Mifflin, 242; Goldsmith, Harry. 1938. "Abraham Lincoln, Invention and Patents." *Journal of the Patent Office Society* 20(1):5–33.

29. Emerson, Jason. 2009. *Lincoln the Inventor*. Southern Illinois University Press, 14–15. The actual model is only about two feet long, not the four feet the witness suggested.

30. Goldsmith, "Invention and Patents," 16; application for patent, in *Collected Works*, 2:32–36.

31. Application for patent, in *Collected Works*, 2:32–36.

32. Ibid.

33. Smith, Chauncey. 1890. "A Century of Patent Law." *Quarterly Journal of Economics* 5(1):44–49, 48; Goldsmith, "Invention and Patents," 18.

34. Emerson, *Lincoln the Inventor*, 88nn53–54.

35. Lincoln to Thomas Ewing, in *Collected Works*, 2:40.

36. Herndon and Weik, *Herndon's Lincoln*, 188; Weik, *Real Lincoln*, 242.

37. Foster, B. G. 1928. *Abraham Lincoln Inventor.* James F. Balsley Bookseller, 8.

38. See "Abraham Lincoln's Patent Model," National Museum of American History, https://americanhistory.si.edu/collections/search/object/nmah_213141.

39. Smith, interview with John Nicolay, July 8, 1865, in Burlingame, *Oral History of Abraham Lincoln*, 18.

40. Cameron, letter to Lincoln, March 10, 1864, Abraham Lincoln Papers, Library of Congress, http://memory.loc.gov/mss/mal/mal1/314/3144000/001.jpg.

41. Anonymous. 1861. "Presidential Patent." *Harper's Weekly*, April 6, p. 210, cols. 2–3.

42. Anonymous. 1860. "The President Elect's Mode of Buoying Vessels." *Scientific American*, December 1, p. 356. Anonymous. 1865. "President Lincoln as an Inventor." *Scientific American*, May 27, p. 340.

43. Berton, *Niagara*, 125, 129.

44. Nichols, Clifton M. 1896. *Life of Abraham Lincoln*. Mast, Crowell & Kirkpatrick, 303.

45. Berton, *Niagara*, 135.

46. Ibid., 138.

47. Ibid., 152.

48. Welles, Gideon. 1911. *Diary of Gideon Welles*. Houghton Mifflin, entry for July 22, 1864; Burlingame, Michael, and John R. Turner Ettlinger, eds. 1999. *Inside Lincoln's White House: The Complete Civil War Diary of John Hay*. Southern Illinois University Press, xvi, 224–25, 238; Burlingame, *Abraham Lincoln*, chap. 33, 3715; Miller, William Lee. 2008. *President Lincoln: The Duty of a Statesman*. Alfred A. Knopf, 381.

Chapter 6: Internal Improvements and the Whig Way

1. Autobiography for Fell, in *Collected Works*, 3:512.

2. Blumenthal, *Self-Made Man*, 45–46.

3. Hudson, John C. 1994. *Making the Corn Belt: A Geographic History of Middle-Western Agriculture*. Indiana University Press, 127.

4. McClelland, Edward. 2019. "Lincoln, Slavery, and Springfield: How Popular Opinion in Central Illinois Influenced Abraham Lincoln's Views on Slavery." MA thesis, Harvard University, 14.

5. Howe, Daniel Walker. 1995. "Why Abraham Lincoln Was a Whig." *JALA* 16(1):27.

6. Burlingame, *Abraham Lincoln*, chap. 9, 955.

7. Lind, Michael. 2004. *What Lincoln Believed: The Values and Convictions of America's Greatest President*. Doubleday, 22–23; Chernow, Ron. 2004. *Alexander Hamilton*. Penguin, 370–87.

8. Guelzo, Allen. 2018. "Reconstruction as a Pure Bourgeois Revolution." *JALA* 39(1):57–58.

9. Address before the Wisconsin State Agricultural Society, September 30, 1859, in *Collected Works*, 3:479.

10. Lundberg, James M. 2020. *Horace Greeley: Print, Politics, and the Failure of American Nationhood*. Johns Hopkins University Press, 5.

11. Richardson, Heather Cox. 2020. *How the South Won the Civil War*. Oxford University Press, 34.

12. Guelzo, "Reconstruction," 55, 58; Burlingame, *Abraham Lincoln*, chap. 17, 1897.

13. See "Communication," in *Collected Works*, 1:5–9, for all quotes in this section.

14. Lincoln had given an impromptu speech in 1830 on navigation of the Sangamon River, see Wilson and Davis, *Herndon's Informants*, 11 (Greene) and 456 (John Hanks).

15. *Illinois State Journal* (Springfield), "President Lincoln's First Speech—an Interesting Reminiscence," November 5, 1864, 2, col. 3. The reminiscence is from James A. Herndon, a cousin to Lincoln's final law partner, May 29, 1865, in Wilson and Davis, *Herndon's Informants*, 16.

16. Herndon, letter to Ward Hill Lamon, February 25, 1870, in Wilson and Davis, *Herndon on Lincoln*, 84–85; Pratt, *Finances of Lincoln*, 19–24.

17. *Sangamo Journal*, June 18, 1836, in *Collected Works*, 1:48.

18. Emery, Tom. 2018. "'Long Nine' Left Colorful, Though Mixed, Legacy in Lincoln Lore." Shaw Local Media, April 22. https://www.shawlocal.com/2018/04/20/long-nine-left-colorful-though-mixed-legacy-in-lincoln-lore/athrlwd/.

19. See *Collected Works*, 1:28.

20. Silvestri and Lairo, *Intellectual Development*, 91.

21. *Laws of the State of Illinois, Passed by the Tenth General Assembly*, Vandalia, Illinois, introduced by William Walters, February 27, 1837, 121–51, GA Session: 10-1, ALPLM, Document #254378.

22. *Vandalia Free Press*, February 21, 1839, in *Collected Works*, 1:144.

23. Temple, *Lincoln's Connections*, 11.

24. Krenkel, John H. 1958. *Illinois Internal Improvements, 1818–1848*. Torch Press, 155; Report of Committee on Finance Regarding the Purchase of Unsold Federal Lands, *House Journal*, Eleventh General Assembly, First Session, pp. 223–25, ALPLM, Document #200154.

25. Burlingame, *Abraham Lincoln*, chap. 4, 342.

26. *Sangamo Journal*, February 9, 1835.

27. Standage, Tom. 2005. *A History of the World in Six Glasses*. Walker & Company, 202.

28. Joshua Speed, interview with Herndon, in Wilson and Davis *Herndon's Informants*, 476.

29. Blumenthal, *Self-Made Man*, 406.

30. Much as William Seward's later purchase of Alaska would be called "Seward's Folly."

31. Krenkel, *Internal Improvements*, 24–46; Temple, *Lincoln's Connections*, 1–8.

32. Temple, *Lincoln's Connections*, 6.

33. Ibid., 78–81; Putnam, James William. 1918. *The Illinois and Michigan Canal: A Study in Economic History*. University of Chicago Press.

34. Loewen, James W. 2000. *Lies across America: What Our Historic Sites Get Wrong*. Touchstone Books, 435.

35. Hall, William Mosely, et al. 1882. *Chicago River-and-Harbor Convention: An Account of Its Origin and Proceedings*. Fergus; Burlingame, *Abraham Lincoln*, chap. 6, 726; Eisendrath, Joseph L. 1974. "Lincoln's First Appearance on the National Scene, July 1847." *Lincoln Herald* 76:59–62.

36. *Daily Missouri Republican* (St. Louis), July 12, 1847, 2:2; ALPLM, Document #237751.

37. Ibid.

38. Speech in the United States House of Representatives on Internal Improvements, June 20, 1848, in *Collected Works*, 1:480–84.

39. Ibid.

40. Wulf, *Invention of Nature*, 288–89.

41. Reply to the Committee of the Republican National Convention, May 19, 1860, in *Collected Works*, 4:51; for platform, see "National Republican Platform, Adopted by the National Republican Convention, Held in Chicago, May 17, 1860," Library of Congress, https://www.loc.gov/resource/lprbscsm.scsm0716/.

42. Annual Message to Congress, December 3, 1861, in *Collected Works*, 5:37.

43. Annual Message to Congress, December 1, 1862, in ibid., 5:526.

44. Lind, *What Lincoln Believed*, 22; Herndon and Weik, *Herndon's Lincoln*, 140–41.

45. Fragment on government, in *Collected Works*, 2:220; Howe, "Why Abraham Lincoln Was a Whig," 27–38.

46. Message to Congress in Special Session, July 4, 1861, in *Collected Works*, 4:438.

47. McPherson, James M. 1991. *Abraham Lincoln and the Second American Revolution*. Oxford University Press, 11. Also see Marc Schulman, "Economics and the American Civil War," History Central, https://www.historycentral.com/CivilWar/AMERICA/Economics.html.

48. McPherson, *Abraham Lincoln*, 37.

Chapter 7: The Science of Slavery

1. Wilkerson, Isabel. 2010. *The Warmth of Other Suns: The Epic Story of America's Great Migration*. Random House, 97–99.

2. Lakwete, Angela. 2003. *Inventing the Cotton Gin: Machine and Myth in Antebellum America*. Johns Hopkins University Press. For accessible background, see "Cotton," Made How, http://www.madehow.com/Volume-6/Cotton.html, and History.com Editors. 2010. "Cotton Gin and Eli Whitney." Histroy.com, February 4. https://www.history.com/topics/inventions/cotton-gin-and-eli-whitney.

3. Julian Rubin, "Eli Whitney: The Invention of the Cotton Gin," https://www.juliantrubin.com/bigten/whitneycottongin.html.

4. Friedman, *Thank You for Being Late*, 208.

5. Everett, Hitchcock, Middleton, and Timms, *Samuel Slater.*

6. Blumenthal, *Wrestling with His Angel*, 120; *Monthly Summary of Commerce and Finance*, United States Department of the Treasury, 1895–1896, 290; Amos Kendall, letter to Lincoln, February 19, 1862, includes newspaper clipping from *Daily National Intelligencer* article titled "Object of the War: Letter No. 3," National Archives and Records Administration (NARA), RG 59, Entry 637, Records of the Bureau of Rolls and Library, ALPLM, Document #237141.

7. Speech at Springfield, Illinois, July 17, 1858, in *Collected Works*, 2:515.

8. Information for this section gleaned from Foner, Eric. 2010. *The Fiery Trial: Abraham Lincoln and American Slavery.* W. W. Norton; Holzer, Harold. 2012. *Lincoln: How Abraham Lincoln Ended Slavery in America.* Newmarket Press; Lubet, Steven. 2010. *Fugitive Justice: Runaways, Rescuers, and Slavery on Trial.* Belknap Press; Maltz, Earl M. 2009. *Slavery and the Supreme Court, 1825–1861.* University Press of Kansas; Striner, Richard. 2006. *Father Abraham: Lincoln's Relentless Struggle to End Slavery.* Oxford University Press; Blumenthal, *Wrestling with His Angel*, 120.

9. Richardson, *How the South Won the Civil War*, 33, citing J. G. Randall.

10. Ibid., 33, citing *American Cotton Planter*, January 1853, 8–13.

11. Olmstead, Frederick Law. 1953. *The Cotton Kingdom: A Traveller's Observations on Cotton and Slavery in the American Slave States.* Modern Library, 7 (originally published 1861).

12. Speech at Peoria, October 16, 1854, in *Collected Works*, 2:274.

13. Blumenthal, *Wrestling with His Angel*, 348; Dickey, Christopher. 2015. *Our Man in Charleston: Britain's Secret Agent in the Civil War South.* Crown, 20.

14. Carden, Allen, and Thomas J. Ebert. 2019. *John George Nicolay: The Man in Lincoln's Shadow.* University of Tennessee Press, 5.

15. Ibid.

16. Kaplan, *Lincoln and the Abolitionists*, 231.

17. Carden and Ebert, *John George Nicolay*, 5.

18. Speech at Peoria, October 16, 1854, in *Collected Works*, 2:262.

19. Speech at Chicago, July 10, 1858, in ibid., 2:291.

20. Loewen, *Lies across America*, 292; Tackach, James. 2019. *Lincoln and the Natural Environment.* Southern Illinois University Press, 45.

21. Tackach, *Lincoln and the Natural Environment*, 45.

22. Ibid., 3.

23. Loewen, *Lies across America*, 292.

24. Ibid.; Kaplan, *Lincoln and the Abolitionists*, 158; Bruce, *Launching of Modern American Science*, 167; Dickey, *Our Man in Charleston*, 20.

25. For example, address before the Young Men's Lyceum, January 27, 1838, in *Collected Works*, 1:108; debate with Douglas in Alton, Illinois, October 15, 1858, in ibid., 3:286.

26. Zeitz, Joshua. 2014. *Lincoln's Boys: John Hay, John Nicolay, and the War for Lincoln's Image.* Viking, 29.

27. Fragment on free labor, September 17, 1859?, in *Collected Works*, 3:462.

28. Helper, Hinton Rowan. 1857. *The Impending Crisis of the South: How to Meet It.* Burdick Brothers, 21–22.

29. Richardson, *How the South Won the Civil War*, xviii.

30. Kendi, Ibram X. 2019. *How to Be an Antiracist*. One World, 63.

31. Bray, "What Lincoln Read," 44; Herndon and Weik, *Herndon's Lincoln*, 264–65.

32. Slotten, Ross. 2004. *The Heretic in Darwin's Court: The Life of Alfred Russel Wallace*. Columbia University Press; Chambers, Robert. 1844. *Vestiges of the Natural History of Creation*. John Churchill; Bruce, *Launching of Modern American Science*, 123; Lander, "Herndon's Auction List," 20; Wulf, *Invention of Nature*, 243.

33. Herndon to John E. Remsburg, in Wilson and Davis, *Herndon on Lincoln*, 329.

34. Bruce, *Launching of Modern American Science*, 124.

35. Kendi, *How to Be*, 50, citing George Best. 1578. *A True Discourse of the Late Voyages of Discoverie*. Henry Bynneman.

36. Haynes, Stephen R. 2002. *Noah's Curse: The Biblical Justification of American Slavery*. Oxford University Press, 322; Goldenberg, David R. 2003. *The Curse of Ham: Race and Slavery in Early Judaism, Christianity, and Islam*. Princeton University Press; Seymour Garte, personal communication.

37. This has caused some confusion among some of the general public. Humans are not descended from apes. Apes, chimpanzees, monkeys, and humans are all descended via various branches from distant common ancestors. Also, the classification scheme can include smaller divisions such as suborders and superfamilies.

38. Boorstin, Daniel J. 1983. *The Discoverers: A History of Man's Search to Know His World and Himself*. Vintage, 464; Kendi, *How to Be*, 42; Rutherford, Adam. 2020. *How to Argue with a Racist: What Our Genes Do (and Don't) Say about Human Difference*. Experiment, 46–47; Brace, C. Loring. 2005. *Race Is a Four Letter Word*. Oxford University Press, 326.

39. Rutherford, *How to Argue*, 48–49; Blumenbach, Johann. 1865. *The Anthropological Treatises of Johann Friedrich Blumenbach*. Anthropological Society of London.

40. Lander, James. 2015. "When Lincoln Borrowed a Book He Didn't Like." *JALA* 36(1):49; Irmscher, Christoph. 2013. *Louis Agassiz: Creator of American Science*. Houghton Mifflin Harcourt, 35; Nott, Josiah Clark, and George Robbins Gliddon. 1854. *Types of Mankind*. Lippincott, Grambo & Co.

41. Bruce, *Launching of Modern American Science*, 125.

42. Gossett, Thomas F. 1997. *Race: The History of an Idea in America*. New ed. Oxford University Press; Morton, Samuel George. 1839. *Crania Americana: A Comparative View of the Skulls of Various Aboriginal Nations of North and South America*. J. Dobson.

43. Renschler, Emily S., and Janet Monge. "The Samuel George Morton Cranial Collection: Historical Significance and New Research." *Expedition* 30(3):30–38.

44. Irmscher, *Louis Agassiz*, 323.

45. Bruce, *Launching of Modern American Science*, 124.

46. For his view, see Tiedemann, Frederick. 1936. "On the Brain of the Negro, Compared with That of the European and the Orang-Outang." *Philosophical Transactions of the Royal Society* 126:497–427. https://royalsocietypublishing.org/doi/pdf/10.1098/rstl.1836.0025.

47. Gould, Stephen J. 1978. "Morton's Ranking of Races by Cranial Capacity: Unconscious Manipulation of Data May Be a Scientific Norm." *Science* 200:503–9; Menand, L. 2001. "Morton, Agassiz, and the Origins of Scientific Racism in the United States."

Journal of Blacks in Higher Education 34:110–13. Some have questioned Gould's own motives, for example, Lewis, Jason E., et al. 2011. "The Mismeasure of Science: Stephen J. Gould versus Samuel George Morton on Skulls and Bias." *PLoS Biology* 9(6):1–6.

48. Delbanco, Andrew. 2018. *The War before the War: Fugitive Slaves and the Struggle for America's Soul from the Revolution to the Civil War.* Penguin, 40, 98.

49. Kendi, *How to Be*, 51, citing Darwin, Charles. 1909. *On the Origin of Species.* Collier, 24.

50. Hart, Richard E. 2020. "Abraham Lincoln's Earliest Encounter of African American Slaves." *For the People* 22(4):6.

51. Letter to Albert G. Hodges, April 4, 1864, in *Collected Works*, 7:281.

52. Debate at Charleston, Illinois, September 18, 1858, in ibid., 3:145–46.

53. Speech at Springfield, Illinois, June 26, 1857, in ibid., 2:405–6.

54. Debate at Charleston, Illinois, September 18, 1858, in ibid., 3:145–46.

55. Speech at Springfield, Illinois, June 26, 1857, in ibid., 2:405–6.

56. Fragment on slavery, April 1, 1854?, in ibid., 2:222–23.

57. Speech at Peoria, October 16, 1854, in ibid., 2:266.

58. Chernow, *Alexander Hamilton*, 513; Jefferson, *Notes on the State of Virginia*, 176–77.

59. Blumenthal, *Wrestling with His Angel*, 56.

60. Blight, David W. 2019. *Frederick Douglass: Prophet of Freedom.* Simon & Schuster, 376; Douglass to Montgomery Blair, September 16, 1862, in Foner, Philip S. 1950. *The Life and Writings of Frederick Douglass.* International Publishers, 3:283–85.

61. Alexander Stephens's "Cornerstone" speech, March 21, 1861, Savannah, Georgia, https://www.battlefields.org/learn/primary-sources/cornerstone-speech.

62. Calhoun, John C. 1843. *Speeches of John C. Calhoun: Delivered in the Congress of the United States from 1811 to the Present Time.* Harper & Brothers, 225; specifically, "Speech on the Reception of Abolition Petitions," February 1837.

63. Fragment on slavery, April 1, 1854?, in *Collected Works*, 2:222.

64. Letter to Henry L. Pierce and others, April 6, 1859, in ibid., 3:375–76.

65. Fragment on proslavery theology, October 1, 1854?, in ibid., 3:204–5.

66. Fragment on slavery, April 1, 1854?, in ibid., 2:222.

67. Preliminary Emancipation Proclamation, in ibid., 5:433–36.

68. Annual Message to Congress, December 1, 1862, in ibid., 5:537.

Chapter 8: The Patent and Technology Cases

1. Fragment, notes for a law lecture, July 1, 1850?, in *Collected Works*, 2:81.

2. Autobiography for Scripps, in ibid., 4:65; Warren, *Lincoln's Youth*, 146–47; Dirck, Brian. 2007. *Lincoln the Lawyer.* University of Illinois Press, 15–16; Burlingame, *Abraham Lincoln*, chap. 3, 294–95.

3. Blackstone, William. 1979. *Commentaries on the Laws of England.* 4 vols. Facsimile ed. with intro. Stanley N. Katz. University of Chicago.

4. Lobban, Michael. 1987. "Blackstone and the Science of Law." *Historical Journal* 30(2):311–35.

5. Boorstin, Daniel J. 1941. *The Mysterious Science of the Law: An Essay on Blackstone's Commentaries.* University of Chicago Press, 3–10.

6. Mayr, Ernst. 1990. "When Is Historiography Whiggish?" *Journal of the History of Ideas* 51(2):301–9.

7. Bray, "What Lincoln Read"; Temple, Wayne C. 2005. "Herndon on Lincoln: An Unknown Interview with a List of Books in the Lincoln & Herndon Law Office." *Journal of the Illinois State Historical Society* 98(1/2):34–50; Steiner, Mark. 2010. "Abraham Lincoln and the Rule of Law Books." *Marquette Law Review* 93(4):1298–99; Lander, "Herndon's Auction List."

8. Lincoln to James T. Thornton, December 2, 1858, in *Collected Works*, 3:344; Lincoln to John M. Brockman, September 25, 1860, in ibid., 4:121.

9. Lincoln to Amos Williams, December 8, 1848, in ibid., 2:14–15.

10. Kent, David J. 2017. *Lincoln: The Man Who Saved America.* Fall River Press, 89–98; Dirck, *Lincoln the Lawyer*, 60; Herndon and Weik, *Herndon's Lincoln.*

11. Herndon and Weik, *Herndon's Lincoln*, 210.

12. Fraker, Guy C. 2012. *Lincoln's Ladder to the Presidency: The Eighth Judicial Circuit.* Southern Illinois University Press, 67; Donald, David Herbert. 1995. *Lincoln.* Simon & Schuster, 104–6.

13. Whitney, Henry C. 1940. *Life on the Circuit with Lincoln.* Caxton Printers.

14. Burlingame, *Abraham Lincoln*, chap. 5, 470; Fraker, *Lincoln's Ladder*, 1; Whitney, *Life on the Circuit.*

15. Kent, *Lincoln*, 99–104.

16. Burlingame, *Abraham Lincoln*, chap. 5, 470; Fraker, *Lincoln's Ladder*, 1.

17. Lincoln to John T. Stuart, January 29, 1840, in *Collected Works*, 1:200.

18. "The Law Practice of Abraham Lincoln: A Narrative Overview," Law Practice of Abraham Lincoln (LPAL), http://www.lawpracticeofabrahamlincoln.org/Reference .aspx?ref=Reference%20html%20files/NarrativeOverview.html.

19. Steiner, Mark E. 2009. "A Docket That Reflects Then and Now." *American Bar Association Journal* 95:39–40; Dirck, *Lincoln the Lawyer*, 60–61.

20. Fragment, notes for a law lecture, in *Collected Works*, 2:82.

21. Steiner, Mark E. 2006. *An Honest Calling: The Law Practice of Abraham Lincoln.* Northern Illinois University Press, 4, 15, 160.

22. Shaw and Burlingame, *Abraham Lincoln Traveled This Way*, 83.

23. Spiegel, Allen D. 2002. *A. Lincoln, Esquire: A Shrewd, Sophisticated Lawyer in His Time.* Mercer University Press, ix; "The Law Practice of Abraham Lincoln: A Statistical Portrait," Papers of Abraham Lincoln, http://www.lawpracticeofabrahamlincoln.org/ Reference.aspx?ref=Reference%20html%20files/StatisticalPortrait.html.

24. David Davis, interview with Herndon, September 30, 1866, in Wilson and Davis, *Herndon's Informants*, 349–50.

25. Bruce, *Lincoln and the Tools of War*, 10–11.

26. Holton, Gerald, and Sonnert, Gerhard. 1999. "A Vision of Jeffersonian Science." *Issues in Science and Technology*, Fall 1999, 62. The two theories of science are named after Isaac Newton and Francis Bacon.

27. Zane, Charles S. 1912. "Lincoln as I Knew Him." *Sunset Magazine* 29:432.

28. For example, *Dawson v. Ennis & Ennis* and *Emerson v. Cole & Wall*. All of Lincoln's cases cited can be found on the LPAL website at http://www.lawpracticeofabrahamlincoln.org/Search.aspx.

29. *Clark v. Stigleman et al.*; *Weyrich and Co. v. Allsup & Allsup*.

30. Warren, Louis A. 1938. "Lincoln and the Logging Industry." *Lincoln Lore* 466 (March 14).

31. *Lewis v. Moffett*; *Lincoln & Herndon vs. Moffett*.

32. *Edmunds v. Hildreth et al.* and other cases; Goldsmith, "Invention and Patents," 19–20.

33. Gross, Daniel. 1996. *Forbes Greatest Business Stories of All Time*. John Wiley & Sons, chapter on "Cyrus McCormick's Reaper and the Industrialization of Farming," 22–38; Casson, Herbert N. 1909. *Cyrus Hall McCormick: His Life and Work*. Books for Libraries Press, 26–45; McCormick, Cyrus. 1931. *The Century of the Reaper*. Houghton Mifflin, 1–33.

34. Lincoln to Peter H. Watson, July 23, 1855, in *Collected Works*, 2:314–15; letter to John Manny, September 1, 1855, in ibid., 2:325.

35. Joseph Gillespie to Herndon, January 31, 1866, in Wilson and Davis, *Herndon's Informants*, 186.

36. Oldroyd, Osborn H., ed. 1882. *Lincoln Memorial Album of Immortelles*. G. W. Carleton & Co., 448–50.

37. *McCormick v. Talcott et al.*; *McCormick v. Manny*; Goldsmith, "Invention and Patents," 19; McMurtry, R. Gerald. 1964. "The Manny Reaper: Some Background Information on the Case." *Lincoln Lore* 1516:1–4; Parkinson, Robert Henry. 1946. "The Patent Case That Lifted Lincoln into a Presidential Candidate." *Abraham Lincoln Quarterly* 4(3):105–22.

38. Wolf, Mark L. 1995. "Thomas Jefferson, Abraham Lincoln, Louis Brandeis and the Mystery of the Universe." *Boston University Journal of Science and Technology Law* 1:1.

39. Spiegel, *A. Lincoln, Esquire*, 22.

40. *Fleming v. Rogers & Crothers*; Hubbard, Charles M. 1997. "Lincoln and the Chicken Bone Case." *American History* 32:31–34, 69; Pratt, Harry E. 1952. "The Famous 'Chicken Bone' Case." *Journal of the Illinois State Historical Society* 45:164–67; Spiegel, *A. Lincoln, Esquire*, 118–19.

41. *People v. Wyant*; Spiegel, *A. Lincoln, Esquire*, 259.

42. Spiegel, *A. Lincoln, Esquire*, 259.

43. *People v. Armstrong*. Also, see the LPAL printed case books, vol. 4, p. 1; Walsh, John. E. 2003. "The Brady Letter: Time for a Serious Look." *For the People* 5(4):4–5; Ferguson, Duncan. 1923. "True Story of the Almanac Used by Abraham Lincoln in the Famous Trial of Duff Armstrong." *Journal of the Illinois State Historical Society* 15(3/4):688–91.

44. Fehrenbacher, Don E., and Fehrenbacher, Virginia, eds. 1996. *Recollected Words of Abraham Lincoln*. Stanford University Press, 270.

45. Olson, Donald W. 1999. "Abe Lincoln and the Leonids." *Sky & Telescope*, November, 34–35.

46. Dominus, Susan. 2019. "Sidelined." *Smithsonian* 50(6):49; Baron, David. 2017. *American Eclipse: A Nation's Epic Race to Catch the Shadow of the Moon and Win the Glory of the World.* Liveright, 36.

47. Herndon and Weik, *Herndon's Lincoln*, 405.

48. Sinnott, Roger W. 1990. "Lincoln and the Almanac Trial." *Sky & Telescope*, August, 186–88.

49. *Johnston v. Jones & Marsh.*

50. Beckwith, Hiram W. 1895. "Lincoln: Personal Recollections of Him, His Contemporaries and Law Practice in Eastern Illinois." *Chicago Tribune*, December 29, p. 32.

51. Lecture by Leonard Swett, Chicago, February 20, 1876, in *Chicago Times*, February 21, 1876; Burlingame, *Abraham Lincoln*, chap. 9, 936.

52. Lincoln to Robert Kinzie, January 5, 1858, in *Collected Works*, 2:430–31.

53. Stowell, Daniel W., ed. 2008. "Johnston v. Jones and Marsh." In *The Papers of Abraham Lincoln: Legal Documents and Cases*, 3:399.

54. Stowell, Daniel W., ed. 2008. "Hurd et al. v. Rock Island Bridge Company." In ibid., 3:321.

55. *Columbus Insurance Co. v. Peoria Bridge Co.*

56. Stowell, "Hurd et al. v. Rock Island Bridge Company," 3:308–12.

57. McGinty, Brian. 2015. *Lincoln's Greatest Case: The River, the Bridge, and the Making of America.* Liveright, 13.

58. Ibid., 61–63.

59. Skilton, John S. 2011. "Abraham Lincoln: A Lawyer 'for the Ages.'" *Wisconsin Law Review* 1:19.

60. Hirsch, and Van Haften, *Abraham Lincoln and the Structure of Reason*, 39.

61. Stowell, "Hurd et al. v. Rock Island Bridge Company," 3:336–59; Skilton, "Abraham Lincoln," 21; speech to the jury, *Chicago Daily Democratic Press*, as reported by Robert Hitt, in *Collected Works*, 2:415–22.

62. Starr, *Lincoln and the Railroads*, 111–12; Stowell, "Hurd et al. v. Rock Island Bridge Company," 3:360; McGinty, *Lincoln's Greatest Case*, 148–57.

63. Kent, *Lincoln*, 105–6; Spiegel, *A. Lincoln, Esquire*, 96–98; McGinty, *Lincoln's Greatest Case*, 4; Dirck, *Lincoln the Lawyer*, 96.

Chapter 9: Working For, and Against, the Railroads

1. Stowell, "Hurd et al. v. Rock Island Bridge Company," 3:336–59.

2. Shaw and Burlingame, *Abraham Lincoln Traveled This Way*, 113.

3. Widmer, *Lincoln on the Verge*, 87–89; White, John H., Jr. 1997. *American Locomotives: An Engineering History, 1830–1880.* Johns Hopkins University Press, 13; O'Donovan, Susan. 2011. "William Webb's World." *New York Times*, February 18.

4. Spiegel, *A. Lincoln, Esquire*, 3; Sagle, Lawrence W. 1948. "Tom Thumb: Little Known Facts about First Locomotive Built in America Slowly Come to Light." *Railway and Locomotive Historical Society Bulletin* 73(73):48.

5. Report on Alton and Springfield Railroad, August 5, 1847, in *Collected Works*, 1:398.

6. Clark, John E. 2004. *Railroads in the Civil War: The Impact of Management on Victory and Defeat.* Louisiana State University Press, 11–12; Burlingame, *Abraham Lincoln*, chap. 9, 905; Blumenthal, *Wrestling with His Angel*, 119.

7. Shaw and Burlingame, *Abraham Lincoln Traveled This Way*, 122. A bronze watermelon statue graces the town square.

8. Blumenthal, *Wrestling with His Angel*, 120.

9. Kenneth Serfass lecture, February 13, 2021; Widmer, *Lincoln on the Verge*, 88.

10. United States Patent Office, *List of Patents for Inventions and Designs, Issued by the United States, from 1790 to 1847.* J. and G. S. Gideon, 1847; Widmer, *Lincoln on the Verge*, 85.

11. Kent, David J. 2016. *Edison: The Inventor of the Modern World.* Fall River Press, 7.

12. Phillips, Ulrich Bonnell. 1968. *A History of Transportation in the Eastern Cotton Belt to 1860.* Octagon Books, 14; Widmer, *Lincoln on the Verge*, 14.

13. McCutcheon, *Writer's Guide to Everyday Life*, 94.

14. Herndon and Weik, *Herndon's Lincoln*, 354.

15. Keyes, Ralph. 1991. *Timelock.* Basic Books, 18; O'Malley, M. 1990. *Keeping Watch: A History of American Time.* Viking; Levine, Robert V. 1997. *A Geography of Time: Temporal Misadventures of a Social Psychologist, or How Every Culture Keeps Time Just a Little Bit Differently.* Basic Books, 63.

16. Levine, *Geography of Time*, 63.

17. "Law Practice of Abraham Lincoln: A Statistical Portrait."

18. Blumenthal, *Wrestling with His Angel*, 93; Blumenthal, *Self-Made Man*, 442.

19. *Barret v. Alton & Sangamon Railroad*; Beard, William D. 1992. "'I Have Labored Hard to Find the Law': Abraham Lincoln and the Alton and Sangamon Railroad." *Illinois Historical Journal* 85(4):209–20.

20. Beard, "'I Have Labored,'" 219; Ely, James W., Jr., "Abraham Lincoln as a Railroad Attorney," *Indiana History*, Railroad Symposium lecture, https://indianahistory.org/wp-content/uploads/51a319bce67b7f5614886cd3a4504ef7.pdf; "Notes of Argument in Law Case," June 15, 1858?, in *Collected Works*, 2:459.

21. Lincoln to William Martin, August 29, 1851, in *Collected Works*, 2:110, referring to February 19 letter to same, ibid., 2:98. Lincoln on February 26 had also written to the railroad's secretary, Isaac Gibson, that "The Books *must* be here"; in ibid., 2:101.

22. He also sued them three times.

23. *Alton & Sangamon v. Baugh*; *Alton & Sangamon v. Carpenter*; Ely, "Abraham Lincoln as a Railroad Attorney," 4–5.

24. "Law Practice of Abraham Lincoln: A Statistical Portrait"; Steiner, *Honest Calling*, 138; Weik, *Real Lincoln*, 194–95. Lincoln also sued them in five cases.

25. *Allen v. Illinois Central Railroad* (several cases); Stowell, *Papers of Abraham Lincoln*, 3:1–23; Steiner, *Honest Calling*, 143, citing Act to Regulate the Duties and Liabilities of Railroad Companies, approved February 14, 1855, 19th General Assembly, Illinois Laws, 173–74.

26. *Illinois Central Railroad v. Morrison & Crabtree*; *Illinois Central Railroad v. Brock, Hays & Company*.

27. *Illinois Central Railroad v. McLean County, Illinois & Parke*; Ely, "Abraham Lincoln as a Railroad Attorney," 8.
28. Lincoln to Jesse Dubois, December 21, 1857, in *Collected Works*, 2:429.
29. Steiner, *Honest Calling*, 144.
30. Ebenezer Lane to W. H. Osborn, August 14, 1857, Illinois Central Railroad Archives, Newberry Library, Chicago, as cited in Steiner, *Honest Calling*, 155.
31. "Law Practice of Abraham Lincoln: A Statistical Portrait"; Richardson, Sarah. 2015. "Casting a Wide Net for Lincoln's Legacy." *Civil War Times* 54(1):26–27.
32. "Law Practice of Abraham Lincoln: A Statistical Portrait."
33. Lincoln to James F. Joy, September 14, 1855, in *Collected Works*, 2:325.
34. Stowell, *Papers of Abraham Lincoln*, 3:385.
35. Ibid., 3:405–7.
36. Ibid., 3:410–11. The amount of $250 is shown on p. 385.
37. *Harris v. Great Western Railroad.*
38. For background on FELA, see "What Is FELA?," Flynn & Wietzke, https://www.felaattorney.com/faqs.
39. *Sprague v. Illinois River Railroad et al.*
40. *Barret v. Alton & Sangamon Railroad*; *Terre Haute & Alton Railroad v. Earp*; Burlingame, *Abraham Lincoln*, chap. 9, 978.
41. *Chicago, Burlington & Quincy Railroad v. Wilson*; Lincoln to Charles Hoyt, January 16, 1856, in *Collected Works*, 2:329.
42. Curran, Dennis J., and Emma Kingdon. 2015. "Abraham Lincoln: A Model for Today's Trial Lawyers." *Massachusetts Law Review* 97(1):5–6.
43. Starr, *Lincoln and the Railroads*, 126–31.
44. Burlingame, *Abraham Lincoln*, chap. 13, 1491–92.
45. Blumenthal, *Wrestling with His Angels*, 136; Starr, *Lincoln and the Railroads*, 135.
46. Clemens died a day after Halley's Comet made its next swing by Earth.
47. Speech at Council Bluffs, Iowa, August 13, 1859, in *Collected Works*, 3:396.
48. Blumenthal, *Wrestling with His Angels*, 239; Oldham, Pamela, with Meredith Bean McMath. 2005. *The CI Guide to the Legacy of Lincoln*. Alpha Books, 203.

Chapter 10: The Science Lectures

1. Temple, Wayne C. 1999. "Lincoln the Lecturer, Part I." *Lincoln Herald* 101(2):94.
2. Neider, Charles, ed. 1996. *The Autobiography of Mark Twain*. Perennial Classics, 211–32.
3. Bruce, *Launching of Modern American Science*, 115–16.
4. Browning, Orville Hickman. 1925. *The Diary of Orville Hickman Browning, Volume 1: 1850–1864*. Illinois State Historical Library, 357.
5. Address before the Young Men's Lyceum, in *Collected Works*, 1:108–15.
6. Temperance address, Springfield, Illinois, February 22, 1842, as reported in *Sangamo Journal*, March 25, 1842, in ibid., 1:271–79.
7. Volk, Kyle G. 2017. *Moral Minorities and the Making of American Democracy*. Oxford University Press, 69–100, 167–205.

8. First debate with Stephen A. Douglas in Ottawa, Illinois, August 21, 1858, in *Collected Works*, 3:14.

9. Briggs, John Channing. 2005. *Lincoln's Speeches Reconsidered.* Johns Hopkins University Press, 58–81.

10. Fragment on Niagara Falls, September 25–30, 1848, in *Collected Works*, 2:10–11.

11. Notes for a law lecture, July 1, 1850?, in ibid., 2:81–82.

12. Bancroft, George. 1854. "The Necessity, the Reality, and the Promise of the Progress of the Human Race." Speech delivered November 20, 1854. See Bancroft, George. 1855. *Literary and Historical Miscellanies.* 2 vols. Harper & Brothers, 2:481–517; Whitney, *Life on the Circuit*, 209; Whitney to Herndon, August 27, 1887, in Wilson and Davis, *Herndon's Informants*, 631, 633.

13. Oldroyd, *Lincoln Memorial Album of Immortelles*, 521–22.

14. Epstein, Daniel Mark. 2004. *Lincoln and Whitman: Parallel Lives in Civil War Washington.* Random House, 14, 32–33, 36.

15. Nicolay, John G. 1894. "Lincoln's Literary Experiments." *Century Magazine* 47:828.

16. Temple, "Lincoln the Lecturer, Part I," 100; Samuel Melvin, letter to Herndon, June 16, 1888, in Wilson and Davis, *Herndon's Informants*, 657.

17. *Daily Pantagraph*, April 9, 1858, p. 3, cols. 2–3; Temple, Wayne C. 1999. "Lincoln the Lecturer, Part II." *Lincoln Herald* 101(4):161.

18. Emerson, *Lincoln the Inventor*, 47.

19. Temple, "Lincoln the Lecturer, Part I" and "Lincoln the Lecturer, Part II."

20. Herndon and Weik, *Herndon's Lincoln*, 271.

21. Nicolay, "Lincoln's Literary Experiments," 831; Emerson, *Lincoln the Inventor*, 51.

22. Briggs, *Lincoln's Speeches Reconsidered*, 185.

23. Miller, Eugene F. 2001. "Democratic Statecraft and Technological Advance: Abraham Lincoln's Reflections on 'Discoveries and Inventions.'" *Review of Politics* 63(3):489.

24. First lecture on discoveries and inventions, April 6, 1858, in *Collected Works*, 2:437–42.

25. Speech of Schuyler Colfax at Central City, Colorado Territory, May 29, 1865, in Sacramento *Union*, June 20, 1858, p. 113.

26. Briggs, *Lincoln's Speeches Reconsidered*, 205.

27. Miller, "Democratic Statecraft," 496.

28. See also Kent, David J. 2015. *Abraham Lincoln and Nikola Tesla: Connected by Fate.* Science Traveler Books.

29. Second lecture on discoveries and inventions, February 11, 1859, in *Collected Works*, 3:356–63.

30. Miller, "Democratic Statecraft," 492–93.

31. Ibid., 494; Schaub, Diana. 2004. "How to Think about Bioethics and the Constitution." American Enterprise Institute, June 7.

32. Miller, "Democratic Statecraft," 498–99.

33. Briggs, *Lincoln's Speeches Reconsidered*, 210.

34. Nicolay, "Lincoln's Literary Experiments," 832.

35. Bates, David Homer. 1995. *Lincoln in the Telegraph Office.* University of Nebraska Press, 218–22.

36. Boorstin, *Discoverers*, 510.

37. Philbrick, Nathaniel. 2016. "Traitors and Haters." *Smithsonian*, May, 46.

38. Second lecture on discoveries and inventions, in *Collected Works*, 3:356–63.

39. Miller, "Democratic Statecraft," 504–5.

40. Ibid., 507–10; Richardson, *How the South Won the Civil War*, 42.

41. Address before the Wisconsin State Agricultural Society, September 30, 1859, in *Collected Works*, 3:471–82; Edwards, Everett E. 1933. "Lincoln's Attitudes toward Farming." United States Department of Agriculture, December 15.

42. Foner, *Fiery Trial*, 115.

43. Simpson, Margaret. 2014. "Mechanization of Agriculture—1889 Fowler Steam Ploughing Engine." Museum of Applied Arts and Sciences. https://www.maas.museum/inside-the-collection/2014/06/23/mechanisation-of-agriculture-1889-fowler-steam-ploughing-engine/.

Chapter 11: Institutionalizing Science

1. Mary Henry Diary, 1858–1863, May 3, 1861, Smithsonian, https://transcription.si.edu/project/6622; *Collected Works*, 7:512.

2. Mary Henry Diary, May 3, 1861.

3. Jahns, Patricia. 1961. *Matthew Fontaine Maury and Joseph Henry: Scientists of the Civil War*. Hastings House, 154–55.

4. Jahns, Patricia. 1970. *Joseph Henry: Father of American Electronics*. Routledge, 87; Miller, William Lee. 2008. *Abraham Lincoln: The Duty of a Statesman*. Alfred A. Knopf, 212.

5. Mary Henry Diary, May 3, 1861.

6. Burleigh, Nina. 2003. *The Stranger and the Statesman: James Smithson, John Quincy Adams, and the Making of America's Greatest Museum, the Smithsonian*. William Morrow, 254ff; Bruce, *Launching of Modern American Science*, 187; Ewing, Heather. 2007. *The Lost World of James Smithson: Science, Revolution, and the Birth of the Smithsonian*. Bloomsbury, 2.

7. Roughly fourteen million in 2020 dollars; Reingold, Nathan. 1985. *Science in Nineteenth-Century America: A Documentary History*. University of Chicago Press, 152–54.

8. Burleigh, *Stranger and the Statesman*, 71.

9. Ibid., 93.

10. James Smithson, last will and testament, October 23, 1826, https://siarchives.si.edu/history/featured-topics/stories/last-will-and-testament-october-23-1826.

11. Burleigh, *Stranger and the Statesman*, 193–94.

12. Hensen, Pamela. 2015. "When Congress Looked James Smithson's Gift Horse in the Mouth." *Smithsonian*, July 30. https://www.smithsonianmag.com/smithsonian-institution/looking-james-smithsons-gift-horse-mouth-180956107/#j6qswaAk8ShmOk5s.03. Lincoln would serve in Congress with John Quincy Adams and was assigned to the committee overseeing Adams's burial when he died in chambers.

13. Bruce, *Launching of Modern American Science*, 256.

14. Joseph Henry to Frederick Barnard, February 23, 1861, in Rothenberg, Marc, ed. 2008. *Papers of Joseph Henry*. Vol. 10. Smithsonian Institution Press, 197–98.

15. Reingold, *Science in Nineteenth-Century America*, 154; Bruce, *Launching of Modern American Science*, 39–40.

16. Rothenberg, Marc. 1992. *The Papers of Joseph Henry*. Vol. 6. Smithsonian Institution Press, xxvi; Ewing, *Lost World of James Smithson*, 326.

17. Jahns, *Matthew Fontaine Maury and Joseph Henry*, 86. The patent office is now the home of the National Portrait Gallery and Smithsonian American Art Museum.

18. Mary Henry Diary, June 1, 1861; Jahns, *Matthew Fontaine Maury and Joseph Henry*, 159; Bruce, *Launching of Modern American Science*, 292. Felton was president of Harvard College (now Harvard University) and a member of the Smithsonian's Board of Regents. He was also Louis Agassiz's brother-in-law.

19. Jahns, *Matthew Fontaine Maury and Joseph Henry*, 159. Gilliss had founded the observatory but was passed over as its first superintendent because Maury was from the secretary of the navy's home state.

20. Bruce, *Launching of Modern American Science*, 8.

21. Rothenberg, Marc, personal interview, March 14, 2018, and correspondence, February 27, 2018.

22. Coffin, *Abraham Lincoln*, 278.

23. Chittenden, Lucius. 1891. *Recollections of President Lincoln and His Administration.* Harper & Brothers, 237.

24. Ibid., 238.

25. Coffin, *Abraham Lincoln*, 278; *Washington Star*, January 4, 1862; James Cravens to Abraham Lincoln, January 5, 1862, Library of Congress.

26. Shaw and Burlingame, *Abraham Lincoln Traveled This Way*, 203.

27. Rothenberg interview, March 14, 2018.

28. Mary Henry Diary, February 6, 1862.

29. Joseph Henry to Alexander Dallas Bache, April 4, 1863, in Rothenberg, *Papers of Joseph Henry*, 10:250.

30. Mary Henry Diary, Tuesday, January 26, 1864.

31. Joseph Henry to Barnard, February 23, 1861, in Rothenberg, *Papers of Joseph Henry*, 10:197–98.

32. Joseph Henry locked book, in Rothenberg, *The Papers of Joseph Henry*, 10:430–431 and n3.

33. Montgomery Meigs to William Seldon, October 8, 1861, Marcus Benjamin Papers, Smithsonian Archives, as noted in Rothenberg, *Papers of Joseph Henry*, 10:431n4; Bruce, *Launching of Modern American Science*, 275; Coulson, Thomas. 1950. *Joseph Henry: His Life and Work*. Princeton University Press, 243.

34. Brooks, Noah. 1895/1971. *Washington, D.C. in Lincoln's Time*. Quadrangle Books, 22–24.

35. Sandburg, Carl. 1959. *Abraham Lincoln: The Prairie Years and the War Years.* Charles Scribner's Sons, 3:400.

36. Joseph Henry to William H. Seward, November 11, 1862, in Rothenberg, *Papers of Joseph Henry*, 10:286.

37. Holzer, Harold. 1993. *Dear Mr. Lincoln: Letters to the President.* Addison-Wesley, 173.

38. Reingold, Nathan. 1958. "Science in the Civil War: The Permanent Commission of the Navy Department." *Isis* 49(3):308.

39. Ibid.

40. Joseph Henry to Asa Gray, April 15, 1863, in Rothenberg, *Papers of Joseph Henry,* 10:302–3n3; Alley, Richard B. 2011. *Earth: The Operators' Manual.* W. W. Norton, 347n4.

41. Reingold, "Science in the Civil War," 310.

42. Joseph Henry to Asa Gray, April 15, 1863, in Rothenberg, *Papers of Joseph Henry,* 10:302–3n3; Joseph Henry to Mary Henry, May 30, 1863, in ibid., 10:314.

43. Letter to Mary Henry, May 30, 1863, in ibid., 10:314; Bruce, *Lincoln and the Tools of War,* 220; "Minutes of the Permanent Commission, Meeting XXXV," in Rothenberg, *Papers of Joseph Henry,* 10:309–12.

44. Joseph Henry to Mary Henry, May 30, 1863, in Rothenberg, *Papers of Joseph Henry,* 10:314.

45. Rothenberg, Marc. "Science Adviser." Smithsonian.com; Lander, James. 2010. *Lincoln & Darwin: Shared Visions of Race, Science, and Religion.* Southern Illinois University Press, 217; Reingold, "Science in the Civil War," 310.

46. Rothenberg, "Science Adviser."

47. John H. Schenck to Abraham Lincoln, January 16, 1864, Abraham Lincoln Papers, Library of Congress, http://memory.loc.gov/mss/mal/mal1/295/2954500/001.jpg (underlining in original).

48. John D. Hall to Abraham Lincoln, March 25, 1864, Naval Records Collection of the Office of Naval Records and Library, NARA, RG45, Entry 36.

49. Charles H. Davis and others to Gideon Welles, May 3, 1864, Abraham Lincoln Papers, Library of Congress, http://memory.loc.gov/mss/mal/mal1/328/3280300/001.jpg.

50. Thomas Schuebly to Abraham Lincoln, October 5, 1863, Naval Records Collection of the Office of Naval Records and Library, NARA, RG45, Entry 36.

51. Reingold, "Science in the Civil War," 310.

52. Kent, *Edison,* 204–5.

53. Joseph Henry to Harriet Henry, October 16, 1861, in Rothenberg, *Papers of Joseph Henry,* 10:226–27n1; Kent, *Edison,* 173–99.

54. National Academy of Sciences, "History," http://www.nasonline.org/about-nas/history/.

55. Reingold, *Science in Nineteenth-Century America,* 200.

56. Note from Abraham Lincoln to Senator Wilson, February 23, 1863, in *Collected Works,* 6:115; Joseph Henry to Stephen Alexander, March 9, 1863, in Rothenberg, *Papers of Joseph Henry,* 10:296–97; Joseph Henry to Asa Gray, April 15, 1863, in ibid., 10:302; Lander, *Lincoln & Darwin,* 217; Bruce, *Launching of Modern American Science,* 302.

57. Cochrane, Rexmond C. 1978. *The National Academy of Sciences: The First Hundred Years, 1863–1963.* National Academies Press, 53, 56; Joseph Henry to Stephen Alexander, March 9, 1863, in Rothenberg, *Papers of Joseph Henry,* 10:296–297nn1–3; Bruce, *Launching of Modern American Science,* 302.

58. Cochrane, *National Academy of Sciences*; Alley, *Earth*, 61.
59. Joseph Henry to Asa Gray, April 15, 1863, in Rothenberg, *Papers of Joseph Henry*, 10:302–3; Joseph Henry to Mary Anna Henry, April 24, 1864, in ibid., 10:303–7. Not long after this, Alexander Dallas Bache suffered a cerebral hemorrhage that incapacitated him for several years. Henry functioned as president during this time and officially became president when Bache died in 1867, serving as both president of NAS and secretary of the Smithsonian until his own death in 1878.
60. Joseph Henry to Stephen Alexander, March 9, 1863, in ibid., 10:296–97n3; Joseph Henry to Asa Gray, April 15, 1863, in ibid., 10:302.
61. Rothenberg interview, March 14, 2018.
62. For more information, visit the NAS website at https://www.nap.edu/.
63. Oldham and McMath, *CI Guide*, 229.
64. Annual Message to Congress, December 3, 1861, in *Collected Works*, 5:46.
65. Bruce, *Launching of Modern American Science*, 317–18; Chaitkin, Anton. 1986. "Abraham Lincoln Imposes Science on American Agriculture." *Executive Intelligence Review*, April 11. http://american_almanac.tripod.com/lincoln2.htm.
66. "An Act to Establish a Department of Agriculture," USDA National Agricultural Library, https://www.nal.usda.gov/topics/act-establish-department-agriculture.
67. Annual Message to Congress, December 1, 1862, in *Collected Works*, 5:526.
68. Joseph Henry to Asa Gray, May 22, 1862, in Rothenberg, *Papers of Joseph Henry*, 10:265n1, citing *U.S. Statutes at Large*, 12:387–88.
69. "The Story of U.S. Agricultural Estimates," USDA, National Agricultural Library, https://archive.org/stream/storyofusagricul1088unit/storyofusagricul1088unit_djvu.txt.
70. Newton, Isaac. 1862. "Report of the Department of Agriculture to Abraham Lincoln." Abraham Lincoln Papers, Library of Congress. http://memory.loc.gov/mss/mal/mal1/207/2076200/001.jpg.
71. Ibid., 48.
72. Ibid., 30.
73. Ibid., 29.
74. The Homestead Act remained in effect until 1976 in most states, and to 1986 in Alaska.
75. Arrington, Todd. 2018. "The Homestead Act, Early Republicans, and the Coming of the Civil War." *Emerging Civil War* blog, January 1, 2018. https://emergingcivilwar.com/2018/01/01/the-homestead-act-early-republicans-and-the-coming-of-the-civil-war/.
76. A major exception was Chinese immigrants, who were ineligible for homesteading and further discouraged from life in the United States by the Chinese Exclusion Act, first signed into law by Chester A. Arthur on May 6, 1882. The Exclusion Act and renewals remained in place until its repeal by the Magnuson Act in 1943. The Homestead Act also continued the displacement of Native American Indian populations and contributed to later environmental issues such as drought, soil erosion, and degradation. See Arrington, "Homestead Act."
77. The Funk family was ahead of their time, as they were pioneers in the development of hybrid corn, wheat, and other better-yield crops. They also electrified their house in

1910, long before anyone in the Midwest knew anything about electricity. Isaac Funk's grandson Deloss had personal consultations with both Nikola Tesla and Thomas Edison. See Kent, *Tesla*; and Kent, *Edison*.

78. Bruce, *Launching of Modern American Science*, 330. For list of land-grant colleges, see https://web.archive.org/web/20130111211111/http://www.aplu.org/page.aspx?pid=249. For HBCUs, see "7 U.S. Code, Section 323. Racial Discrimination by Colleges Restricted," https://www.law.cornell.edu/uscode/text/7/323.

79. Rothenberg interview, March 14, 2018; Bruce, *Launching of Modern American Science*, 287, 330.

80. For example, Bordewich, Fergus M. 2020. *Congress at War: How Republican Reformers Fought the Civil War, Defied Lincoln, Ended Slavery, and Remade America*. Alfred A. Knopf.

81. Schaff, Jon D. 2019. *Abraham Lincoln's Statesmanship and the Limits of Liberal Democracy*. Southern Illinois University Press, 143.

82. *Cincinnati Daily Gazette*, February 13, 1861, in *Collected Works*, 4:203.

83. Schaff, *Abraham Lincoln's Statesmanship*, 181.

84. Ibid., 185.

85. "Communication to the People of Sangamon County," March 9, 1832, *Sangamo Journal*, March 15, 1832, in *Collected Works*, 1:5–9; Schaff, *Abraham Lincoln's Statesmanship*, 193.

86. Wilson, Robert. 2006. *The Explorer King: Adventure, Science, and the Great Diamond Hoax—Clarence King in the Old West*. Scribner, 8–9.

87. Abraham Lincoln, response to John Conness, November 18, 1863, in *Collected Works*, 7:13; Kurzius, Alexa Z. 2014. "These 1861 Photos Helped Convince Abraham Lincoln to Preserve Yosemite for the Public." *Smithsonian*, June 5.

88. Muir, John. 1912. *The Yosemite*. Century Co., 106.

89. Abraham Lincoln to Charles Maltby, March 25, 1865, "California in the Civil War," California Department of Parks and Recreation, http://www.parks.ca .gov/?page_id=26775.

90. Johnson also urged Muir to found the Sierra Club to advocate for preservation of the Sierra Nevada region. Johnson went on to publish the serialization of John Nicolay and John Hay's *Abraham Lincoln: A History* prior to its release in book form. Johnson himself wrote a four-volume treatise called *Battles and Leaders of the Civil War*, published in 1887. Muir sometimes attended Johnson's gala parties in his New York mansion, along with other frequent guess that included Nikola Tesla and Mark Twain. See Kent, *Tesla*, 211.

91. Mary Henry Diary, January 25, 1865; Ewing, *Lost World of James Smithson*, 1–8; *Daily Intelligencer*, January 24 and 25, 1865; *Evening Star*, January 24 and 25, 1865; *Report of the Special Committee of the Board of Regents of the Smithsonian Institution Relative to the Fire*, February 1865, Senate Report No. 129.

92. Mary Henry Diary, January 26, 1865.

93. Burleigh, *Stranger and the Statesman*, 159.

94. Mary Henry Diary, January 25–26, 1865; Ewing, *Lost World of James Smithson*, 5–7.

95. Bruce, *Launching of Modern American Science*, 301. Amount is approximately two million in 2020 dollars.

96. Henson, Pamela H. 2015. "The Burning of the Smithsonian." Smithsonian Archives, January 23. https://siarchives.si.edu/blog/burning-smithsonian.

97. Ewing, *Lost World of James Smithson*, 10; Johnson, Walter R. 1844. *A Memoir on the Scientific Character and Researches of James Smithson, Esq., F.R.S.* Barrett and Jones.

98. Henry desk diary, January 26, 1865, in Rothenberg, *Papers of Joseph Henry*, 10:463.

99. *Collected Works*, 5:521–22.

100. Ibid. The transcontinental railroad would be completed with an elaborate ceremony on May 10, 1869, shortly after Ulysses S. Grant was sworn in as president of the United States.

Chapter 12: The Technology of War

1. For example, Edwin D. Morgan to Lincoln, October 31, 1862, NARA, RG 45, Entry 36, Records of the Office of the Secretary of the Navy, 1798–1921, Miscellaneous Letters Received, ALPLM, Document #291813.

2. Joseph G. Totten to Lincoln, January 2, 1862, Abraham Lincoln Papers, Library of Congress, ALPLM, Document #216550; Paul Reverend Franklin Jones to Lincoln, January 4, 1862, Abraham Lincoln Papers, Library of Congress, ALPLM, Document #216558.

3. January 8, 1862, Borrower's Ledger 1861–1863, 114, Archives of the Library of Congress; see the Lincoln Archives Digital Project at http://www.lincolnarchives.org/cgi -bin/lincoln?a=d&d=&sf=&d=Drg94-159-01-14-lr-186201&page=1; Halleck, Henry Wager. 1846. *Elements of Military Art and Science.* D. Appleton & Co.

4. Taliaferro, Adam L. 2017. "Lincoln & Clausewitz: An Examination of Lincoln's Military Strategy as Compared to the Great Military Theorist." *Lincoln Herald* 119(4):225–36; McPherson, James. 2008. *Tried by War.* Penguin, 142; Christopher Hamner, George Mason University, personal communication, February 17, 2020.

5. See "Brevet Brigadier General James W. Ripley," Ordnance Corps, https://goord-nance.army.mil/history/chiefs/ripley.html.

6. Bruce, *Lincoln and the Tools of War*, 126–27.

7. Lincoln to War Department, August 21, 1864, in *Collected Works*, 7:510; Lincoln to Benjamin Butler, September 13, 1864, in ibid., 8:3.

8. Lincoln to Dahlgren and Dahlgren to Lincoln, both June 10, 1861, in ibid., 4:399.

9. Lincoln to Ripley, May 5, 1862, in ibid., 10:133.

10. Bruce, *Lincoln and the Tools of War*, 190.

11. Blumenthal, *All the Powers of Earth*, 625.

12. Hamner, personal communication, February 17, 2020.

13. Burlingame and Ettlinger, *Inside Lincoln's White House*, 311n127.

14. Morrison, Jed. 2013. "Target Practice with Mr. Lincoln." *New York Times*, August 19; Bartlett, W. A. 1921. "Lincoln's Seven Hits with a Rifle." *Boston Transcript*, reprinted in *Magazine of History* 19(73); Burlingame and Ettlinger, *Inside Lincoln's White House*, 75.

15. Burlingame and Ettlinger, *Inside Lincoln's White House*, 311n127; Austerman, Wayne. 1984. "The Northern Spencer Goes South." *Civil War Times* 23(3):26–30.

16. Lincoln to Ripley, August 17, 1861, in *Collected Works Supplement*, 10:92.

17. Lincoln to Ripley, December 19, 1861, in *Collected Works*, 5:75.

18. Lincoln to Stanton, August 9, 1862, in ibid., 5:365.

19. Richard J. Gatling to Lincoln, February 18, 1864, NARA, Box 7, RG 156, Entry 994: Records of the Office of the Chief of Ordnance, Miscellaneous Records, Ordnance Department Special File, 1812–1912, Correspondence Relating to Inventions, 1812–1870.

20. Bruce, *Lincoln and the Tools of War*, 291.

21. Ibid., 219; Pohl, Robert. 2018. "Lost Capitol Hill: An Explosion at the Navy Yard." TheHillIsHome.com, June 25. https://thehillishome.com/2018/06/lost-capitol-hill -explosion-navy-yard/.

22. Hawley, David. 2011. "Engineering the Union's Victory." *History Channel Magazine*, July/August, 33–38; Larson, C. Kay. 2013. "How Trains Saved the Union." *New York Times*, November 1.

23. Ditmeyer, Steven R. 2013. "Railroads, Herman Haupt, and the Battle of Gettysburg." *Railroad History*, Spring/Summer, 46–51; Turner, George Edgar. 1972. *Victory Rode the Rails: The Strategic Place of the Railroads in the Civil War*. Greenwood Press, 31–33.

24. Pinkerton to Felton, January 27, 1861, in Wilson and Davis, *Herndon's Informants*, 267–68, 312; Felton to Pinkerton, December 31, 1867, in Pinkerton, Allan. 1868. *History and Evidence of the Passage of Abraham Lincoln from Harrisburg, Pa. to Washington, D.C. on the 22d and 23d of February, 1861*. Privately printed, 15.

25. Haupt, Herman. 1901. *Reminiscences of General Herman Haupt*. Wright & Joys, 49; Stokes, G. P. 1991. "Herman Haupt's Railroads: Beanpoles and Cornstalks." *Civil War Times*, November–December, 12–21, 76.

26. Stokes, "Herman Haupt's Railroads," 12–21, 76; Gallagher, Gary W. 2019. "Off the Tracks: The Confederacy Failed to Take Advantage of Railroad Technology." *Civil War Times* 58(8):22–24.

27. Charles H. Haskins to Lincoln, June 19, 1864, NARA, Box 258, RG 107, Entry 18: Records of the Secretary of War, Record Series Originating during the Period 1789–1889, Correspondence, Letters Received (Main Series), 1801–1889, Microfilm M 221, Roll 252, Frames 841–845, ALPLM, Document #211728; Daniel C. Bolton to Lincoln, June 13, 1864, NARA, Box 257, RG 107, Entry 18, Microfilm M 221, Roll 250, Frames 933–935, ALPLM, Document #211728.

28. Anonymous. 2019. Noted in the "News!" page in *Civil War Times* 58(8):12.

29. Special Field Orders from General William T. Sherman, July 18, 1864, on 7th Pennsylvania Calvary, https://7thpennsylvaniacavalry.com/special-field-orders-from -major-general-william-t-sherman-to-july-18-1864/; Nye, Logan. 2020. "Sherman's Bow Ties Were an Ultimate 'Screw You' to the South." We Are the Mighty, August 7, 2020. https://www.wearethemighty.com/mighty-history/sherman-neckties-civil-war -history/.

30. Hodges, Robert R. 2009. *American Civil War Railroad Tactics*. Osprey, 7, 12–15.

31. Whyte, William. 2015. "Hastily Produced Union Ironclads Ruled the Western Theater's Waterways." *Civil War Times* 54(1):38–45.

32. Holloway, Anna Gibson, and Jonathan W. White. 2018. *Our Little Monitor: The Greatest Invention of the Civil War*. Kent State University Press, 34ff.

33. Ibid., 34; Church, William Conant. 1890. *The Life of John Ericsson*. 2 vols. Charles Scribner's Sons, 1906–1907, 1:246–47.

34. Stoddard, William O. 2000. *Inside the White House in War Times: Memoirs and Reports of Lincoln's Secretary*. Ed. Michael Burlingame. University of Nebraska Press, 20.

35. Lincoln to Welles, March 10, 1862, in *Collected Works*, 5:154.

36. Keeler, William Frederick. 1964. *Aboard the USS Monitor, 1862: The Letters of Acting Paymaster William Frederick Keeler, US Navy, to His Wife, Anna*. Ed. Robert W. Daly. US Naval Institute.

37. Norder, Steve. 2020. *Lincoln Takes Command: The Campaign to Seize Norfolk and the Destruction of the* CSS Virginia. Savas Beatie, 93.

38. Chase to his wife "Nettie," May 11, 1862, in Diary of Salmon P. Chase, Chase Papers, Library of Congress; Norder, *Lincoln Takes Command*, 270–71.

39. Hamner, personal communication, February 17, 2020; Symonds, personal communication, November 17, 2019.

40. Brutus de Villeroi to Lincoln, September 4, 1861, NARA, vol. 13, RG 45, Entry 36, Naval Records, Microfilm M124, Roll 383, Document 121, ALPLM, Document #291646; de Villeroi to Lincoln, March 8, 1862, NARA, vol. 1, RG 45, Entry 36, Microfilm M124, Roll 400, Document 136, ALPLM, Document #291696; Louis Hennet and others to Lincoln, March 29, 1862, NARA, vol. 3, RG 45, Entry 36, Naval Records, Microfilm M124, Roll 402, Document 247, ALPLM, Document #291719; Wyatt, Kingseed. 2001. "The North's Only Submarine, *Alligator*, Did Not Live Up to Her Reputation as a 'Monster' and a 'Terrible Engine.'" *America's Civil War* 14(5):26–29.

41. Evans, Charles M. 2002. *War of the Aeronauts: A History of Ballooning in the Civil War*. Stackpole Books, 28.

42. Lincoln to Scott, July 25, 1861, in *Collected Works*, 4:460.

43. Evans, *War of the Aeronauts*, 86–87.

44. Kevin Knapp, notes from a lecture, February 11, 2016.

45. Ibid.

46. Thaddeus S. C. Lowe telegram to Lincoln, June 18, 1861, Abraham Lincoln Papers, Library of Congress, ALPLM, Document #215052; Holzer, *Dear Mr. Lincoln*, 179.

47. Edward D. Tippett to Lincoln, May 11, 1861, NARA Box 30, RG 156, Entry 994, Records of the Office of the Chief of Ordnance, ALPLM, Document #275658; Tippett to Lincoln, May 25, 1861, NARA Box 30, RG 156, Entry 994, Records of the Office of the Chief of Ordnance, ALPLM, Document #301857; Tippett to Lincoln, February 9, 1865, Abraham Lincoln Papers, Library of Congress, ALPLM, Document #227853; Holzer, *Dear Mr. Lincoln*, 191–93.

48. Bates, *Lincoln in the Telegraph Office*, 4; Mueller, Marilyn. 2010. "Tapping into the New Technology: Lincoln's Earliest Telegraphic Message." *Lincoln Editor* 10:7–8; Holst, Erica. 2009. "Lightning Line on the Prairie: Lincoln's Use of Telegraphy." *Lincoln Editor* 9(2):6–8.

49. Kortenhof, Kurt. 2011. "What Hath God Wrought?" *History Magazine*, May/June, 13; Howe, Daniel Walker. 2007. *What Hath God Wrought: The Transformation of America, 1815–1848*. Oxford University Press.

50. Kent, *Edison*; Wheeler, Tom. 2006. *Mr. Lincoln's T-Mails: The Untold Story of How Abraham Lincoln Used the Telegraph to Win the Civil War*. HarperCollins.

51. Wheeler, *Mr. Lincoln's T-Mails*, 3.

52. Bates, *Lincoln in the Telegraph Office*, 40.

53. Burlingame, *Abraham Lincoln*, chap. 23, 2495–96.

54. *National Intelligencer*, February 26, 1862.

55. Wheeler, *Mr. Lincoln's T-Mails*, 36.

56. *New York Tribune*, October 28, 1861; Leland Stanford to Lincoln, October 25, 1861, NARA, Record Group 107, Entry 34, Telegrams Sent and Received by the War Department Central Telegraph Office.

57. Lincoln to McClellan, October 13, 1862, in *Collected Works*, 5:460–61; Lincoln to McClellan, October 25, 1862, in ibid., 5:474.

58. Burlingame, *Abraham Lincoln*, chap. 26, 2885–88; Lincoln to Fremont, May 24, 1862, in *Collected Works*, 5:231.

59. Jepsen, Thomas C. 1991. "The Telegraph Goes to War." *Civil War* 9(6):58–62; Wheeler, *Mr. Lincoln's T-Mails*, 98.

60. Memorandum concerning his probable failure of reelection, August 23, 1864, in *Collected Works*, 7:514.

61. Ramirez, Ainissa. 2020. "The $60,000 Telegram That Helped Abraham Lincoln Abolish Slavery." *Time*, May 6. https://time.com/5832758/abraham-lincoln-slavery -telegram/.

62. Annual Message to Congress, December 6, 1864, in *Collected Works*, 8:146.

Chapter 13: The Science of War

1. Alexander Bache to Lincoln, April 26, 1861, letter and map, Abraham Lincoln Papers, Library of Congress, ALPLM, Documents #214647 and #214664.

2. All four border states rejected multiple attempts at gradual compensated emancipation.

3. Burlingame, *Abraham Lincoln*, chap. 29, 3164, citing William L. Shea and Terrence J. Winschel. 2003. *Vicksburg Is the Key: The Struggle for the Mississippi River*. University of Nebraska Press, 1.

4. Thompson, Clive. 2016. "How Data Won the West." *Smithsonian*, July–August, 26; Carleton, Genevieve. 2020. "The Map That Helped Convince Lincoln That Slavery Had to End." *Ranker*, July 8. https://www.ranker.com/list/map-that-convinced-lincoln-to -end-slavery/genevieve-carlton.

5. Recognized in remarks by President Barack Obama on April 29, 2013, the 150th anniversary of the creation of the National Academy of Sciences, https://notes.nap .edu/2013/04/30/president-barack-obamas-speech-to-the-national-academy-of -sciences-full-transcript/.

6. Smith, Glenn S. 2017. "Joseph Henry's Role in the Discovery of Electromagnetic Induction." *European Journal of Physics* 38(1):015207; Kent, *Edison*; Kent, *Abraham Lincoln and Nikola Tesla*.

7. Herndon and Weik, *Herndon's Lincoln*, 116.

8. Ibid., 116; Joshua Speed to Herndon, ibid., 478.

9. Speech at Chicago, July 10, 1858, in *Collected Works*, 2:500.

10. Alley, *Earth*, 60–62; True, Frederick W. 1913. *A History of the First Half-Century of the National Academy of Sciences*. Lord Baltimore Press, 216–17.

11. Alley, *Earth*, 60–62; True, *History of the First Half-Century*, 81.

12. Cochrane, *National Academy of Sciences*, 80–90; True, *History of the First Half-Century*, 213–30.

13. Speech to the Springfield Scott Club, August 14, 1852, in *Collected Works*, 2:149.

14. Second lecture on discoveries and inventions, in ibid., 3:357.

15. Debate with Stephen A. Douglas at Charleston, Illinois, September 18, 1858, in ibid., 3:184. A cuttlefish is actually a cephalopod similar to octopus and squid, all of which squirt "ink" to create a distraction that allow them to escape predators. It was common to use the terms interchangeably at that time, especially far away from the ocean.

16. Chittenden, *Recollections of President Lincoln*, 247–50; Burlingame and Ettlinger, *Inside Lincoln's White House*, 193; Lincoln to Don C. Buell and Henry Halleck, January 13, 1862, in *Collected Works*, 5:98.

17. Baron, *American Eclipse*, 152.

18. Burlingame, *Abraham Lincoln*, chap. 30, 3280; Noe, Kenneth W. 2020. *The Howling Storm: Weather, Climate, and the American Civil War*. Louisiana State University Press.

19. Memorandum concerning Francis L. Capen's weather forecasts, April 28, 1863, in *Collected Works*, 6:190–91.

20. Rothenberg, Marc. "Joseph Henry, Lincoln's Science Advisor." Papers of Joseph Henry, Smithsonian.

21. Ross, Charles. 2001. *Civil War Acoustic Shadows*. White Mane Books, 23. This book is an excellent source of information on this little-known phenomenon and the battles affected.

22. Lincoln to McClellan, May 31, 1862, in *Collected Works*, 5:254.

23. Hirsch and Van Haften, *Abraham Lincoln and the Structure of Reason*; Hirsch, David, and Dan Van Haften. 2019. *The Tyranny of Public Discourse: Abraham Lincoln's Six-Element Antidote for Meaningful and Persuasive Writing*. Savas Beatie. The six elements are Enunciation, Exposition, Specification, Construction, Proof, and Conclusion. These six elements should not be confused with the "Six Books" of Euclid's *Elements*.

24. Humes, James C. 1996. *The Wit and Wisdom of Abraham Lincoln*. Gramercy Books, 124–25.

25. Ruane, Michael. 2013. "Empire of Science." *Smithsonian* 44(1):18.

26. Hancock, Harold B., and Norman B. Wilkinson. 1964. "'The Devil to Pay!': Saltpeter and the *Trent* Affair." *Civil War History* 10:20–32; Bruce, *Launching of Modern American Science*, 311.

27. Lincoln to the Senate of the United States, January 26, 1863, in *Collected Works*, 6:79.

28. Diller to Lincoln, October 31, 1863, in Holzer, *Dear Mr. Lincoln*, 189.

29. Lincoln to Diller, December 15, 1862, in *Collected Works*, 6:3–5; Lincoln endorsement, January 15, 1863, in ibid., 6:59.

30. Memorandum of instructions for test of Diller's powder, November 2, 1863, in ibid., 6:559–61; Holzer, *Dear Mr. Lincoln*, 189; Bruce, *Launching of Modern American Science*, 311.

31. For example, see "'That When a Lady Lifts Her Skirt, She Shoots a Horrid Yankee': The Story of Confederate Women's Urine and the Manufacture of Gunpowder," Civilian Military Intelligence Group, https://civilianmilitaryintelligencegroup.com/12836/that-when-a-lady-lifts-her-skirt-she-shoots-a-horrid-yankee-the-story-of-confederate-womens-urine-and-the-manufacture-of-gunpowder.

32. Lincoln to Garrett, January 10, 1865, in *Collected Works*, 8:208.

33. Shoaf, Dana. 2017. "Fuel for the Fires." *Civil War Times* 56(4):12–13; Richardson, Sarah. 2016. "Interview with Peter Shulman." *Civil War Times* 55(1):22–23.

34. For a good discussion of the science behind the Crater, see Ross, Charles. 2000. *Trial by Fire: Science, Technology and the Civil War*. White Mane Books, 3–25.

35. Thompson to Lincoln, April 11, 1861, Abraham Lincoln Papers, Library of Congress, reported in the *Lincoln Log* for April 10, 1861.

36. Rothenberg, *Papers of Joseph Henry*, 10:268nn1–4; Scheips, Paul J. 1952. "Lincoln and the Chiriqui Colonization Project." *Journal of Negro History* 37:443–45; handwritten report from Lesley to Joseph Henry, no date, Abraham Lincoln Papers, Document #218431, Library of Congress.

37. Rothenberg, *Papers of Joseph Henry*, 10:280n5.

38. Ibid., 281n11.

39. Lincoln to Stanton and Welles, February 16, 1861, in *Collected Works*, 6:107.

40. Hasegawa, Guy R. 2015. *Villainous Compounds: Chemical Weapons and the American Civil War*. Southern Illinois University Press, 126.

41. James Cornelius, personal communication, April 20, 2016.

42. Green, James L., and Scott Boardsen. 2006. "Duration and Extent of the Great Auroral Storm of 1859." *Advances in Space Research* 38:130–35; Green, James L., et al. 2006. "Eyewitness Reports of the Great Auroral Storm of 1859." *Advances in Space Research* 38:145–54.

43. Lincoln to Butterfield, May 11, 1863, in *Collected Works*, 6:209.

44. Gillespie to Herndon, December 8, 1866, in Wilson and Davis, *Herndon's Informants*, 506.

45. Benson, Kirk R. 2014. "Lincoln and the Cosmos." *Astronomy Magazine* blog, July 14. http://cs.astronomy.com/asy/b/astronomy/archive/2014/07/14/lincoln-and-the-cosmos.aspx.

Chapter 14: Assassination Science

1. Leale, Charles A. "Report on the Death of President Lincoln." RG 112, Records of the Office of the Surgeon General (War), entry 12: Central Office, Correspondence,

1818–1946, 1818–1890, Letters Received, Box 56, NARA, Washington, DC; Papaioan-nou, Helena Iles, and Daniel W. Stowell. 2013. "Dr. Charles A. Leale's Report on the Assassination of Abraham Lincoln." *JALA* 34(1):40–53; Kaufman, Michael T. 1995. "Medicine on a Good Friday 6 Score and 10 Years Ago." *New York Times*, April 15.

2. Steers, Edward, Jr. 2010. *The Lincoln Assassination Encyclopedia*. Harper Perennial, 458.

3. *New York World*, July 3, 1881, reported by Elliff, John T. 2015. "A Vivid Description by a Surgeon Who Saw President Lincoln Shot and Watched Him Die." *Lincoln Forum Bulletin* 38:2–3, 11.

4. White, Jonathan W. 2017. *Midnight in America: Darkness, Sleep, and Dreams during the Civil War*. University of North Carolina Press, 151–56.

5. Major R. O. Ackerman to Ranger Wally Shaw. 1988. "Der(r)inger Defined." *Lincolnian* 6(4):6.

6. *New York World*, July 3, 1881; Leale, "Report on the Death"; Papaioannou and Stow-ell, "Dr. Charles A. Leale's Report"; Temple, Wayne C. 2015. *Lincoln's Surgeons at the Assassination*. Mayhaven; also see "'His Wound Is Mortal; It Is Impossible for Him to Recover': The Final Hours of President Abraham Lincoln," National Museum of Health and Medicine, https://www.medicalmuseum.mil/index.cfm?p=visit.exhibits.current.col-lection_that_teaches.lincoln.page_01.

7. See sources in note 6.

8. Cornelius and Knorowski, *Under Lincoln's Hat*, 142.

9. Graham, Donald. 2019. "Medical Care in the Time of Lincoln." *For the People* 21(3):5–8; Hirschhorn, Norbert, Robert G. Feldman, and Ian A. Greaves. 2001. "Abra-ham Lincoln's Blue Pills." *Perspectives in Biology and Medicine* 44(3):315–32; Abel, E. Lawrence. 2020. *Lincoln's Jewish Spy: The Life and Times of Issachar Zacharie*. McFarland, 67; testimonial for Issachar Zacharie, September 22, 1862, in *Collected Works*, 5:436.

10. Goldman, Armond, and Frank Schmalstieg. 2007. "Abraham Lincoln's Gettysburg Illness." *Journal of Medical Biography* 15(2):104–10; Graham, "Medical Care in the Time of Lincoln," 5–8.

11. Civil War Preservation Trust. 2003. *Two Week Curriculum for Teaching the Civil War*. National Museum of Civil War Medicine, 175–80. Also see "Frightful Realities of the Civil War," https://www.battlefields.org/learn/head-tilting-history/frightful-realities -civil-war.

12. Schroeder-Lien, Glenna R. 2012. *Lincoln and Medicine*. Southern Illinois University Press, 56–58.

13. Golden, Janet. 2013. "Civil War's Record Deaths Led to Major Advances in Public Health." *Philadelphia Inquirer*, July 23. https://www.inquirer.com/philly/blogs/public_ health/Civil-Wars-record-death-toll-led-to-major-advances-in-public-health.html.

14. Thompson, Helen. 2015. "Six Ways the Civil War Changed American Medicine." *Smithsonian*, June 17, p. 5. https://www.smithsonianmag.com/science-nature/six-ways -civil-war-changed-american-medicine-180955626/.

15. Ibid., 3.

16. Humphreys, Margaret. 2017. "Five Things That Will Surprise You about Civil War Medicine." Johns Hopkins University Press blog, March 20. https://www.press.jhu.edu/ newsroom/five-things-will-surprise-you-about-civil-war-medicine.

17. Herzog, Norbert, and David Niesel. 2019. "Medical Discovery News: High School Student Solves Civil War Mystery of Glowing Wounds." *Abilene Reporter News*, January 1. https://www.reporternews.com/story/life/2019/01/01/medical-discovery-news-civil-war-mystery-glowing-wounds-solved/2450888002/; Russell, Shahan. 2017. "The 'Glowing Angels' Who Saved Civil War Soldiers Turned Out to be Luminous Parasitic Bacteria." *War History Online*, February 4. https://www.warhistoryonline.com/american-civil-war/glowing-angels-saved-civil-war-soldiers.html; Soniak, Matt. 2012. "Why Some Civil War Soldiers Glowed in the Dark." *Mental Floss*, April 5. https://www.mentalfloss.com/article/30380/why-some-civil-war-soldiers-glowed-dark.

18. Schroeder-Lien, *Lincoln and Medicine*, 78; see ibid., 78n12, for others.

19. Stone, Robert. 1865. "Abraham Lincoln's Final Hours, Death, and Autopsy Report Documented by Dr. Robert Stone, April 15, 1865," https://www.shapell.org/manuscript/doctor-of-abraham-lincoln-obervation-of-presidents-last-hours-alive-and-postmortem/#transcripts; Temple, *Lincoln's Surgeons at the Assassination*; see Lincoln Digital Archives Project for reports by Leale, Woodward, and Barnes: http://www.lincolnarchives.us/cgi-bin/lincoln?a=d&d=&sf=&d=Dassassination-autopsy&page=1.

20. Schroeder-Lien, *Lincoln and Medicine*, 78.

21. Welles, *Diary of Gideon Welles*, 2:287.

22. Schroeder-Lien, *Lincoln and Medicine*, 78. See also Barnes's and Stone's autopsy reports.

23. Purtle, Helen R. 1958. "Lincoln Memorabilia in the Medical Museum of the Armed Forces Institute of Pathology." *Bulletin of History of Medicine* 32(1):68–74; Curtis, Edward A. 1865. "Last Professional Service of the War." *Glimpses of Hospital Life in War Times* 4:63–65.

24. "'His Wound Is Mortal; It Is Impossible for Him to Recover': The Final Hours of President Abraham Lincoln—More on Lincoln's Autopsy," National Museum of Health and Medicine, https://www.medicalmuseum.mil/index.cfm?p=visit.exhibits.current.collection_that_teaches.lincoln.page_04.

25. Steers, Edward, Jr., and Harold Holzer. 2009. *The Lincoln Assassination Conspirators: Their Confinement and Execution, as Recorded in the Letterbook of John Frederick Hartranft.* Louisiana State University Press.

26. Ibid.

27. Swanson, James. 2015. "The Final Hours of John Wilkes Booth." *Smithsonian*, April 8. https://www.smithsonianmag.com/history/final-hours-john-wilkes-booth-180954853/?all; Oster, Grant. "Boston Corbett and the Year of the Mad Hatter." *Hankering for History.* https://hankeringforhistory.com/boston-corbett-and-the-year-of-the-mad-hatter/.

28. Barnes to Stanton, April 27, 1865, RG 94, Lincoln Archives Digital Project, http://www.lincolnarchives.us/cgi-bin/lincoln?a=d&d=&sf=&d=Drg94-tr132-05-1.

29. Good general-audience coverage of these events can be found in two books by James L. Swanson: 2006. *Manhunt: The 12-Day Chase for Lincoln's Killer.* William Morrow; 2010. *Bloody Crimes: The Chase for Jefferson Davis and the Death Pageant for Lincoln's Corpse.* William Morrow.

30. Widmer, *Lincoln on the Verge*.

31. Leavy, Michael. 2015. *The Lincoln Funeral: An Illustrated History*. Westholme, 35, 42–42, 121; Sotos, Wendy J. 2018. "1,700 Miles of Mourners: Abraham Lincoln's Funeral Train Traveled across Seven States." *HistoryNet*. https://www.historynet .com/1700-miles-mourners-abraham-lincolns-funeral-train-traveled-across-seven-states .htm.

32. Anonymous. 2019. "Booming Business." *Civil War Times* 58(8):72; Hennessey, John. 2017. "Variable Pricing for the Dead." *Mysteries and Conundrums*, National Park Service, December 31. https://npsfrsp.wordpress.com/2017/12/31/variable-pricing-for-the -dead/.

33. Walsh, Brian. 2017. "How Lincoln's Embrace of Embalming Birthed the American Funeral Industry." *Conversation*, October 30. https://theconversation.com/how-lincolns -embrace-of-embalming-birthed-the-american-funeral-industry-86196.

34. Stone autopsy report, Shapell Manuscript Foundation, https://www.shapell.org/ manuscript/doctor-of-abraham-lincoln-obervation-of-presidents-last-hours-alive-and -postmortem/#transcripts.

35. Craughwell, Thomas J. 2007. *Stealing Lincoln's Body*. Belknap Press, 6–9.

36. Steers, Edward, Jr. 2001. *Blood on the Moon: The Assassination of Abraham Lincoln*. University Press of Kentucky, 280–81; *New York Times*, April 25, 1865, reported in Leavy, *Lincoln Funeral*, 43.

37. Pallardy, Richard. 2018. "Preserving the Body: Embalming Practices Began during the Civil War." Earth.com, December 11. https://www.earth.com/news/body -embalming-civil-war/; National Museum of Civil War Medicine. 2016. "Embalming and the Civil War." February 20. https://www.civilwarmed.org/embalming1/; Jeffrey Jones, personal communication.

38. White, *Midnight in America*, 151–56.

39. Burlingame, *Abraham Lincoln*, chap. 1, 45–47.

40. Anonymous. 2015. "DNA Tests: Nancy Hanks Is Daughter of Lucey Hanks." *For the People* 17(4):3.

41. Eschner, Kat. 2016. "People Have Spent Years Trying to Diagnose Mary Todd Lincoln from beyond the Grave." *Smithsonian*, December 13. https://www.smithsonianmag .com/smart-news/people-have-spent-years-trying-diagnose-mary-todd-lincoln-beyond -grave-180961405/; Emerson, Jason. 2007. *The Madness of Mary Lincoln*. Southern Illinois University Press; Sotos, John G. 2015. "'What an Affliction': Mary Lincoln's Fatal Pernicious Anemia." *Perspectives in Biology and Medicine* 58(4):419–43; Dr. Jon Willen, personal communication.

42. Gordon, Abraham. 1962. *Journal Kentucky Medical Association* 60:249; Schwartz, Harold. 1964. *Journal of the American Medical Association* (*JAMA*) 187:473; three letters to *JAMA*, July 12, 1864, 164–65; Davidson, Glen W. 1996. "Abraham Lincoln and the DNA Controversy." *JALA* 17(1):1–20; Steers, *Getting Right with Lincoln*, 126–32; Reilly, Philip R. 2000. *Abraham Lincoln's DNA and Other Adventures in Genetics*. Cold Spring Harbor Laboratory Press, 3–13; Dr. Jon Willen, personal communication.

43. Sotos, John G. 2008. *The Physical Lincoln: Finding the Genetic Cause of Abraham Lincoln's Height, Homeliness, Pseudo-Depression, and Imminent Cancer Death*. Mount Vernon

Book Systems, 240; Steers, *Getting Right with Lincoln*, 132–34; Dr. Jon Willen, personal communication.

Epilogue

1. Cole, John Y. 2019. *On These Walls: Inscriptions and Quotations in the Library of Congress*. Meadows & Wiser. https://www.loc.gov/loc/walls/.

2. Grant Goodrich to Herndon, December 9, 1866, in Wilson and Davis, *Herndon's Informants*, 510.

3. Speech at Chicago, July 10, 1858, in *Collected Works*, 2:500.

4. For more information on Lincoln's connections with Joseph Henry, Thomas Edison, and Nikola Tesla, see Kent, *Abraham Lincoln and Nikola Tesla*.

5. Cole, *On These Walls*, https://www.loc.gov/loc/walls/jeff1.html#mrr.

6. Kent, *Abraham Lincoln and Nikola Tesla*.

7. Address at Cooper Institute, February 27, 1859, in *Collected Works*, 3:522–50.

8. "House Divided" speech, June 16, 1858, in ibid., 2:461.

9. Speech at Springfield, Illinois, June 26, 1857, in ibid., 2:405.

10. Message to Congress in Special Session, July 4, 1861, in ibid., 4:438.

11. Lincoln to James C. Conkling, August 26, 1863, in ibid., 6:409.

12. Last public address, April 11, 1865, in ibid., 8:403.

13. Fragment on government, April 1, 1854?, in ibid., 2:220.

14. Striner, Richard. 2015. "What Lincoln Means to Me—and Not Necessarily to Others." *Lincoln Lore* 1909:11–14.

15. Remarks on April 29, 2013, by President Barack Obama at the National Academy of Sciences, Washington, DC.

16. See Kent, David J. 2020. "The Thomas Edison–Abraham Lincoln Connection." April 24. http://www.davidjkent-writer.com/2020/04/24/the-thomas-edison-abraham -lincoln-connection/.

17. Benjamin Franklin was the other. See Silverman, Jason. 2015. "Abraham Lincoln and the Physicist." *Lincoln Herald*, Winter 2015, 212–31; Kent, *Tesla*.

18. Annual Message to Congress, December 1, 1862, in *Collected Works*, 5:537.

BIBLIOGRAPHY

Abel, E. Lawrence. 2020. *Lincoln's Jewish Spy: The Life and Times of Issachar Zacharie.* McFarland.

Alford, Terry. 2015. *Fortune's Fool: The Life of John Wilkes Booth.* Oxford University Press.

Alley, Richard B. 2011. *Earth: The Operators' Manual.* W. W. Norton.

Angier, Natalie. 2007. *The Canon: A Whirligig Tour of the Beautiful Basics of Science.* Houghton Mifflin.

Atkinson, Eleanor. 1908. *The Boyhood of Lincoln.* McClure.

Baber, Adin. 2002. *A. Lincoln with Compass and Chain.* Illinois Professional Land Surveyors Association.

Baron, David. 2017. *American Eclipse: A Nation's Epic Race to Catch the Shadow of the Moon and Win the Glory of the World.* Liveright.

Bartelt, William E. 2008. *There I Grew Up: Remembering Abraham Lincoln's Indiana Youth.* Indiana Historical Society Press.

Bartelt, William E., and Joshua A. Claybourn, eds. 2019. *Abe's Youth: Shaping the Future President.* Indiana University Press.

Basler, Roy P., ed. 1953. *The Collected Works of Abraham Lincoln.* Rutgers University Press. [This nine-volume set, plus two addendum volumes, is the ultimate resource for most Abraham Lincoln documents. It is also available in searchable format online at http://quod.lib.umich.edu/l/lincoln/.]

Bates, David Homer. 1995. *Lincoln in the Telegraph Office.* University of Nebraska Press.

Bedini, Silvio A. 1990. *Thomas Jefferson: Statesman of Science.* Macmillan.

Bedini, Silvio A. 2002. *Jefferson and Science.* Thomas Jefferson Foundation.

Berton, Pierre. 1992. *Niagara: A History of the Falls.* Excelsior Editions.

Beveridge, Albert. 1928. *Abraham Lincoln 1809–1858.* Houghton Mifflin.

Blackstone, William. 1979. *Commentaries on the Laws of England.* Facsimile ed. with introduction by Stanley N. Katz. University of Chicago.

Blight, David W. 2019. *Frederick Douglass: Prophet of Freedom.* Simon & Schuster.

Blumenbach, Johann. 1865. *The Anthropological Treatises of Johann Friedrich Blumenbach.* Anthropological Society of London.

Blumenthal, Sidney. 2016. *A Self-Made Man, 1809–1849: The Political Life of Abraham Lincoln.* Simon & Schuster.

Blumenthal, Sidney. 2017. *Wrestling with His Angel, 1849–1856: The Political Life of Abraham Lincoln.* Simon & Schuster.

Blumenthal, Sidney. 2019. *All the Powers of Earth, 1856–1860: The Political Life of Abraham Lincoln.* Simon & Schuster.

Boorstin, Daniel J. 1941. *The Mysterious Science of the Law: An Essay on Blackstone's Commentaries.* University of Chicago Press.

Boorstin, Daniel J. 1983. *The Discoverers: A History of Man's Search to Know His World and Himself.* Vintage.

Bordewich, Fergus M. 2020. *Congress at War: How Republican Reformers Fought the Civil War, Defied Lincoln, Ended Slavery, and Remade America.* Alfred A. Knopf.

Bowers, Claude. 1945. *The Young Jefferson, 1743–1789.* Houghton Mifflin.

Bray, Robert. 2010. *Reading with Lincoln.* Southern Illinois University Press.

Brewster, George. 1943. *A New Philosophy of Matter Showing the Identity of All the Imponderables and the Influence Which Electricity Exerts over Matter in Producing All Chemical Changes and All Motion.* A. W. Maddocks.

Briggs, John Channing. 2005. *Lincoln's Speeches Reconsidered.* Johns Hopkins University Press.

Brookhiser, Richard. 2014. *Founders' Son: A Life of Abraham Lincoln.* Basic Books.

Brooks, Noah. 1901. *Abraham Lincoln: His Youth and Early Manhood with a Brief Account of His Later Life.* G. P. Putnam's Sons.

Brooks, Noah. 1895/1971. *Washington, D.C. in Lincoln's Time.* Quadrangle Books.

Browning, Orville Hickman. 1925. *The Diary of Orville Hickman Browning, Volume 1: 1850–1864.* Illinois State Historical Library.

Brownstein, Elizabeth Smith. 2005. *Lincoln's Other White House: The Untold Story of the Man and His Presidency.* John Wiley & Sons.

Bruce, Robert V. 1956. *Lincoln and the Tools of War.* Bobbs-Merrill.

Bruce, Robert V. 1987. *The Launching of Modern American Science, 1846–1876.* Alfred A. Knopf.

Burleigh, Nina. 2003. *The Stranger and the Statesman: James Smithson, John Quincy Adams, and the Making of America's Greatest Museum, the Smithsonian.* William Morrow.

Burlingame, Michael, ed. 2006. *An Oral History of Abraham Lincoln: John G. Nicolay's Interviews and Essays.* Southern Illinois University Press.

Burlingame, Michael. 2008. *Abraham Lincoln: A Life.* Johns Hopkins University Press. [This two-volume set is perhaps the most comprehensive contemporary biography of Lincoln's life. An unedited online version is also available on the Knox College website. All page numbers cited refer to the online manuscript version at https://www.knox.edu/about-knox/lincoln-studies-center/burlingame-abraham-lincoln-a-life.]

Burlingame, Michael, and John R. Turner Ettlinger, eds. 1999. *Inside Lincoln's White House: The Complete Civil War Diary of John Hay.* Southern Illinois University Press.

Calhoun, John C. 1843. *Speeches of John C. Calhoun: Delivered in the Congress of the United States from 1811 to the Present Time.* Harper & Brothers.

Campanella, Richard. 2010. *Lincoln in New Orleans: The 1828–1831 Flatboat Voyages and Their Place in History.* University of Louisiana at Lafayette Press.

Carden, Allen, and Thomas J. Ebert. 2019. *John George Nicolay: The Man in Lincoln's Shadow.* University of Tennessee Press.

Carpenter, Francis B. 1867. *Six Months in the White House: The Story of a Picture.* Hurd and Houghton.

Casey, John. 1885. *The First Six Books of the Elements of Euclid.* 3rd ed. Hodges, Figgis & Company.

Casson, Herbert N. 1909. *Cyrus Hall McCormick: His Life and Work*. Books for Libraries Press.

Chernow, Ron. 2004. *Alexander Hamilton*. Penguin.

Chittenden, Lucius. 1891. *Recollections of President Lincoln and His Administration*. Harper and Brothers.

Clark, John E. 2004. *Railroads in the Civil War: The Impact of Management on Victory and Defeat*. Louisiana State University Press.

Cochrane, Rexmond C. 1978. *The National Academy of Sciences: The First Hundred Years, 1863–1963*. National Academies Press.

Coffin, Charles Carleton. 1892. *Abraham Lincoln*. Harper & Brothers.

Cohen, I. Bernard. 1995. *Science and the Founding Fathers: Science in the Political Thought of Thomas Jefferson, Benjamin Franklin, John Adams, and James Madison*. W. W. Norton.

Cole, John Y. 2019. *On These Walls: Inscriptions & Quotations in the Library of Congress*. Meadows & Wiser.

Cornelius, James M., and Carla Knorowski. 2016. *Under Lincoln's Hat: 100 Objects That Tell the Story of His Life and Legacy*. LP Books.

Craughwell, Thomas J. 2007. *Stealing Lincoln's Body*. Belknap Press.

Crump, Thomas. 2009. *Abraham Lincoln's World: How Riverboats, Railroads, and Republicans Transformed America*. Continuum Books.

Daboll, Nathan. 1817. *Daboll's Schoolmaster's Assistant (Daboll's Arithmetic)*. E & E Hosford.

Delbanco, Andrew. 2018. *The War Before the War: Fugitive Slaves and the Struggle for America's Soul from the Revolution to the Civil War*. Penguin.

Denny, Mark. 2007. *Ingenium: Five Machines That Changed the World*. Johns Hopkins University Press.

Dilworth, Thomas. 1796. *Dilworth's Spelling Book, Improved: A New Guide to the English Tongue*. John McCulluch.

Dirck, Brian. 2007. *Lincoln the Lawyer*. University of Illinois Press.

Dirck, Brian R. 2017. *Lincoln in Indiana*. Southern Illinois University Press.

Dirck, Brian. 2019. *The Black Heavens: Abraham Lincoln and Death*. Southern Illinois University Press.

Dodge, Daniel Kilham. 1900/2000. *Abraham Lincoln: The Evolution of His Literary Style*. University of Illinois Press.

Donald, David Herbert. 1948. *Lincoln's Herndon*. Alfred A. Knopf.

Donald, David Herbert. 1995. *Lincoln*. Simon & Schuster.

Duncan, Kunigunde, and D. F. Nickols. 1944. *Mentor Graham: The Man Who Taught Lincoln*. University of Chicago Press.

Emerson, Jason. 2007. *The Madness of Mary Lincoln*. Southern Illinois University Press.

Emerson, Jason. 2009. *Lincoln the Inventor*. Southern Illinois University Press.

Epstein, Daniel Mark. 2004. *Lincoln and Whitman: Parallel Lives in Civil War Washington*. Random House.

Evans, Charles M. 2002. *War of the Aeronauts: A History of Ballooning in the Civil War*. Stackpole Books.

Everett, Griff, Stepanie H. Hitchcock, Jane Middleton, and Rosemary H. Timms. 2006. *"Samuel Slater—Hero or Traitor?"* Maypole Promotions.

Ewing, Heather. 2007. *The Lost World of James Smithson: Science, Revolution, and the Birth of the Smithsonian.* Bloomsbury.

Fehrenbacher, Don E., and Virginia Fehrenbacher, eds. 1996. *Recollected Words of Abraham Lincoln.* Stanford University Press.

Flint, Abel. 1830. *A System of Geometry and Trigonometry with a Treatise on Surveying.* 6th ed. Cooke and Company.

Foner, Eric. 2010. *The Fiery Trial: Abraham Lincoln and American Slavery.* W. W. Norton.

Foner, Philip S. 1950. *The Life and Writings of Frederick Douglass.* International Publishers.

Fornieri, Joseph R., and Sara Vaughn Gabbard. *Lincoln's America, 1809–1865.* Southern Illinois University Press.

Foster, B. G. 1928. *Abraham Lincoln Inventor.* James F. Balsley Bookseller.

Fraker, Guy C. 2012. *Lincoln's Ladder to the Presidency: The Eighth Judicial Court.* Southern Illinois University Press.

Fraker, Guy. 2017. *A Guide to Lincoln's Eighth Judicial Circuit.* Southern Illinois University Press.

Friedman, Thomas. 2016. *Thank You for Being Late.* Farrar, Straus and Giroux.

Goldenberg, David R. 2003. *The Curse of Ham: Race and Slavery in Early Judaism, Christianity, and Islam.* Princeton University Press.

Gossett, Thomas F. 1997. *Race: The History of an Idea in America.* New ed. Oxford University Press.

Gross, Daniel. 1996. *Forbes Greatest Business Stories of All Time.* John Wiley & Sons.

Hall, William Mosely, et al. 1882. *Chicago River-and-Harbor Convention: An Account of Its Origin and Proceedings.* Fergus Printing.

Halleck, Henry W. 1862. *Elements of Military Arts and Science.* D. Appleton & Co.

Hanna, William F. 1983. *Abraham Among the Yankees: Abraham Lincoln's 1848 Visit to Massachusetts.* Old Colony Historical Society.

Harris, Ann G., Esther Tuttle, and Sherwood D. Tuttle. 1997. *Geology of National Parks.* 5th ed. Kendall Hunt.

Hart, Richard E. 2019. *The Collected Works of Thomas Lincoln: Carpenter and Cabinetmaker.* Pigeon Creek Series.

Hasegawa, Guy R. 2015. *Villainous Compounds: Chemical Weapons and the American Civil War.* Southern Illinois University Press.

Haupt, Herman. 1901. *Reminiscences of General Herman Haupt.* Wright & Joys.

Haynes, Stephen R. 2002. *Noah's Curse: The Biblical Justification of American Slavery.* Oxford University Press.

Helper, Hinton Rowan. 1857. *The Impending Crisis of the South: How to Meet It.* Burdick Brothers.

Herndon, William H., and Jesse W. Weik. 2006. *Herndon's Lincoln.* Annotated and edited by Douglas L. Wilson and Rodney O. Davis. University of Illinois Press. [Originally published in 1889, this annotated volume provides the best resource available to modern readers.]

Hertz, Emanuel. 1938. *The Hidden Lincoln*. Viking.

Hirsch, David, and Dan Van Haften. 2010. *Abraham Lincoln and the Structure of Reason*. Savas Beatie.

Hirsch, David, and Dan Van Haften. 2019. *The Tyranny of Public Discourse: Abraham Lincoln's Six-Element Antidote for Meaningful and Persuasive Writing*. Savas Beatie.

Hodges, Robert R. 2009. *American Civil War Railroad Tactics*. Osprey.

Hoekstra, J. M., et al. 2010. *The Atlas of Global Conservation: Changes, Challenges, and Opportunities to Make a Difference*. University of California Press.

Holloway, Anna Gibson, and Jonathan W. White. 2018. *Our Little Monitor: The Greatest Invention of the Civil War*. Kent State University Press.

Holzer, Harold. 1993. *Dear Mr. Lincoln: Letters to the President*. Addison-Wesley.

Holzer, Harold. 2012. *Lincoln: How Abraham Lincoln Ended Slavery in America*. Newmarket Press.

Holzer, Harold. 2014. *Lincoln and the Power of the Press*. Simon & Schuster.

Holzer, Harold, and Norton Garfinkle. 2015. *A Just and Generous Nation*. Basic Books.

Houser, M. L. 1942. *Young Abraham Lincoln and Log College*. Lester O. Schriver.

Houser, M. L. 1943. *Young Abraham Lincoln Mathematician*. Lester O. Schriver.

Houser, M. L. 1957. *Lincoln's Education and Other Essays*. Bookman Associates.

Howe, Daniel Walker. 2007. *What Hath God Wrought: The Transformation of America, 1815–1848*. Oxford University Press.

Howells, William D. 1938. *Life of Abraham Lincoln*. Abraham Lincoln Association.

Hudson, John C. 1994. *Making the Corn Belt: A Geographic History of Middle-Western Agriculture*. Indiana University Press.

Humes, James C. 1996. *The Wit and Wisdom of Abraham Lincoln*. Gramercy Books.

Irmscher, Christoph. 2013. *Louis Agassiz: Creator of American Science*. Houghton Mifflin Harcourt.

Jahns, Patricia. 1961. *Matthew Fontaine Maury and Joseph Henry: Scientists of the Civil War*. Hastings House.

Jahns, Patricia. 1970. *Joseph Henry: Father of American Electronics*. Rutledge Books.

Jefferson, Thomas. 2002. *Notes on the State of Virginia*. Edited and with notes by David Waldstreicher. Bedford/St. Martins.

Kaplan, Fred. 2008. *Lincoln: The Biography of a Writer*. HarperCollins.

Kaplan, Fred. 2017. *Lincoln and the Abolitionists: John Quincy Adams, Slavery, and the Civil War*. HarperCollins.

Keeler, William Frederick, with Robert W. Daly, eds. 1964. *Aboard the USS Monitor, 1862: The Letters of Acting Paymaster William Frederick Keeler, US Navy, to His Wife, Anna*. US Naval Institute.

Kendi, Ibram X. 2019. *How to Be an Antiracist*. One World.

Kent, David J. 2013. *Tesla: The Wizard of Electricity*. Fall River Press.

Kent, David J. 2014. "A Christmas Gift for Abraham Lincoln." *Smithsonian Civil War Studies*, December 8, 2014.

Kent, David J. 2015. "The Majesty and the Math of Niagara Falls." *Lincolnian* 33:10–14.

Kent, David J. 2015. *Abraham Lincoln and Nikola Tesla: Connected by Fate*. Science Traveler Books.

Kent, David J. 2016. *Edison: The Inventor of the Modern World*. Fall River Press.

Kent, David J. 2017. *Lincoln: The Man Who Saved America*. Fall River Press.

Keyes, Ralph. 1991. *Timelock*. Basic Books.

Kirkham, Samuel. 1999. *Kirkham's Grammar: The Book That Shaped Lincoln's Prose*. Octavo Press.

Klingaman, William K., and Nicholas P. Klingaman. 2013. *The Year without Summer: 1816 and the Volcano That Darkened the World and Changed History*. St. Martin's Press.

Krenkel, John H. 1958. *Illinois Internal Improvements 1818–1848*. Torch Press.

Lakwete, Angela. 2003. *Inventing the Cotton Gin: Machine and Myth in Antebellum America*. Johns Hopkins University Press.

Lamon, Ward Hill. 1872/2013. *The Life of Abraham Lincoln*. Reprint ed. including letter from Theo. Lemon. Echo Library.

Lander, James. 2010. *Lincoln & Darwin: Shared Visions of Race, Science, and Religion*. Southern Illinois University Press.

Leavitt, Dudley. 1826. *Pike's System of Arithmetick, Abridged*. Jacob B. Moore.

Leavy, Michael. 2015. *The Lincoln Funeral: An Illustrated History*. Westholme.

Lee, Hilde Gabriel. 1992. *Taste of the States: A Food History of America*. Howell Press.

Levine, Robert V. 1997. *A Geography of Time: Temporal Misadventures of a Social Psychologist, or How Every Culture Keeps Time Just a Little Bit Differently*. Basic Books.

Lind, Michael. 2004. *What Lincoln Believed: The Values and Convictions of America's Greatest President*. Doubleday.

Livio, Mario. 2002. *The Golden Ratio*. Broadway Books.

Loewen, James W. 2000. *Lies Across America: What Our Historic Sites Get Wrong*. Touchstone Books.

Lubet, Steven. 2010. *Fugitive Justice: Runaways, Rescuers, and Slavery on Trial*. Belknap Press.

Lundberg, James M. 2020. *Horace Greeley: Print, Politics, and the Failure of American Nationhood*. Johns Hopkins University Press.

Lyell, Charles. 1830. *Principles of Geology*. John Murray.

Maltz, Earl M. 2009. *Slavery and the Supreme Court, 1825–1861*. University Press of Kansas.

Marx, Leo. 1964. *The Machine in the Garden: Technology and the Pastoral Ideal in America*. Oxford University Press.

McClelland, Edward. 2019. "Lincoln, Slavery, and Springfield: How Popular Opinion in Central Illinois Influenced Abraham Lincoln's Views on Slavery." MA thesis, Harvard University.

McCormick, Cyrus. 1931. *The Century of the Reaper*. Houghton Mifflin.

McCullough, David. 2019. *The Pioneers: The Heroic Story of the Settlers Who Brought the American Ideal West*. Simon & Schuster.

McCutcheon, Marc. 1993. *The Writer's Guide to Everyday Life in the 1800s*. Writer's Digest Books.

McGinty, Brian. 2015. *Lincoln's Greatest Case: The River, the Bridge, and the Making of America*. Liveright.

McPherson, James M. 1991. *Abraham Lincoln and the Second American Revolution.* Oxford University Press.

McPherson, James M. 2008. *Tried by War: Abraham Lincoln as Commander in Chief.* Penguin.

Mearns, David C. 1948. *The Lincoln Papers.* Doubleday and Company.

Meyer, Balthasar H. 1917. *History of Transportation in the United States before 1860.* Carnegie Institution.

Miller, William Lee. 2008. *President Lincoln: The Duty of a Statesman.* Alfred A. Knopf.

Morton, Samuel George. 1839. *Crania Americana: A Comparative View of the Skulls of Various Aboriginal Nations of North and South America.* J. Dobson.

Muller-Schwartz, Dietland, and Lixing Sun. 2003. *The Beaver: Natural History of a Wetlands Engineer.* Comstock.

Neider, Charles, ed. 1996. *The Autobiography of Mark Twain.* Perennial Classics.

Newton, Isaac. 1862. *Report of the Department of Agriculture to Abraham Lincoln.* Abraham Lincoln Papers, Library of Congress, Washington, DC.

Newton, Joseph Fort. 1910. *Lincoln and Herndon.* Torch Press.

Nichols, Clifton M. 1896. *Life of Abraham Lincoln.* Mast, Crowell & Kirkpatrick.

Nicolay, John G., and John Hay. 1890. *Abraham Lincoln: A History.* Century. [Original ten-volume biography by Lincoln's private secretaries under Robert Lincoln's authority.]

Norder, Steve. 2020. *Lincoln Takes Command: The Campaign to Seize Norfolk and the Destruction of the* CSS Virginia. Savas Beatie.

Nott, Josiah Clark, and George Robbins Gliddon. 1854. *Types of Mankind.* Lippincott, Grambo & Co.

Oldham, Pamela, with Meredith Bean McMath. 2005. *The CI Guide to the Legacy of Lincoln.* Alpha Books.

Oldroyd, Osborn H. 1883. *The Lincoln Memorial: Album-Immortelles.* G. W. Carleton & Co. Press.

Olmstead, Frederick Law. 1953. *The Cotton Kingdom: A Traveller's Observations on Cotton and Slavery in the American Slave States.* Modern Library.

O'Malley, M. 1990. *Keeping Watch: A History of American Time.* Viking.

Phillips, Ulrich Bonnell. 1968. *A History of Transportation in the Eastern Cotton Belt to 1860.* Octagon Books.

Power, John Carroll, and Sarah A. Power. 1876. *History of the Early Settlers of Sangamon County.* Edwin A. Wilson.

Pratt, Harry E. 1943. *The Personal Finances of Abraham Lincoln.* Abraham Lincoln Association.

Rayner, William H., and Milton O. Schmidt. 1955. *Elementary Surveying.* D. Van Nostrand.

Reilly, Philip R. 2000. *Abraham Lincoln's DNA and Other Adventures in Genetics.* Cold Spring Harbor Laboratory Press.

Reingold, Nathan. 1985. *Science in Nineteenth Century: A Documentary History.* University of Chicago Press.

Rice, Allen Thorndike. 1886. *Reminiscences of Abraham Lincoln*. North American Publishing.

Richardson, Heather Cox. 2020. *How the South Won the Civil War*. Oxford University Press.

Ross, Charles. 2000. *Trial by Fire: Science, Technology and the Civil War*. White Mane Books.

Ross, Charles. 2001. *Civil War Acoustic Shadows*. White Mane Books.

Rothenberg, Marc. 1992. *The Papers of Joseph Henry*. Vol. 10. Science History Publications.

Rutherford, Adam. 2020. *How to Argue with a Racist: What Our Genes Do (and Don't) Say about Human Difference*. Experiment.

Sandburg, Carl. 1926. *Abraham Lincoln: The Prairie Years*. Harcourt, Brace, and Co.

Sandburg, Carl. 1959. *The Prairie Years and the War Years*. 6 vols. Charles Scribner's Sons.

Schaff, Jon D. 2019. *Abraham Lincoln's Statesmanship and the Limits of Liberal Democracy*. Southern Illinois University Press.

Schroeder-Lien, Glenna R. 2012. *Lincoln and Medicine*. Southern Illinois University Press.

Scripps, John Locke. 2010. *Vote Lincoln! The Presidential Campaign Biography of Abraham Lincoln, 1860*. Boston Hill Press.

Shaw, Robert, and Michael Burlingame. 2012. *Abraham Lincoln Traveled This Way*. Firelight.

Silvestri, Vito N., and Alfred P. Lairo. 2013. *Abraham Lincoln's Intellectual Development 1809–1837*. Wasteland Press.

Skeen, C. Edward. 2003. *1816: America Rising*. University Press of Kentucky.

Sotos, John G. 2008. *The Physical Lincoln: Finding the Genetic Cause of Abraham Lincoln's Height, Homeliness, Pseudo-Depression, and Imminent Cancer Death*. Mount Vernon Book Systems.

Spears, Zarel C., and Robert S. Barton. 1947. *Berry and Lincoln Frontier Merchants: The Store That "Winked Out."* Stratford House.

Spiegel, Allen D. 2002. *A. Lincoln, Esquire: A Shrewd, Sophisticated Lawyer in His Time*. Mercer University Press.

Standage, Tom. 2005. *A History of the World in Six Glasses*. Walker & Company.

Starr, John W., Jr. 1927. *Lincoln and the Railroads*. Dodd, Mead & Company.

Steers, Edward, Jr. 2001. *Blood on the Moon: The Assassination of Abraham Lincoln*. University Press of Kentucky.

Steers, Edward, Jr. 2010. *The Lincoln Assassination Encyclopedia*. Harper Perennial.

Steers, Edward, Jr. 2021. *Getting Right with Lincoln*. University Press of Kentucky.

Steers, Edward, Jr., and Harold Holzer. 2009. *The Lincoln Assassination Conspirators: Their Confinement and Execution, as Recorded in the Letterbook of John Frederick Hartranft*. Louisiana State University Press.

Steiner, Mark E. 2006. *An Honest Calling: The Law Practice of Abraham Lincoln*. Northern Illinois University Press.

Stewart, Amy. 2009. *Wicked Plants: The Weed That Killed Lincoln's Mother and Other Botanical Atrocities*. Algonquin Books of Chapel Hill.

Stoddard, William O. 2000. *Inside the White House in War Times: Memoirs and Reports of Lincoln's Secretary.* Edited by Michael Burlingame. University of Nebraska Press.

Stowell, Daniel W., ed. 2008. *The Papers of Abraham Lincoln: Legal Documents and Cases.* University of Virginia Press.

Striner, Richard. 2006. *Father Abraham: Lincoln's Relentless Struggle to End Slavery.* Oxford University Press.

Struik, Dirk J. 1967. *A Concise History of Mathematics.* Dover.

Swanson, James L. 2006. *Manhunt: The 12-Day Chase for Lincoln's Killer.* William Morrow.

Swanson, James L. 2010. *Bloody Crimes: The Chase for Jefferson Davis and the Death Pageant for Lincoln's Corpse.* William Morrow.

Tackach, James. 2019. *Lincoln and the Natural Environment.* Southern Illinois University Press.

Taylor, Daniel Cravens. 2019. *Thomas Lincoln, Abraham's Father.* Beacon.

Temple, Wayne C. 1986. *Lincoln's Connections with the Illinois & Michigan Canal, His Return from Congress in '48, and His Invention.* Illinois Bell.

Temple, Wayne C. 2004. *"The Taste Is in My Mouth a Little . . .": Lincoln's Victuals and Potables.* Mayhaven.

Temple, Wayne C. 2015. *Lincoln's Surgeons at the Assassination.* Mayhaven.

Thayer, William M. 1863. *The Pioneer Boy and How He Became President.* Walker, Wise and Company.

Townsend, George Alfred. 1867. *The Real Life of Abraham Lincoln: A Talk with Mr. Herndon, His Late Law Partner.* Publication Office, Bible House.

True, Frederick W. 1913. *A History of the First Half-Century of the National Academy of Sciences.* Lord Baltimore Press.

Turner, George Edgar. 1972. *Victory Rode the Rails: The Strategic Place of the Railroads in the Civil War.* Greenwood Press.

Turner, Justin G., and Linda Levitt Turner. 1987. *Mary Todd Lincoln: Her Life and Letters.* Fromm International.

Twain, Mark. 1883. *Life on the Mississippi.* James R. Osgood & Company.

Varhola, Michael J. 1999. *Everyday Life during the Civil War.* Writer's Digest Books.

Volk, Kyle G. 2017. *Moral Minorities and the Making of American Democracy.* Oxford University Press.

Waltmann, Henry G. 1975. *Pioneer Farming in Indiana: Thomas Lincoln's Major Crops, 1816–1830.* Association for Living Historical Farms and Agricultural Museums, Smithsonian Institution.

Warren, Louis A. 1959. *Lincoln's Youth: Indiana Years Seven to Twenty-One 1816–1830.* Appleton Century Crofts.

Weik, Jesse W. 1922. *The Real Lincoln: A Portrait.* Houghton Mifflin.

Welles, Gideon. 1911. *Diary of Gideon Welles.* Houghton Mifflin.

Wells, David A., ed. 1850. *The Annual of Scientific Discovery, or, Year-Book of Facts in Science and Art.* Gould, Kendall, and Lincoln.

Wert, Jeffry D. 2018. *Civil War Barons: The Tycoons, Entrepreneurs, Inventors, and Visionaries Who Forged Victory and Shaped a Nation.* De Capo Press.

Wheeler, Tom. 2006. *Mr. Lincoln's T-Mails: The Untold Story of How Abraham Lincoln Used the Telegraph to Win the Civil War.* HarperCollins.

White, John H., Jr. 1997. *American Locomotives: An Engineering History, 1830–1880.* Johns Hopkins University Press.

White, Jonathan W. 2014. *Emancipation, the Union Army, and the Reelection of Abraham Lincoln.* Louisiana State University Press.

White, Jonathan W. 2017. *Midnight in America: Darkness, Sleep, and Dreams during the Civil War.* University of North Carolina Press.

White, Ronald C., Jr. 2005. *The Eloquent President: A Portrait of Lincoln through His Words.* Random House.

Whitney, Henry C. 1907. *Lincoln the Citizen.* Current Literature Publishing.

Whitney, Henry C. 1940. *Life on the Circuit with Lincoln.* Caxton Printers.

Widmer, Ted. 2020. *Lincoln on the Verge: Thirteen Days to Washington.* Simon & Schuster.

Wilkerson, Isabel. 2010. *The Warmth of Other Suns: The Epic Story of America's Great Migration.* Random House.

Wilson, Douglas L., and Rodney O. Davis. 1998. *Herndon's Informants: Letters, Interviews, and Statements about Abraham Lincoln.* University of Illinois Press. [Wilson and Davis annotate the thousands of letters and interviews conducted by William Herndon after Lincoln's death. The ultimate resource.]

Wilson, Douglas L., and Rodney O. Davis. 2016. *Herndon on Lincoln: Letters.* University of Illinois Press.

Wilson, Robert. 2006. *The Explorer King: Adventure, Science, and the Great Diamond Hoax—Clarence King in the Old West.* Scribner.

Wulf, Andrea. 2015. *The Invention of Nature: Alexander Von Humboldt's New World.* Alfred A. Knopf.

Zeitz, Joshua. 2014. *Lincoln's Boys: John Hay, John Nicolay, and the War for Lincoln's Image.* Viking.

INDEX

Abraham Lincoln Presidential Library and Museum, 55

Abraham Lincoln Presidential Library Foundation Leadership Prize, 248

acoustic shadows, 217–18

Adam and Eve, 107, 157, 160, 244

Adams, John Quincy, 85, 170–71

Affordable Care Act, 247

Agassiz, Louis, 35, 110, 152, 172; in Lincoln administration, 33, 199; NAS, role in creation of, 179–80, 181; racial prejudices of, 107, 111, 115, 245

agriculture, 13, 14, 103, 105, 158; agricultural economy, 4, 87, 98; Department of Agriculture, 182–4, 185, 247; Wisconsin State Agricultural Society address, 163–66

agronomy, 3, 9–11, 215, 243

Alexander, Joseph B., 236

Alexander, Stephen, 181

Alice in Wonderland (Carroll), 234

Allen, James, 204

Allen, Wilson, 143

Alton & Sangamon Railroad, 141, 142, 146, 147

amalgamation concept, 112

Ambulance Corps, 231

American Association for the Advancement of Science (AAAS), 171

American Cotton Planter (periodical), 101

American exceptionalism, 171

"American System" of economic development, 69

Ames, Horatio, 195

amputations and plastic surgery, 232

Anderson River, 40, 43

"Angel's Glow" phenomenon, 232–33

Annual of Scientific Discovery series, 33

Archimedes principle, 76

Armstrong, George, 146–47

Armstrong, Hannah, 129

Armstrong, William (Duff), 129, 130

Atherton, William, 39

atmospheric churn, invention of, 127

Augur, Christopher, 233

Bache, Alexander Dallas, 288n59; Coast Survey, as superintendent of, 177, 211; compass magnetism, working on problems with, 212, 214; *Lazzaroni* group, as part of, 171–72; NAS, role in creation of, 179, 180–81

Bacon, Francis, 32, 126, 160, 279n26

Baird, Spencer, 181

Bale, Hardin, 77

balloon surveillance, 191, 193, 204–5, 223, 246

Baltimore & Ohio Railroad, 138, 199, 221

Bancroft, George, 154

Banks, Nathaniel P., 230

Barnard, Frederick Augustus Porter, 171, 180

Barnes, Joseph K., 229, 233, 235

Barret, James A., 141, 147

Barret v. Alton & Sangamon Railroad, 147

Barrett, Oliver, 155

Basler, Roy P., 154–55

Bates, David Homer, 161, 206–7

Battle of Antietam, 207, 208

Battle of Shiloh, 232–33

Battle of the Crater, 221

Baugh, George, 142

Beecher, Henry Ward, 151, 175

Bell, Robert, 32

Hanks, Joseph, 55, 238
Hanks, Lucey, 238
Harding, George, 128
Harper's Weekly (periodical), 80
Harris, Clara, 227
Harris, Jasper, 146–47
Harvey, William, 115
Haupt, Herman, 199–200
Hay, John, 154, 156, 188, 197
Hayes, Isaac Israel, 152
Hays, Isaac I., 174–75
Hazel, Caleb, 21
Helmholz, Hermann von, 32
Helper, Hinton Rowan, 105
Henry, Anson, 62
Henry, Joseph, 191, 199, 245, 248;
    commissions and memberships of,
    171, 177–78, 179, 217, 246–47; fire
    as destroying papers, 189–90; NAS
    affiliation, 180–81, 214, 288n59; as
    science advisor to Lincoln, 174–75,
    221–22, 242; as Smithsonian
    Institution director, 169, 172–76, 189,
    205; telegraph technology and, 206,
    212, 216
Henry, Mary Anna, 177, 180, 189, 190
Herndon, Hinton Rowan, 51, 105
Herndon, William, 59–60; book collection
    of, 34, 106, 122; as chronicler of
    Lincoln's life, 23–24, 27, 28, 29–30,
    57, 76–77, 106, 140, 154, 242;
    friendship with Lincoln, 58, 73–74,
    79, 156; as law partner of Lincoln, 22,
    33, 34, 51, 122, 124, 127, 140, 146,
    161, 213, 238
Hill, Samuel, 59
Hirsch, David, 28, 133, 219
historically black colleges and universities
    (HBCUs), 186
Hitt, Robert, 131
Holmes, Thomas, 236
Homestead Act, 96, 97, 185–86, 187,
    288nn74–76
horological cradles, 127

Houser, M. L., 25
Hoyt, Charles, 147
Humboldt, Alexander von, 106
Hungerford, Henry James, 170
Hunt, William Leonard (The Great
    Farini), 81
Hurd, John, 132
Huxley, Thomas, 106
hydrography, science of, 47
hydrology, 4, 10, 72, 74, 79, 215, 243

Illinois and Michigan Canal, 74, 92–94,
    95, 97, 138, 191, 224
Illinois Central Railroad: Lincoln as
    working for, 141, 143, 146, 148;
    Stephen Douglas, connection to, 141,
    149; taxes and, 138, 144–45
Illinois River, 47, 50, 89–91, 93, 132,
    138, 191
Illinois River Railroad, 147
Impending Crisis of the South (Helper), 105
industrial revolution, 162
insanity defense cases, 129
Introduction to Astronomy (Olmsted), 31
ironclad warships, 201–4

Jackson, Andrew, 61, 85, 170, 195, 218,
    233, 234
Jackson, Stonewall, 208
Jacksonian Democrats, 85–86
Jefferson, Thomas, 20, 35, 63, 86, 102, 116,
    211; classical education of, 19, 173;
    Euclid, study of, 26–27, 219; as a
    plantation owner, 104, 173; science
    and, 114, 126; Thomas Jefferson
    Building, 241, 242
Johnson, Edward, 218
Johnson, Lyndon, 247
Johnson, Robert Underwood, 188–89,
    289n90
Johnston, John D., 41, 42, 44, 46
Johnston, Joseph, 199
Johnston, William, 131, 230
Jones, Paul Franklin, 193–94

Mount Tambora volcano, 6
Mudd, Samuel, 234
"mud-sill theory," 164
Muir, John, 188–89
multiple endocrine neoplasia 2B (MEN 2B), 240
multishot gun weaponry, 197–98
Musick, Samuel, 91

Napoleon III, 201
National Academy of Sciences (NAS), 179–81, 214–15, 247–48
National Revenue Commission, 34
Nevada, 190, 208–9
New and Easy System of Geography and Popular Astronomy (O'Neill), 30
The New Complete System of Arithmetick (Pike), 23, 25, 88
New Deal, 247
New Orleans steamboat, 43, 50
A New Philosophy of Matter (Brewster), 32
New York World (periodical), 29
Newton, Isaac, 183–4
Niagara Falls, 69–74, 81, 94, 111, 153, 244, 254
Nicolay, John, 154, 155, 156
Nolin River, 10, 39, 43
Norris, James, 129
Northern Cross Railroad, 138, 140
Northwest Ordinance, 63, 99, 102
Northwest Territory, 16, 67, 99
Notes on the State of Virginia (Jefferson), 114
Nott, Josiah Clark, 110, 111, 115
Novum Organum (Bacon), 32

Obama, Barack, 247
Offutt, Denton, 30, 46–47, 52, 53, 58–59, 75
Ohio River, 30, 39–40, 42, 46, 50, 89, 137
Old Fogies *vs.* Young America, 159–60
Olmsted, Denison, 31
On Floating Bodies (Archimedes), 76

On the Correlation of Physical Forces (Grove), 32
"On the Variety of Mankind" (Blumenbach), 109
On These Walls (Cole), 241
O'Neill, John, 30–31
opium production, 5
Ord, Edward, 218
On the Origin of Species (Darwin), 106, 107, 111

Pacific Railroad Act, 97, 187, 191
Pascal, Blaise, 88
Pate, Samuel, 41
patents, 100, 122, 125, 126, 139, 163, 172, 183; *Annual of Scientific Discovery*, as listed in, 33; commissioner of patents, Harding declining position, 128; Lincoln as a patent lawyer, 35, 127, 244; Lincoln obtaining, 68, 78–80, 82, 158, 244; Parker v. Hoyt waterwheel patent case, 242
Peirce, Benjamin, 172, 180
Percy, Hugh, 170
Permanent Commission, 176–79, 193, 246–47
Petersen's boarding home, 229, 233
Phillips, Wendell, 152, 175
Pierce, Franklin, 94
Pierce, Henry L., 116
Pike, Nicholas, 23, 25, 88
"Point of Beginning" obelisk, 67
Polk, James K., 67, 94, 102
polygenism, 107, 110
Price, Sterling, 218
Pupin, Michael, 248

race and racism, 27, 186, 221, 247; Agassiz, racial prejudices of, 111, 245; Lincoln's examination of race, 112–17, 222, 246; scientific racism, 106–12
Radford, Reuben, 59

About the Author

David J. Kent is a Lincoln researcher and an award-winning career scientist. He is currently president of the Lincoln Group of the District of Columbia, treasurer and Executive Committee member of the Board of Directors of the Abraham Lincoln Institute, a member of the Board of Advisors of the Lincoln Forum, and an active member of the Abraham Lincoln Association. He is the author of several previous books on Abraham Lincoln, Nikola Tesla, and Thomas Edison, including *Lincoln: The Man Who Saved America*, which was nominated for multiple awards. He has written about Lincoln in *Civil War Times*, the *Lincoln Herald*, the *Smithsonian Civil War Studies* online newsletter, the *Bulletin of the Lincoln Forum*, and the *Lincolnian*. An avid reader, his Abraham Lincoln book collection exceeds 1,600 volumes, and he reads twenty to thirty new Lincoln books a year. His research focuses on Lincoln's interests in science and technology. His website is http://www.davidjkent-writer.com/.